THE LATIN AMERICA F
Series edited by Robin Kirk and Orin

The Buenos Aires Reader

THE

BUENOS

AIRES

READER

HISTORY, CULTURE, POLITICS

Diego Armus and Lisa Ubelaker Andrade, editors

DUKE UNIVERSITY PRESS   *Durham and London*   2024

Names: Armus, Diego, editor. | Andrade, Lisa Ubelaker, editor.
Title: The Buenos Aires reader : history, culture, politics /
Diego Armus and Lisa Ubelaker Andrade, editors.
Other titles: Latin America readers.
Description: Durham : Duke University Press, 2024. |
Series: The Latin America readers | Includes bibliographical references
and index.
Identifiers: LCCN 2023053849 (print)
LCCN 2023053850 (ebook)
ISBN 9781478030843 (paperback)
ISBN 9781478026600 (hardcover)
ISBN 9781478059851 (ebook)
Subjects: LCSH: Buenos Aires (Argentina)—History. | Buenos Aires (Argentina)—
Civilization. | Buenos Aires (Argentina)—Intellectual life. | Buenos Aires
(Argentina)—Social life and customs. | Buenos Aires (Argentina)—Description and
travel. | BISAC: HISTORY / Latin America / South America | TRAVEL /
South America / Argentina
Classification: LCC F3001.2 .B88 2024 (print) | LCC F3001.2 (ebook) |
DDC 982/.11—dc23/eng/20240430
LC record available at https://lccn.loc.gov/2023053849
LC ebook record available at https://lccn.loc.gov/2023053850

Cover art: Gastón Pérez Mazás, *Obelisco Campeón*, December 18, 2022.
Buenos Aires, Argentina.

To Lauri, my *porteña* in New York City
—Diego

To Nico, Olivia, and Simón, my favorite *porteños* of all
—Lisa

And to Buenos Aires, which gave us both a lifetime
of questions and curiosity

Contents

Acknowledgments

This book is meant to piece together the many voices of Buenos Aires; as such, it builds on a bounty of scholarship, journalism, art, and collective knowledge. We are grateful to those who allowed us to include fragments of their work. We are also indebted to several colleagues who contributed critical feedback at different stages of the manuscript; particular thanks go to Jennifer Adair, Anahí Ballent, Rodrigo Booth, Lila Caimari, Paulo Drinot, Jorge Fondebrider, Wendy Gosselin, Roy Hora, Matt Karush, Flavia Macías, and Lía Munilla. Samuel Amaral, Isabella Cosse, Daniel James, Cecilia Palmeiro, Analía Rey, Sylvia Saítta, Guido Segal, Mariano Siskind, and Dani Yako indicated potentially useful sources, lent advice, and provided contacts. Many others helped in different capacities, and while naming all of them is impossible, we are appreciative of their generosity. The work of then-Swarthmore students Ryan Arazi, Naomi Caldwell, Amy DiPierro, Liliana Frankel, and Tiffany Wang offered valuable young readers' input. Catalina Vydra's organizational skills were critical. At Duke University Press, Miriam Angress's expertise and patience made this manuscript a book; we are particularly grateful for her flexibility in working with us to create a city *Reader* that experimented with format. Swarthmore College assisted with its Hungerford Funds and, crucially, helped this coauthorship take form.

This *Reader* also owes its existence to a spirit of collaboration, and its contents—its syntheses and its inevitable shortcomings—are the result of many years of ongoing conversations, debates, discussions, and compromises over how and what to translate and share of the city's story, and how to interpret it. The result is a text that reflects two paths: Diego, who is from Buenos Aires, has lived and taught Argentina's history in the United States since the late 1990s; Lisa, who is from the United States, encountered Buenos Aires (at Diego's introduction) in 2004 and has lived and taught there since 2013. In the university classroom, we have both taught Argentina's past, but as immigrants, we also have faced more everyday questions that leave us scattering for answers: every *porteño* living abroad has been asked to explain, "How did you end up here?"; every foreigner who has immigrated to Buenos Aires has been asked, "Why are you here?" We wanted to tell this city's history as we have always wished to have explained it, to create a book that made Buenos

Aires legible without oversimplification, and to share our love for its particularities without over-romanticization. In the process, and as we debated each line of writing, points of momentary disagreement and conflicting generational perspectives became rather refreshing opportunities for us to rediscover, better communicate, or even relearn the city's past and present. In this way, each book page, with its flaws and successes, reflects that collaboration.

Introduction

"The City of Fury": That is the nickname locals have bestowed on the city of Buenos Aires. The title comes from a 1988 rock anthem of the same name—a hit performed by the band Soda Stereo, written by lead vocalist Gustavo Cerati. In the song, the narrator awakes in the evening and spends the night flying through the streets of Buenos Aires, a place teeming with energy. The melody and rhythm transmit the beat of the streets still humming in the early hours of morning; the lyrics reflect the city's poetry, its spirit of creativity. In the chorus, you can hear the echoes of nocturnal crowds: a city alive.

The nickname stuck because the song not only conveyed Buenos Aires's vibrant energy but also reflected a shared, unsettling sense of struggle. Cerati's song was written during a period when Buenos Aires and Argentina had recently emerged from the depths of state terror; the violence of a dictatorship had been brought to light. The song was first recorded in a year marked by record inflation, when the value of the Argentine currency plummeted daily. Cerati sings of a city that is his but that "belongs to no one"; and as the sun rises, the narrator collapses. "The City of Fury" expressed entangled feelings of love for the life and ingenuity of Buenos Aires, as well as the fraught experiences of instability and turmoil.

Cerati was not the first to pair such contrasting feelings about Buenos Aires in song. Long before the golden age of Argentine rock, tangos spoke of a city that was both thrilling and challenging. The iconic singer Carlos Gardel crooned an ode to "nocturnal Corrientes Street, its *milongas* [tango halls], its night owls, and finer people [. . .] the brilliance of its spectacular lights, dizzy and grinning; it was there that I lost my youth." The writer Ernesto Sabato also wrote of a "frenzy and hardness" of Buenos Aires in his tango "Al Buenos Aires que se fue" ("The Buenos Aires That Is No More"); the narrator in that piece looks for relief by walking the city's quieter streets and flowered plazas. In songs like these, experiences of love and coming of age in Buenos Aires's more quaint neighborhoods contrasted against the lively seductions of its nightlife downtown and the enthralling cultures of horse racing and soccer. The songs often included words in *lunfardo*—a local slang still in use today that modifies and combines words from Spanish and Italian, as well as French, English, Guaraní, Quechua, Portuguese, Bantu, and other African languages. They emanated the diverse experiences and origins of the city's working and middle classes during many decades of the twentieth century.

The Buenos Aires that appears in these songs bears little resemblance to the clichéd representation of Buenos Aires as the "Paris of South America." This phrase, often used in travel guides, points visitors toward the city's majestic domes and turrets, its most elegant cafés, and the many landmarks built by the wealthy elite at the turn of the twentieth century.

While these spaces are a critical part of Buenos Aires and its history, residents and visitors who have tried to understand Buenos Aires with any depth have inevitably had to contend with a more nuanced reality. In fact, the city's best-known writers have lamented their inability to neatly convey its multifaceted complexity. Julio Cortázar wrote of a city so populated by ideas and diverse realities that it was impenetrable: Buenos Aires was, he said, "unattainable, enigmatic, impossible; one can't ring every doorbell. [. . .] We have invented Buenos Aires as friend, as servant, but it rejects us, it belongs to no one, though we attempted to possess it through love, violence, wanderings, in the dark poetry of bars and labor."[1] Jorge Luis Borges, who returned to Buenos Aires as a subject time and again, wrote in one of his early poems, "The city is in me, like a poem that I have not been able to put into words."[2] The writer Victoria Ocampo commented that any Argentine who read those lines by Borges would feel a sense of recognition and surprise, akin to looking in a mirror.[3]

How can we ever grasp this elusive Buenos Aires? We see these descriptions as an invitation to view the city as a place with many faces and pathways of entry, a home to people with vastly different experiences. We bring together (and translate into English) texts that reflect a multitude of viewpoints and forms of expression, including essays and documents as well as photographs, letters, comics, articles, poems, songs, manifestos, fiction, interviews, paintings—a vast array of testimonies.

Buenos Aires is revealed here as a city of creativity and arts, one made up of the aromas of *asado* (barbecue), the clattering of restaurants crowded with family and friends; quiet plazas where *mate* (a shared drink) is passed and neighbors mingle; soccer stadiums where rowdy fans jump while chanting *canciones de cancha* (stadium songs). Yet it is also a city marked by political upheavals and conflict, the struggles of staggering economic crises, as well as inequality, deep poverty, diverse middle classes, and ostentatious displays of wealth. It is both a city of the night and a daytime cauldron, bubbling with the energies of protestors, graffiti, street art, and commentators of all kinds. These voices make their demands heard in the street, on the walls, and in the press—a tradition of entrenched disagreements peppered with moments of shared joy and celebration.

The Buenos Aires Reader brings together stories and accounts of this city that might otherwise be inaccessible to English readers. The *Reader* is built around seven themes that we believe are important entry points to understand the uniqueness of Buenos Aires. We chose these themes because they are significant ways that *porteños* (the people of Buenos Aires) view themselves and because they are topics that writers and residents have repeatedly returned to as central to the city's story. They are also common areas of curiosity and fascination for the city's many visitors.

In each of its seven parts, the *Reader* provides an opportunity to take a deeper look at a theme, as well as to investigate ideas and debates about gender, class, sexuality, race, religion, inequalities, and politics. A short introduction at the beginning of each part offers an overview of the subject and connects its selections with each other and to the larger picture.

Our hope is that you explore this *Reader* as you might a city. Although you can certainly read this book in order, from beginning to end, the introductions to each part can also be used as a field guide to form your own itinerary of exploration. By following your own interests and curiosity, you can embark on a personalized journey, deepening your understanding through the wide array of testimonies and documents.

You might begin by walking the cobblestone streets in the historic downtown neighborhood of San Telmo or strolling the central square of the Plaza de Mayo. Part I, "The Living City," looks closely at how the city built out from this historic center to become a sprawling metropolis. It invites you to consider window shopping on Florida Street but also to veer off this typical tourist circuit and see the eclectic architecture of historic homes in the city's many neighborhoods, to enjoy the culture of its plazas and neighborhood parks.

This part also shows how epidemics impacted the city map and highlighted the struggles of the most marginalized neighborhoods. It offers tribute to the city's history of public transport, including its buses and their eccentric decorations. It illuminates the contrasts of Greater Buenos Aires—a zone beyond the city borders that features sprawling, luxury gated-community developments as well as millions of people struggling to get by.

A typical scene downtown, where a crowd of protestors drums, grills, and waves banners, turns you toward part II, "Taking to the Street," which tells the long history of mass celebration, collective action, and protest in Buenos Aires. It highlights street mobilizations past and present: early festivities in the plazas, religious and labor rallies, mass gatherings for Peronism, the solemn protest of the Mothers of the Plaza de Mayo during the dictatorship, public demonstrations following the return to democracy, and the performances and marches of the contemporary feminist movement, among others.

Part II also guides you through streets covered in colorful graffiti, murals, and banners—and explores the rich tradition behind the millions of people gathered at the Obelisk monument to celebrate Argentina's 2022 World Cup win.

Part III, "Eating in Buenos Aires," invites you to rethink the cultures and roots of Buenos Aires's food traditions, searching through its legendary café-lined streets and considering the stories behind the city's most typical foods. Drinking *mate*, for example, brings friends and family together in a social ritual and a celebration of life. Other selections explore the political action behind the city's famous *factura* pastries, celebrate the city's emblematic cake (the dulce de leche–layered chocotorta), or consider the impact of migrations, class, and gender on how, where, and what *porteños* eat.

It is impossible to know Buenos Aires without discussing its most passionate pastime. Part IV, "*Hinchas, Cracks*, and *Potreros* in the City of Soccer," traces Buenos Aires's intense love for *fútbol* (soccer). Local team allegiances run deep. Encounter the intensity of *hinchas* (fans) in their poems, songs, stories, and interviews; discover the sport's legendary beginnings, historic rivalries, and fans' emotional investment in their neighborhood clubs. This part also examines soccer's histories of politics, violence, and exclusion. The sport has shaped local identities, created icons, and—some have argued—nurtured a distinctive local style of play.

The city's many bookstores offer a quiet counter to the rowdy thrill of the stadium. These cherished spaces reflect Buenos Aires's reputation as a city of readers (and writers). Part V, "Reading, Watching, and Listening in Buenos Aires," delves into the profound and prolific presence of print media: the city's publishing industry and its newspapers and magazines; the risks and collusions connected to printing during times of censorship; and the importance of film, radio, and television industries in making Buenos Aires a vital producer of Spanish-language media.

Part VI, "The City at Night," explores Buenos Aires's dynamic nightlife as a space of creativity. The city comes alive long after sunset, spilling over with new energy. You can enjoy vanguard theater and the sounds of tango, the city's most iconic dance. You can consider other realms of the night—the echoes of rebellion and state repression in Buenos Aires rock, and the persistence of youth cultures despite censorship. The cloak of night was a setting for violent kidnappings during the 1976–83 civic-military dictatorship, as well as enduring LGBTQ+ nightlife in the face of police oppression.

Finally, part VII, "Written Cities," explores artists' and writers' abundant representations of the city, its people and character. We invite you to consider how the city has been envisaged through collage, photography, and paint; and to listen to fervent debates about Buenos Aires's character from those who see it as "middle class," "cosmopolitan," "modern," "fragmented," "inclusive," and unequal. In the pens of its many writers, we find stories of resistance under authoritarianism and odes to a spirit of resilience and survival.

There are many itineraries that you might take with this *Reader*. Our hope is that we have communicated the diversity, energy, and often-inharmonious perspectives of Buenos Aires in such a way that readers will be able to appreciate the city's rich past and present.

Finally, we want to point out two key supplementary texts: first, the very brief chronological summary of five hundred years of history, located just after this introduction; and second, "Suggestions for Further Reading," where you can find a list of works of scholarship that have shaped *The Buenos Aires Reader*, as well as recommended films and fiction that will deepen your experience of the City of Fury.

Notes

1. From Alicia D'Amico, Sara Facio, and Julio Cortázar, *Buenos Aires, Buenos Aires* (Buenos Aires: Sudamericana, 1968), 45–46.
2. Jorge Luis Borges, "Vanilocuencia," in *Fervor de Buenos Aires* [poems] (Buenos Aires: Imprenta Serantes, 1923).
3. Victoria Ocampo, "Visión de Jorge Luis Borges," *Cuadernos: Revista Mensual*, no. 55 (December 1961): 18.

Buenos Aires: A Brief History of the Last Five Hundred Years

1500s–1810s: Querandí Resistance and the Atlantic Port

Before there was a "Buenos Aires," the territory where the city now stands was the land of the Querandí, a native tribe of nomadic game hunters, fishers, and foragers. The Querandí successfully warded off colonizing Spanish forces several times, frustrating settlers who tried to build on the shores of the Río de la Plata in 1516 and again in 1536. A third attempt at colonization took place in 1580: launched from the nearby city of Asunción rather than Spain, it was an effort to improve communication between colonial Paraguay and the Crown. This effort proved more sustainable. The outpost of the Spanish Empire remained small, but following the arrival of a series of military units in the late 1600s, the number of residents of Buenos Aires grew, trades diversified, and streets were built. For much of the 1600s, however, the Spanish colony remained a rather unimpressive port town.

After two centuries of marginal existence—in which the port city became best known for smuggling silver from Potosí—Buenos Aires's colonial relevance began to grow in the late 1700s. It became the capital of the Viceroyalty of the Río de la Plata in 1776. At the time, there were twenty-four thousand inhabitants in the city; by 1810 the number had nearly doubled. The port city had also expanded its footprint. By the early 1800s, most residents lived in the thirty blocks that surrounded the Plaza Victoria (today called the Plaza de Mayo), but other residents were dispersed over another 260 more rustic adjacent streets.

Political organization centered on the city's cabildo—a colonial town council—where residents with the title of *vecino* could debate and vote on local issues. *Vecino* was, at least on paper, a flexible category; it did not make any explicit exclusions on the grounds of race, property ownership, or place of birth; in practice, however, it referred to a degree of social standing or prestige, a vague construction that did not encourage diversity.

During this period, Spanish and *porteño* merchants gained power and presence, as did upper clergy and colonial officials. Working peoples included a diverse group of *criollos* (European descendants born in America), African descendants both free and enslaved (a gradual abolition law was passed in 1813, but slavery was not abolished in the city until 1861), and Indigenous and mestizo residents. Cafés, churches, and *pulperías* (a type of country store and tavern), as well as the plaza itself, were places where city inhabitants socialized and discussed events of the day.

In 1810, while crisis marked a weakening of the Spanish Crown, an open cabildo was held; its members, by then representing a lively port that sought economic independence from the empire, began a revolution. A longer period of republican experimentation began.

1820s–1850s: Porteños *and the Interior in the Early Republic*

Amid a process of independence, new ephemeral political configurations emerged. In the 1820s, the cabildo was dissolved, and new debates and reforms related to political rights and city governance took place. An enduring conflict between the port city of Buenos Aires and the other provinces that made up the former colonial viceroyalty emerged. Initially, the provinces chose to operate as sovereign entities, joining together in a loose confederation. However, commerce and access to the Atlantic World made the port a major source of fiscal resources. Over the following decades, pastoral products—mainly salted beef and hides—became important exports; and as the division between the port city and the provinces became more pronounced, the role of Buenos Aires in the regional economy and political system became a subject of contention. Residents of Buenos Aires began to refer to the vast terrains and disparate cities of the other provinces as, simply, the country's "Interior" and to themselves as "people of the port," or *porteños*. Tensions over the power of Buenos Aires boiled over into politics. Federalists (those who wanted the provinces to remain loosely connected sovereign states) and Unitarians (who looked to see those provinces united under a central government in the capital city) were at odds.

Both factions made their impact on Buenos Aires. The Unitarian Bernardino Rivadavia first led the city as minister of the government of Buenos Aires (1821–26) and then as president of Argentina (1826–27). The period was characterized by plans for urban modernization and the expansion of education services; the city government also launched initiatives to pave and add lighting to streets, build new avenues, and make improvements in hygiene—for example, by moving slaughterhouses to the city's outskirts. Some reforms materialized, and others did not, but all of them signaled new priorities: to make the city more "modern" while ensuring political order.

From 1829 to 1852, Juan Manuel de Rosas, a Federalist from Buenos Aires Province became governor and a powerful leader of Argentina, controlling city governance with the support of an acquiescent legislature in the province of Buenos Aires. Urban reforms slowed, though they did not vanish. Under a confederation in which Buenos Aires had an undoubted hegemonic power, Rosas forged an alliance with elites of the other provinces. His political opposition, many of whom were in exile, suggested that Rosas's strong rule, cruel treatment of dissidents, and paternalist relation with popular classes magnified the perceived political differences between a port-based liberal elite and the cultures and politics of the Interior.

By the middle of the nineteenth century, it had become quite clear that the capital city was acquiring a viewpoint and standing distinct from other parts of the country. An enduring paradox was emerging: although Buenos Aires had become the political, economic, and cultural epicenter of the nation, it was, at the same time, fundamentally different, in each of these respects, from the rest of the country.

1850s–1910s: Immigration and New Urban Cultures in the Making

In the second half of the nineteenth century, with Rosas out of power, the liberal elite returned to their efforts to modernize Buenos Aires. Politics was seen as entering a new era, with notable growth in parties, participation, and press. A diverse network of associations and clubs that had begun to form in the 1820s expanded in the 1860s and '70s. They mobilized during elections. Street demonstrations and military-civil insurrections were also tools of political action.

During this period, the capital city housed the national executive, but that office was not in control of city governance. In the 1880s, this political relationship again changed. Buenos Aires became the capital of the young republic of Argentina in 1880, and three years later, a law established that a city mayor would be nominated by the national president and confirmed by the national Senate; a thirty-member city council (the Concejo Deliberante) was chosen by voting residents. In 1883, the city's newly appointed mayor, Torcuato de Alvear, revived the reformist project, updating urban and port infrastructure and building government agencies. The neighborhoods of Flores and Belgrano were officially added to the city map. As the borders of the "Federal Capital" came into clearer view, so too did the division between the *porteño* and the provincial.

Meanwhile, other changes were afoot. Wool—and, later, grains and refrigerated beef—were making their way to European markets as exports. Trade brought immense wealth into the country, but particularly to the port city and landowning elite, cementing Buenos Aires's role as Argentina's economic center. By the 1870s there was no question that port-driven wealth and governing power were transforming urban life.

However, it was a dramatic change in demographics that would catapult the city's social and cultural dynamics into a new era. Immigrants from Italy and Spain had begun to arrive in the 1850s, but by the following decade it was clear that a more massive wave of immigration was underway; this trend would continue into the early twentieth century. The 1869 city-wide census counted 92,000 foreign-born persons among its population of 187,000; by 1896, those numbers had grown to 345,000 among 663,000, and in 1936, there were 870,000 foreign-born persons in a total population of 2.45 million. The majority of the immigrants who settled in Buenos Aires heralded from Italy and Spain. Middle Easterners and Eastern Europeans also arrived in substantial numbers. Although the number of British migrants was, by comparison, quite small, their connections to the agro-export and railroad industries also permitted them to leave a mark on city culture. In nonelite neighborhoods, immigrants intermingled with longer-standing residents, including the city's *criollo,* mestizo, and Black populations.

New mixed cultures emerged out of these connections and relationships. Popular trends like tango and football took shape; new foods became staples of the city's diet. The tango, for example, can trace its origins to the meeting of cultures in this era. In the early nineteenth century, the *candombe* and *milonga* dances initiated by the Afro-descendant community of Montevideo and Buenos Aires livened meeting spots, and the spaces they met were referred to as *tangos* (and these three words—*candombe, milonga,* and *tango*—reflect African heritage). Amid the waves of immigration in the second half of the nineteenth century, a flurry of new influences and styles intermixed. Instruments like the bandoneón—a kind of accordion—met popular dances like waltzes, polkas, the mazurka, and the habanera. A new tango dance and culture emerged. In bars, in the street, and in brothels and dance halls, the word *milonga* began to refer to the event, and *tango* began to refer to three entangled elements—a style of music with powerful instrumentation, a new close-contact dance, and characteristic lamenting lyrics that told of love, loss, and life in Buenos Aires.

Although a diverse array of mestizos, *criollos,* Afro-Argentines, and more recent immigrants shared these social spaces, there was no question that the racial dynamics of the city were in flux. Nor was this coincidental. In the nineteenth century, the nation's elite had encouraged this wave of immigration from Europe with a whitening agenda in mind. Although they had initially sought to entice northern Europeans to come to Argentina, the arrival of immigrants who were mostly from the southern part of the continent nonetheless fulfilled their aim of building a population of European origin. Numerically, the massive arrival of immigrants diminished the proportion of mestizo and Black people in the city. A city census taken in 1778, for example, suggested that Afro-descendants (counting those persons classified as *negro* as well as those categorized as *mulato*) made up nearly a third of the colonial population (29.7 percent of 24,205 persons total), but by 1887 that percentage had dropped dramatically, to 1.8 percent, within a general population that had swelled to 433,375 persons. For some time it was suggested that this drop could be explained by the disproportionate number of Black men sent to fight in the Paraguayan War (1864–70), as well as epidemics that devastated areas of the city where many Black residents lived. However, it is clear that racism and a political culture that emphasized homogenization and whiteness as social goals not only encouraged European immigration but also often affected census counts and racial identification. Many mixed persons are thought to have either identified as, or been counted as, white (or other categories bestowed with relative racial privilege). Thus, while the cultural composition of society was becoming in some ways quite diverse and mixed, the erasure of racial identities was also emerging as a key part of social politics. In fact, after that 1887 census, it was no longer possible for residents to identify as Black on the city census—the category was eliminated. It was restored in 2010, the result of a campaign by the city's Black community; in 2022, when the census specifically asked residents if they self-identified as an Afro-descendant or had any African or Black heritage, 40,670 in the capital city responded affirmatively.

As the lower sectors were developing new local cultures in the late nineteenth century, powerful elites became entrenched in the mandate that they had assigned themselves of modernizing and ordering the city and the nation. They were an insular group that was experiencing an economic heyday; using their growing wealth, they busily and avidly imitated and adapted (with varying success) the latest fashions from Europe. Local cultures emerged in the process, but the influence of European high culture was quite visible in every realm of daily life, from their choice of restaurants and architectural styles to their acquisition of fine art and preferred sports (e.g., horse racing, polo, and fencing).

Nineteenth-century elites were also reluctant to open the political system to the lower sectors. Political parties, whether liberal or conservative, were rooted in personal relationships, and political and economic commonalities. Although the electorate in Buenos Aires was very broad, the vote was neither compulsory nor entirely universal. All free, male residents of age could vote. Restrictions were tighter to run for office—elected officials had to reach certain levels of wealth and education, depending on the post.

These oligarchical tendencies in politics were vocally challenged. Anarchists, socialists, and other groups brought labor rights to the fore; civilian-military revolts also made the political panorama more complex. Conservative elite contingents cracked down on all these interventions in the name of preserving order, but others entertained the idea of a more inclusive political system, envisaging universal and obligatory male suffrage as a cornerstone of future democracy. By the end of the nineteenth century, new political parties emerged. Two grew in significance in the capital city and offered defined political programs: the Unión Cívica Radical (UCR) and the

Socialist Party. Socialists engaged a discourse based in workers' rights; the UCR appealed to a sense of republicanism. Both parties drew from heterogeneous social sectors.

Immigration was also impacting other realms of urban life. Among the enduring echoes of cultural mixture from this period was a drastic change in everyday language. In the course of a generation, most city residents spoke Spanish in addition to another language or dialect. Though multilingualism was a trait the social classes held in common, the meanings of speaking more than one language was quite different across groups. For the elite, speaking several languages was often the reflection of education and worldliness; it was used as a sign and tool of high status, of international connection. In the lower and working classes, multilingualism reflected heritage. Those in power expressed concern at the languages of the poor, and in particular their use of *cocoliche*—a transitional language that mixed words of various Italian dialects with Spanish.

The use of *cocoliche* declined as immigrants and their children further integrated into the local culture, though the persistence of some of the new words and its hybrid rhythm, which mixed Italian and Spanish intonations and expressions, became evident in the city's distinctive and enduring *porteño* accent. A local slang, known as *lunfardo*, also became part of everyday speech. It originated in prisons and combined words and expressions from many languages. Gradually and over time, it formed part of a shared urban lexicon; thousands of words used today—for example, *guita* (money), *pibe* (boy), *mina* (girl), and *cancha* (stadium)—reflect these origins. At the beginning of the twentieth century, social divides persisted, but a shared urban culture was emerging.

1910s–1950s: A Shared Mass Culture, a Growing Industrial Belt, and the Rise of Peronism

Daily life in the early twentieth century was still profoundly shaped by class, but it was abundantly clear to many that one's position in the social hierarchy was far from written in stone. For many immigrants and their descendants, Buenos Aires offered the opportunity of upward mobility.

Evidence of this change could be seen in the city map. For much of the nineteenth century, broad swaths of Buenos Aires were difficult to access from downtown. They were seen as rustic outskirts, known in urban lore as *arrabales*: tango lyrics and nostalgic poetry mythologized these spaces and the outsider characters who populated them. However, advances in infrastructure in the early decades of the twentieth century began to slowly convert these areas into lots for the construction of new homes and storefronts. Streets were gradually paved; networks of sewage, drinkable water, and street lighting expanded; a new cemetery and hospitals were built. This development was uneven—some areas received services faster than others—but the sense that Buenos Aires's urban world was expanding was quite evident. Many immigrants and their descendants, driven by a desire to live in a house of their own, left downtown tenements, known as *conventillos*, and set out to occupy emerging neighborhoods farther from the city center.

Over time, and especially as a transport system made up of buses, trains, and subway expanded and public works stabilized, these new areas became even more attractive. The neighborhood, outside the city center, became a bedrock of working- and middle-class lifestyles; there families found opportunities to participate in community organizations and build small businesses. Neighborhood associations, local branches of political parties, parishes, soccer clubs, and libraries consolidated as a rich ground for new, sometimes quite homogeneous, identities.

The expanding public sector and the transportation system that connected neighborhoods and workplaces downtown also allowed residents access to white-collar jobs outside their immediate neighborhood. Some used the rather inclusive system of public education to access professional positions, and many saw hard individualized work as a path to an improved life.

Others toiled long hours as laborers but found that a period of economic expansion in tandem with collective organizing for expanded labor rights generated relative economic security. At the beginning of the century, socialists and anarchists—and, later, anarcho-syndicalists, communists, liberal radicals, and Social Catholics—prioritized the idea of collective bargaining as a way to improve social standing; by the 1920s and 1930s labor had carved out an important role in society and politics.

Electoral participation also expanded in these decades. In 1912, voting was made obligatory, secret, personal, and universal for all native-born and naturalized men. In 1917 this was applied to city elections; nonnaturalized residents of Buenos Aires were also permitted a more limited vote for the thirty-member city council. The mandatory vote, in particular, made the ballot an obligation rather than a mere right; a new confidentiality, combined with reforms that encouraged minority party representation, also hastened the emergence of a number of small parties, some centering on specific issues and others drawing from class politics. In city politics, the change further reinforced the power of the Unión Cívica Radical and the Socialist Party. Although the city's mayor was still nominated by the nation's president, local elections were held for city council. To win these votes, the two parties sought to consolidate their bases using neighborhood organizations: the UCR used systems of patronage and neighborhood committees to gain votes; the Socialists used neighborhood organizations as well as education campaigns.

The world of the neighborhood was distinct from the bustle of downtown, but these two zones of urban life were connected. The city built diagonal roads and other major avenues that broke with the rigid grid but generated a flow of street traffic that reinforced—rather than minimized—the traditional center of the city as a point of convergence and ceremony. Corrientes Avenue, which departs from the city's downtown and crosses horizontally along the city map, served as one bridge between the two worlds, offering a seemingly endless array of nocturnal delights by the 1930s. As it neared downtown, the avenue was lined with theaters, cinemas, dance halls, kiosks, cabarets, cafés, and pizzerias and *confiterías*—refined coffee and tea salons. A boom in mass media, including diverse, widely consumed magazines, radio programs, and films, further connected the geographically divided neighborhoods with a shared mass culture.

These cultural changes appeared to solidify Buenos Aires as a city with a vast and diverse middle class (or at least persons who saw themselves that way). Indeed, by midcentury the notion of being "middle class" expanded in use and in relevance. Persons with significant economic differences identified with the idea, making the category both inclusive and, at the same time, increasingly imprecise in meaning. The characterization of Buenos Aires as a "middle-class city" could also serve to overshadow ongoing struggles and social and economic exclusions. As Buenos Aires was the seat of national government, it was also the stage for political movements that reflected real inequalities sometimes at odds with the self-image that *porteños* conveyed in their shared mass culture.

Ultimately, such exclusions became impossible to ignore. The military took over the national government in 1930, asserting itself as an arbiter of the political arena that would intervene when it saw elected officials as unable to manage crisis. Political parties continued to struggle for power, and limited elections were held, but the decade was marked by political corruption, state repression of workers' movements, and fraudulent voting. In the city, the Unión Cívica Radical and Socialists continued to dominate electorally, despite divisions in party politics that led to the formation of smaller, ephemeral organizations.

Amid the global economic crisis of the early 1930s, some also began to envision alternatives to an economy they saw as overly reliant on exports. A state policy of "import-substitution industrialization"—regulations that encouraged the replacement of imported goods with locally produced industries—resulted in a greater concentration of factories in Buenos Aires and its surrounding areas. In tandem, young migrants from the Interior arrived in Buenos Aires and its industrializing suburbs in search of jobs. By 1938, the area just outside the capital city was home to 74 percent of national industry and 72 percent of its workers and employees. The numbers reflected a new era of dramatic demographic change, defined not by overseas immigration but by internal migration to the city's outskirts.

Authorities in the capital did not respond to this growth. Instead, city governments like that of Mariano de Vedia y Mitre (1932–38) focused on modernizing initiatives within the city limits: they enlarged avenues, expanded the subway network, and built a beltway that only further demarcated the political limits of the capital. The city's population reached 2.5 million, at which point it plateaued.

Yet the growth in Buenos Aires's larger metropolitan area was undeniable. In 1948, in recognition of this new reality, Greater Buenos Aires was formally established as the sum of several municipalities that surrounded the capital city. By that year there were more than 1.5 million inhabitants living in the area outside city limits. Some migrants and impoverished sectors also moved to the city itself, and over the next two decades *villa miserias*—precarious settlements on unused public or private lands—expanded in size and number. In Greater Buenos Aires the new industrial labor force, organized by seasoned leadership, had also mobilized to improve working conditions.

A military coup in 1943 catalyzed new changes. The military junta suspended the elected city council. The growing industrial laborers of Greater Buenos Aires, however, found a sympathetic ear in Secretary of Labor Colonel Juan Domingo Perón, who responded to long-standing demands for wage regulation, worker's compensation, and specialized labor courts to hear workers' claims, among other reforms. Perón's rising popularity—and power—generated tensions in the military government, and in 1945 he was asked to step down. He was taken into state custody. Labor leaders and thousands of factory workers, most from the industrial neighborhoods just outside the city limits, staged a mass demonstration in the Plaza de Mayo; the show of political force catalyzed Perón's release, to the shock of many of the city's more established residents and political actors. Perón began his campaign for the presidency.

In 1946, after a decisive but hard-fought national election, the first experiment in Peronism began. In Buenos Aires, the rise of Peronism generated debate over the social and economic character of the city and its peoples. Some avid anti-Peronists spoke of the new political movement as an "invasion." This perception was steeped in classist and racist ideas that imagined the city as made up of European immigrants and saw Perón's working-class supporters as nonwhite provincials. Another example of this was the use of the epithet *cabecita negra* (literally, "little black heads"): this racist term mocked migrants' Indigenous, *criollo*, or mestizo (mixed European and Indigenous) heritage, dark hair, and features and insinuated that Perón's followers were racially and culturally inferior to *porteños*.

This type of hostile language not only made social fissures more visible but also underestimated Peronism's appeal. While the capital city developed a reputation as a center of anti-Peronist organizing and discourse and was often contrasted to the pro-Perón industrial city outskirts, in reality the geographic borders of political opinion were not so stark. Electoral records suggest that the Peronist Party actually gained ground with capital city voters during the first decade of Perón's presidency, in particular by winning over voters in working-class neighborhoods and earning many more votes when women's voting rights were secured in 1947.

During this initial period, many of Perón's supporters viewed *Justicialismo* (Perón's political movement) as capable of addressing inequalities in both the city and its outskirts. The government put in place important nationalist and social justice policies and used the tools of the city's mass culture to promote this vision—and to censor criticism and opposition. By 1954, however, a sputtering economy contributed to a growing political opposition, which included former allies in the military and the Catholic Church. Rivals criticized this economic decline as well as Perón's cult of personality, his treatment of dissidents, his incitement of violence among followers, and his control of the media.

The capital city thus became a backdrop for Peronist aspirations and its tragedies. There was no clearer example of this than the events of June 16, 1955, when the Armed Forces bombed the Plaza de Mayo in an attempt to oust the president, killing and wounding hundreds of civilians. Following Perón's subsequent exile the following September, a campaign of de-Peronization was set in motion. Military leaders not only eliminated the Peronist Party but also razed any sign of Perón or Peronism across the city landscape, changing street names, demolishing buildings, and removing statues. Urban and political history became enmeshed in acts of erasure.

At the same time, as dramatic as these hallmarks of political history were, they had a relatively lesser impact on the world of the neighborhood or the daily life of many of the city's residents. Life in the city's neighborhoods continued in relative calm, with opportunities expanding and contracting with the vagaries of the economy. City council elections resumed in 1958. The city of Buenos Aires seemed to retain much of its middle-class profile.

Certainly, however, the political language of the 1940s and 1950s opened new questions about the city's social and political identity as well as the relationship between *porteños* and the migrants building their own neighborhoods beyond the city limits. Greater Buenos Aires also continued to grow as an archipelago of urbanized spaces, largely made up of rather humble neighborhoods and industrial urbanized zones. For many, the area offered terrain on which they might be able to build a small family home. Yet by the end of the 1950s, new movements—and a new generation of urbanites—began to call into question what it meant to be middle class or *porteño*. Ideological and cultural divisions became more visible as the decade marched on.

1960s–1970s: Fragmentation and Polarization

The second half of the twentieth century brought new experiences of social and cultural fragmentation. The culture of the city's downtown boomed.

Corrientes Avenue flourished as an epicenter of the city's nightlife; the construction of high-rise buildings in various neighborhoods underlined a wave of renovation. These novelties, however, were not accompanied by updates in basic infrastructure. At the same time, Greater Buenos Aires continued to expand in size and population, and its own social and community organizations became more consolidated. By 1960 Greater Buenos Aires's population had grown to 4 million, and by 1970 to 5.5 million.

Meanwhile, across the city, young people were adopting and developing new fashions and political ideas that were connected to global trends but grounded in local experiences. The youth that came of age in the 1960s did so amid an era of de-Peronization, limited democracy, Cold War ideologies, expanded international and national consumerism, and a return to military rule. General Juan Carlos Onganía led a coup, once again under the premise that military rule would generate conservative order. City governance echoed these swings toward authoritarianism: in periods of dictatorship, the city council was suspended and the city mayor remained an executive appointee.

Onganía's dictatorship (1966–73) was characterized by oppressive measures used to restrain brewing ideas of free expression and political questioning. Such efforts had only limited success. Labor demands continued and conflicts erupted; the cultures of rock, rebellion, and experimentation persisted despite crackdowns in the name of traditional moral values.

The city's vast population participated in new trends to varying degrees, and they also reacted to authoritarianism in a number of ways. Some resented the repeal of democracy. Some praised a sense of restored order; others still actively fought against the regime, some by vocally and publicly questioning the status quo, and others by organizing in left-wing, militant, armed political groups.

By the early 1970s, when the military regime looked to transfer the government to civilian power, the decades-long effort to "de-Peronize" society was revealed as a failure. Distinct political groups, which ranged from rightist conservatives to leftist revolutionaries, rallied around the figure of Perón, still in exile. These divided factions, at odds with one another, each interpreted Peronism as reflecting their political visions and claimed the leader as their own. Perón's return to Argentina in 1973 was accompanied by a massive demonstration at the airport that devolved into a violent confrontation between these disparate groups.

The clash escalated after the leader's reelection to the presidency. The most reactionary sectors of this heterogeneous Peronist mandate came to the forefront of the government and invited the armed forces to annihilate leftist and Peronist guerrilla groups and all those they deemed "subversive." Perón died within the year, leaving the vice president—his wife, Isabel Martínez de Perón—as his successor. Violence, economic uncertainty, and massive street demonstrations culminated in a generalized sense of insecurity. As conflict between rightist paramilitaries and leftist/Peronist guerrilla groups escalated, the government failed to address public uncertainty. Various sectors of society condoned a military intervention, seeing it as inevitable or even necessary. On March 24, 1976, a dangerous authoritarian junta took control.

1976–1983: The Civic-Military Dictatorship and the Reign of State-Led Terror

The military coup marked the beginning of the most brutal military dictatorship in Argentina's history, an era of state-led terror. The National Congress was suspended, as was the city council. In social and political realms of everyday life, the military regime, its civilian allies, and most of the Catholic Church hierarchy took up a mantle of "social order" and began a campaign of violence. They kidnapped, illegally detained, and tortured—and, in many cases, killed—an estimated thirty thousand dissidents (and supposed dissidents), most of them young people. Many of the regime's victims, known as the "disappeared," were held captive in clandestine detention centers embedded within the city landscape—at military and police buildings like the campus known as the ESMA (Escuela de Mecánica de la Armada), as well as sites that, from the street, took on a more ordinary appearance: a mechanic shop, a bus depot, a Ford auto plant, an old traditional mansion, or other public buildings. Several of the mothers of disappeared persons began to march, resolutely and silently, in the Plaza de Mayo once a week. Donning white kerchiefs and requesting news of the whereabouts of their children, they began what would become a decades-long crusade for justice. Meanwhile, the regime razed cultural and social institutions and decimated the city's once thriving press using threats, censorship, and violence.

Amid this campaign of terror, the authoritarian government attempted to paint itself as a beacon of "order." It spoke of a plan to "recover" the city for the "decent" middle classes and revived the promises of unfinished infrastructural projects. Without public debate (or consent), the military offered large infrastructural projects to a concentrated group of business and economic elites, many of them accomplices in the state's violence. The city government obsessed over what it called "cleanliness." It demolished the city's poorest neighborhoods and informal urban settlements with brutality. The *villa* residents, whom they referred to as a blight on the city, were expelled to Greater Buenos Aires. At the same time, new developments were promised: highways to improve transit and an ecological "green belt" that would circle the city. Although some of those schemes were completed, many were abandoned, and, as in the 1960s, such proposals were not paired with a renovation of the city's basic—aging—services and infrastructure. Amid corruption, economic decay, state terror, a failed Malvinas/Falklands War with Britain, social unrest, and increasing pressure from local and international human rights organizations, the military dictatorship came to an end in 1983. Elections were held. Democracy would return.

1980s–1990s: The Return to Democracy and the Rise of Neoliberalism

In the wake of authoritarianism, Buenos Aires experienced a recovery of public space. The people could once again voice their concerns. Neighborhood associations and communities saw something of a revival (though they did not return to the central position they held at the beginning of the century), and the city's once-inhibited cultural industries experienced a powerful comeback.

Recognition of the military's violent regime also felt suddenly plausible. The new democratically elected president, Raúl Alfonsín, assembled a historic truth commission that would make the heinous acts undertaken by the military dictatorship a part of public record. Human rights organizations supported activists and survivors as they recorded and testified to the oppression and extreme state violence that took place. The military leadership was put on trial, and some were given a life sentence. But the historical power of the military had not vanished; democracy was still fragile. It was not long before the state passed a series of laws narrowing the scope of prosecutions and issuing pardons for lower-ranking officers, permitting many of those who committed acts of torture to live their lives freely. By the early 2000s, after two decades of democracy and a repudiation of state terror, the military's credibility, and its traditional role in politics, seemed to have weakened. Pardons were rescinded, and trials resumed.

The military had also left Argentina with a shattered economy: a skyrocketing national debt, rising unemployment, and dilapidated public services. The democratic government struggled to jump-start a recovery. In the 1980s, those in need of housing built up informal settlements once more; city infrastructure began to buckle, demonstrating the need for renovation. By the late 1980s and early 1990s, two episodes of heightened inflation threatened a sense of overall economic stability, aggravating social divisions and generating a context of downward mobility for some.

In the 1990s, important reforms to city politics took place. In 1994, a revised constitution proclaimed the Ciudad Autónoma de Buenos Aires an autonomous territory. City residents would elect not only legislative representatives but also their mayor. For the first time, the city executive could hail from a party that was different, even oppositional to, the national executive. In that first mayoral election, the candidate from the Unión Cívica Radical won.

Meanwhile, in national politics, President Alfonsín's successor, Peronist president Carlos Menem, invited a neoliberal turn and engaged in a process of deregulation and privatization. These changes had sweeping effects. A powerful local currency (the Argentine peso was pegged to the US dollar), together with the lowered trade tariffs, created an influx of imported consumer products, further integrating the local economy into the global market and stimulating consumer tastes. Shopping malls dotted the city, as did new high-income living developments and condominiums—signposts of a new wave of modernization that pleased some but lacked a coherent or socially grounded urban plan. Feelings on this period reflect this divide: the upper sectors of society remember the 1990s as a period of prosperity and access to the privatized and global market; the lower (and some of the middle) sectors, however, were more likely to feel the effects of rising unemployment, disinvestment from public institutions—including education and health care—and the costs of a dollarized economy. Nevertheless, many were enthusiastic about the lack of inflation.

Patterns in Greater Buenos Aires echoed these growing inequalities. There, the decade saw the multiplication of gated communities—manicured, exclusive neighborhoods, known as "countries," that resembled US suburbs and offered heightened security and a range of amenities; in parallel, the decade was marked by a rise in the number of residents living in precarious settlements and underserved communities. Those residents often lacked access to electricity, paved roads, and water and suffered the impacts of regular flooding. Although the traditional barrios of Buenos Aires retained a similar look and feel, it was clear that a more severely fragmented society was taking shape.

2000s–the Present: Crisis and Survival

Buenos Aires greeted the twenty-first century in an economic descent that appeared to threaten the legacy of the so-called middle-class city. In December 2001, after a national default on the country's debt, the local currency was devalued, and the national government employed drastic measures to try to curtail the damage. Many of those who had made it through the rising unemployment and price inflation at the end of the 1990s struggled to escape the economic perils of crisis. As the savings of much of the middle sectors evaporated, the relative power of the wealthiest increased. An even more powerful distrust of banks followed amid rapid government turnover and a shredded credit system. In its wake, a cash economy dominated in daily life, upheld by a general lack of confidence in institutions.

Following the 2001 crisis, the country—and the city—underwent a gradual process of economic recovery fueled by a global commodities boom and the rise of new key national exports, like GMO soybeans. The city and the nation once again turned inward as local industries slowly reemerged and social policies broadened their reach. A new wave of diverse protests, mobilizations, and demands also took over public space. Groups made up of both unemployed persons and informal workers (holding jobs without formal contract or legal protections) blocked city traffic. Demonstrations both for and against the national and city governments grew in number.

Political divisions within the city certainly existed, but the electoral divide between those who lived within the city limits and those beyond its borders became more pronounced. Peronism had never found its most captive audience in the capital, particularly in contrast to most districts in Greater Buenos Aires, considered by many to be the party's electoral stronghold. In the twenty-first century, this political geography became more notable as the city became a cradle for opposition politics. While the nation elected Peronists Néstor Kirchner (2003–7) and Cristina Fernández de Kirchner (2007–15), city elections showed an opposing trend, electing the conservative Mauricio Macri as city mayor in 2007. Macri went on to run for president and succeed Fernández de Kirchner with an opposition coalition, winning in the 2015 election. This win was a surprise to many. Despite losing the presidency in 2019 to Peronist Alberto Fernández (with Cristina Kirchner serving as vice president), Macri's party—with its stronghold in the capital—retained national electoral viability as well as control of the city government. As mayor, Macri and his successor, Horacio Rodríguez Larreta, became known for their focus on urban infrastructure, with initiatives like a high-speed bus system, bicycle lanes, and elevated train tracks to improve transit; renovations in the city's plazas; and plans to urbanize the city's *villas*. At the same time, residents protested that city government's resources were unevenly distributed in what had become a predictable pattern: southern neighborhoods saw less investment than wealthier northern neighborhoods. They also decried the deteriorating public health and education systems, the revised zoning and construction contracts that favored private investors, the privatization of public lands, and the still-minor inroads to urbanizing the city's *villas*.

Amid the ongoing recovery from the 2001 economic crash, the idea that the capital was a city with a vast middle class remained, but the notion of what constituted a middle class appeared to fluctuate drastically. To be middle class in the wake of crisis was also to live with a sense of precarity. In the early 2010s and 2020s, most residents no longer expected to experience much upward mobility. The future was uncertain. Some found (and find) ways to take advantage of the vagaries of the new economic reality and prosper from it. The vast majority developed infinite strategies to persevere even as their income declined. Many keep up appearances of what might broadly be called a middle-class lifestyle, relying on the accumulated wealth of previous generations, finding ways to reduce their expenses and focusing on but one of the myriad aspects of life that were important to previous experiences of upward mobility: housing and stable work, access to private healthcare and hospitals, or a secure retirement. Education can also affirm a sense of middle-class belonging; some acquire access through the free public system and others through private options.

Buenos Aires and Argentina navigated the 2020 pandemic with strict restrictions on circulation but, at least initially, a sense of agreement between the federal (Peronist) government, led by Alberto Fernández, and the city government, led by Rodríguez Larreta (Propuesta Republicana, or PRO). The severe confinement, however, spurred debates over individual liberty and had political costs. A spiraling economy, combined with sustained charges by anti-Peronists of corruption, enlivened conservative critiques. Rapid inflation left some looking back on the neoliberal 1990s—when the peso was stable because it was pegged to the US dollar—with renewed nostalgia. Most lamented the lack of political alternatives as they struggled to make ends meet, wages stagnated, and prices rose. By the end of 2023, an estimated 45 percent of the population of Greater Buenos Aires was living in poverty.

The lack of political solutions generated frustration. Although voters in the capital city and the province of Buenos Aires reelected the standing parties in their mayoral and gubernatorial elections, when it came to the presidency, the "anarcho-libertarian" rightist Javier Milei gained traction. In the final presidential runoff, Milei carried the majority in nearly all the neighborhoods of the capital city; although Peronism won out in many neighborhoods in Greater Buenos Aires, it was often by a tight margin.

Along with promises to "take a chainsaw" to government, cut budgets and social programs, and deregulate the market, Milei's campaign also revived conservative talking points that had, in recent decades, diminished in political discourse. The new party challenged some of the legal and social achievements made by feminist and LGBTQ+ movements, teased the possibility of fighting crime by deregulating gun ownership, spoke to the idea of restoring individual liberty, and, to the shock of many, revived long-debunked dictatorship-era discourse that suggested state terror was part of a two-sided "war" against extremists.

Many voters suggested that it was frustration with the dire economic reality and the political status quo rather than a resounding agreement with these types of statements that compelled their vote, but nevertheless, the candidate found clear support across class and geographical lines. Although many supported initiatives to downsize government bureaucracy, Milei himself offered little salve to personal economic woes, as subsidies were lifted, social budgets were slashed, and the cost of living skyrocketed.

The parts of the city most observable to tourists can conceal some of these political and economic tensions. The vibrant use of renovated public spaces, a diverse gastronomy, and a seemingly endless array of shops, small businesses, niche theaters, bookstores, bars, cultural centers, and cafés are often pointed to as testaments to the resilience and constant renovation of the city's spirit. They sometimes also disguise the economic struggles, disparities, and instability that saturate daily life. Nevertheless, it is clear that despite its struggles, the city continues to offer some a promise of opportunity. In recent decades, immigrants from Latin American countries—Bolivians, Paraguayans, Peruvians, Colombians, and Venezuelans—have built significant communities in the city and in Greater Buenos Aires. Others from farther abroad—like China, Taiwan, South Korea, and Senegal—have also made the city home. Although these newer immigrant sectors have perhaps not yet had the dramatic demographic effect of those who arrived at the beginning of the previous century, their contributions are evident across many domains of city life; new generations have thus brought to light a renewed diversity in Buenos Aires, a city that has loosened its ties to Europe but retained its legacy as a space of cultural mixture.

I

The Living City

Buenos Aires began as a backwater port, a relatively small Spanish colony that accessed the Atlantic Ocean at the mouth of the Río de la Plata. The town initially grew in a rather slow fashion, but by the late twentieth century it was a "megacity," an immense grid that incorporated the flat land of the surrounding plains, known as the pampas, and brought smaller towns into the fold of a vast urbanized zone. The results of this growth, and in particular the physical changes in the urban space—its neighborhoods, public and private spaces, architecture, and transportation—serve as the backdrop for residents' ever-changing experiences of life in the city.

From Port City to Modern Metropolis

At the end of the nineteenth century, the twin catalysts of mass immigration and rising agro-wealth transformed Buenos Aires in ways evident to even the most casual viewer. The government and the upper classes were investing in majestic and ornate buildings in the art deco and eclectic styles in vogue in Europe, and older colonial landmarks were progressively overshadowed by a mix of these new trends in architecture. At the centennial celebration in 1910, the city housed 1.5 million residents; electric lights festively decorated the Plaza de Mayo, and celebrants lauded the beauty of elaborate buildings like the newly renovated Teatro Colón. The recently widened Avenida de Mayo was presented as a landmark of modernity that stood ready to host the trail of cars, buses, trams, subways, and other traditional forms of transportation, like horse-drawn carts, that busy city residents would use to traverse the city. Florida Street offered a scattering of modern department stores that stocked imported goods and contemporary European fashions, drawing crowds. (See "Shopping in the City," the first selection below.) Decorative cupulas garnished multistory buildings on major street corners: the adornments, each one unique, seemed to punctuate a "golden age" in the city's architectural history.

The buzz of the centennial celebrations was billed as a kind of historic culmination after decades of change. A generation before, the city's wealthiest sectors had lived not far from the city center in large mansions with internal patios; on weekends and in the summer, they would escape to luxurious country homes. By the 1860s and 1870s, infectious diseases (and fear of them) began to alter the urban map, guiding an initial internal migration within city borders. Over the following decades, more and more residents who lived in the southern sector of the city and could afford to move joined them, aspiring to new homes along the northern corridor. By the 1890s the wealthiest sectors relocated to neighborhoods like Recoleta, where some moved into decorated mansions and, at the turn of the century, into new spacious apartments. Today, some buildings still use the same wrought-iron elevators that debuted in the most modern buildings at the beginning of the twentieth century. The city's elite often furnished their homes inside and out in a Parisian aesthetic, collected European arts and imports, and sought every opportunity to bring the high culture and fashions of the Old World to Buenos Aires.

When they fled to these northern neighborhoods, wealthy families had abandoned their former residences downtown. Their migration cemented their former neighborhoods as spaces where working and immigrant cultures would dominate. Homes that had once been inhabited by single families and a team of servants were quickly transformed into shared housing for the working classes. In these styles of residences, known as *conventillos* and *inquilinatos*, tenants, many of them immigrants, occupied rooms and converted the patios, bathrooms, and kitchens into communal spaces. For residents, these crowded homes lacked a great deal of privacy and were not without conflict, but they were also sites of significant exchange: as immigrants from various backgrounds intermingled, new hybrid cultures—food, music, language—and social organizations emerged. For outsiders, the *conventillo* also became a subject of debate—particularly during outbreaks of disease. Critics only saw disorder, nests of rebellion, moral decay, and bad taste, and they stigmatized residents. Urban reformers, even those in government positions, also looked on with a critical eye. (See "From Yellow Fever to COVID-19: Epidemics and Inequalities in the City.")

Although they never housed more than a quarter of the city's population, *conventillos* obtained an important place in popular memory and nostalgia. They served as the setting for countless tangos, and, as the musical style popularized, the buildings became a celebrated and romanticized part of folk culture. Today, *conventillos* in La Boca, like the decorative mausoleums for the elite in Recoleta Cemetery, are billed as tourist attractions.

Buenos Aires's flirtation with modernity and grandeur at the turn of the century, although impressive, did not extend across the urban map. The dense center of the city was dotted with an eclectic mix of European-style buildings, monuments, and meticulously planned plazas, but modernization was uneven. While visiting in 1891, *Harper's* journalist Theodore Child noted this, writing that "Buenos Aires will be a stupendous city but it will be eight or ten years before this happens; in the meantime, today's city is like a provisional incomplete sketch." Modern amenities expanded slowly. In 1887, a mere 14 percent of houses in Buenos Aires were serviced with clean water, and by 1910 that number had climbed to 53 percent. By the middle of the 1920s, vast sectors of the city had street lighting—but there were still large gaps. Only in the 1930s did services like gas begin to reach the more densely populated neighborhoods; coal stoves slowly began to be replaced with gas alternatives.

Despite this uneven development, there was no question that the city map

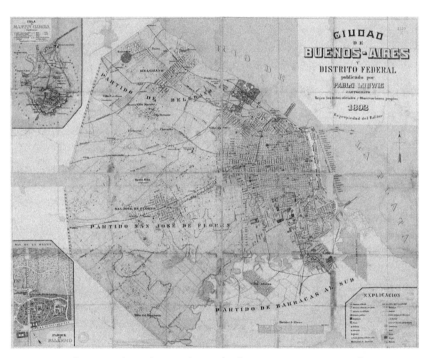

Buenos Aires has gone through several periods of expansion. A sequence of maps from 1892, 1933, and 2003 demonstrates the city's growth. In this 1892 map, downtown areas are marked out in a neat grid; the contemporary city neighborhoods of Flores and Belgrano appear here as separate towns, distant from the urbanized center even if technically within city limits. *Source: Ciudad de Buenos Aires y Distrito Federal*, by Pablo Ludwig, 1892. Courtesy of the Biblioteca Nacional Mariano Moreno.

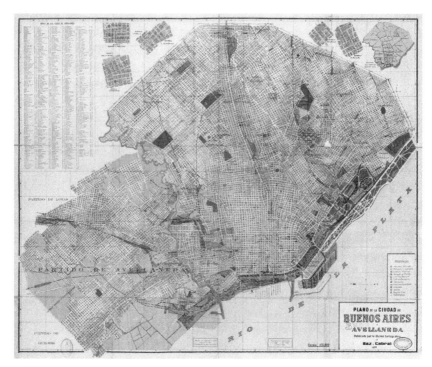

In this map from 1933 the city is undergoing a process of urbanization and expansion. Although the city has been organized into a grid, construction is still uneven: dark gray areas delineate paved roads and developed city blocks where buildings have been constructed; white streets are unpaved; light gray city blocks are undeveloped. Across the river, Avellaneda shows significant development, a sign of the emergence of industry in the city outskirts. *Source: Plano de la Ciudad de Buenos Aires y Avellaneda*, by Oficina Cartográfica de Baz y Cabral, 1933. Courtesy of the Biblioteca Nacional Mariano Moreno.

was gradually filling out. The introduction of new forms of transportation was a key element of this expansion. For much of the nineteenth century, Buenos Aires was a horse-drawn city. It had one of the highest numbers of horses per capita in the world, in no small part because the animals proliferated at incredible rates in the surrounding pampa region and could be acquired for cheap. Horses pulled the city's first line of *bondis* or *colectivos,* a colloquial term for shared transportation, used today to refer to buses. These horse-drawn carts traveled through city streets and offered laborers a shared ride to work. A railway, built in 1857, better connected the city to the countryside. Urban passenger trains quickly followed, and in 1897 the first electric trolley was inaugurated. Residents marveled at the speed with which it traversed the city, "devouring distances" at a then-notable twenty miles per hour.

In 1913 the city inaugurated its underground rail, the *subte*—the first of

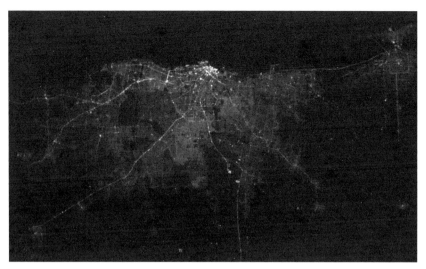

In this photograph taken from the NASA space station in 2003, urbanized Greater Buenos Aires illuminates the night sky. Electric lights stream out into the suburbs, marking population density and making urbanization so visible that there appears to be no break between the capital's city limits and the once distant cities. *Source: Buenos Aires at Night*, by Earth Science and Remote Sensing Unit, NASA, Johnson Space Center, February 2003, https://eoimages.gsfc.nasa.gov/images/imagerecords/3000/3295/ ISS006-E-24987.JPG. Courtesy of the Earth Science and Remote Sensing Unit, NASA Johnson Space Center.

its kind in Latin America. The wooden cars dashed under the city streets and marked out Buenos Aires as a city on the cusp of modernity. It was this novelty, along with the adoption of the automobile, that most dramatically changed movement. Although at first automobiles were only for the wealthy, it was not long before innovative drivers adapted models to create a new style of *colectivo*: by the late 1930s a number of cars ran on fixed routes and charged a price for a shared ride. (See "The *Colectivo*, an Innovation for the Modern City.") Modern transport revolutionized getting around in the city. It allowed for swift access from the city's downtown to its borders and connected once-disparate neighborhoods; working families could move out of their cramped living quarters downtown and head inland to build new homes and neighborhoods in areas that had once been considered outside the comforts of urban living. In these emerging neighborhoods, like Caballito, Villa Crespo, and Floresta, there were also *conventillos*, but they were not as common as in La Boca or downtown; the buildings that came to dominate the landscape were instead modest houses that began as simple dwellings and over time became larger, more solid, more permanent constructions. (See "New Neighborhoods and the Expansion of City Life.")

For residents, the new neighborhoods, and specifically, the even smaller

In the 1930s horse-drawn carriages still coexisted with newer methods of transportation. In this photograph, an electric trolley shares the road with an automobile and, to the far left, a horse-drawn cart. *Source: Los tranvías (Alsina y Defensa)*, by Anonymous, 1930. Courtesy of the Archivo General de la Nación Argentina Dpto. Doc. Fotográficos. Inv: 486:145653.

Commuters travel in the city's first subway line. When it was built, the Buenos Aires *subte* was the only underground rail in Latin America and the thirteenth constructed worldwide. More lines were added in the following decades, though expansion slowed in the 1940s. *Source: Subte Leonardo N. Alem*, by Anonymous, 1938. Courtesy of the Archivo General de la Nación Argentina Dpto. Doc. Fotográficos.

space known as the *barrio chico* (small neighborhood), functioned as an epicenter of daily life and local identity. In a four- or five-square-block radius, neighbors might share a school, a library, a church, shops, cafés, a police station, a sports club, and a corner store. Public spaces like the neighborhood plaza—which often included benches, small paths, shaded green areas, and a playground for children—teemed with life. (See "Green Spaces.") Residents formed *sociedades de fomento* (neighborhood associations) that facilitated a profound sense of belonging. (See "Neighborhood Associations.")

At the same time, while neighbors often expressed a sense of devotion and "love" for their individual *barrios*, lifestyles were not that different across these spaces. More established areas like El Once, La Boca, San Telmo, and Recoleta were associated with certain ethnic or social classes (and to a certain degree these were also generalizations). (See "El Once, The Changing Character of an Iconic Jewish Neighborhood.") However, the neighborhoods possessed similar institutions and habits, with small variations. In particular, newer neighborhoods like Villa Lugano, Caballito, Chacarita, and Boedo were most characterized by diversity—residents represented a range of social backgrounds and national origins. In these new spaces, laborers, semi-skilled workers, artisans, small business owners, and educated professionals became neighbors. The mixed character of these communities also spoke to the reality that Buenos Aires had become a city with industries rather than an industrial city: neighborhood life centered not on a specific kind of work but on a social and cultural living space. By midcentury, these experiences also cemented perceptions of the city as a predominantly middle-class space, albeit one with noted pockets of wealth and poverty.

As neighborhoods were populated, many residents aspired to live in a single-family home. (See "The Single-Family Home as a Cultural and Political Ideal.") Typical urban houses in the city are one- or two-story residences built around a long internal patio and decorated or updated with unique art deco façades and details. Yet even at their peak, most families did not occupy these homes alone; in 1943, 54 percent of households shared their street address with extended family or rented out part of a home. Apartment-living was extremely common. By midcentury, some apartment buildings offered modest living quarters with a bathroom and a kitchen; others were more sophisticated and attracted the more accommodated sectors. Over time it became clear that the city built upward, not just outward, and by 1980, 73 percent of the city's population lived in rented or owned apartments. (See "Vertical Living.")

New Extremes and a More Fragmented City

The idea that the neighborhood served as an epicenter of daily life—so pivotal in the 1920s and '30s—began to fade by the end of the twentieth century.

Although in some neighborhoods new high-rise developments and other cultural transformations have been the strongest catalysts of change, other pernicious factors contributed. The repressive climate brought on by the 1976 military coup, followed by a period of intense political neoliberalism in the 1990s and a stark economic crisis in 2001, left many public spaces in relative decline until more recent renovations. Privatization, combined with a society deeply damaged by a diminished economy, meant further disregard for the former cornerstones of the old neighborhood culture: the plaza, local sports clubs, and *sociedades de fomento* (neighborhood associations).

Other recent private real estate ventures radically changed the face of neighborhoods. In the 1990s, private investments converted Puerto Madero, a long-abandoned port, into a modern, expensive residential and commercial area. The development was completed in the early 2000s, immediately after an economic crisis had left much of the city in disarray. Given the context, its tight grid of towers, pristine paved boardwalks, recycled architecture, yacht club, and high-end restaurants seemed a study in contrast. There was no question that the new neighborhood's residents would represent the wealthiest sectors, and its postcard-worthy scenes would make it a tourist attraction. Over time, however, the area's public outdoor spaces, pedestrian bridge, and scenic views have also drawn more diverse crowds: on weekends the area fills up with passersby from all social sectors.

For some, Puerto Madero is a success story—a sign of Buenos Aires's constant renovation and an example of a new type of modern city with high-density luxury condominiums, orderly streets, and manicured public spaces. For others, it is a peculiar space that serves as a sign of inequalities; it is set near the Casa Rosada (the administrative building for the executive power) and not far from two informal housing settlements (Villa 31 / Barrio Mugica and Rodrigo Bueno). The contrast serves as a reminder of the state's longstanding failures to address the housing needs of its poorest residents.

Privatized ventures like Puerto Madero have worked in tandem with state investment, but by and large, and throughout the twentieth century, state initiatives to construct low- and middle-income housing both in the city and in Greater Buenos Aires have been few. Rare examples include the construction of Ciudad Evita, a suburban neighborhood imagined as an idealized worker's neighborhood during the first Peronist period; "monoblocks" in the city outskirts during the 1960s, using funds, in part, from the US Alliance for Progress; and the low-income housing of Fuerte Apache, which began in the 1960s but was further populated when the military regime (1976–83) forcibly removed *villa* residents from the capital city. For the most part, however, governments—civilian and military—have been quite ineffective in offering solutions to the lack of accessible housing.

One of the consequences of the state's erratic and limited approach to resolving housing problems in the city has been the growth of informal settlements, which are home to tens of thousands of city residents. The history of Buenos Aires's *villas* goes back many decades. When migrants arrived in large numbers during the 1930s and '40s, they were propelled by a combination of increasingly precarious working conditions in the rural Interior and industrializing policies that encouraged output of urban factories. Many of these migrants moved to Greater Buenos Aires in search of jobs and gradually built homes there; others struggled to find affordable housing and, as a result, began to build their own living quarters on empty lots and marginal, undeveloped public lands near work opportunities. These spaces lacked basic urban services and, at first, were composed of rather rudimentary single-story shacks built out of found and recycled materials, including zinc paneling, brick, and concrete. When they first began to appear, politicians and other residents believed the neighborhoods were temporary improvised "solutions" to a housing emergency; thus, they were called *villas de emergencia* (emergency settlements). Despite this name, these makeshift neighborhoods—like Villa 31 / Barrio Mugica, which saw its first residents set up camp in the 1930s—became somewhat hidden but permanent parts of the landscape for the next century.

Reactions from outside the *villa* were mixed: academics and scholars studied these sites as a new phenomenon in the modern capitalist urban periphery. Politicians questioned what was to be done. Some activists, including *villa* residents, looked to foster change and improve living conditions through social action and, later, pushed the state to formalize and urbanize the neighborhoods. By the late 1960s and early 1970s, the *villero* movement was quite active: political radicalization garnered the involvement of students, leftist priests, and community organizers who fought for land rights, housing, and job security for residents. At the same time, during the 1976–83 civic-military dictatorship, the government argued that *villas* should be demolished and the area "cleaned." (See "Dictatorship and the Razing of the City's *Villas*.") These proposals often meant the violent destruction of residents' homes without the offer of any alternative. It is estimated that in 1976, 215,000 people lived in *villas*; in 1981, 14,000 were left. While some moved to formal housing projects outside the city, many who evacuated had little choice but to set up new informal settlements in Greater Buenos Aires.

In both the city and Greater Buenos Aires, *villa* residents continue to face both stigmatization and the unrelenting challenges of equipping their neighborhoods with basic infrastructure and services such as paved streets, drinkable water, street lighting, access to public transportation, and school and primary health care centers. Outsiders often paint the *villa* as a forbidden and dangerous space built out of delinquency, but voices from the inside describe a more complex culture, in which the violence of poverty coexists with a resilient, diverse, and hard-working community. (See "The Permanence of 'Emergency' Settlements.") By the 2010s, a growing acceptance among city officials that these neighborhoods are part of the social fabric of the city gave way to calls that the government recognize inhabitants' rights to live there, equip the neighborhoods with services, and integrate them as recognized neighborhoods. These initiatives, however, have been uneven and in many cases incomplete; some have also questioned the level of community involvement and express fears that urbanization may also be connected to speculation on land value.

These policies came in tandem with other city initiatives to update an aging urban infrastructure. Over the last two decades, a scattering of other urban planning strategies—bike lanes, an elevated railway, bus lanes, renovated playgrounds at city plazas, traffic control cameras, and outdoor food courts—have made an impact. Although some hail these developments as much-needed updates in the making of a contemporary "global city," others criticize them as top-down measures that prioritize the needs of tourists and speculative investors, continue to prioritize wealthier northern neighborhoods over their southern counterparts, and endanger long-standing neighborhood traditions. Some residents criticize that the proliferation of condominiums with amenities has often meant the demolition of older art nouveau and art deco homes, depriving neighborhoods of their traditional architecture and character. Revisions of the urban code and the challenges of crisis have incited some to rejoin neighborhood assemblies and hold organizational meetings against the demolition of historic constructions and green spaces, among other changes.

The Megacity and the Vast Urban Landscape

While the city has seen steady growth over the last fifty years, the primary marker of Buenos Aires's transformation from bustling port city to a sprawling metropolis is the intense urbanization that has taken place just beyond its borders. The population of "Greater Buenos Aires"—the metropolitan area surrounding the city (10.8 million at the time of the 2022 census)—long ago eclipsed that of the capital city (3.1 million that same year). Its social geography has also been marked by two rather different styles of migration and construction.

On the one hand, since the 1940s, the possibility of finding work and more affordable housing attracted generations of migrants and immigrants to Greater Buenos Aires. By the 1960s, tens of thousands of persons, many from Paraguay, Bolivia, and the Interior of Argentina, had come to reside in expansive neighborhoods and urbanized areas just outside the city's limits. Four processes marked efforts to build working-class housing: residences constructed by private industries; state-constructed housing; occupation of lands for the construction of informal housing; and self-construction. In this final option—the most common—a family purchased a small lot, often in installments, and gradually built on that lot of land, making additions as necessary and possible. Processes of urbanization took place rapidly, and today some bordering cities like Ramos Mejia (around 100,000 inhabitants) or Quilmes (with 600,000 inhabitants) visually resemble neighborhoods of the capital city; other areas offer more rustic infrastructure.

On the other hand, and particularly over the last forty years, less urbanized areas of Greater Buenos Aires have witnessed a smaller (but environmentally impactful) migration of wealthy, upper middle-class, and middle-class families who moved out of the capital to new suburban enclaves. Generations before, elite families in the nineteenth century developed the custom of getting away from the bustle of the city to spend summer months in *casas quintas,* homes in the countryside in towns like Tigre, Flores, Victoria, Olivos, and San Isidro. More than a century later, in the late 1980s and early 1990s, families with money were seeking out a similar sensation of "escape"—and sense of security. They purchased lots in new developments marketed as "countries." These US-style suburban communities were used as weekend residences and included facilities for sports and organized activities, curated green spaces, and private pools, as well as twenty-four-hour security, an electric-fenced perimeter, and secured entryway.

Over the years, a flurry of similar neighborhoods—known as *barrios cerrados*—have been built to be used as primary residences. One of the largest, Nordelta, was conceived of in the early 1990s as a luxurious town behind walls; by 2023, its linked gated neighborhoods, which include man-made lakes, golf courses, and a yacht club, housed forty-five thousand residents. That same year there were more than 870 gated communities in Greater Buenos Aires of varying sizes and styles, from the modest to the luxurious. A scattering of private schools and shopping centers serve these wealthier communities; working-class neighbors enter the walled suburbs to labor as household workers, maintenance and upkeep, and security, among a range of other positions.

These contrasting migrations to the city's outskirts have generated a geography of vivid socioeconomic contrasts in which enclosed pockets of sought-after suburban living spaces border vast and densely populated townships and cities inhabited by the some of the country's poorest communities. Although inequality is certainly not new, the unequal allocation of resources has become all the more marked in periods of economic crisis and inflation. At the close of 2023, twelve thousand new homes were approved for construction in gated communities of Greater Buenos Aires; meanwhile, poverty rates beyond their walls rose steadily—a parallel study calculated that over 40 percent of residents in the metropolitan area outside the capital city were living under the poverty line. Conditions were projected to worsen as an economic crisis deepened.

There is no doubt that the "megacity" of the Buenos Aires metropolitan area is a landscape of strikingly unequal experiences. The capital city remains, for the most part, a vast and walkable urban space in which persons with differing experiences move about its streets and make use of its public spaces. When one strays from the city's most typical tourist attractions, an eclectic array of architectural markers come into view: high-rise luxury condos tower alongside 1920s art deco and art nouveau houses; luxurious hotels stand in close proximity to less visible housing settlements; generations of neighbors gather at local plazas and parks and use a vast network of buses, subways, trains, highways, avenues, and cobblestone streets. A far cry from the colonial port town it once was, a vast urban space extends outward in all directions from the historic city center.

Shopping in the City

Ezequiel Martínez Estrada

In the nineteenth century, shopping became an important part of elite culture. From roughly 1880 to 1940, Florida Street served as a promenade where luxurious imports could be bought and displayed. Wealthy residents strolled the blocks in their finest, and all types of consumer goods—imported and national—filled store windows. Two major department stores became monuments to consumer culture at the turn of the century: a locally owned Gath & Chaves and the only Harrods department store outside the British Empire. In this excerpt from his famous essay Radiografía de la Pampa, *which succinctly critiqued the imbalances of modern Argentina, the writer Ezequiel Martínez Estrada notes that Calle Florida was not just significant for those who could afford to shop there; it also figured prominently in the imagination of middle and lower classes as a place of glamour.*

Since that time, shopping habits have changed. During the first two Peronist administrations, consumer culture became an important component of policies that made it possible for some workers to access lifestyles once out of reach. In the 1990s, several major shopping malls (known as shoppings*) were constructed. These US-style consumer settings were often built over renovated historic buildings, like Abasto (once a food market and entry point for agricultural goods), Patio Bullrich (a former thoroughbred auction house in Recoleta), and Galerías Pacífico (previously a railway headquarters and department store). Before it was restyled as a shopping mall in 1989, the latter was also used as a clandestine detention center during the 1976–83 civic-military dictatorship.*

The consumer turn of these buildings reflected economic trends. During the 1990s, with the peso pegged to the US dollar, the availability of cheap imported goods was a marker of powerful local currency and neoliberal economic policies. In the wake of the 2001 crisis, purchasing power plummeted. Importation restrictions saw the fabrication of new local brands, but widespread unemployment, a loss of savings and wages, and a return to unstable currency made many of the goods sold in those restored consumer palaces far too expensive for most residents. Shoppings nevertheless drew crowds—as did shop-lined streets like those in Palermo, along with outside markets and fairs held in plazas. As on Florida Street decades before, participating in consumer culture did not always require a purchase: passersby were there to window-shop, peruse products, and stroll.

Florida Street (1933)

Ezequiel Martínez Estrada

Florida is the Sunday suit of Buenos Aires, a suit that it wears every day. [. . .] Maybe Florida is Florida because it is so narrow that we are unable to take a step back and contemplate its shop windows from a comfortable distance, disentangling ourselves from its fiction. Like in the movies, Florida dreams of fortune and love. The luxury of the window displays, with jewels, decor, silks, perfume, books, radios, and projectors, makes Florida the shop window of our ambitions. And that's how Florida, like the filmmaker, uses its magic to take us into the palaces of multimillionaires, into spanking clean and perfectly outfitted homes, into little country houses with no mosquitos or stagnant waters, and we share the eventful lives of the world's most important men and industry bigwigs, the life of thieves and artists; or at thirty, we fall in the kind of love we dreamed of when we were eighteen. [. . .] Those shop windows also allow us to grasp at the shadows of the big screen, at that which is beyond our reach, beyond our destiny and behind the glass. All that those people walking around at noon and at dusk dream of at night, or while they work, all of the dreams captured in the gem, in the gorgeous woman, in the book the critics raved about, they are all there, as accessible as the light and shadows of the big screen. There's the Jockey Club, which is like an indoor shop window on Florida, where one dreams of family trees that have yielded over one thousand cubic meters of wood this year, and of the drop of the price of live cattle in Liverpool, and of gambling, which is the machinery of hope. There on Florida are the bars where artists dream, the jewelry shops and the stores of women's dreams, the bookstores of writers' dreams.

The beautiful part of this enormous fiction is that everyone wants to fool themselves into believing it for no good reason, that everyone is a little bit in on the secret and accepts the appearances at face value, imbuing them with reality. And if someone thinks that it's all a lie—as some do in church, or in the theater—no one says a word, and Florida continues to exist in the souls of the faithful.

Translated by Wendy Gosselin and Jane Brodie

From Yellow Fever to COVID-19: Epidemics and Inequalities in the City

Benigno Lugones, Guillermo Rawson, Andrés D'Elía, Nora Cortiñas, and Adolfo Pérez Esquivel

Like the more contemporary COVID-19 pandemic, recurrent cycles of disease in the nineteenth century—particularly the yellow fever epidemic of 1871—exposed Buenos Aires's economic and infrastructural inequalities. In "A Study of Conventillo Housing in Buenos Aires" from 1885, hygienist and politician Guillermo Rawson portrays the conventillos—crowded living spaces that housed many working families—as epicenters of contagion. During the 1871 emergency, the first cases of yellow fever were found in southern neighborhoods of the city, like San Telmo, but the disease spread rapidly in areas with poor hygiene infrastructure and polluted groundwater. Illness ravaged the city, and the population declined. Many died (on some days the death toll neared one thousand); others fled in fear. In "Death in the City in 1871," journalist Benigno Lugones recalls the horrid death toll in the major national newspaper, La Nación. Lugones himself eventually died of tuberculosis at the age of twenty-seven. Infectious diseases remained the most common causes of death until the city made notable (and rather successful) improvements in basic urban infrastructure, like drinkable water, sewers, paved roads, and garbage collection.

The COVID-19 pandemic similarly brought attention to economic divides. In March 2020, with only a handful of cases reported and with the daunting uncertainty of a newly declared pandemic, the city's mayor, in accordance with Argentina's president, announced a total lockdown. Residents without special permits were not allowed to assemble for any reason and could circulate only within their neighborhoods to purchase basic goods. As the photograph illustrates, persons walking in pairs, taking public transport, or found outside the perimeter of their neighborhoods were required to present a license to circulate.

These policies also exposed inequalities. While the middle classes scrambled to move work and school online and stayed cooped up in small apartments, many working people were deemed "essential workers" and kept the city functioning. Informal laborers, by contrast, often found themselves without pay. In the poorest sectors of the city, a lack of basic services—including, in some places, running water or internet connection—generated a digital and sanitary divide. In "COVID-19 and Inequality in the Twenty-First Century," human rights activists criticize city officials for the conditions in city's poorest neighborhoods.

Death in the City in 1871 (1872)

Benigno Lugones

One day they counted more than nine hundred dead. In the cemetery, the coffins sat without tombs, forming immense pillars which rose into the open air, beneath a gray, sad sky. That day, the whole city suffered a tremor of horror, a new tremor adding onto all those it had already suffered, because it had never seen such a horrible tragedy. The cruelest surprises continued without end, infinitely varied in form but always identical in substance. [. . .] [People] spoke slowly and in whispers. There was only one thing to communicate: deaths. And each new story was an exacerbation of the horror. For that reason, relatives fled from relatives and friends fled from friends, to escape the contagion. [. . .] But the masses are ignorant and fear is idiotic. [. . .] In the tenements, in the narrow, short, small, dark, dirty rooms, the Neapolitans and the Galicians, covered in filth, died by the dozens, by carts per room, by hundreds per whole house. The authorities met them with a hard hand.

Translated by Liliana Frankel

A Study of Conventillo Housing in Buenos Aires (1885)

Guillermo Rawson

When we, comfortably accommodated in our houses, see the faces of scarcity and misery parading before us, it seems that we complete a religious and moral obligation by giving them assistances. [. . .] But let's follow them, if only in our minds, to the desolate space that shelters them; alongside them we enter the dark corner, narrow, humid and infested, where they pass their time, living, sleeping, where they suffer the pains of illness and are taken by premature death. [. . .] Let's think of that accumulation of hundreds of people, of all ages and conditions, lumped in their cramped, unhealthy rooms, let's remember that there they grow and reproduce by the thousands, under those lethal influences, the germs so efficient at producing infections and the poisoned air which slowly escapes with its charge of death, spreading in the streets. [. . .] The tropical illnesses and contagions which tend to spread widely have their origin in the less cared-for neighborhoods of the south, which alone proves that these are the sections in which the health of the city is least tended-to. [. . .] The rental houses, with rare exceptions, are old buildings, poorly constructed from the beginning, now decadent, but which were never intended for their current use.

Translated by Liliana Frankel

Restricted Circulation during the 2020 Lockdown (2020)
Andrés D'Elía

Courtesy of the photographer.

COVID-19 and Inequality in the Twenty-First Century: A Petition (2020)
Nora Cortiñas and Adolfo Pérez Esquivel

We appeal to our public officials to take responsibility, to the media outlets to fulfill their commitments, and to the conscience of our society as a whole, to shed light on the magnitude and severity of the violations of the most basic of human rights that are taking place in Villa 31 in Retiro, where more than fifty thousand people have been without water for nine days. The day before yesterday, a woman from the neighborhood, from the Bajo Autopista sector, died of coronavirus. But she did not die only of coronavirus. She was eighty-four years old, in good health, and lived in an enormous, impoverished community located in the wealthiest city of Argentina. She died from the same abandonment and apathy that 350,000 human beings overcrowded in the worst living conditions suffer in silence. This cannot be allowed to occur in a democracy. This cannot be allowed to occur in silence. This cannot be allowed. The first victim of Barrio Mugica—and there could be many more due to the lack of an emphatic social repudiation of the situation and absence of an immediate response from the state—lived in a nine-square-meter room with her eighty-five-year-old husband and her daughter, who contracted the virus; they share a bathroom with eleven other people. Because they were asymptomatic, they were refused a swab test. They were also not told to isolate; it took forty-eight hours after their daughter's diagnosis for someone to ask for "her parents' phone number" from her colleagues at *La Poderosa* [a media outlet that covers news from the *villas*], who have a screenshot to prove it. [. . .] The curve of infections in Villa 31 grew 1,900 percent in just four days, and yet the public received no official data about what was happening in the slums of Buenos Aires. There was no [information] between Thursday morning and Sunday afternoon, when there was finally some slight recognition of the information the community had been shouting at the top of its lungs. "Confirmed cases have jumped to 182 in the impoverished neighborhoods of the capital city," of which 107 occurred in an area that had only three cases before being left without water. [. . .] Are we really going to make a scandal out of the images of "crowded passageways" when people had to leave their homes seven times a day in order to fill a bucket, get food supplies, or go to their informal jobs? How can they say so blithely that "some neighbors do not want to isolate," as if they had no idea of the conditions created by their own housing policies?

Translated by Leslie Robertson

The *Colectivo*, an Innovation for the Modern City

Anonymous and César Fernández Moreno

A popular legend credits Buenos Aires with the invention of the bus. Even if this claim may be exaggerated, it is true that residents have come up with many creative forms of shared transportation. Long before automobiles entered the city landscape, residents shared horse-drawn carriages to get around. In the 1920s cars took over: although in 1923 there were 19,300 license plates registered for motor vehicles in Buenos Aires, in the short span of seven years, nearly 50,000 cars were registered. Some, known as colectivos, were used for shared rides; the cars connected once-disparate neighborhoods along regular routes. The photograph shows how early automobile colectivos served as a form of worker transport. The text, by the writer and urban chronicler César Fernández Moreno, illustrates how bus culture evolved: by the 1970s, hundreds of bus lines connected the city. Although they were regulated by city government, buses were privately owned, and drivers often decorated their vehicles in extravagant ways. Among the most popular form of decoration was the fileteado style, a typical local embellishment characterized by lines that billow into spirals, bold colors, and symmetry. It also became common to add colorful curtains, floor lights, and all types of decorations to the interior of the cabin. A representation of this style can be found in the color insert to this volume, in the painting Con música de Tito Rodríguez, *by Marcia Schvartz.*

Getting to Work by Colectivo *in the 1930s (ca. 1931)*

Anonymous

Courtesy of the Archivo General de la Nación Argentina Dpto. Doc. Fotográficos, Inv: 6483.

The Colectivo *(1972)*

César Fernández Moreno

Colectivos are an entirely Argentine creation. [. . .] To understand *colectivos*, you need one very *porteño* ability: craftiness. [. . .] The passenger must bring to bear his craftiness as soon as he boards the *colectivo*: he must board quickly, without wasting a single second as it pauses at each stop before lurching off again. He then must pay for his trip just as the driver shifts into first gear. When the driver shifts into second, the passenger gets his ticket and change. The craftiness then involves figuring out how to get a seat when the *colectivo* is full: he must stand as far back as possible, where he's most likely to get a seat. [. . .] And boy, is the bus driver crafty. [. . .] He's like a pianist, able to move different parts of his body to entirely different tunes. He drives with his left hand. Sometimes he smokes and even turns the dial on a portable radio. Despite the traffic, he guides his little mastodon with the ease of a bike rider. With his right hand, he tears the ticket and makes change. He can talk courteously to the policeman or to the friend who is riding next to him, standing up. The bus driver is like the captain of a ship at sea: his power is absolute. [. . .] From his seat, he berates the passengers reluctant to move toward the back and toward the side. [. . .] There are different types of drivers.

[. . .] There's the mature, the calm, the cool drivers. There's the aggressive driver, the skeptic. The driver who makes sarcastic comments. [. . .] There's the young, almost infantile driver, who doesn't have much authority but who imposes respect merely because he sits on the throne. [. . .] When these drivers are behind the wheel, passengers are subject to the forcefulness of youth: the sudden bursts of speed, the slamming on of brakes, the sudden swerves [. . .]. The *colectivo* invites reflection, inside and out. [. . .] There are bourgeois *colectivos* filled with well-dressed ladies speaking softly and chitchatting as if attending a fancy party. [. . .] There are *colectivos* for the poor that start and end in the rusty heart of the slums. It's a pleasure to use the entire system of *colectivos* to get from one neighborhood to the next, as if playing an enormous organ with pipes of different colors. Like an abstract bridge that connects our house and our office: we are nearing the ideal of the moving sidewalk. [. . .] The bodies of its fleet are still covered with flowers, tiny painted flourishes, curtains with tassels, bright splashes of plastic on ceiling and walls, shiny scales of mother-of-pearl or gemstones decorating the wheel.

Translated by Wendy Gosselin and Jane Brodie

New Neighborhoods and the Expansion
of City Life
Conrado Nalé Roxlo, Alberto Vázquez, and Pablo Riggio

Buenos Aires's growth from 1900 to 1940 was quite pronounced, largely propelled by the urbanization of neighborhoods located farther out from the city center. This expansion was the result of a deliberate modernization—some of it state-led, some of it privately funded—and a slightly more haphazard growth guided by individual investments: families moved out in search of affordable plots of land where they might build a modest home, either on their own or with the help of a small contractor. The government regulated lot sizes and the supply of basic services such as water, sewage, pavements, and electricity, a task that coincided with new sanitary standards and aesthetics. The neighborhoods of Villa Urquiza and Flores changed considerably during this period. Flores was once considered a separate town in the countryside, where some members of the elite built summer residences. In "Memories of Flores," writer Conrado Nalé Roxlo recalls the feeling of being in the countryside.

Villa Urquiza was likewise remote. When neighborhood resident Alberto Vázquez was born there a century ago, the area was called La Siberia and was mostly empty lots. It slowly populated over the course of the 1930s, first with the arrival of the factory, and then later, when bus routes began to run from downtown. On the event of his hundredth birthday, Vázquez recounted his memories to the neighborhood newspaper El Barrio, *noting that the typical neighborhood lifestyle emerged in a gradual way: when his parents arrived, buildings were few and far between; when he was a boy, he played soccer with other kids in the empty lots, but by the time he was an adult, community life was more vibrant—he bought food in a crowded local market on the weekends and met his wife at a neighborhood dance.*

Memories of Flores (1978)

Conrado Nalé Roxlo

I was very small, and I don't have a clear sense of the degree to which Flores was separated from the city center, but I know that the young folks would hang out in the train station awaiting the arrivals, as still happens today in remote towns. Other charms of the Flores of my youth included the estates, the truly grand estates with their artistically wrought gates and gardens populated with white statues. For many of those families, these were habitual residences, and for others, they were summer homes. They would hold sumptuous dances, organize brilliant equestrian events. I remember [it was] like an English picture card: the *amazonas* in long skirts and crested hats riding atop their graceful purebred horses.

Translated by Liliana Frankel

A Hundred Years in the Neighborhood (2017)
Alberto Vázquez and Pablo Riggio

In what was called La Siberia, there wasn't anything more than a few houses, all of them on long plots of land extending out from the street. The roads were made of dirt and each had a trench in front of the homes; the rainwater flowed through them to what [. . .] used to be a swamp. There were enormous fields in the whole area. Just before the mid-'20s, they paved Burela Street, then Cullen, and that's how the neighborhood began to grow. [. . .] The "medieval" solitude of La Siberia saw its sun set with the arrival of the Avanti cigarette factory in 1902, located on the block between Roosevelt, Cullen, Ceretti, and Burela Streets. The number of employees, a majority of whom were children of immigrants, continued to increase with the passage of time, and according to Vázquez, the area experienced a true revolution without any type of official planning. "My father built rooms onto our house and we rented them to the people who came to the factory," he recalls. [. . .] There were about fifty workers in the 1920s. I would see them leave at eleven, and by five in the afternoon, the women would have their hands browned from kneading tobacco. More and more families arrived to La Siberia, and the Gorriti School—which was much smaller than it is now—could not cope, so they opened a primary school on Congreso and Triunvirato. Kids organized soccer games between the different blocks. "The ball was made of rags, when a rubber one appeared everyone was up in arms!" he says. The main weekend attraction was the silent theater called General Urquiza. Ten cents was enough to enjoy three movies. Dances were held on Sunday nights in the Círculo Urquiza social club; there he met his wife, Nelly, to whom he was married for sixty-eight years.

Translated by Liliana Frankel

Green Spaces

Ricardo Lorenzo, "Borocotó"

The plaza is an essential part of community life. Many of the city's major parks were designed by landscape architect Carlos Thays at the end of the nineteenth century to integrate aspects of local Argentine ecology with French and British garden designs. The Bosques de Palermo remains the largest green space. In the nineteenth century it was an important place for elite social life, but by the twentieth, it, like many other green spaces, was no longer so exclusive. Social reformers regarded both the smaller neighborhood plazas and the larger elaborate green spaces as the "lungs" of the city, boosting health and "civility." The photograph captures neighbors in a playground and plaza in 2022, and the essay "The Neighborhood Plaza" (from 1938) fondly recalls these spaces as a center of neighborhood activity; today there are over six hundred plazas within the city limits, and most include an aging carousel, shaded park benches, a flag pole, renovated play spaces for children, and a scattering of monuments.

A Neighborhood Plaza (2022)

Courtesy of the photographer, Lisa Ubelaker Andrade.

The Neighborhood Plaza (1938)

Ricardo Lorenzo, "Borocotó"

We all had "our plaza"; in the afternoons, after school, a piece of bread in hand, we met at the bench and set up the match; we played until the gardener who walked with a country gait shooed us off and left us to wonder, is all that grass just to look at? At dusk, our playing field was only as wide as the streetlamp's reach; sometimes we played tag while the girls sang and our mothers talked about us, while the old men sat in the middle of the plaza, talking about wars, one reading the paper aloud to the others; they argued and sauntered off to their houses, sure they had convinced the others.

Translated by Lisa Ubelaker Andrade

Neighborhood Associations

Corporación Mitre, Boedo Neighborhood Association,

and Unión Vecinal

As city neighborhoods became more populated, many residents looking for new homes placed a high premium on the idea of having a "private life." Yet urban living also meant they would need to negotiate the use of shared public spaces. The neighborhood association—known as the sociedad de fomento—*became a central institution. In these texts, local newspapers discuss the role and purpose of these associations, seeing them as the engine behind local "progress" and community identity. The notion of "loving one's neighborhood" emerges as an important idea, guiding a sense of participation as well as belonging.*

Creating a Neighborhood (1927)
Corporación Mitre

The Mitre Corporation has taken up the task of disseminating culture, creating a library, giving classes and talks, founding our newspaper, promoting music and entertainment, and despite the opinion of those who think with their gut, this work is its greatest reward.

Translated by Liliana Frankel

Love for Boedo (1940)
Boedo Neighborhood Association

To love one's neighborhood is to desire its progress and its material and spiritual value: to buy everything that one needs in one's neighborhood, to choose *its* spectacles, *its* cafes, *its* schools, *its* meeting places.

Translated by Liliana Frankel

Unión Vecinal

The Unión Vecinal should be free of ideological differences or credos. If one wants to play politics they should go to the [Peronist] *unidad básica* or the [Radical Party] *comité*, because in the neighborhood association one should only find the neighbor, in his condition as such.

Translated by Liliana Frankel

El Once: The Changing Character
of an Iconic Jewish Neighborhood

César Tiempo and Marcelo Cohen

Although many neighborhoods of Buenos Aires are associated with unique character-istics or connected to a particular class or niche identity, today most are more diverse than such classifications would let on. Good examples include Villa Crespo and El Once. By 1920, the Jewish population of Argentina reached 150,000, and the major-ity resided in the capital city. These two neighborhoods became important centers for Jewish life. While the neighborhoods still contain community centers, eateries, temples, and many Jewish-owned businesses, El Once and Villa Crespo are also now home to a more diverse community. In the following accounts, two writers describe the neighborhood of El Once, nearly fifty years apart.

Enclave in El Once (1937)

César Tiempo

On Lavalle Street up toward Pueyrredón, the appearance of Jewish life changes, as if immersed in a fog. Here, next to the typical junk shops and watchmakers, next to the bakeries in whose windows challah, that braided, sometimes-sweet bread, and *beigalej* blossom, is a cluster of old houses and *conventillos*, vestibules with fruit stands and balconies where private bed-clothes are aired, while slobs and blundering peddlers crisscross a hellish Ba-bel. Next to that new building that until just yesterday was home to half the Jewish community and is now a gaping parking garage, we come upon the synagogue and the Talmud á B'nei Israel. We can see the ritual undertakings from the street when, at sunset, a group of the faithful raise their prayers to Adonai under the guidance of the supple and booming voice of a tall and wil-lowy Jew wrapped in a prayer shawl.

Translated by Wendy Gosselin and Jane Brodie

Diversity in El Once (2007)

Marcelo Cohen

From Rivadavia to Córdoba Avenues and from Callao to Pueyrredón, the neighborhood of El Once, more like a few-block appendage that the spirit of a neighborhood overtook to the south and west, is ninety square blocks of motley buildings—cheap eight-story real estate developments, unpolished pearls of rationalist architecture, and fortresses in the best Parisian bourgeois style—with an average, in the sixty densest blocks, of 120 storefronts per block, many of them wholesale outlets. Fabric and leather shops, dressmakers, home supply stores, gift shops. Billions of pesos in sales each year. Churches, religious schools, gyms, a hundred-year-old German school, Buddhist temples, and a wide variety of synagogues; film distributors; bargain video stores; and used bookshops. Lebanese, Syrians, Ashkenazi and Sephardic Jews, Armenians, Turkish Jews, Koreans, Chinese, Peruvians, Paraguayans, Bolivians, and now Brazilians as well, blasély vying for customers among the constant stream of people that converges in Plaza Miserere to take the western-bound trains, wandering slowly in the delicious stupor of possible purchases. The emporium of cheap knockoffs. Those who will never buy anything on the internet will shop here, alongside—indeed, one with—camp-lovers in search of oddities and middle-class families who have seen better days looking for an affordable outfit for their daughter's fifteenth birthday party.

Translated by Wendy Gosselin and Jane Brodie

The Single-Family Home as a Cultural and Political Ideal

Sameer Makarius and Mundo Peronista

As the urban map filled out in the 1930s, the single-family home became an idealized form of living, even if it remained an elusive goal for many. The casa chorizo—*so named because its dimensions made it resemble a chorizo sausage—was a style of construction typical of the era. Built on 30-by-165-foot lots, the* casa chorizo *features an outdoor patio that runs along one side and a line of high-ceiling rooms running opposite. Owners decorated the façade with details and ornamental designs, many in art deco style. The* casa cajón *was another common layout—it resembled, as its name suggests, a simple box, but it left space for the owner to build additions when the means became available. Writers and social reformers of all stripes lauded these models of housing as important contributions to modern urban family life, purporting that the single-family home facilitated community and moral living. A revised style of* casa cajón, *the* chalet californiano, *began to dominate the popular imagination in the 1940s, and during the first Peronist era (1946–55) a more modest version nicknamed the* chalecito peronista *appeared as an option for few sectors of the working classes. These houses were held up as a symbol of change, of a new universally accessible consumer culture and a growing feeling of Buenos Aires as a city where workers could reach a higher standard of living.*

"This Is My Neighborhood" is an excerpt from the pro-Peronist magazine Mundo Peronista, *printed in 1953. It suggests that not only was the Peronist government building single-family homes for the nation's workers, but neighborhoods of such houses were also "improving" the habits and culture of those who lived there. State-led housing (Peronist or otherwise) never came to dominate the landscape, but descriptions like these connected the single-family home to an idealized upward mobility. In the photograph* A Quiet Neighborhood Street *by Sameer Makarius, a midcentury photographer who dedicated a large portion of his work to chronicling the urban landscape, one can view a more typical scene: houses alongside multifloor apartment buildings.*

A Quiet Neighborhood Street (ca. 1953)

Sameer Makarius

Calle de Barrio, by Sameer Makarius, ca. 1953. Courtesy of Karim Makarius.

This Is My Neighborhood (1952)

Mundo Peronista

Come with me for a bit.

Take a good look, from up here. It is situated in front of General Paz Avenue and was inaugurated just three years ago.

It is a new neighborhood. But I am one of the old inhabitants of these same spaces.

Now, come along with me. Let's keep walking. I live there, in that beautiful chalet on the right. I live comfortably, as people should live.

It's all a question of habit.

At the beginning, when we came to this neighborhood, when they gave us this house, I admit we were not so comfortable in it. The house was just too pretty, and we had always lived in a poor house made of wood. We had never had electric light or gas for cooking. We didn't know what it was like to walk on a waxed floor. But that is what some people said—maybe you were among them—that giving us these houses was like "throwing daisies to the pigs."

They forgot just one thing. That in life, perfecting one's habits is a question of time.

How we have changed!

Now I have surprised even myself with the ways we have changed. Look at my chalet. Do you see those pleasant curtains? They were made by my wife on a sewing machine that I bought her with the fruits of my labor. You might ask why we didn't have curtains in the house where we used to live. If you ask, it is because you don't know how we used to live: earning less than what we needed, spending to live, out of work; with no space for recreation, schools, churches . . .

In little time we have changed so much that the people who live here are not the same people they were before. They are new people. [. . .] Here there are laborers, employees, civil servants . . . But despite all that we are equals. Because the dignity of work makes us equals. We leave our home at an early hour. And almost always at the same time our women begin their housekeeping. [. . .] You see those women cutting flowers in the garden? They form part of one of the many families in my neighborhood and they are cutting flowers to decorate their homes, finishing their daily chores. And what do you say of those four people calmly sitting in the clearing between the grass and the garden? Is that not a truly admirable picture?

Translated by Lisa Ubelaker Andrade

Vertical Living

Homero Expósito

Although many residents idealized the single-family home, most live in apartments; those who live in houses often share their dwelling with other occupants or renters. Although apartment living is very common, it has often been depicted in a critical light, as isolating and even damaging. In 1929, the writer Roberto Arlt, famous for his sharp depictions of urban living, reflected, "We, the people of the city, are accustomed to a sixteen-square-meter space. To the darkness of the apartment. To all the frankly abominable [conditions] that progress, the stingy property owners, and city housing regulations have mounted on our heads." Years later, Juan Cafferata, a formidable voice in debates over housing, echoed: "The apartment, which offers amenities of technical progress, has simply forgotten about the children. The home is a golden cage; but it lacks soul. The egoism, the landlords' eagerness for profit, the desire for the easy life, has created [. . .] elegant conventillos *that produce no emotion and retain no memory." In this tango by Homero Expósito titled "Sexto piso" ("The Sixth Floor"), the author observes a city of apartment buildings as a backdrop for traitorous love.*

The Sixth Floor (1955)

Homero Expósito

Picture window on the sixth floor
You're lost, I'm done in
and this pain that ails me . . .
Picture window, and the men below so small
and the poor and the rich
all so small . . .
Down there they run around like ants:
all worn out, but bread's not cheap.
Picture window, a lens that
transmits my pain for the city.
Alone,
without your love, down and alone
I fly

through the clouds of sleepless nights.
Oh! The bitter taste of
seeing this hell, once the balcony
of a sixth heaven!
No! Nothing to do but live
like this, clenched and trampled down on the ground.
If sorrow
makes the mediocre poor,
how you must have suffered! [. . .]
Picture window, and this poisonous pain
so tired of living and the endless waiting.

Translated by Wendy Gosselin and Jane Brodie

Dictatorship and the Razing of the City's *Villas*

City Housing Office, Magtara Feres,

and Eduardo Blaustein

During the 1976–83 dictatorship, the military began a violent process of "eradicating" the city's informal settlements. As "A City Ordinance" shows, the military saw the irregularity of constructions, the lack of services and infrastructure, and the racial and ethnic makeup of its residents as incompatible with its ideal. They began to demolish the neighborhoods and vacate their occupants, often citing sanitation and health as a reason. In "Recollections of a Demolition" resident Magtara Feres recalls how families were put out on the street and their homes and belongings destroyed. Some were relocated to low-quality housing miles outside the city. The operation was conducted in four stages: "freezing," which sought to stop the expansion of villas *within the city; "discouragement," which looked to push the population out by cutting off electricity, stopping trash collection, cutting water, removing public transportation, and engaging in verbal threats; and "eradication," which encouraged residents to move elsewhere—by their own accord, by paying transport back to their country or town of origin, or, ultimately, by force. The final stage was demolition. The media—by then extremely censored and curtailed—voiced approval and depicted* villas *as violent, crime-infested, and opaque. The process of demolition intensified as the opening night of the 1978* FIFA *World Cup—hosted in the city—neared. The* villas *located near the River Plate stadium were the first to be razed, followed by Villa 31 in Retiro and, in 1979, the largest, in Bajo Flores. Residents resisted the measures. They petitioned and stood in protest. Urban* villas *decreased in size but did not disappear. Following the return to democracy, some were rebuilt; their initiatives gained more public acceptance, and politicians and media outlets began to call for measures to urbanize the spaces rather than demolish them.*

A City Ordinance (1976)

City Housing Office

The mayor's office hereby informs the population that, in accordance with its policy of freezing the growth of *villas* in the city, no new dwellings will be built in such areas, and the expansion of existing dwellings is strictly prohibited. Those who fail to comply with this order are warned that any new construction will be torn down and legal measures will be taken against those who violate the legitimate rights of dominion that the city exercises over its territories. [. . .] The city, as the authority responsible for the urbanization and the upkeep of the city, neither can nor should tolerate the spread of precarious constructions, which are counter to the basic material and spiritual needs of human life, and thus also a threat to public health.

Translated by Wendy Gosselin and Jane Brodie

Recollections of a Demolition (2001)
Magtara Feres and Eduardo Blaustein

Magtara Feres recalls the day her old house was torn down.

> MF: It was six in the morning. A neighbor told us what was happening. We knocked on our neighbors' doors to warn them. [. . .] There were army tanks and trucks. We sent our kids away so they wouldn't end up in jail. Then I heard a noise like a stampede. That was when the first house fell, and I started crying. Every time I remember it, I start crying all over again.

How many houses did they ultimately manage to tear down?

> MF: Four hundred and ten.

Did you ever try to resist at all?

> MF: We tried. The women lay down in front of the bulldozers. But they always came at daybreak and started shooting . . . what's the name of that stuff that smells and makes you feel like you're choking?

Tear gas.

> MF: I remember we put blankets over the windows to keep from choking. And we had to take the people who had asthma or heart trouble over to Cobo Avenue.

Did they shoot the gas on a day when things got out of hand or . . . ?

> MF: No. They shot it every night so that people would stay indoors. And they would say, "If you don't leave, we'll tear your house down."

Translated by Wendy Gosselin and Jane Brodie

The Permanence of "Emergency" Settlements

Anonymous, David Fernández, and Dalma Villalba

The first settlements in what came to be known as Villa 31 appeared near the Retiro railway station at the beginning of the 1930s. These makeshift communities grew in the wake of the economic crisis and as migrants from the country's Interior arrived in the city but were unable to find affordable housing. Initially they were thought to be temporary. The first photo represents this initial settlement in 1932; the second, taken in the same area nearly eighty years later, shows how the neighborhood has grown. Today Villa 31, renamed Barrio Mugica, is still behind Retiro train station's loading docks and, as can be seen in the photograph, is just steps from Recoleta, one of the wealthiest neighborhoods in the city. Recent decades have seen efforts toward greater inclusion and urbanization of neighborhoods like Villa 31 / Barrio Mugica, though results have been quite uneven. The neighborhood's residents, like journalist and activist Dalma Villalba, have also sought to combat the stigma and stereotypes of "being from the villa*" by noting the diversity and resilience of the many immigrants who live there, and the value neighbors place on their community.*

The First Informal Housing Settlements Near Retiro Train Station (1932)

Anonymous

Villa Desocupación, Retiro. Courtesy of the Archivo General de la Nación Argentina Dpto. Doc. Fotográficos.

A View of Villa 31 / Barrio Mugica and Neighboring Retiro (2009)

David Fernández

Villa 31 desde la autopista, by David Fernández, 2009. Courtesy of *Clarín*.

A Heart Beats in "Little" Latin America (2020)

Dalma Villalba

In the *villas* of the city of Buenos Aires, we breathe, we live differently. Here, colors, smells, flavors, idiosyncrasies mix, are made new, are reborn—the mixing of different migrations to Argentina (some from neighboring countries, others in economic exile from brethren countries farther away). This "cosmopolitan" city, the one inside the *villa*, has a different accent, because here are cultures from Perú, Colombia, Bolivia; here we all know some words in Guaraní, we destroy that Argentine presumption that Chileans are "bad"; here we all know something about each other's countries; we've all tried ceviche, *arroz chaufa, sopa de chairo, chipa guazú, sopa paraguaya, salchipapa, leche de tigre, asados* in the street. They say we are lazy or thieves, or that the women here get pregnant so they can receive welfare, but these are ideas that are so false, so banal, that its only worth contending them with a single truth—90 percent of the people who live in the *villas* are doing all of the tasks that the rest of society doesn't want to do—most of the city's construction workers are Paraguayan; Bolivians produce and sell most of the fruits and vegetables the city eats. The women of our neighborhood are some of the greatest economists—with only two *mangos* [pesos] they find a way to cook a meal for everyone and an extra treat for their kids. The *villas* are the cradle of the true *"Patria Grande"*; and do you know how we are able to do that? Because here there is a concept of neighborliness; we still have the pleasure of seeing our kids play in the street, without fear, because our neighbors are part of our families. Our cultural diversity brings us joy, power, and hope to go on, to bet on a better life, and that [one day] we might share our life experiences, our knowledge, and our fears with the rest of the society—a society of which we are a part, even though often it seems they do not wish we were.

Translated by Lisa Ubelaker Andrade

Contrasts in Greater Buenos Aires

Various Authors and Claudia Piñeiro

Greater Buenos Aires—the large metropolitan region around the capital city of Buenos Aires—is a vast urbanized zone and home to living spaces with marked inequalities. The city of Quilmes grew steadily as an industrial center in the 1930s and became home to hundreds of factories by the mid-1940s. The possibility of employment, combined with the relative affordability of land, made it a site where social mobility seemed possible for many. In the late 1970s and early 1980s, new waves of migrants and former residents of villas in the capital city began to occupy and build on marginal lands. As soon as political conditions permitted, those who settled there fought to acquire land rights and basic urban infrastructure. In "An Open Letter to the Mayor of Quilmes," activists, priests, students, union leaders, and politicians from diverse political backgrounds express support for the occupants and protest the lack of housing solutions in the area.

Meanwhile, lands in Greater Buenos Aires were also being bought and developed for countries, *gated suburbs used as weekend getaways. Soon after, similar neighborhoods were designed for use as permanent homes, especially among those who saw investment in a lot as an idealized escape from city life. The homes in these gated communities tend to be eclectic in style, with manicured public spaces rid of "visual pollution." In their most ostentatious renditions, the communities can feature venues for sailing, horseback riding, boating, golf, and a range of sports and activities; others offer fewer amenities but have twenty-four-hour security and houses with gardens and square footage at more affordable prices than in the city. In "Thursday Night Widows," Claudia Piñeiro describes one such community at the beginning of the 2000s, just as inflation and a brewing economic crisis appeared to mark the end of an era.*

An Open Letter to the Mayor of Quilmes (1982)

Various Authors

Dear Mr. Mayor,

Over the past few weeks, approximately twenty thousand people have come to the neighborhoods [. . .] in Quilmes. [. . .] The socioeconomic crisis that is part of this country's brutal reality is clearly expressed in the spontaneous move of thousands of Argentine families. In recent times, the closure of numerous places of employment and the progressive deterioration of salaries has led to a dangerous uptick of social exclusion. Among the many problems affecting the country today, housing is a particularly pressing one, and an immediate solution is required in order to restore a decent standard of living for the Argentine family. Those who have come [. . .] have attempted to resolve their lack of housing by building homes on empty lots—lots which, according to unconfirmed media sources, were already earmarked for expropriation and for the construction of public housing. The thousands of women, men, and children who have come are homeless and destitute; they do not have access to even the most essential infrastructure (running water, lights), and they receive no medical attention, which is particularly alarming given the state of health of the children. The occupied lands are currently surrounded around the clock by a barricade of Buenos Aires province police officers. This makes it impossible to get food to these people. There is no question that these people are crying out for an act of solidarity. It is a cry that should invoke the sense of humanitarianism of our society.

Translated by Wendy Gosselin and Jane Brodie

Thursday Night Widows (2009)

Claudia Piñeiro

Our neighborhood is a gated community, ringed by a perimeter fence that is concealed behind different kinds of shrub. It's called the Cascade Heights Country Club. Most of us shorten the name to "The Cascade" and a few people call it "The Heights." It has a golf course, tennis courts, swimming pool and two club houses. And private security. Fifteen security guards working shifts during the day, and twenty-two at night. That's more than five hundred acres of land, accessible only to us or to people authorized by one of us.

There are three ways to enter our neighborhood. If you're a member, you can open a barrier at the main gated by swiping a personalized magnetic card across the electronic reader. There's a side entrance, also with a barrier, for visitors who have received prior authorization and can supply certain information, such as an identity card number, car registration number and other identifying numbers. For tradesmen, domestic staff, gardeners, painters, builders, and all other laborers, there's a turnstile where ID cards have to be presented, and bags and car trunks are checked. All along the perimeter, at fifty-yard intervals, there are cameras which can turn 180 degrees. There used to be cameras that could turn 360 degrees, but they were invading the privacy of some members whose homes were close to the perimeter fence, so a few years ago they were deactivated, then replaced.

The houses are separated from one another by living fences—bushes, in other words. But these are not any old bushes. Privet is out of fashion, along with that erstwhile favourite, the violet campanula that grows by railway lines. There are none of those straight trimmed hedges that look like green walls. Definitely no round ones. The hedges are cut to look uneven, just this side of messy, giving them a natural appearance that is meticulously contrived. At first glance, these plants seem to have sprung up spontaneously between the neighbors, rather than to have been placed deliberately, to demarcate properties. [. . .] Wire fencing and railing are not permitted, let alone walls. The only exception is the six-foot-high perimeter fence which is the responsibility of the Club's administration and which is shortly going to be replaced by a wall, in line with new security regulations. Gardens that back onto the golf course may not be contained on that side even by a living fence; close to the boundary you can make out where the gardens end because the type of grass changes but, from a distance, the gaze is lost in an endless green vista and it is possible to believe that everything belongs to you. Those of us who move to Cascade Heights say that we have come in search of "green," a healthy life, sports, and security. Trotting out these reasons means not having to confess, even to ourselves, the real reasons for coming. And after a while we don't even remember them.

Translated by Miranda France

II

Taking to the Street

Some of the most iconic images of Buenos Aires's history are of the city's central plaza occupied: the crowds of workers that descended on the Plaza de Mayo on October 17, 1945, to demand the release of General Juan Perón; the silent but impactful circle of vigilant protest of the Mothers of the Plaza de Mayo every Thursday afternoon during the civic-military dictatorship, demanding to know the whereabouts of their disappeared children; police and protesters in confrontation as a dispersed crowd yelled "¡Que se vayan todos!" (They all must go!) at government officials amid the 2001 economic crisis fallout. These demonstrations of public discontent have become markers of the country's—and the city's—social and political history.

As exceptional as these events were, they were also part of a much more everyday tradition of public protest—and celebration. Regular morning news programs announce which downtown streets have been shut down or blockaded by marches, and residents have become entirely accustomed to encountering parades of groups demonstrating support for a particular cause, unions either on strike or engaging in a public action, or massive crowds blocking off major arteries. Nor are such displays confined to a certain class, social sector, or cause: drawing massive crowds, stopping traffic, and participating in a public march through city streets have been taken up by conservatives, leftists, populists, rich, and poor; regular marches and mass gatherings have been used as a method of commemorating public memory of the victims of state terror, as well as a tool to legitimize authoritarian rule. Congregating in public spaces has been and remains a form of celebrating a shared sense of joy; sometimes acts of protest and celebration appear to intertwine, with demonstrations taking on a spirit of a party. Taking to the street is, in this way, a deeply embedded tradition, an expected reaction to major events, a show of force or impulse suited to almost any notable occasion and cause.

Celebration and Demands in the Nineteenth Century

Like many cities of the Spanish colonies, Buenos Aires was designed around a main plaza, an open space bordered by buildings representing society's guiding institutions—an area where public life converged. (See "Celebrations in the Plaza in the Early Nineteenth Century," the first selection below.) As the geographic center of public life, the plaza quickly became a focal point for all kinds of demonstrations. By 1810, amid the brewing revolution for independence, public actions often culminated there. Leaders of the revolutionary movement first gathered at private spaces like the Café de los Catalanes and the Fonda de las Naciones to plan their action, but when events were set to escalate, their eyes turned to the city center as a site of protest. (See "The Plaza and the Demands of the People.") Over the following decades, celebrations commemorating the May Revolution and other festivities, like Carnaval, became highly anticipated events that saw diverse crowds converge on city streets. (See "The Streets of Revelry: Carnaval.") Processions—particularly religious demonstrations and funerals—were also viewed as important public affairs.

Almost all elements of life in Buenos Aires were forever changed by mass immigration at the turn of the twentieth century, and the use of public space in the city was no exception. By the late 1860s, street mobilizations became common. These demonstrations were grounded in the right to protest but were expressive of a growing conflict around the lack of universal suffrage. A nascent labor movement guided the tenor and direction of public demonstrations, while a workers' press stimulated organization. One of the earliest such publications came out of the Black community—the paper *El Proletario* intersected notions of race and class to make demands for rights; as European immigrants became more numerous, a range of papers from a variety of ideologies and backgrounds, and in a number of languages, began to bolster demands.

In the 1880s, the first strikes took place in Buenos Aires. By the end of that decade, workers were better organized, more numerous, and more active. Between 1888 and 1891 thirty-six strikes were held in the country, most of them in Buenos Aires. Regular protests took place outside factories and in the neighborhoods where workers lived and organized, like in present-day La Boca, Abasto, El Once, Almagro, and Barracas, and made demands for improved working conditions and raises. In a few years, the act of taking to the street had become associated with workers' mobilizations and petitions for voting rights. May 1 became a significant event in the city that mixed celebration and protest. (See "Workers Take to the Street.") The events also pointed to the clear cosmopolitan character of Buenos Aires workers' organizations, which harbored strong ties to labor movements in Europe and elsewhere and were rooted in a variety of ideologies, including anarchism, socialism, anarcho-syndicalism, communism, and Social Catholicism.

Protest and celebration in the street were a regular occurrence by the 1900s, but although public displays could be rowdy, violence was rare. Debates over which types of street demonstrations were legitimate uses of public space, and which were dangerous, destructive, or incited by "foreign" ideologies, were common during the early twentieth century. The Ley de Defensa Social (Law of Social Defense) of 1910 particularly clamped down on anarchist gatherings, and, as the letter of the law was vague, it empowered the state to engage in rather arbitrary uses of force against oppositional groups. In 1912, the Saénz Peña Law was passed, guaranteeing suffrage and the secret vote to male citizens. Despite the expansion of voting rights, the street remained a key forum for public expression, its use expanding in parallel to formal electoral politics.

During the presidential election of 1928, for example, the federal police granted permission for 2,462 gatherings and 411 public demonstrations. Rather than inciting violence, these manifestations normally engendered competition: opposing groups sometimes chose to organize parallel demonstrations for the same date, each seeking to convene a larger crowd and garner more attention than their rival. This also meant that demonstrations were not always dominated by the political left or the working classes: the nationalist right, conservative religious groups, and other more moderate political factions—namely the Radical Party—were each known to make public gatherings, marches, and processions a key element of their public voice.

On notable occasions, however, conflicts between those who were making demands and those who called for "order" boiled over into violence. Labor groups launched fourteen general strikes in the first fourteen years of the twentieth century, and between these there were hundreds of smaller demonstrations. Several erupted into more significant points of tension, action, or violence, or conflict with state representatives. The Semana Trágica, or Tragic Week, in 1919, serves as one of the most important examples of the outbreak of violence. A strike at a factory, initially a rather ordinary affair, escalated quickly when protesting workers fired on police. Several workers were killed, and during their funeral procession a few days later, some participants began to set fire to objects and buildings in their path. When police were deployed, the violence spread, and mobs took to the city; workers specifically targeted British-owned businesses, and rightist counter-marchers intermixed classist and anti-Semitic sentiments, turning their violence toward the city's Jewish neighborhoods.

Events like these fed the flames of a voracious ongoing debate over the origins of protesters' demands, the influence of "foreign" ideologies, and the state's right to suppress street activity and "subversive" political movements. The elite and the press argued over the degree to which protests should be

Abraham Vigo, a member of the group Artistas del Pueblo, often depicted labor conditions and emphasized workers' power in the streets. *Source: La Huelga,* by Abraham Vigo, 1935, from the series *Luchas proletarias.* Courtesy of the Museo Nacional de Bellas Artes (Argentina).

allowed to intervene in the public's "right to order" and "freedom to move" about the city.

Others, including writers and artists, insisted on the importance of taking to the street as an essential cultural component of urban life. At a moment when many painters saw the vast pampas as the primary setting for narratives of national identity, a group known as the Artistas del Pueblo (Artists of the People), themselves of more humble origins, found inspiration in the inequalities of the urban social landscape and the workers' movements. Abraham Vigo was one of these artists: his sketches and prints offered a rugged but clear aesthetic and sought to represent the world of workers, the conditions of their labor, and their demonstrations in the streets.

Over the following century, these same issues would come up time and time again, as objectors questioned protesters' behavior and social origins and postulated whether they were making legitimate claims or whether they had been "incited" by outsiders. In 1932, in the wake of a military coup, a new police directive defined how the public could use the street, favoring "order" and freedom of movement over freedom to protest, redefining police control over public spaces, and isolating leftist workers (described as radical and foreign) from what the right deemed to be the "true Argentine laborer." It was

In 1907, strikers protested the cost of renting rooms in *conventillos*—the tenements that housed immigrant families and other working-class persons. During a period of rising inflation and taxes, property owners chose to pass along higher costs to renters, many of whom occupied substandard buildings that lacked basic services. When renters organized and refused to pay the higher rates, they were confronted by the police, who evicted many of them onto the streets. This photo, originally printed in *Caras y Caretas*, one of the city's major magazines, illustrates how women and children played a key role in this strike over domestic spaces. *Source: La huelga de los inquilinos*, by Anonymous, 1907. Courtesy of the Archivo General de la Nación Argentina Dpto. Doc. Fotográficos, *Caras y Caretas* collection.

amid this climate of ideas that one of the largest demonstrations to take place before the advent of Peronism—the International Eucharistic Congress of 1934—drew hundreds of thousands of congregants in Buenos Aires. A major gathering began in Palermo and coalesced in a public mass in the Plaza de Mayo. The historic procession highlighted both the power of the Catholic Church as well as its friendly relationship with the political and military establishment. (See "The Church in the Street.")

The media made special note of women's presence in the mass Eucharist events, but it was not the first time that they were key participants in public demonstrations. Before women acquired the right to vote (in 1949) or rose to leadership in electoral politics, they played a role in the organization of local elections and participated in philanthropy as well as regular labor and political manifestations. When they took a more prominent role, their presence often mobilized around ideas about domestic life. One example was a 1907 renters' strike. Rising housing prices affected the domestic space; thus, women became central participants and organizers and, along with their children, took to the street with brooms in hand. They used the symbols of the home to suggest that the law endangered the welfare of "its most vulnerable" residents.

Peronism, Graffiti, and the Politics of the Plaza

Mass public demonstrations were certainly not a new phenomenon when thousands of men and women (many from the city's new industrial belt) descended on the central Plaza de Mayo in 1945 to, in the words of one protester, "rescue" General Juan Perón from imprisonment. (See "The Plaza de Mayo and Juan Perón.") Nevertheless, the October 17 mobilization remains one of the most significant and impactful in the history of the city. The demonstration jump-started the Peronist political movement; it also became a mobilization by which all other political gatherings at the plaza would be measured. For the nascent Peronist opposition, the presence and determination of this unified crowd generated a new era of critical commentary about *who* appeared at the plaza, *how*, and *why*. It also spurred a number of counter-protests that sought to define the opposition, as well as annual Peronist celebrations, in which followers returned to the Plaza for the "Day of Loyalty" in a type of commemoration of the initial demonstration. There is little doubt that the events of October 17 were singular in their symbolism, even if the compulsion to express a kind of collective, popular voice by forming a crowd was, by then, a common occurrence.

Marching was not the only way to "take to the street." The city's streets themselves have long been canvases onto which city residents paint, plaster, and hang banners with calls to action, poems, demands, declarations of love, and other forms of public expression. These kinds of public messages are left for passersby to read, contemplate, enjoy, or disparage. With their authors absent, they often take on a certain potency, appearing to evoke a message from the city itself, as if its walls could talk. When the messages become crowded, they visually display the cacophony of voices of *porteño* public life. (See "The Writing on the Wall.")

Nor are they a new phenomenon. By the first Peronist political campaign, in 1945, painted graffiti, known as *pintadas,* and plastered posters, known as *afiches,* were already an important component of political campaigns. De-

Graffiti and posters have long lined city streets. In this photograph from 1945, a man pastes a poster for presidential candidate José Tamborini, covering up signs for Juan Perón underneath. *Source: Carteles*, by Anonymous, 1945. Courtesy of the Archivo General de la Nación Argentina Dpto. Doc. Fotográficos.

bates over the aesthetics and propriety of these street campaigns also pre-date Peronism, but in that election, the rivalry between political movements made a notable mark on the city's walls. Competing factions took to the streets at night and in early hours of the morning to strip the walls of op-posing movements' posters and place their own, and in some cases to update their messages; during the first Peronist campaign anti-Peronists often left the message "Perón Nazi" at night, only to find it "edited" by their rivals to become "Peronazo" (*-azo* being an augmentative suffix that emphasized the power of the movement) in the morning.

Over the next several years, the messages on city walls echoed a brewing political tension that would ultimately dovetail in episodes of violence. On June 16, 1955, the military attempted to oust Perón from government by un-leashing twenty-eight military planes to fire on the Casa Rosada, the CGT, the presidential residence, and the Plaza de Mayo. A crowd of Perón's support-ers had descended on the plaza; also present were ordinary civilians going about their day. With no warning, the military planes dropped bombs and massacred at least 308 persons, some of them children aboard a trolley. The violent attack and the disregard for civilian life drew repudiation; it foreshad-owed the military's extreme capacity of violence as well as growing political polarization.

The comic strip *Mafalda* became an important expression of observations about 1960s–70s society's internal contradictions and, in particular, the tensions between conformity and protest; here, the cartoon depicts Buenos Aires's graffiti-covered city streets. In the first box, Mafalda encounters Don Manolo, the owner of her neighborhood corner store; she asks him, "Are you [a] good [person]?" He answers, "What a question, of course I am!" She leaves the store, thinking, "It is surprising! Every person I ask says that they are a good person. It seems the whole world is good." She walks in front of a wall covered in reminders of political and social conflicts: "Stop hunger and layoffs!" says one message; "Murderous Yankees, out of Vietnam!" says another; a third, "And what did you do in Hungary?"; "Justice for the teachers" is covered by the words "Lazy people!" Mafalda continues in thought, "It is just so comforting to know." Source: *Mafalda*, by Quino, 1971. Courtesy of Julieta Colombo.

Over the following tumultuous thirty years, the walls of the city became an even more important battlefield of symbols—a space in which competing narrations of urban life could be expressed, erased, and reasserted under the darkness of night, disrupting the imposition of a sense of consensus put in place by oppressive governance, or complacent media.

In the early 1970s, the question of armed political action—particularly in public spaces—became a central point of contention. (See "Public Violence.") Some leftist groups viewed armed protest as part of a path to revolution. The military and its allies on the right used this discourse to justify a violent campaign to eliminate all those they suspected of being associated with the left. Following a coup in 1976, their operations became broad; public gatherings were restricted, marches were eliminated, and the military secretly abducted, tortured, and murdered citizens while publicly justifying their regime as necessary to maintain order.

In the depths of this state violence, a group of women, mothers of young people who had been abducted, built on the symbols of maternity to stage one of the most poignant and powerful protests of their age. Originally a group of only a few, the Mothers began their weekly protests in 1977, silently demanding answers to the whereabouts of their children. (See "The Mothers of the Plaza de Mayo.") They slowly marched in circles in front of the Casa Rosada—the administrative seat of the executive branch. In little time, the group had grown to over a hundred women; they would regularly appear carrying photographs of their disappeared daughters and sons. Although the mothers' actions were not immediately put down by the military (as had been the case for other displays of protest), the group was infiltrated, and as their numbers grew and their efforts more insistent, several of the founding members were tortured, killed, and disappeared. The military leaders and their allies sought to discredit the women publicly by referring to them as "madwomen"; the characterization swapped the gendered image of a grieving mother with that of a hysterical or irrational woman.

The military junta in power also looked to use the plaza and the symbols of mass mobilization to promote a public image that they had unanimous mass approval. In 1982, for example, following their announcement that Argentina would go to war against Britain for the Malvinas/Falkland Islands, a crowd gathered in the plaza to show support. The event was billed as a show of "consensus" in the pro-military press. (See "The Plaza as a Site of 'Consensus.'") The moment was short-lived; the war was a debacle, a brutal defeat that unraveled military power and, alongside an economic decline and local and international pressure regarding human rights violations, an emerging but limited social unrest catalyzed the return to democracy.

Democracy, Freedom, and New Forms of Making Demands

Amid the transition to democracy, the public's power in the streets gradually recovered; a new era of public expression began. Graffiti reemerged as a part of youth culture, and the city's walls saw a new eruption of poetic phrases, commentaries, artistic interventions, and ironic statements. Over the following two decades, several groups reclaimed public spaces as sites to remember victims and incite justice. (See "The Escrache.")

In the 1990s and 2000s, economic crisis and a sense of freedom of expression also stirred up a return of urban street art traditions and some new innovations. Murals and street art grew in number, building on a history of afiches, public interventions, and graffiti. It also became popular to string up pasacalles— rudimentary banners that hang across a street or along lampposts and are used to make public declarations of love, commemorate an anniversary, a graduation, or make a very public apology. These are often light-hearted and can be funny: in a southern neighborhood of Buenos Aires one such banner read, "Valeria, you aren't Google, but you have everything I am searching for."

In this new economic and political era, the act of taking to the street also took new forms. When inflation rose and economic downturns and deindustrialization destabilized the city (and, even more so, the outskirts in Greater Buenos Aires), mass mobilizations voiced a strong criticism of the neoliberal moment, using a variety of new and old tactics. In the 1990s, protesters took up the controversial method of blocking streets, occupying public spaces with semipermanent encampments, and disrupting urban traffic and highways with protests that lasted days. In 1997, for example, teachers set up what was known as La Carpa Blanca (the White Tent) in front of the National Congress to demand pay raises and more money for education. The encampment became a plaza fixture for 1,003 days, during which time it became a powerful symbol of protest against the deep cuts taken against public spending and social welfare in the 1990s. (See "A White Tent Occupies the Plaza.") At the same time, other disenfranchised groups began to organize *piquetes*. These protests sought to disrupt everyday life by blocking roads and making demands on employers, or, in the case of the unemployed, on the government. Debates over these new methods of making demands revived an age-old question of competing rights: the right to "circulate freely" in the city versus the right to protest.

At moments of political and economic crisis, a sense of indignation pushed masses into the streets. In 2001, when Argentina defaulted on its debt, bank accounts were frozen, the peso was devalued, unemployment skyrocketed, and large sections of the middle class lost their life savings. Men and women without specific political affiliations descended on the plaza repeating the refrain "Que se vayan todos" (They all must go). Others watched on television from their homes as police cracked down on the protestors and threw tear gas. Thirty-nine people were killed. The president evacuated the Casa Rosada (the executive building) by helicopter. These events, like the Semana Trágica (Tragic Week) almost a century earlier, would reverberate in public memory precisely because their deterioration into violence was so shocking.

Over the following years, daily *piquete* activism made road stoppages the subject of the morning news. Critics of these types of protests questioned the sincerity and legitimacy of those who participated, portraying them as violent or, more often, claiming that they were paid, compelled, and bussed to the marches by corrupt leaders. They also criticized the *piquetes* as often resembling celebrations, complete with music and *choripanes* (grilled chorizo sausage on bread). Supporters responded that these were the legitimate protests of a disenfranchised sector, the result of neoliberal economic policy and decades of corruption. The apparent air of celebration, they noted—the sound of drums, the chants—were part of a long culture of cooperative resistance that in no way discounted the legitimacy of their claims. (See "Public Kitchens and *Piquetes*.") Under relative economic recovery in the 2000s, the frequency of *piquete* protests subsided slightly. However, in periods of crisis, of rapid inflation and escalating poverty, the *piquete* and the march reemerged as a part of daily life.

Without a doubt, the impetus to take to the street lives on—in moments of celebration, as protest, and also as expression of broad social issues. The city government has also attempted to channel this desire for public life in the street in a more top-down organized fashion, temporarily closing public avenues for "museum night," public concerts, or the night of the bookstores—open festivities that convene a diverse crowd in public spaces.

Although political allegiances still fuel protests and parties continue to use crowds as evidence of legitimacy, some important street mobilizations have also crossed traditional partisan lines. In April 2024, for example, 150,000 marchers descended on the city center to voice support for the free public university system in the face of ongoing budget cuts. At least in its initial years, the movement known as Ni Una Menos (Not One Less) serves as another example. The first demonstration, in 2015, was a relatively small poetry and performance art action organized by journalists and activists to protest domestic violence and recent femicides, a slew of killings of young women. The movement grew when organizers communicated their outcry on social media using the hashtags and slogan #NiUnaMenos and #VivasLasQueremos (#NotOneLess, #WeWantThemAlive). The reference to the disappearance of women echoed human rights campaigns of decades' past but also showed the power of social media in convening a new generation of street demonstrators. (See "Ni Una Menos, Not One Less.") When a larger march was organized in June 2015, its trajectory also became significant: by walking to the steps of the Congress rather than the Plaza de Mayo, participants put the weight of their criticism on civil society and representative government, underlining femicide as both a legislative and a social issue. Members of the movement returned to the plaza in front of the Congress in the coming years with a new hashtag, *#QueSeaLey* (#LetItBeLaw), demonstrating a consolidated political agenda, criticizing conservative parties, and prioritizing demands for free and legal abortion rights. (See "Pañuelazo," located in the color insert of this volume.)

The site of a massive march remains an important component of its message, even when the act of "taking to the street" is unplanned. When Argentina made it to the World Cup final and won in 1986 and in 2022, *porteños* found themselves desperate to share in public celebration. In 2022, millions decided to convene at the Obelisk, a national monument at the center of the city's major avenue. The Obelisk was a site for universal celebration, a place dissociated enough from political division that residents could gather there and briefly rejoice in a state of euphoria. (See "Streets of Celebration.") Amid divided political loyalties, causes for celebration as well as despair, the local impetus to take to the street—in joy, in anger, frustration, or hope—is without question an enduring part of the city's spirit and a vibrant part of everyday life.

Celebrations in the Plaza in the Early Nineteenth Century

Carlos E. Pellegrini, John Parish Robertson, and William Parish Robertson

Buenos Aires was built around a central plaza. Even initially, the buildings that bordered the plaza—the cabildo (city hall), the cathedral, a market, a military fort—represented the major pillars of civic life. Over time, the buildings were modified: the Casa Rosada, which today houses the executive branch of government, replaced the fort, and the headquarters of the Central Bank were added in the twentieth century. The changes only emphasized the plaza's importance as a symbolic, centrally located gathering point for all types of protests and public celebrations. This 1841 painting by the architect, engineer, and painter Carlos E. Pellegrini depicts women, children, and men of various classes and races commemorating the anniversary of the revolution. The idea of the plaza as a public space and a site for inclusive celebration would become a recurring theme in late nineteenth-century painting, when the city's artists looked to give the nation, and the city, a visual rendering of its foundational moments and culture. In the text, a travel memoir published in London in 1843, two British merchants take note of the festive spirit of these commemorations.

Nineteenth-Century Independence Celebrations in the Plaza (1841)

Carlos E. Pellegrini

Fiestas Mayas en la Plaza Victoria: Recuerdos del Río de la Plata, 1841. Courtesy of the Museo Nacional de Bellas Artes (Argentina).

Letters on South America (1843)

John Parish Robertson and William Parish Robertson

The hymn having been sung, and the children having retired, the square gradually filled during the forenoon with well-dressed people. The troops appeared in new uniforms; and a grand procession of the public bodies, including the governor, his staff, the corps diplomatique, and all the field officers, proceeded from the fort or government house to the cathedral, where high mass, with Te Deum, was celebrated. In the afternoon and during the whole evening bands of military music played popular airs on the balcony of the cabildo or town hall; the inhabitants in gay attire crowded the streets, as well as the plaza mayor or great square, and here a grand display of fire-works took place at nine o'clock, when several thousand assembled to witness them; the night closing in with *tertulias* [regularly scheduled gatherings] given by many of the principal families, and with patriotic assemblages in all the principal cafés of the city. It was for several years remarked, during the fervid course of the revolution, that the 25th of May always brought good news; and these creating an enthusiasm which animated all classes and throwing down for the moment the dikes of classism, it was wonderful to see what general hilarity distinguished the "Fiestas Mayas" throughout.

The Plaza and the Demands of the People

José María Tagiman and Vicente Fidel López

Vicente Fidel López's early history of the 1810 revolutionary movement, La Gran Semana de Mayo, *includes a number of letters that describe the growing rebellion against the Spanish colonial power. In this letter, the observer, José María Tagiman, tells of revolutionaries meeting in cafés and* pulperías *(rustic bars) to plan a demonstration in the plaza. The rebels charged that the viceroy should be publicly hanged and called for an "open cabildo"—that is, an open meeting of local male residents, persons who held the social title of* vecino *(neighbor). They warned that if their demands for representation were not met, they would organize a march—a show of public force that would demonstrate the will of the people. Ultimately, six hundred armed men descended on the plaza to demand that the viceroy step down and that an open cabildo commence. When the cabildo meeting included only the more prominent men in the city, a more diverse crowd of men, women, and children gathered outside in the plaza, inventing what would become the first in a long succession of famous public chants to demand government action and public accountability. As most schoolchildren still learn, the crowd in the plaza roused those inside by repeating the call "The people want to know!" Even though a select strata of men were the only ones voting in local government, politics was something that a broader cross section of society could participate in by taking to the street and making their opinions known.*

From the Café to the Plaza (1810)

José María Tagiman and Vicente Fidel López

At the Café de los Catalanes and La Fonda, with the wide sidewalk, the young people are out in force. Pancho Planes has put himself in charge [. . .] to go around agitating the crowd and pulling people toward the center of town, where they are chanting relentlessly: "Open Cabildo! Down with the viceroy!" I don't know at what time these devils go to sleep, because they stay up all night going from house to house and from room to room. Who would have thought that there would be such energy and public spirit in Buenos Aires against the tyrants? This has to blow up today or tomorrow; it can't stay like this.

Translated by Liliana Frankel

The Streets of Revelry: Carnaval

Anonymous and Eustaquio Pellicer

As early as the eighteenth century, the streets and the plaza became spaces for celebration. All social classes—wealthy and poor, enslaved and free—took part in Carnaval, an annual holiday celebration that allowed a certain degree of social role reversal. Participants dressed in costumes, held public dances and parades, and doused one another with water. Yet even while such popular celebrations were accepted, they were also contested. During the colonial period, the public revelry of the poor, and particularly celebrations by free and enslaved Blacks, came under criticism in the press, which charged that the lowest sectors of the social hierarchy (especially people of color) were capitalizing on the spirit of the celebration to take vengeance. In response, Governor Juan José Vértiz moved Carnaval dances to closed quarters in 1771, perceiving such public behavior as "immoral." When Carnaval revived in the early nineteenth century, elaborate parades and music became the norm, often led by the Black community. Elite voices continued to decry Carnaval as a "barbarous" affair, and one local paper implored the city's "cultured" inhabitants to refrain from participating. Over time, Carnaval changed. In Eustaquio Pellicer's "Carnaval," the author captures some of the tension surrounding the celebrations. In the early twentieth century, celebrations began to be organized by neighborhoods, and increasingly it was European immigrants and their descendants who took up the drums and dancing; participants often donned blackface, a practice that went largely unquestioned until recently. The two photographs—taken thirty years apart—both capture celebrations on the Avenida de Mayo. Today, Carnaval continues to be celebrated. In 2023, twenty-two streets were closed for celebrations and at least 130 murgas—groups of musicians and dancers who participate in neighborhood Carnaval shows—organized workshops and practiced in their neighborhood plazas for months before the event.

Residents Ready for a Carnaval Parade (1939)

Anonymous

Courtesy of the Archivo General de la Nación Argentina Dpto. Doc. Fotográficos.

A Crowd Gathers at Carnaval (1968)

Anonymous

Courtesy of the Archivo General de la Nación Argentina Dpto. Doc. Fotográficos. Inv: 298838.

Carnaval (1899)

Eustaquio Pellicer

This year we were so close to having a Carnaval without crimes—only six or eight were committed, and in the last days. This would have been the peak of decadence because no matter what people claim, Carnaval is a festival destined to awaken people's hostile instincts, to stimulate their aggression; it's possible to imagine it without almost any of its usual characteristics, but not without the edge which gives it its nature, its essential fighting spirit.

Who hasn't felt a little bloodthirsty once abandoned to the ardor of the Carnaval game? All one must do is observe the progressive fury attacking those who play adversaries in the battle reenactments in order to understand the undoing to which they are susceptible. To begin with, it was satisfying to throw confetti, mainly if one manages to get a lot of it in the eyes of their chosen target. Later, people took to using streamers, which allow for bruising when fired impetuously to hit against an unmasked mouth. Later, water was adopted, used in the quantities suitable for putting out a fire. [. . .] We aren't of the type who let Carnaval turn them on to the point of blindness: but frankly, we declare that on the last Tuesday we realized we were only a step away from vertigo, and moments from a state in which, lacking streamers, we would have thrown bottles at the heads of our opponents.

Translated by Liliana Frankel

Workers Take to the Street

Anonymous and Various Authors

May Day, the international day of the worker, was a significant holiday at the beginning of the twentieth century. As these excerpts from newspapers highlight, the day's festivities served a variety of aims and diverse groups took part. The city's major daily newspaper, La Nación, *depicts May Day as a cause of celebration, detailing the flags and banners waved, the music and scene; the socialist paper* La Vanguardia *lauds their peaceful but politically assertive demonstration. By contrast, the magazine* Caras y Caretas *reports from an anarchist march in which participants argued that May Day should be not a cause for celebration but a more serious occasion for making demands. The photograph depicts a socialist May Day march in 1909.*

Socialist Alfredo Palacios Addresses Workers on May Day (1909)

Anonymous

Courtesy of the Archivo General de la Nación Argentina Dpto. Doc. Fotográficos.
Inv: 21750.

Many May Days (1897–1904)

La Nación (1904)

A march of between three and four thousand participants with signs and red flags, whose inscriptions were as follows: "Long live May 1," "Long live social emancipation," "Down with militarism," "Club Balvanera," "Pilar Socialist Center," "Northern Barracas Socialist Center," "Karl Marx Club," "Workers' Socialist Center," "Workers' Federation," "University Socialist Center," "We want eight hours," "Carriage builders," "Tanners' Society" [. . .].

The line was led by a security guards' picket and a musical band which during the route toward the Plaza Rodríguez Peña awoke great enthusiasm in the marchers, playing the workers' anthem and the Marseillaise. [. . .] The whole way, they made the point of showing that order was being preserved. [. . .]

When the crowd arrived at the plaza, various young women threw flowers with red ribbons from a balcony to the demonstrators. [. . .] The faces of the assembled showed a sense of satisfaction and success as they happily celebrated the Day of the Worker.

La Vanguardia *(1897)*

We testify that the socialists conducted themselves in the most pacific manner, which is to say, a democratic socialist demonstration, whose most aggressive tone was the red tint of its flags and the flower pins which shone from the coat buttons and hairdos of the excited women workers, who formed a painterly group in the crowd, adorned with starched dresses and packets. After twenty blocks of free speech and movement, the demonstrators rode a wave of exaltation that made possible and even probable some kind of outbreak. But nothing of the sort occurred.

Caras y Caretas *(1899)*

An extremely long line of demonstrators with about five or six thousand people squashed in [. . .] two women leading with red flags behind the musical band "The Height of Disgrace" [. . .]; at the end, a large sign on a white background read: "Greetings from the workers' societies to the universal proletariat. May First isn't a party, but a protest."

Translated by Liliana Frankel

The Church in the Street

Anonymous and Caras y Caretas

In 1934 Buenos Aires served as the host of the International Eucharistic Congress. The city's residents witnessed, for the first time, a truly massive congregation of hundreds of thousands of persons in their streets. The cause was a celebratory reassertion of Buenos Aires—and Argentina's—Catholicism. In a city that would become known for its secularity, the 1934 Congress signaled a historical moment in which conservative and Catholic groups held sway. The success of the gathering led many to believe that Buenos Aires might become a stronghold for the Church. Although the event marked a reignition of the powerful bond between the military and the Church, as well as a growing popular religiosity, Buenos Aires did not shake its secular spirit. The next gathering of this size would be at the onset of Peronism, which initially built on Church and military allegiances but also integrated new sectors and ideas to create a political movement.

A Mass Procession to Celebrate the International Eucharistic Congress
Arrives at the Cathedral (1934)

Anonymous

Courtesy of the Archivo General de la Nación Argentina Dpto. Doc. Fotográficos.

An Incredible Crowd (1934)

Caras y Caretas

People of all social classes took to the stepped streets, balconies, and rooftop terraces to applaud the distinguished cardinal as he descended from his carriage at Plaza de Mayo. [. . .] The borders and sidewalks of Plaza de Mayo were completely packed. Hundreds of thousands of people had come to receive communion. Plaza de Mayo was engulfed in a swarm of human activity as it filled with a crowd that, at once, spilled onto the Avenida de Mayo and into the Plaza de Congreso. It was an emotional scene that culminated in a night of triumph for Catholicism.

Translated by Leslie Robertson

The Plaza de Mayo and Juan Perón

Anonymous and Mundo Peronista

While serving as labor secretary in a military government, Colonel Juan Domingo Perón galvanized support from workers by responding to long-standing union demands; when his popularity became an issue for military leaders, he was removed from office and detained, sparking a mass demonstration to demand his release. Large crowds descended on the Plaza de Mayo; the gathering—largely made up of working people and migrants to the city and its outskirts—shocked members of the upper classes and other city residents. In an expression of disgust, some publicly mocked the crowd as dirty "shirtless ones," or cabecitas negras—*literally, "little black heads." Juan Perón, Evita (Juan Perón's wife), and their followers would eventually reclaim many of those terms and celebrate their identity as* descamisados *(shirtless ones). At the same time, the ability to convene a truly massive crowd of supporters became a critical marker of the Peronist political movement, which, in the path to the presidency, drew support not only from workers, but also from members of the nationalist and Catholic right, among other groups. Peronist media outlets regularly detailed reports of the crowds that congregated in the plaza to greet the leader. The text, an excerpt of a 1951 article from the Peronist magazine* Mundo Peronista, *mentions the first uses of television and dramatizes the beginning of one such gathering: it effuses that the sun always shines when Perón speaks and evokes the crowd's emotional response to the appearance of a then-ill Evita. In the photograph, Perón, flanked by his advisers, approaches a microphone to address a crowd in 1952. Supporters wave banners and scale lampposts and monuments to catch a glimpse, and the eye, of the leader. In the near distance, there is a large sign referring to the* CGT, *the Confederación General de Trabajo (General Confederation of Labor), the massive and powerful labor union that formed the backbone of the workers' movement.*

A Crowd Gathers to Hear Juan Perón on Loyalty Day, October 17, in 1952 (1952)

Anonymous

Previously published in Samuel Amaral and Horacio Batalla, *Imágenes del peronismo, fotografías/photographs, 1945–1955* (Caseros: Editorial de la Universidad Nacional de Tres de Febrero, 2010). Courtesy of the Archivo General de la Nación and Samuel Amaral.

Perón and Evita Speak (1951)

Mundo Peronista

From the early morning hours, Perón's people began to flow into the historic square. Although the main event was to take place at 6:00 p.m. numerous groups of women, men, and children milled about the square, passing by the reception areas and below the balconies of the presidential palace. The children fed flocks of gentle pigeons by hand. In the middle of the square, those who arrived early had already set up their posters and banners. The adjoining buildings were also decorated with the slogans and signage of the various trade unions.

However, a little after midday, it began to rain. Some sought refuge under awnings or trees; others stood stoically in the middle of the square, despite the rain. Youngsters perched themselves on the monument, lying in the arms of Belgrano or riding his horse. [. . .] "It will not rain, the sun always shines when Perón speaks." [. . .]

"Evita is here as well," they said to each other.

And yes, Evita was there, with her arms raised, held up high by the General. Evita was there, greeting the people. For those of us who were near the Presidential Palace, and those who watched on television, we were able to see how the emotions of that immense crowd greeting Eva Perón—waving their handkerchiefs and shouting their love and affection—reached Evita's heart, and she was overwhelmed with tears.

Thousands of voices, thousands of roaring throats . . .

"YES GENERAL, YES GENERAL, *PRESENTES!* . . . WE ARE HERE, WE ARE HERE! WE ARE HERE!

Translated by Leslie Robertson

The Writing on the Wall

Anonymous, Alejo Santander, and Tano Verón

Like its plazas, the city's walls have long served as canvases for public displays of political—and personal—ideas. Today pintadas *(graffiti), street art, and* afiches *(poster paste-ups) cover walls with colorful messages that vary wildly in substance and style. Yet they are hardly novelties. The magazine* Caras y Caretas *satirized the incredible number of posters on the city's walls as early as 1900. The first photograph below depicts a rather rudimentary* pintada *during the presidential elections of 1946; it reads, "Vote Perón-Quijano, the people's formula against the capitalist oligarchy, voting for them will ensure the well-being of Argentina's workers." A second image depicts a contemporary wall covered in signs that read, for example, "We have not come to this world to give up," "What an idiot I am," and "Attention: Don't sell your freedom for anything in the world." Finally, contemporary street artist Tano Verón reflects on why and how he began to leave his own messages on city streets.*

Graffiti in Favor of Juan Perón's Candidacy (1946)

Anonymous

Courtesy of the Archivo General de la Nación Argentina Dpto. Doc. Fotográficos.
Inv: 55613.

Courtesy of the photographer, Lisa Ubelaker Andrade.

Street Art (2017)

Alejo Santander and Tano Verón

Verón pasted posters in front of an old two-story house in the 2100-block of Uriarte, where he has permission to do so and which is an area that, in recent years, has transformed into an open-air gallery for local urban artists. A colorful collage in the heart of the Palermo neighborhood, three posters, three messages, and a bit of yellow and blue aerosol paint; he goes about the work with some sentimentality, knowing that it may be one of the last times he does it. In November, the building will be demolished and replaced with an apartment tower. The urban art scene in Buenos Aires arrived in 2001, hand in hand with the severe social crisis and the need of many people to speak out. The stencil was the central element seen in those years. The messages conveyed were disruptive and critical of the politics of the day, of multinational corporations and of consumer society, a formula that today's brands try to turn on its head by camouflaging their advertising campaigns as street art. The pulse of the city was always evident in the graffiti, paintings, and posters, as was the need to leave one's mark in the public space as a witness to the present, free of any intervening interests. [. . .] "I want to see people react, stop for a moment, and try to understand what they just read," says Verón, explaining why he leaves a phrase painted in a corner for others to read, turning it into, as he defines it, laughing, "an urban self-help wall." He says that he has always been an aspiring writer, working almost in secret. "I would write down my thoughts and ideas. I read a lot, and the phrases of different authors were always etched in my mind. One day I thought that I could write too, but using the things that I am already familiar with as a poster designer: eye-catching appeal, a quick read, and the merging of images and words. Making short phrases that are easy to read, easy to share, and easy to repeat. And then go out and paste them everywhere. Because that is what street art is, repetition."

Translated by Leslie Robertson

Public Violence

Fuerzas Armadas Revolucionarias–Montoneros

Street protests are usually peaceful and take place without any confrontation. On occasion, minor standoffs result in tensions between marchers and authorities; truly violent encounters are rare. Perhaps because of their rarity, those public acts that devolved into violence have been notable events in history, often evidencing deep political and social fissures. The introduction discussed two of these moments: La Semana Trágica, a weeklong episode of mass violence in January 1919, and the bombing of the Plaza de Mayo on June 16, 1955, when Argentina's own navy and air force planes attacked the city's central plaza in an initial attempt to oust then-president Juan Perón. In 1973, political tensions devolved into another major episode of public violence. On the outskirts of the city, at the Buenos Aires Airport in Ezeiza, millions of Perón's supporters of all stripes had gathered to welcome the leader from his nearly twenty-year exile from the country. In his absence, however, Peronism had fractured and was reinterpreted by groups with opposing views. At the scene were rightist Peronist supporters as well as groups on the far left. Each laid claim to the leader. "On the Ezeiza Massacre" is an excerpt of a flier circulated in the streets by the Fuerzas Armadas Revolucionarias–Montoneros, a leftist guerrilla faction that had taken up arms to realize their vision of a left-oriented Peronist society. As they note, the group was convinced that upon his return to Argentina, Perón would take up their struggle. Tensions were high as the crowd awaited the leader. Then, armed right-wing Peronists began firing on the crowd, killing several attendees. The text interprets the day's events from the FAR-Montoneros perspective.

On the Ezeiza Massacre (1973)

Fuerzas Armadas Revolucionarias–Montoneros

An historic event has taken place in our homeland: the final return of General Perón, to reunite with the Argentine people and continue leading in the path to liberation. Our people understood the significance [of this event] and offered an appropriate response—an encouraging 4 million *compañeros* from all parts of the country came out. However, the great celebration of liberation took a dark turn amid the abnormal events witnessed: a handful of assassins bearing armbands from the Ministry of Social Welfare, the Concentración

Nacional Universitaria (CNU), and Comando de Organización (CdeO) took fire from the stage and from the woods and slaughtered the people with the sick aim of preventing the much desired reunion between General Perón and the 4 million *compañeros*. They wanted to prevent our reunification because this is how they hold siege of our leader, acting as intermediaries, lying to Perón about what the people say and think and lying to the people about what Perón says and thinks. That is why they committed this absurd shooting that they alone were prepared for; then they tried cancel the event, citing Perón's own safety.

[. . .]

Let it thus be made evident that the Ezeiza massacre was caused by a group of mercenary lackeys at the service of imperialism who attacked the people, of which we are a part. Because of their actions many *compañeros* were killed and wounded; among these anonymous martyrs of this struggle is our fighter, the Montonero Horacio Simona. Our objectives will be achieved only through the organization and mobilization of the people to defeat the infiltrators and the enemies of the homeland. This work must continue, despite the provocations and intimidations that aim to discourage them. Our weapons and our lives have not been and will not be at the service of secondary interests; they are and they will be used at the service of the interests of the homeland and of the people, and in particular of the working class.

Translated by Lisa Ubelaker Andrade

The Mothers of the Plaza de Mayo

Eduardo Longoni, Adriana Lestido, Renée Epelbaum,

and Marjorie Agosín

Among the most important mobilizations in the history of Buenos Aires were those of the Mothers of the Plaza de Mayo. During the 1976–83 civic-military dictatorship, the military abducted, threatened, tortured, and "disappeared" citizens. Criticism, or its public manifestation, was restricted. Mothers of persons who had been disappeared bravely gathered in the central Plaza de Mayo; they solemnly and quietly walked in a circle, white bandannas tied to their heads, staying in movement so as not to be counted, requesting information on the location of their sons and daughters who had been kidnapped and "disappeared" by military agents. As one of the founders of this movement, Renée Epelbaum, recounts in this testimony, at first they were few in number, and they had much to fear in breaking the silence and bringing their search for their sons and daughters to such a public place. She notes that they were depicted as madwomen in the press. Despite fear of being kidnapped, tortured, and killed themselves, they remained consistent in their search; their presence at the plaza became one of the few interventions in the public sphere that intimated the profound violence of the state. The photographs illustrate these protests: in the first, the Mothers' march is put down by military police on horseback in 1982. In the second photograph, taken the same year, a mother and daughter demonstrate in a plaza in Greater Buenos Aires against the disappearance of the woman's brother, a laborer last seen in 1976.

Since the end of the dictatorship, the Mothers of the Plaza de Mayo have continued to mobilize each week, circling the plaza as an act of remembrance and sustained activism. The Grandmothers of the Plaza de Mayo have also continued to use all means possible to locate their lost grandchildren—many of the kidnapped young women were pregnant and gave birth in clandestine detention centers, their children taken from them and placed into adoption. Following the return to democracy, the Grandmothers began a campaign to encourage persons who were born between 1976 and 1982 and who questioned their true identities to undergo DNA testing; using this method they have successfully matched and identified more than a hundred grandchildren.

Eduardo Longoni

La marcha por la vida. Courtesy of the photographer.

A Mother and Daughter Protest the Dictatorship (1982)

Adriana Lestido

Madre e Hija de Plaza de Mayo. Courtesy of the photographer.

In the Beginning We Were a Powerless Group (1990)

Renée Epelbaum and Marjorie Agosín

In the beginning, when we would first meet in the Plaza, we were a power-less group. People laughed at us. When it rained, we looked like a bunch of heads smothered by enormous white kerchiefs. In the beginning of 1983, with a democratic Argentine government facing a discredited military regime we became stars because we had legitimacy in the eyes of the new government. Remember this word well, *legitimacy*. Our battle was legitimate; that of the military was something hidden, monstrous, and illegal. You must also remember that, during the Malvinas/Falklands War, we were viciously attacked. In the newspapers there were caricatures of us as horrible old women with huge knives in our backs, showing that we were traitors against the great Argentine nation. [. . .] I repeat that we began and continue as a movement because we are mothers, we became involved because our children disappeared. I remember that María Adela (one of the founders of the Mothers of the Plaza de Mayo) went to the Plaza on April 30, 1977. She and her three sisters were there alone, completely alone. You cannot imagine how afraid they were, it is almost impossible to explain. [. . .] In this way, mothers began to meet in the Plaza. At first, there weren't fourteen, there were three or four. We formed strategies such as petitioning for writs of habeas corpus, because we wanted to recover the bodies or for the military to at least tell us where they were. We were desperate, but we were also rationally searching for an immediate solution. We always thought our children would reappear, and so we went from court to court, from police station to police station. At three-thirty p.m. on the dot we continued to meet to share our news.

Translated by Janice Molloy

The Plaza as a Site of "Consensus"

Revista Gente

In 1982, Gente, an entertainment and news magazine that offered a consistently pro-military editorial position during the 1976–83 civic-military dictatorship, described the thousands of persons who gathered in the plaza in support of the military's decision to reclaim the Malvinas/Falkland Islands alongside images. During the international conflict, the heavily censored press legitimized the actions of the authoritarian regime using the image of the crowded plaza to suggest that there was vast public support. Images like these reinforced the myth that the military regime had the backing of the majority and that objectors were radical outliers. Although the effort to reoccupy the Malvinas/Falkland Islands and extract them from British control did stoke latent and diverse ideas of nationalism, the display of support described here was, in reality, quite ephemeral. The dictatorship was in its final hour.

The Plaza in Dictatorship (1982)

Revista Gente

Saturday the 10th: Plaza de Mayo, 200,000 people, an act in which the Argentinians consolidated their sense of sovereignty: this time, the plaza was for everyone. Neither official communications nor days of planning were necessary to organize the event. Just one call the day beforehand had been enough to awaken a latent impulse. It wasn't the protest of a single sector, it wasn't the march of the few against the few. But indeed, it was like so many other occasions—asking for something, although something for everyone, that wouldn't be undone—for the defense of sovereignty. This was the testimony of a people newly united after a long time. Big and small, of every age, of every sector . . . So were the unions. [. . .] From the terrace of the Casa Rosada, the interior minister, General Alfredo Saint-Jean, and the governor of Buenos Aires, Jorge Aguado, contemplated the giant protest. In their transmissions to the outside world, the French news agency AFP said that "About 100,000 people facing the Capitol were shouting 'America for the Americans!'"

Translated by Wendy Gosselin and Jane Brodie

The *Escrache*

Julieta Colomer and Anabella Arrascaeta

In the late 1980s and early 1990s, a series of measures granted pardons to military personnel who had been tried for their involvement with state terrorism activities from 1976 to 1983. As a result, individuals who had participated and facilitated acts of torture and disappearance were allowed to go free, living normal lives across the city. In response, two groups, HIJOS (Hijos e Hijas por la Identidad y la Justicia contra el Olvido y el Silencio, or Children for Identity and Justice and against Silence and Forgetting) and a collective known as the Mesas de Escrache (Escrache Collectives), began to organize public interventions to bring awareness about where those persons lived and what crimes they had committed. They referred to these acts as "escraches," a slang term that means "to bring to light." They organized in the neighborhoods where known torturers lived by circulating pamphlets, drawing pintadas (graffiti), and hanging afiches (posters) with information about the individual's crimes. These acts culminated in a rally in which neighbors marched to the perpetrator's home. In "Escrachar: To Make the Oppressor's Name Known" and the accompanying photograph, organizer Julieta Colomer describes the escrache. She highlights that rather than take a tenor of anger, the acts were designed to evoke a feeling of coming together, akin to a block party. The pardons were rescinded in 2003 and military personnel were put on trial, but the escrache suggested that even when justice was difficult to find in the courts, organizers would not permit the crimes of the civic-military dictatorship to be ignored in the street.

This Assassin Lives in Our Neighborhood: A Poster Announces an Upcoming Escrache *(2001)*

Julieta Colomer

Este asesino vive en nuestro barrio. Courtesy of the photographer.

Escrachar: *To Make the Oppressor's Name Known (2016)*

Julieta Colomer and Anabella Arrascaeta

Taking politics into our own hands, taking everyday problems and finding solutions together: the *escrache*, or public condemnation, arises from this idea. It has nothing to do with revenge, compulsive finger-pointing, insults, or coming to blows. It took place in a context and against a backdrop where impunity was absolutely naturalized, part of our normal daily life. We would cross paths in the street with the perpetrators of genocide, perpetrators of the most heinous crimes we suffer as a society. For those of us who were the children [of disappeared persons], who were part of a generation trying to understand genocide, suffering it firsthand, having more questions than answers, it was unacceptable. [. . .] The *escrache* was a response to injustice. It was a tool developed by a generation of youth, first from rage and later to deepen reflection and the collective effort to denounce the impunity of the murderers who should have been serving their sentences in the shared cells of our country's prisons. Then came a collective creation that included many other young people who supported the *escraches* and who identified with us, as we all understood that we had all experienced the dictatorship and we were all children of the same history. [. . .] It went from being a simple denunciation to an entire process. A process of constructing meaning in community, conversing face to face with neighbors, distributing flyers door to door, doing open radio programs in neighborhood plazas, speaking at cultural centers, talks with students and teachers at schools, deploying an entire means of communication through which we could [. . .] question the meaning of justice, memory, truth, [. . .] to question the institutional models and the mass media, or those who said "they did what they did for a reason" or [of the disappeared] "they must have done something."

Translated by Lisa Ubelaker Andrade

A White Tent Occupies the Plaza

Luis Bruschtein

La Carpa Blanca (The White Tent), a lengthy demonstration and occupation held by teachers in front of the National Congress, became a regular fixture downtown and a focal point for expressions of discontent with the neoliberal policies of the 1990s. The protest began with teachers who demanded more funding for public schools, but other issues were integrated into the protest, including a broader rejection of free-market policies and budget cuts. In its nearly three years of existence, the tent hosted around 3 million visitors. Under the tarp, protestors held concerts and performances and housed and cared for hunger strikers. Once again, the image of children, women, and workers taking to the street provoked discussion, as did the connection between celebration and protest. In the following article, printed in the newspaper Página/12, *reporter Luis Bruschtein narrates the emotional dismantling of the tent in 1999.*

After 1,003 Days the Teachers Pack Up "the White Tent" (1999)

Luis Bruschtein

They started taking down the White Tent at exactly 8:30 last night. There were colored sparklers, thundering firecrackers, and León Gieco songs. But, more than anything else, there was emotion. Hundreds of teachers collecting pieces of tarp as if it were their school flag. The writings on the fabric vanished as it was rolled up. One of the last ones that could be read said, "The White Tent: where the people's utopian dreams nestle." "At first, nobody dreamed it would last so long. Then nobody ever dreamed we would take it down one day," exclaimed one teacher. And another chimed in, "We've been doing everything under the sun to keep it up for almost three years. I can't believe it won't be here anymore." The last group of hunger strikers continued their fast until the tent was taken down. Only when all that was left were the bare metal bars did someone hand out some crackers. But by then everyone—union members and rank-and-file teachers with their families—was enveloped in a tangle of embraces under the metal skeleton that had been the tent. Some danced in each other's arms to the *chamamés* that Gieco sang, only letting go to embrace another dressed in a white teacher's uniform. Some laughed and others wept with emotion, wearing their uniforms proudly. They were proud to be teachers. [. . .] They read what the over eighty groups of hunger strikers who had spent time in the tent over the course of those two years and nine months had written on the fabric. [. . .] "When we decided to set up the tent," recalled Marta Maffei, "we didn't think we would be here for a month, or even two months, let alone a year or two years and nine months. But we managed to stick it out because this tent was greater than any of us. It was a speck of hope in a country engulfed in frivolity. [. . .] This is the first time since the onset of this vile commodification of everything—the commodification of Argentines' rights and needs, of their culture and education—that a policy has been rescinded.

Translated by Wendy Gosselin and Jane Brodie

Public Kitchens and *Piquetes*

Hilda

In the years approaching the 2001 economic crisis, unemployed persons, workers, and recently impoverished middle classes protested the growing economic injustice. They used old and new strategies to leave their mark: blocking roads to disrupt traffic (piquetes), parading while banging on pots (cacerolazos), or setting up public kitchens (ollas populares) to make demands on the government. The unemployed pushed for state-led plans to address their plight, for allowances to form cooperatives to construct popular housing, or for the provision of basic services in the wake of crisis. Some even organized to wrest control of their failing places of employment, bargaining for a collective workers' ownership. These collectively owned businesses became known as empresas recuperadas. *Some of these acts, like the* olla popular, *had been used before, but their magnitude and frequency were quite unprecedented. Rather than simply occupy public spaces, march, or go on strike, the* piquete *drew attention to a particular issue by blocking a major avenue or highway, intercepting in the daily life of other citizens. This aspect of disruption also made it a highly criticized form of protest. In the year 2002,* piquetes *reached their peak: some 2,336 roadblocks were held that year. In the text, a protestor, "Hilda," describes her involvement and notes that that these new kinds of protests often involved the entire family, and women played a particularly important role.*

Community, Food, and Protest at an Olla Popular (2002)

Hilda

We first set up the *olla popular* because people were hungry. The problem was how to get food to put in the pot and food for the people in the neighborhood. Some said it was degrading to ask for food. But the *olla* stayed open; it was a gathering place for individuals and for community groups. It was there that we first talked about going to city hall to demand unemployment benefits and sacks of food. We wanted refills every fifteen days. There were more than a thousand families from some twenty neighborhoods at the mobilizations. A lot of men were there too. I'm not sure, but I have the feeling that when we mobilize to ask for unemployment benefits, men come along.

But they don't go to the *olla popular*. It's us women that keep that going. Men are less willing to participate. I think that's because we women are tougher, more confrontational. Or maybe it's because of our kids. If you don't have anything to give your little ones to eat or shoes for their feet, you'll do whatever it takes.

Translated by Liliana Frankel

Ni Una Menos, Not One Less

Ni Una Menos, Verónica Abdala,

and Carolina Yuriko Arakaki

In the 2010s, the city's streets and plazas continued to be a space for public demonstration and celebrations. In 2015, a movement organized under the hashtag #NiUnaMenos (#NotOneLess) drew hundreds of thousands to march in protest against recurrent femicides and the culture of violence against women. The phrase "not one less" referred to the idea that participants would not accept any more of their fellow women going "missing" only to be later found dead at the hands of male violence. In "A Manifesto for a Movement," a text read in front of the National Congress on June 3, 2015, organizers voice the movement's purpose and lay out aims for legal reform, social change, and a transformation in the way women and women's issues were presented in media.

Over the following several years, consistent and creative demonstrations marked a "fourth wave" of feminist demonstration. Young women, members of the old guard (including several members of the Madres de la Plaza de Mayo), and the intermediate generations mobilized. Protests regularly combined strikes and marches, street and performance art, and online organizing. "Women's Bodies in Plastic Bags" describes one instance of performance art at a 2018 march.

That year, an emboldened feminist movement also adopted the hashtag #QueSeaLey (#LetItBeLaw) to advocate for abortion rights. Supporters of the movement began to don green scarves, a nod to the white scarves worn by the Mothers of the Plaza de Mayo, tying them on school backpacks, around wrists, or on their purses. (See "Pañuelazo" in the color insert.) The scarves have appeared in movements to legalize abortion around the region.

The focus on reproductive rights also marked a political turn; it spurred a reactionary counterprotest of conservatives who began their own marches and donned a light blue bandanna. After finding defeat in Congress in 2018, abortion was taken up a second time amid a more favorable political landscape in 2020. Late that year, abortion was declared free and legal. By 2023, efforts to repeal the legalization of abortion and critiques of the feminist movement became part of the growing right-wing agenda.

A Manifesto for a Movement (2015)

Ni Una Menos

The private is political. A woman who dares to say *"Basta* [Enough]," who wants to stop being a victim and become a survivor, challenges the whole structure of *machista* violence. But that is also her moment of greatest vulnerability; that's when, in an act of rage, he may try to kill her, and thus, it is when she most needs others, men and women, who can help her maintain her resolve: social and affective networks, state assistance, and strong political activism that insists on telling her that she is not alone and that it's not her fault. So that her *"BASTA"* can be said aloud, can be sustained. And that is what we are doing today in this public plaza. The violence that takes place in the domestic sphere is connected to social questions that must be debated in the public sphere. [. . .] We affirm our right to say no to whatever it is that one does not desire, be it a partner, a pregnancy, a sexual act, a predetermined way of life. [. . .] The fight against [femicide] requires a multifaceted response, of all the powers of the state [. . .] but also a response from all of civil society, and in particular by journalists and the media, where public dialogues are formed.

We say, "Not one less," with the pain of all of the victims, a pain that grows and grows. This massive, shared sentiment, this enormous and committed social participation, is a unanimous cry. It is the path we've found, in all the country's plazas, with mobilization, shared pain, the worry and urgent necessity of beginning coordinated actions that can attack the problem from its source—patriarchal culture—and until its end: the beaten woman, the assassinated woman.

Translated by Liliana Frankel

Women's Bodies in Plastic Bags (2018)

Verónica Abdala and Carolina Yuriko Arakaki

The artistic collective Expresión Mole performed an act on Wednesday that had a huge impact on those attending the march against the "Patriarchal Justice System" that in late November acquitted the men accused of sexually abusing and killing Lucía Perez. According to the justice system, no one is responsible for her October 2016 death, which prompted the first national women's strike that same year. The corner of Diagonal Norte and Florida Streets is frequented by a large number of people entering and leaving the subway station, or walking through the area. The location allowed for a gathering of a "crowd of people who do not belong to the art world and who are often indifferent even to events reported in the press, or who do not participate in demonstrations," explained Carolina Yuriko Arakaki, one of the promoters of the street intervention.

Expresión Mole is an aerial dance company that uses harnesses and acrobatics in its plays and public events, and artists from the company participated, hanging naked while wrapped in plastic bags during the intervention. They remained motionless for close to two hours.

They did not alert the press to the intervention, and they did not even hang a sign announcing the name of the group. Nevertheless, within moments of their arrival, they were surrounded by the public and photographers that recorded the scene.

Arakaki stated, "We wish to make a clear allusion to the pile of dead bodies left by the femicides that occur in Argentina. We are trying to represent the women who are victims of abuse and neglect, which often includes rape and murder, and other actions that are sometimes simply symbolic. That is why we put ourselves into bags, to refer not only to death but also to the garbage that the patriarchy wants us to believe we are. [. . .] Hundreds of men passed by that corner and looked at the scene and were mobilized by what they saw. We believe that art has a transformative power. While it may not achieve a radical change, it plants a seed."

Translated by Leslie Robertson

Streets of Celebration

Gastón Pérez Mazás and Pedro Lipcovich

The impetus to take to the street is felt not only in moments of protest but also in moments of celebration. When the national soccer team advances in the World Cup final or experiences a significant victory, it is customary for crowds to spontaneously descend on the Obelisk downtown. The photograph, taken from above, shows just a small portion of the crowd that gathered there when Argentina won the World Cup in 2022. The massive crowds that took to the streets of Buenos Aires that day, said to have numbered in the millions, led many newspapers to nickname the celebrations "the biggest party in all history." Though the particular event was historic and the numbers of people in the street remarkable, the tradition runs deep; the article excerpt that follows recounts a similar moment in 2014, when Argentina made it to the semifinals of the World Cup, and relates the multiple reasons that the persons who gathered there felt compelled to leave their houses and "meet at the Obelisk."

Record Crowds Celebrate Argentina's World Cup Win at the Obelisk *(2022)*

Gastón Pérez Mazás

Obelisco Campeón. Courtesy of the photographer.

A Sea of People and Flags at the Obelisk *(2014)*

Pedro Lipcovich

Everyone went to the Obelisk last night. Some of them, the youngest, were celebrating their first World Cup where Argentina made it to the finals and, because they had not been alive, they did not suffer from the pain or guilt of the 1978 World Cup. There was the man who named his son after Diego [Maradona], and another who said, "I'm happy," while his young daughter, wrapped in the flag, sat on his shoulders. There were those who blew air horns and others with hats shaped like soccer balls. [. . .] Tens of thousands, yelling, singing, jumping, taking pictures, filming themselves with their phones, celebrating through the night, from Corrientes to Callao, along the southern and northern sides of 9 de Julio, and down Diagonal to the Plaza de Mayo. [. . .] Horns blaring like it was New Year's Eve. An enormous inflatable Christ the Redeemer statue, similar to the one in Rio de Janeiro, was there as a symbol either of devotion or of sarcasm, but it could not take to the sky. More and more people arrived. They sang, "Volveremos, volveremos / volveremos otra vez / volveremo' a ser campeones / como en el '86" [We'll be back, we'll be back / we'll be back again / we'll be champions / just like 1986], and, of course, "Ar-gen-tina!" At intervals and in waves groups broke out jumping, singing: "Y ya lo ve, y ya lo ve, el que no salta es un inglés" [And you see, and you see, he who does not jump is an Englishman]. But Argentina did not play against England, so perhaps they should have sung "he who does not jump is a Dutchman"? [. . .] Many were debuting their new, powerful air horns. "We didn't think we would come out," said Guillermo, forty-five, surrounded by his large family. "We thought we would come out for the final, but it has been so long since we have celebrated." [. . .] The moon was high and a bit clouded over. "Although I didn't feel well, I came. I like this World Cup better than the one in '78. Back then, we were young, ignorant. We ignored a lot of things," said Daniel, fifty-seven. At 9:20 p.m. an impromptu *batucada* parade broke out on Cerrito. The Christ the Redeemer had finally managed to rise up over the avenue.

Translated by Leslie Robertson

Eating in Buenos Aires

At its most elemental level, the story of food in Buenos Aires reflects a history of mixture. *Porteños* have developed unique traditions and rituals that reflect the city's hybrid cultures, histories of colonialism, empire, and the movements of peoples. They have long made creative use of ingredients—meat, dairy, and grains (some native to the Americas but many brought from Europe)—that found fertile ground in the pampas outside the city limits. A few staples, like the ubiquitous ritual of drinking *mate*, hint at the resilience of regional Indigenous traditions. (See *"Mate* as Ritual," the first selection below.) When examined more closely, the culinary landscape in Buenos Aires also tells a story of social change. In a country where beef and the idea of "plenty" have served as symbols of national pride and well-being, food has also become a charged point of political conflict, a signpost of the ups and downs of the economy, and a window into ever-evolving changes in class, gender, and the effects of globalization.

At Home

Unlike in other nineteenth-century Latin American cities, where the lower classes relied on plant-based carbohydrates (beans, potatoes, rice, or corn) for nourishment and upper sectors had a more diverse diet that also included animal-based products (dairy, beef, and other meats), the Buenos Aires diet was quite similar across class lines. (See "Nineteenth-Century Meals.") An abundance of cattle and wheat from the countryside meant that these products were quite accessible in the capital city. Yet all things were, of course, not equal. The wealthy had access to abundance: although the poor and emerging middle classes often ate similar foods as wealthy *porteños*, they consumed them in far smaller amounts and used lesser-grade products.

By the end of the century, however, the less wealthy sectors were also infusing Buenos Aires meals with new diversity. The millions of immigrants who arrived in Argentina between 1860 and 1930 brought their food traditions with them; they adapted their "Old World" recipes to new conditions. At the same time, the wealthy were highlighting culinary ties to Europe:

the *criollo* elite hosted formal dinners with complicated menus that demonstrated their fashionable European taste. But Buenos Aires's humbler residents were changing its culinary landscape in a more rustic fashion, from the bottom up. The *milanesa napolitana* remains one of these most cherished food contributions. It is a thin cut of veal, breaded and fried—or baked—in beef fat or oil, topped with tomato sauce and cheese (and sometimes ham), and toasted in the oven. Far more ubiquitous than the legendary Argentine *asado*, it embodies the essential elements of basic *porteño* fare: its primary ingredients are major agriculture products (beef, grains, and dairy), and the *napolitana*'s flavors (and name) emphasize an Italian heritage. Some often incorrectly assume that the dish is from Naples; it is, in fact, a local innovation, first created in the 1920s at a restaurant downtown.

The *milanesa* made use of a rather economical cut of the national prize export: beef. Cattle were first brought to the pampas in the sixteenth century by European settlers. In those vast plains, the animals thrived, and by the turn of the twentieth century, when chilled and frozen beef could be transported overseas, Argentine meat found its market. The beef industry, which also made an impact through the construction of industrial meatpacking plants just beyond the city limits, became a central focus of political and economic life. It also shaped the *porteño* diet. Even today the most prestigious cuts (taken from the lower back) are either set aside for export or available domestically at high prices; most locals live off an ample supply of cheaper cuts of meat taken from the rest of the cow. The vast national demand for beef has meant that butchers are able to sell virtually every part of the carcass, from the diaphragm to the tongue; and most cooks know how each cut should be served, considering its fat content and tenderness. The most expensive include the *lomo* (tenderloin); the *ojo de bife* (a boneless ribeye); and the *bife de chorizo* (a thickly cut steak). Those looking for slightly cheaper options purchase the flavorful *vacío* (hanger steak), *asado de tira* (beef rib), and *entraña* (skirt steak), and those on a tight budget often access higher-fat and bone-in cuts like the osso buco, *cuadril* (rump), and roast beef (chuck). Other parts of the cow, like *chinchulines* (chitterlings), *riñones* (kidneys), and *mollejas* (sweetbreads), make regular appearances at *parrillas* (meat-based restaurants) and the traditional barbecue, known as the *asado*.

Beef's central place in the economy, local diet, and culture has made its accessibility and price a recurring political issue. On the one hand, politicians have made a point of ensuring that local consumers have access to beef at reasonable prices, regulating the export industry if necessary. (See "Anti-imperialism and Beef.") On the other hand, meat has been so widely and regularly consumed that public health initiatives have occasionally focused on the challenge of diversifying the local diet.

Amid moments of high inflation, the cost of beef and other basic pantry items has also become a way for households—and policymakers—to measure the cost of living. Many residents recall good economic times by how often they were able to put meat on the table for dinner. In times of prosperity, it is often said that beef should be eaten "at least twice a week"; in moments of economic downturn or rising food prices, however, beef makes it to the table far less often; ordinary diets rely more on pasta, vegetables, and a range of carbohydrates. In recent decades, escalating poverty and a cycle of economic crises have also made food inequality a prominent social issue. (See "Food and Crisis.") At the end of the civic-military dictatorship (1976–83), for example, the long lines at soup kitchens and the unaffordable food prices for the urban poor served as a powerful indictment of the regime's inadequate economic governance.

When elections were announced in 1982, presidential candidate Raúl Alfonsín campaigned with the slogan "In a democracy, one eats, one is cured, one is educated," and, once elected, he launched policies to address food inequality. But questions about food access and economic policy reemerged not long after. In 1989, amid drastic hyperinflation, food prices surged 70 percent over the course of only days. Supermarkets were looted—an act that was understood by many to be a protest of unlivable economic conditions.

A little more than a decade later, in December 2001, the scene seemed to repeat again. In the midst of a major economic tailspin and political crisis, banks closed and the government limited withdrawals of cash; businesses laid off workers, middle-class families lost their savings and jobs, and the poorest sectors of the city became unable to pay for even the most basic supplies. Once again, amid a dire political and economic crisis, lines at community-based soup kitchens (known as *comedores* and *merenderos*) and the prevalence of food insecurity would resonate as images of economic failure and political abandonment.

During such periods of crisis, the grilled feast that most typifies Argentine cuisine, the *asado*, was a rarity, an image of far-off abundance or of wealth. In times of economic stability, it could be an ordinary affair, modified to fit the group's budget. In an *asado*, families and friends gather at a long table staged in front of the outdoor grill—known as the *parrilla*. The table is lined with wine, salads, and traditional *criolla* and chimichurri salsas. Attendees spend the afternoon chatting as the *asador* grills and supplies a perfectly timed parade of chorizos and entrails, followed by three or four other cuts (quality and quantity depend on the budget). At the meal's end, those eating "applaud" the *asador*, traditionally a man; his skills served as a sign of masculinity. Like many meals connected to a sense of national identity, the *asado* traces its origins to the countryside. It was not until the late 1940s that the meal became fully integrated into the urban scene. Then, newly constructed homes and apartment buildings began to include built-in *parrillas*—a style of cement outdoor grill with a chimney and a grate that can be lowered and raised to control heat exposure. When those more permanent structures were not available, however, the meal might be prepared in an empty lot or on a makeshift grill. (See "The *Asado*: A Food Ritual.")

Cooking done indoors, by contrast, was traditionally viewed as women's labor. For much of the city's history, women were charged with the task of providing healthy meals for the family, an act that has often been represented as patriotic. (See "Patriotic Cooking.") Governments at times encouraged women to select national (not imported) products if there was a surplus, or asked them not to cook meat when there was a shortage.

By the mid-twentieth century, the rising accessibility of gas stoves and other new appliances was advertised as liberating women from some of their most arduous domestic tasks. Yet even while they adopted modern technology in the kitchen, many women found it important to distinguish Argentine culinary culture from US processed food. Well into the 1960s, Argentina's first lady of the kitchen, television star and cookbook writer Petrona Carrizo de Gandulfo (known as "Doña Petrona") insisted that Argentine women did not "cook from a can." Her refrain echoed a common response to the rapidly modernizing kitchen, though there was no question that canned and packaged foods were becoming popular. Nevertheless, mastery of basic cooking, including the ability to make homemade pastas, bread, pastries, and meat dishes—like the *milanesa*—was considered part of a woman's duty.

In their own homes, working- and lower middle-class women went about these activities on their own or with family help. Families of more means hired domestic workers. Petrona's television show and her cookbooks highlighted the role of paid domestic workers, marking out tasks that could be assigned; she also cooked alongside her own employee, Juana Bordoy (known as "Juanita"), demonstrating a classed, often fraught on-air relationship. (See "Domestic Labors.") Today Petrona's most time-consuming recipes are rarely cooked in the city's family kitchens. While the idea that women should take care of the household has not entirely disappeared, less laborious and more time-efficient recipes have risen in popularity—like the iconic birthday cake, the chocotorta. (See "The Chocotorta and Changing Ideas of Women's Work.")

Buying Food

Today, calling for delivery has become a popular alternative to more elaborate home dining. It is, however, a tradition with deep roots of its own. By the early twentieth century, Buenos Aires's streets were crowded with traveling food vendors. Some carried their wares in baskets that hung from a long stick hoisted over their shoulders, while others transported food using a horse-drawn cart, a pushcart, or, later, a bicycle; the streets flooded with the sounds of merchants singing out the names of the products on offer. Downtown,

For much of the nineteenth century residents bought food at open-air markets, but following a series of epidemics, initiatives arose to build indoor markets to improve sanitary conditions. The Mercado del Abasto, the interior of which is pictured here, was one such project. The market was first inaugurated in 1893. The Mercado del Abasto was renovated in the 1930s, and the resulting multistory, arched building became an emblematic landmark of the Abasto neighborhood. It served as an important site for agricultural commerce until the 1980s, when the much larger distribution center, the Mercado Central de Buenos Aires, opened outside the city limits. In the late 1990s the Mercado del Abasto building was converted into a shopping mall. Although some nineteenth-century markets have shared a similar destiny, others, like the Mercado de Progreso in Caballito and the Mercado de San Telmo—a popular tourist destination—are still in use today. *Source: Mercado del Abasto,* by Anonymous, 1898. Courtesy of the Archivo General de la Nación Argentina Dpto. Doc. Fotográficos. Inv: 12396.

workers also enjoyed a variety of street foods: copper-kettle-roasted peanuts became a typical street snack, and the milkman could often be seen carting his cow, stopping and offering fresh milk by the bottle—and carrying individual glasses for passersby.

Then, as today, locals did much of their shopping at small neighborhood stores, larger indoor markets, and outdoor food fairs. Although chain supermarkets are now routinely visited for pantry staples, buying food can still entail visiting a butcher for meat, a market for fruits and vegetables, a corner store for dry goods, a pasta shop for pasta, and a bakery for breads and pastries. (See "Anarchist Pastries.") These small businesses also reflect the lasting traces of the immigrant cultures that brought them into existence. (See "Neighborhood Businesses.") Indoor markets like Mercado de San Telmo, Mercado del Progreso, and Mercado de Belgrano were created at the turn of the twentieth century as a way to improve sanitation and organization; several of these enormous indoor structures continue to house family businesses that have been passed down across generations, and a few have seen stalls reinvented with more contemporary food court options.

For a long time, most residents could acquire many basic goods at a corner grocery, or *almacén,* that sold dry goods, cigarettes, wine, and cured meats. They were typically owned by Spanish immigrants who operated with an informal credit system for the entire neighborhood, keeping tabs of debt owed in a small notebook at the counter. During the 1960s, these small businesses encountered new competition from larger chain stores, some local and others with international investors. The new supermarkets replicated the US model and came in a variety of sizes, and while they marketed themselves as clean and efficient and found relative success, they never came to fully replace the neighborhood specialty stores. By the 1990s, with chain supermarkets gaining ground but still inconveniently dispersed, the opportunity opened for a new generation of immigrant entrepreneurs. Two new phenomena appeared: the twenty-four-hour corner kiosk, and small supermarkets often referred to as *supermercados chinos*—their name a reference to the stores' Chinese-immigrant ownership. These new establishments were usually constructed out of simple, tiled spaces outfitted with industrial refrigerators and shelving. Most also included vegetable and fruit stands, often managed by other immigrants, many from Bolivia and Perú. In 2004, like the Spanish-owned *almacenes* before them, Chinese supermarket owners created a formal organization, the Cámara de Supermercados Chinos (Chinese Supermarkets Association of Argentina), to integrate their business into the commercial economy, encourage further growth, and collectively combat discrimination.

Dining Out

In the late 2010s, Buenos Aires emerged as a food destination—its mix of top-ranking restaurants, traditional eateries, and accessible global prices elevated its prominence in the culinary world. *Porteños* have a long tradition of dining out, but the diversity and creativity of contemporary restaurants is relatively new. In the nineteenth century, informal eateries, like *fondas,* offered improvised basic fare; formal restaurants were less common. The few that existed were elegant salons on the perimeter of downtown, some inside in high-end hotels.

Greater in number were cafés. Since the city's beginnings, cafés were a critical place for social life, a place where the coffee itself was merely a pretext. Early in the city's history, neighbors gathered in cafés to discuss politics, and during the independence movement they became a place in which the possibility of revolution could be debated. A century later, café-bars were more numerous, diverse in style, and often stayed open late into the night. Today cafés of all kinds are still found on nearly every street: some are elegant and others rustic; some are historic sites of interest faithful to custom; many are basic spots where *tostadas* (toasted bread), *medialunas* (a sweet sticky croissant), and simple lunch offerings are served. A variety of local chains joined the scene in the last few decades, and even more recently, trendy specialty coffee spots offer the drink to go. Traditionally, however, cafés are small businesses where coffee is ordered from a table and patrons can sit and linger—reading, chatting, or staring out a window—for as long as they please. (See "The Café.")

At the turn of the twentieth century, a few rather formal restaurants offered extensive menus that listed pages upon pages of pastas, meat, fish, chicken, and potato dishes and difficult-to-pronounce names in a mixture of European languages. One customer complained, "Is there someone out there who can actually read these hotel restaurant menus? They are a terrible corruption of Spanish, Italian, English, German." Most *porteños* did not realize that some of their favorite foods were local creations; today, many pasta-lovers are surprised to hear that *sorrentinos*—large round ravioli—cannot be found outside Argentina.

In working-class neighborhoods, residents unpretentiously created new kinds of eateries and innovations based on favorite foods from their own cultures of origin. Among these was a local rendition of pizza and, with it, the pizzeria. The pizzeria Banchero was among the first in the city. It began as a bakery; the owner started to use leftover dough to make *fugazza*, a traditional Genovese bread covered in onion. When bakers began to pile on *muzzarella*, a denser white cheese than the Italian mozzarella, they renamed it the *fugazzeta*; it erupted in popularity. Pizza was also offered with *fainá*, a pizza-like crust made of garbanzo flour, water, oil and salt, which could be eaten alone or on top of pizza (to the chagrin of Italians). Several appeared on Corrientes Avenue and served late into the night. (See "Pizza.") The wine industry in Argentina also took its place at the pizzeria in the early twentieth century; cups of moscato, an affordable wine, were paired with pizza; the act of having these three items late at night became such an iconic experience that it inspired a rock song titled "Moscato, Pizza, and Fainá" in 1988: the band Memphis la Blusera described the meal as a classic way to "end the night."

By the 1940s, pizzerias were popular and affordable spots to eat at midday or during a long night out. Some family businesses were passed down among generations; other new pizzerias opened in neighborhoods, far from the lights of Corrientes; their owners were often no longer immigrants, but first- or second-generation Argentines of mixed backgrounds. They were faithful observers of new innovations of *porteño* pizza, dishing out the *pizza al molde* (baked in a dish), *a la piedra* (baked on the floor of the oven or stone), *media masa* (a special, dense crust), or *a la parrilla* (on the grill).

In the decade previous, migrants from other provinces in Argentina moved to Buenos Aires attracted by jobs in the growing industrial enclaves outside the capital city limits; they also made an impact on culinary culture. Pizzerias, for example, integrated the *empanada criolla* into their menus. Empanadas can be traced back to Arabic influences in Portuguese and Spanish cuisine, and in Latin America they exist in seemingly innumerable renditions (often reflecting local ingredients). In Argentina, a classic empanada is made from a wheat- and animal-fat-based dough and filled with beef (chopped rather than ground) and other ingredients, then baked or fried. Although empanadas were not new to Buenos Aires, the increasingly traditional inclusion of *empanadas de carne* and even *empanadas de humita* (filled with corn and cheese) on the menus at city pizzerias was suggestive of how *criollo* recipes made their way into these popular eateries. Today, an order of empanadas (by the dozen) can include a range of options that reflect the city's culture mixture: spinach and greens; *caprese* with tomato, cheese, and basil; and—a local favorite that mirrors the *fugazzeta*—melted cheese and onion. Each type of empanada is identifiable by its *repulgue* (braided closure).

The *choripán* is another city staple: a grilled chorizo sausage served on a simple bread roll. It is most often found outside the city's restaurant circuit, sold as street food or at an *asado*. At the beginning of the twentieth century, beef cuts were sold on bread from small carts, but in the 1940s a version of the *choripán*, the *sanguche de chorizo* (chorizo sandwich), grew in popularity as a food served at soccer stadiums; other popular stadium foods were the *pizza canchera* (pizza with only sauce) and the *milanesa* sandwich. Eating chorizo and entrails along with a heaping spoonful of chimichurri remains a mainstay at carts stationed along the river, in parks, and in streets downtown. (See "Food and Nostalgia.") In the twenty-first century the *choripán* also became a symbol of political clientelism. It was often grilled at large protests, and critics, attempting to delegitimize a demonstration, would allege that the marchers were "there for the free *choripán*."

A chorizo (without the bread) can also be enjoyed at a specific kind of restaurant, the *parrilla*. *Parrillas* first appeared as a kind of extension of the rural asado tradition in Mataderos, a neighborhood on the farthest edge of the city that was once known for its many slaughterhouses; these types of restaurants began to appear across the city in the 1940s. *Parrillas* combined a meat-centered menu with the ambiance of another classic, unpretentious restaurant, the *bodegón*, where abundant plates of favorite homemade dishes were served alongside accessibly priced Argentine wine (often served in a pitcher resembling a penguin). The informal ambiance of the *bodegón* has made it an enduring and popular destination for a meal out. (See "The *Bodegón*.")

The city's archetypical café-bars are still popular today. Friends gather for long chats or to grab a bite to eat. *Source: Café-Bar*, by Roberto Pera, 2021. Courtesy of the photographer.

In the late 1980s, the city opened its doors to US-style fast food. Before, the middle and upper classes had enjoyed US-style burgers at a small local chain, Pumper Nic, which renamed the burger the *paty*. The international corporation McDonald's first set up shop in 1986 in the well-to-do neighborhood of Belgrano; Burger King followed in 1989. When developers converted the old central market—Abasto—into an indoor shopping mall in 1998, the food court swelled with families enjoying a variety of fast food on the weekends. The burger saw another heyday in the twenty-first century as local cooks made use of beef to offer their renditions of the inexpensive meal.

These new trends appeared alongside a notable rise of chef-led small restaurants that were drawing up innovative menus. The strong culture of dining out has proved fertile ground for an eclectic contemporary restaurant industry in which a new generation of chefs combine classic tastes with creative freedom. They have built a globally recognized food scene and held food fairs to highlight local ingredients and talent. Those at the head of the kitchen—and cooks in the line—have showcased new cultures of mixture in Buenos Aires cuisine. (See "A Twenty-First-Century Culinary Scene.")

Mate as Ritual

Lalo Mir

Although many of the culinary traditions of Buenos Aires hint at the city's historic connections to the Old World, a few underline the resilience of Indigenous cultures. Drinking yerba mate is among the most important and ubiquitous of these. Though mate can be enjoyed alone, it is a social drink, a ritual with its own rules and meanings. Those who drink mate carry a thermos for hot water and a bag of yerba with them wherever they go. The yerba—made of tiny green leaves—is put in a hollowed-out gourd, steeped in hot (never boiling) water, and sipped using a bombilla, a straw with a filter; the cebador, the person serving the mate, holds the thermos, fills the gourd with water, and passes it among his or her companions; one by one, they each take their time to finish completely before returning it. After some time, the cebador must change the yerba, as it runs out of flavor. Unlike coffee, mate is never enjoyed in a restaurant—it is disconnected from commercial spaces and instead is enjoyed at home, at work, in plazas or parks. The drink also inspires a different rhythm: the act of passing the gourd and waiting one's turn becomes part of a shared moment and conversation. In this poem, radio host Lalo Mir expands on this idea, seeing mate, and all the habits that surround it, as a universal part of local culture and one of the few rituals that crosses all social lines.

A Mate *and a Love* (2009)

Lalo Mir

Mate is not a drink.
Well, yes. It is a liquid and enters through the mouth.
But it is not a drink.
In this country, nobody has *mate* because they are thirsty.
It's more of a habit, like scratching oneself.
Mate is the exact opposite of television: it makes you talk if you're with
    someone, and it makes you think when you're alone.
When someone arrives to your house the first greeting is "hello"
and the second "a *mate*?"
This happens in every house.
In the houses of the rich and those of the poor.

It happens between chatty, gossiping women,

and it happens between serious men, or immature ones.

It happens between old folks in a home and between teenagers while
they study.

It is the only thing that parents and their children share without arguing
or reprimands.

Peronists and Radicals serve *mate* with no questions.

In summer and in winter.

It is the only thing that makes us alike,

victims and executioners; good and bad.

When you have a child, you begin to give them *mate* when they ask you.

You serve it a little warm, with a lot of sugar, and they feel grown up.

You feel an enormous pride when a kid of your flesh and blood begins to
drink *mate*.

Your heart jumps from your body.

Later, as years pass, they will choose whether to drink it bitter, sweet,

very hot, chilled, with orange peel, with wild herbs, with a spritz of
lemon.

When you meet someone for the first time, you will drink a few *mates*.

A person will ask, when they aren't sure: "Sweet or bitter?"

The other responds: "However you drink it."

The keyboards of Argentina have their letters full of *yerba*.

Yerba is the only thing that is always there, in every house.

Always. With inflation, with hunger,

with the military, with democracy, with any of our plagues and

eternal curses.

And if one day there's no *yerba*, a neighbor has it and gives it to you.

Yerba isn't something you deny to anyone.

This is the only country in the world where the decision to stop being a
child and

to begin being a man happens on one day in particular.

[. . .] The day on which a child puts the kettle on the stove and drinks
their first *mate* without anyone else in the house,

in this moment, they've discovered that they have a soul.

or they are dying of fear,

or they are dying of love, or something: but it's not just any day.

None of us remember that day on which we first drank a *mate* alone. But
it should have been an important day for each of us.

Inside, there are revolutions.

A simple *mate* is a demonstration of values, nothing more and nothing
less . . .

It is the solidarity of sitting through a watered-down *mate* because the
conversation is good.

The conversation, not the *mate.*
It is respect for the rhythms of talking and listening,
you speak while the other drinks
and it is the sincerity to say:
Enough, this *yerba* needs to be changed!

Translated by Wendy Gosselin and Jane Brodie

Nineteenth-Century Meals

Lucio V. Mansilla

Lucio V. Mansilla, born to a traditional elite family, recalls life as an adolescent in the mid-nineteenth century and, in particular, the kinds of foods he ate. He notes that one of the most common dishes was the puchero criollo, *a rich broth filled with beans, garbanzos, chicken or beef, odds and ends. The dish became a staple for all classes. For the rich, it was a stew of abundance; for the poor, it was a way of serving many on very little. Mansilla describes food at that time as "genuine"—while he accepts the presence of what he views as "international" cuisine, his comments suggest a underlying criticism of the ways new immigrants appear to be altering the city's culinary repertoires.*

My Memories (1904)

Lucio V. Mansilla

The dinners were [. . .] extremely varied: a *puchero* of meat or chicken, always with squash, rice, and celery and sometimes with potatoes and corn (not cabbage, because of the smell); farina; *quibebe* [a winter-squash stew] that had been special-ordered; and pastries, of the variety which the Black pastry chefs sold at the houses of their usual customers on a cutting board covered with cloth, then cotton (though never white, so as to preserve the batch's heat). But they tasted good. Very occasionally there would be empanadas, which were very heavy. [. . .] And when there wasn't *puchero*, fried eggs and sandwich meat, or soup and sometimes ham. *Café con leche* [coffee and milk] for the adults, tea with milk for the kids, with a little bread and butter and *mazamorra* [a traditional dessert made of white rice, milk and vanilla]. There are people who believe that during that era, people didn't eat well. Those people should be corrected. We ate moderately. Times were hard. But not bad. And everything was genuine. Not like nowadays, when lots of things are falsified. And back then you ate the real thing. While now, with the invasion of fakes from the world over, names are one thing, while their referents may be something else entirely. Obviously I'm not referring to any hotels, guesthouses, or restaurants in particular, nor to a particular house with chefs, butlers, and white-gloved valets: neither am I referring to those straightforward establishments where everything is abundant, where one can go at any time of day [. . .] for all the courses, beginning with the ravioli and meat with the skin still on and finishing with the omelet, soufflé, or plum pudding; rather, I refer to the crowd that likes to employ chefs carrying cookbooks who are later discovered ignorant of how to beat eggs with oil for a mediocre mayonnaise, revealing that they were previously drivers and quartermasters, French, Italian, Spanish, or Portuguese, anything you could imagine, besides what they had told themselves in the hope that they too could embody the proverb "the kitchen makes the cook."

Translated by Liliana Frankel

Anti-imperialism and Beef

Lisandro de la Torre, José Peter, and Caras y Caretas

During the first half of the twentieth century, the question over who exactly profited from Argentina's vast beef and agriculture production became a central issue in national politics. The beef industry expanded rapidly under British financing. A wealthy elite prospered. In 1933, Argentina signed the Roca-Runciman Agreement with Great Britain, a deal that guaranteed a market for its beef exports and fixed tariffs on grains. The deal came at a cost: Argentina agreed to purchase British coal, railroad materials, and other imports and allowed British businesses contracts to circumvent local labor laws, among other advantages. Critics, including Senator Lisandro de la Torre, rallied against the deal as a grossly imperialist project that brought millions to the few, endangered workers, all while pushing Argentina into the fold of British economic power. In "Report to the National Senate Denouncing the Roca-Runciman Pact," de la Torre expresses his disdain for the new agreement and suggests that Argentina was not only humiliated but also worse off than any of that empire's formal colonies. The meat industry and, in particular, the trade relationship with Britain continued to rile anti-imperialists throughout the 1930s and into the 1940s. In "Tales from the Proletariat," José Peter, a union leader and communist, connects anti-imperialism to workers' struggles to improve labor conditions in meatpacking plants in the 1930s.

When Juan Perón came to power in 1946, regaining some control of the meat industry and recovering lost profits was a focal point of nationalist policy. The two-frame cartoon from the magazine Caras y Caretas *(1952) illustrates a perception that became quite common during the first Peronist period: in the first drawing, titled "From Abroad Will Come He Who Will Eat Yours," the obese British Empire personified as John Bull eats an enormous steak, leaving the tiny Argentine to consume the miserable leftovers; in the second panel, titled "From Abroad Will Come He Who Will Eat Your Leftovers," a stout laborer named Juan Pueblo (who resembles Juan Perón) eats two slices of steak as a tiny, elegantly dressed British man waits for leftovers. In the images, the availability of meat signals pride in an anti-imperialist government that would feed its people first.*

The critiques mark what would become a series of diverse policies that sought to ensure profits from the beef industry and guarantee the availability of beef to the domestic market. While a number of administrations attempted to reserve certain cuts of meat for domestic consumption, put in place price controls, or impose taxes on exports, these policies often faltered in the face of inflation, making access to beef and local beef prices a subject of public debate.

Report to the National Senate Denouncing the Roca-Runciman Pact (1934)

Lisandro de la Torre

The Argentine minister, Mr. Duhau, appears to be like the ministers of some of the British dominions. The Minister of Agriculture knows perfectly well that the meatpacking plants constitute a monopoly of scandalous proportions. [. . .] Noncompliance with laws; the suspension of the collection of fines; a lack of oversight of the payment of taxes, a bargain at 25 percent of foreign currency; tolerance for the appropriation of exchange rate benefits; concealment of the low purchase prices of steers through publishing inaccurate statistics, equally matched by the official ignorance of sales prices; prosecution of Argentine meatpacking companies; the gift to the foreign meatpackers pool of 11 percent of the quota for two years; the acceptance of the fact that Argentines are being suppressed and England has the monopoly on the export of 85 percent of Argentine meat, and that it chooses the importers—a depressing condition that it has not even dared to impose on its own dominions. [. . .] The British government tells the Argentine government: We shall not permit you to encourage the organization of companies that compete with foreign meatpackers. Under these conditions, it cannot be said that Argentina has become a British dominion, since Britain does not take the liberty of imposing such humiliations on British dominions. British dominions each have their own meat import quotas and they manage them themselves. Argentina is the only one that will not be able to manage its quota. I wonder, after all of this, whether we will be able to continue to sing the line of the anthem, "To the great Argentine people, good health."

Translated by Leslie Robertson

Tales from the Proletariat (1968)

José Peter

Anti-imperialist hate was made incarnate among the masses. The antinational and anti-working-class policy followed by corporations was clear to everyone. And the most outrageous of all, and which would be immensely difficult to qualify, is that the government and police were in favor of them and against the workers of the country, who leave their own lives in tatters to produce the wealth that feeds their economy. Neither one thought of the misery and hunger that thousands of families would have to endure. The "patriotism" of the government was dedicated only to looking after the petty interests of the companies.

Translated by Leslie Robertson

Imperialism, Peronism, and the Worker's Right to Beef (1952)

Caras y Caretas

Caras y Caretas, August 1952, 54–55. Artist unknown.

Food and Crisis

Juan González Yuste

At several points in recent history, food inequality and scarcity has emerged as a powerful image of political failure. In this article, written at the very end of Argentina's civic-military dictatorship, the Spanish newspaper El País *reports of "hunger in the breadbasket of the world." This refrain was meant to suggest an irony: the common perception that Argentina was a major global provider of beef, wheat, and other grains made it all the more striking that its poorest families might be struggling to put food on the table. Journalist Juan González Yuste explains that while more accommodated sectors were experiencing long lines at the butcher and a decline in weekly beef consumption, rising food prices resulted in a much more significant struggle for the urban poor: an increase in community-run soup kitchens and persons traveling from Greater Buenos Aires to the urban center to rummage for food scraps. Observations like these served as clear testaments to the economic failures of the civic-military dictatorship. The issue would reemerge under democratic governments. In mid-1989, wages had an annual increase of 200 percent, but the cost of bread jumped by more than 500 percent, milk more than 400 percent, and cheese more than 1,000 percent; the situation spurred episodes of supermarket looting, both spontaneous and organized. In 2002, in the aftermath of a December default and staggering inflation, the question of food inequality, and in particular, the struggles of the growing poor to pay for basic pantry ingredients reemerged, and news of "food riots" again made headlines.*

The topic of food prices persisted in the following decades. By 2020, women who ran comedores *or* merenderos—*kitchens that feed many by pulling together state resources and donations, and holding fundraisers—found demand escalating. Although state programs brought resources to the community-based kitchens during the pandemic, these initiatives were cut and riled in controversy by early 2024: despite rising demand at community kitchens, new austerity policies razed federal budgets for social programs. Amid scarce donations, cooks lacked basic staples. Protestors again took to the streets to march against hunger.*

Food Struggles in the So-Called "Breadbasket of the World" (1982)

Juan González Yuste

Six years after the coup d'état that overthrew Perón's widow and six months after the disastrous military adventure in the Malvinas/Falkland Islands, something unusual is happening in Argentina today: the people of the breadbasket of the world are hungry. Despite the pressure placed on the Argentine media from the ruling military junta, the newspaper *Clarín* stated: "The journalistic chronicle has recorded the treks by many women from the suburbs to the capital city in search of free bread doled out at some establishments and scraps discarded from the restaurants and markets downtown. We also know of a rising number of people systematically searching for waste in the garbage dumps."

Adolfo Pérez Esquivel, winner of the 1980 Nobel Peace Prize for his work in human rights, categorically affirms: "Today there is hunger in Argentina. I have denounced it publicly, because I have seen children eating in the garbage; I have seen children fighting for scraps with the pigs in the Province of Santa Fe. But there is no need to go that far. You can see it here in Buenos Aires. There are *ollas populares* [soup kitchens] that try to alleviate the hunger, and I have visited parishes where they give the children *mate* with milk and a loaf of bread. That is their food for the whole day . . ." Just half an hour from Buenos Aires [. . .] groups in Buen Pastor parish have organized one of these *ollas populares*, an emergency canteen visited twice a day by 150 children. [. . .]

Argentina, the country known for meat, is struggling to put beef on the table. According to the National Beef Board, compared to an average annual per capita consumption over the past twenty years of 87 kilograms, the figure for last September was the lowest in history: 52 kilos. The weekly paper *El Nacional* gave an even more dire outlook, quoting the Coordinadora de Actividades Mercantiles Empresarias (Coordinator of Commercial Business Activities): "Meat consumption dropped from 115 kilos per inhabitant to only twenty-two." Buenos Aires restaurants have been restricted from selling meat on Thursdays and Fridays. *Humor Registrado*, one of the magazines that would like to see an end to the military regime, ironically commented that in Argentina, where everyone is trying to offload blame for the Malvinas/Falkland Islands War, the foreign debt and questions over the disappeared, "there is such hunger that, if a scapegoat appears, it gets eaten immediately."

Translated by Lisa Ubelaker Andrade

The *Asado*: A Food Ritual

Eduardo Archetti, Anonymous, and Nicolás Olivari

Beef has long served as a staple of Buenos Aires diets—it is used in a myriad of dishes and, when the economy is strong, eaten regularly. The asado—*a traditional meal in which a selection of meat and entrails is grilled and served—is an important part of local identity. In "Manhood and the Asador," the anthropologist Eduardo Archetti analyzes the culture of the* asado *and examines the way the ceremonious meal is constructed around ideas of masculinity. The artist Marcos López's staged photograph* Asado en Mendiolaza *(2001), located in the color insert of this volume, captures some of these characteristics and also alludes to the association of the* asado *with good economic times: modeled after Leonardo Da Vinci's* The Last Supper *and taken just before the 2001 economic crisis, López's scene offers a sense of foreboding. Set in the Córdoba countryside, the photograph also references the* asado's *rural roots. Yet, as the texts in this chapter suggest, the* asado *also made its mark on the capital city. Although some urbanites have grills installed in their apartment rooftops or backyards, others come up with more spontaneous solutions: the photograph illustrates one such scene—construction workers in 1930 build a grill from metal parts at lunchtime. The text "Lunch at the Construction Site," part of an essay by urban chronicler Nicolás Olivari, describes a remarkably similar scenario taking place more than thirty years later.*

Manhood and the Asador (1999)

Eduardo Archetti

Asado, the product of the pampa, is a ceremony of national hospitality and one of the most recurring Argentinian manias. [. . .] Borges liked to say (or at least we attribute him this quote as with so many others) that grilling is an excellent pretext for the ritual of "conversant friendship." The world of *asado* is one of outdoorsmen, and the man who grills is the central character of the ritual. One of my informants established a parallel between this activity and the gaucho saying that best sums up their old nomadic lifestyle: "outdoors and with fatty meat." If there is a consensus on anything in Argentina, it's the fact that grilling is a "virile and very Argentinian ceremony." [. . .]

There are as many practices and secrets of *asado* as there are *asadores* [persons who grill]. *Asado* is public but, at the same time, eminently "secret" in the sense that the individual aspect of it is difficult to transmit. The world of *asado* establishes a hierarchy between men that, in general, is totally accepted and permits legitimate exclusions. It's always preferable to declare oneself bad at grilling as opposed to submitting oneself to a hell of ridicule if the *asado* goes badly. It's very difficult, then, not to know who is the best *asador* among a group of friends, or in a family. Consequently, it's thought that while a cook is self-made, taking courses, trying and trying until he is skilled at a recipe, a real master of *asado* is born. [. . .] *Asado* allows for an attentive table to experience (or better, to imagine, if one is so inclined) the reconstruction of the dead animal's body. *Asado* is based in the individuation of the parts and on the order in which one begins, first with the viscera, continuing with the ribs (thrown on) and finishing with the muscles (the skirt, the belly, and the sirloin). The mixture of parts observed in an isolated bowl of *puchero*, or in the meat made into a *milanesa*, doesn't allow for a complete reconstruction of the original body. [However,] it is possible to conceptualize [. . .] eating meat from the grill as both deconstructive act, and an analytical process, made possible in the evident death of the animal. In the words of an informant, "We speak so much of *asado* in terms of what is eaten, how are the gizzards, or is the finished product tough or is it tender, because it is a process which takes place over time, hours, and moves from one part of an animal to another" (and, I might add, in which the whole body is expressed in its parts).

Translated by Liliana Frankel

Construction Workers Grill on Their Lunch Break (ca. 1930)

Anonymous

Courtesy of the Archivo General de la Nación Argentina Dpto. Doc. Fotográficos.
Inv: 322327.

Lunch at a Construction Site (1966)

Nicolás Olivari

There is one hour of rest in their day. When the time comes for their afternoon break, the construction workers come down from their still-inaccessible workplaces and begin to prepare lunch. A carnivorous display is laid out and presented on an improvised grill made from twisted iron found on the site. An abundance of meat. Chorizos toasting to a golden color. How many people stop and look on with desire at the makeshift grills that materialize at construction sites? The sacred hour of this midmorning snack! More than a few rich men, very rich from the look of them, stop their luxury cars in front of the workers. They pretend it is for some other reason, but the truth is that the smell has stopped them in their tracks—literally. The scent of grilling meat so subtly evaporates into the air—the scent of *asado*.

Translated by Liliana Frankel

Patriotic Cooking

Cía Sansinena

During the first half of the twentieth century, women were expected to create nutri-
tious meals for their families. Girls were trained in the "art and science" of domestic
work, which provided instruction on basic homemaking, nutrition, and preventing
illness. This 1940 cookbook also suggests that Argentine women fulfill an important
patriotic duty by cooking recipes that support national agricultural industries and
food products. A few years later, under Peronism, the ideas of housework, woman-
hood, and patriotism became further entangled. In the 1940s and 1950s, Peronist pub-
lications underlined that cooking healthy foods and managing the household economy
by finding affordable prices was a women's patriotic duty. At the same time, recipes
that once had foreign-sounding names were often retitled to allude to more humble or
national roots: Papas a la Croquignole in Sansinena's 1940 cookbook (a simple recipe
of boiled potatoes with a cream sauce) became Papas a la Crema (Cream Potatoes);
Papas Maître d'Hôtel became Papas Campesino.

An Introduction to Fine Cooking (1940)

Cía Sansinena

Modern existence, where trifles often seem as important as basics, fills the art
of eating and, thereby, the art of cooking with nuance. [. . .] It often warms
up friendships and spices up homes. And then there is that unquestionable
Spanish saying "Food is the way to a man's heart . . ." Of course, in these
busy times, elaborate and costly dishes are reserved for special occasions.
We go for something quick and easy that is nonetheless flavorful and nutri-
tious. The art of cooking must be democratized, so to speak. Indeed, it must
be guided to reasonable nationalist ends—patriotic ends, it could be said,
without falling into excess or affectation. That is to say, an Argentine cuisine
suited to Argentina and its possibilities, one that makes use of the products
of the native soil. That would ensure the sale of those products and the excellence of dishes based on them.

Translated by Wendy Gosselin and Jane Brodie

Domestic Labors

Marisa Avigliano

Doña Petrona rose to popularity in the 1940s and 1950s as the author of the most-sold cookbook in Argentina. Later she became the star of Argentina's first major cooking show. Her elaborate recipes, particularly her decorated cakes, often presumed a great deal of skill in the kitchen. The show also highlighted local particularities: Petrona altered recipes to adapt to fluctuations in the economy and taught her followers about new kitchen technologies, particularly the use of a gas stove.

The show also foregrounded the labor of paid household laborers in middle- and upper-class homes. Petrona appeared on air with her assistant, Juanita Bordoy. This 2016 essay, looking back on the life of Bordoy, recalls the way the presence of the two women on television impacted viewers, highlighting questions about the dynamics of domestic labor—a relationship that usually transpired behind closed doors. Obtaining labor rights and guarantees for paid household employees has been a long-fought effort led by the sector's workers. Historically, domestic service was not included in general labor laws; contracts were often informal, and it was difficult or impossible to regulate the conditions of labor performed in private homes, all of which left workers vulnerable. In the late 1940s, Eva Perón spoke to the idea that domestic workers and housewives should be granted labor rights and a salary; she also proposed that if women were paid for their housework they may not feel the need to look for what she referred to as "less natural" work outside the home. In recent decades, the labor and women's movements have taken up the issue and legislative advancements were made. Plans for housewife compensation never came to pass (though a retirement plan was put in place in 2005), but household workers did acquire labor rights—at least on paper; many still work without formalized legal contracts or protections and are paid without benefits, under the table.

Juanita Bordoy, the Other Star (2016)

Marisa Avigliano

A pair of arms holds up a roasting pan that slides onto one of the oven racks. The camera shows buns and egg-glazed pastries with pastry cream; the oven door closes and the camera forgets all about the arms. It's not the first time the body to which those arms belong has been seen in parts—it is almost never shown whole—just half of it leaning in. The brightly lit close-ups are the domain of Doña Petrona, the first TV star of Argentine cooking, and in the background, we see her assistant, Juanita, who never poses. Petrona speaks in the first person, "I put it in a medium-high oven. Do you see which rack I use?" Petrona speaks and Juanita acts. Both are as impeccable and "posh" as a housewife was expected to be in the sixties. [. . .] Juanita never stands still: she wipes down counters, separates eggs, washes and dries slotted spoons, preps dishes, and warms up whatever Petrona will need. [. . .] It was said even back then that Petrona mistreated poor Juanita, who did everything she asked without even a hint of chagrin. "I'm not your Juanita!" "I want a Juanita of my own!" said the housewives who would copy every last word of the recipes [. . .] read at the end of the show. Children would play house and pretend to be Petrona and Juanita (the host always got to be Petrona and order the guest around). [. . .] "Check on the oven for me," "Don't take it away, I'm not done yet!" "Juanita, roll up my sleeves please" (When Petrona's sweater sleeves were in her way Juanita had to drop whatever she was doing to roll them up): those were just some of the phrases from the liturgy uttered by the impatient cook (they sound like something out of *Gosford Park* or *Downton Abbey*). Together the two women would decide what would later appear on screen (Petrona's husband was part of the team, but no one remembers him—Petrona and Juanita were the couple to be reckoned with); together they cooked before the camera for over thirty years; and together they lived until Petrona died. She was called "La Morocha" [a nickname that alludes to someone with darker features] in her native province of La Pampa until she arrived in Buenos Aires in 1945, where she became Juanita. The use of the diminutive "Juanita" erased any sign of the countryside, underscored matriarchy—there were twenty years between them—and turned Juanita into a housekeeper with a room of her own next to the one belonging to the lady of the house: an iron loyalty that faltered only once, when an auditorium full of the duo's fans gave Juanita a larger round of applause than Petrona. Everything quickly got back to normal, though, hierarchies restored, when with mathematic rigor the assistant blushed as she reminded those present, "The star is the lady of the house."

Translated by Wendy Gosselin and Jane Brodie

The Chocotorta and Changing Ideas of Women's Work

Marité Mabragaña and Hernán Firpo

Cooking habits changed considerably during the second half of the twentieth century. Many middle-class women departed from their expected role as housewives and cooks when they worked outside the home. Marité Mabragaña was one such woman. She describes herself as a member of the first generation of women who worked in white-collar professions—in her case, at a major advertising agency. Mabragaña was the inventor of the chocotorta, the 1990's working mothers' answer to Doña Petrona's elaborate and time-consuming birthday cakes. As she recounts here, she came up with the idea for the cake while working with two major packaged food brands.

Her major claim to fame also draws attention to the history of national packaged food brands, which by the end of the twentieth century were a growing sector of the food market. One of the three key ingredients in the chocotorta is the packaged Chocolina cookie, a product created by a national brand, Bagley, in 1975. Bagley was founded in the late nineteenth century when its owner acquired permission to import machinery to mass produce snacks, generating some local competition in a market dominated by foreign imports. Bagley produced snacks for the merienda—*a four or five p.m. sweet treat common in most Argentine households. Their first product was a sweet wafer called Operas, and then an emblematic cracker called Criollitas. By the 1960s, as the demand for packaged foods rose, they offered more variety. The Chocolina, a chocolate cookie, made it to the map of favorite snacks after Mabragaña's advertising campaign. Working mothers and children embraced the easily prepared, no-bake dessert, the Chocotorta, making it the quintessential birthday cake by the 1990s.*

Working Women and the Invention of the Chocotorta (2012)

Marité Mabragaña and Hernán Firpo

"I was among the first generation of women that climbed the hierarchical ladder in this country. [At our advertising agency] we had accounts with many large companies, including those that made Mendicrim [a cream cheese] and Chocolinas [a chocolate cookie]. Running the accounts of these companies, as well as working as a housewife and cooking all the time, I knew that the

combination of dulce de leche and cream cheese made for one of the best flavors in the world. At that time, Mendicrim was *the* brand of cream cheese—
there were no other brands. In our house, we ate vanilla wafers in cream
and I suppose that the idea came from there: If one could join a drenched
Chocolina cookie with cream cheese and dulce de leche and make layers,
how would it taste?"

She brought it to the office, where it received high praise.

"I thought up the name chocotorta. In the original recipe, one wets the
chocolate cookies with port, mixes dulce de leche with cream cheese and layers cookies and dulce de leche. It's very easy. What I loved about it was that
you didn't need to put it in the oven and it was like a game that brought your
husband and the kids into the kitchen. We worked for about a year to get the
two companies to be part of what would be a different kind of advertisement.
[. . .] They finally accepted, [and] today that's called co-branding."

After that, the chocotorta took on a life of its own.

Translated by Liliana Frankel

Anarchist Pastries

Anonymous and El Obrero

Buenos Aires bakeries sell a range of small, sweet pastries known as facturas *that shoppers purchase by the dozen and serve as a morning or afternoon snack. Many bakers at the turn of the century were active participants in labor strikes, consumer boycotts, and demonstrations, and a number participated in the anarchist movement. In the photograph, taken in 1902, the bakers wipe their table clean during a major strike; firearms can be seen hanging on the wall. In the text "Strike and Boycott of La Princesa Bakery," one workers' association declares a strike and boycott on a bakery, inciting readers of the periodical* El Obrero *to join them.*

This spirit of protest and the key influence of the anarchist movement also shaped the names and forms of the pastries the bakers sold. The story once circulated that the medialuna—the sweeter and syrupy local rendition of the croissant—owed its name to a seventeenth-century protest staged by bakers in Vienna when the city was being occupied by the Ottoman Empire; its crescent shape was meant to mimic the symbol on the Ottoman flag. Anarchist bakers in Buenos Aires decided to imitate this joke with a collection of local innovations. Even today, when shoppers choose their dozen factura *pastries, they select among a range of treats with shapes and names designed to mock the police, the army, the Church, and the banks. With an ironic and raunchy sense of humor, bakers sold* cañoncitos *(tiny cannons),* suspiros de monja *(nun's sighs),* sacramentos *(sacraments),* bombas *(bombs), and* bolas de fraile *(friar's balls). Even the name* factura—literally, "an invoice"—is said to allude to debts still owed to the workers.

Anonymous, 1902. Courtesy of the Archivo General de la Nación Argentina Dpto. Doc. Fotográficos. Inv: 21878.

Strike and Boycott of La Princesa
Bakery (1902)

El Obrero

The Sociedad Cosmopolita de Resistencia y Colección de Obreros Panaderos (Cosmopolitan Society of Resistance and Bakery Workers' Collective) informs all unions in the capital that the Bakery Workers Assembly, held on January 12, has declared a strike and boycott of the La Princesa bakery because its owners all too often commit abuses against union workers, as well as due to the insults and slander directed at this Society.

It is war against the La Princesa bakery!

And no bakery worker shall work at that bakery.

And may no one purchase bread at that bakery.

We shall find out the names of any traitor that works at the bakery and publish it in the next bulletin.

Translated by Leslie Robertson

Neighborhood Businesses

Bernardo González Arrili

During the 1920s and 1930s, small or family-run businesses began to dot the landscape and color the experience of community in city neighborhoods. These businesses also captured some of the ways in which cultural mixture informed everyday life. The writer Bernardo González Arrili, born in 1892 in Buenos Aires, remembers two of these neighborhood food traditions in detail: the ice cream cart and the bakery. In the 1920s and 1930s, immigrants (many from Naples) began to sell ice cream on carts in the hot summer months, calling out to passersby on their routes. Not long after, artisan ice cream shops became popular; by the 1940s, the family-run stores were a fixture of neighborhoods; today, several remain, having navigated changes in the industry and retaining a faithful clientele. At these shops, new classic flavors were made. The contemporary citywide favorite, dulce de leche granizado *(dulce de leche with chocolate flakes), made its debut in the mid-twentieth century.*

Ice Cream Carts and Bakeries in the Neighborhood (1952)
Bernardo González Arrili

At dusk, when the lights in the shop windows and foyers, the lights on street corners, were turned on, the horn on the ice cream cart would begin to sound. It was a two-wheeled cart and, on its poles, the hefty man who drove it would rest his considerable gut or, when it came to a stop, his buttocks, always crammed into creased trousers. On top of the cart were six round brass-plated lids resting on as many vats. To prevent spills and evaporation, wet strips of burlap were coiled around the edges. Inside were the delicious "Naples-style" ices: slightly yellow "pure egg" cream, chocolate, and lemon. The other three vats must have been spares holding more or, perhaps, they were empty—all we ever tasted was the simple cream-chocolate-lemon combo. [. . .]

Before there was a bakery on every corner, [. . .] bread, crackers, and cakes were baked in every house, and if there was a home without an oven, the loaves were ordered or bought from a neighbor or a relative. [. . .] The [home-made] bread didn't have the same shape as the bakery loaf—though more roughly finished, it was far tastier. [. . .] [In our neighborhood] there were three or four neighborhood bakeries . . . One was on Esmeralda Street. [. . .] The shop, which was not very big, was three white marble steps off the curb; I don't think it had display windows to show off its goods. In the midafternoon, people would go in to buy *facturas*. The bakery's claim to fame was its *trenzas* (braided breads) and *medialunas* (a sticky sweet croissant). [. . .] The allegedly Welsh proprietor was a thick man with a mane of white hair. When we would show up, he would be sitting in a corner, leaving the office unattended. On hot days, he would take his chair out to the stoop next to the front door and fan himself with his large palm. His wife, a slight woman, was at the counter, waiting on customers. A block and a half from Corrientes Street, north on Esmeralda, there was another pastry shop with two display cases bursting with sweet breads, glazed cookies, and chocolates.

Translated by Wendy Gosselin and Jane Brodie

The Café

Alberto Mario Salas and Anonymous

Buenos Aires streets are lined with cafés. In these spaces, coffee has always been an excuse, merely a reason to sit, meet friends and colleagues, or read, reflect, and pass the time. In the text Alberto Salas notes that until the end of the 1950s, cafés remained male-dominated spaces; in the photograph, men at a café show their cards in a traditional game of truco. In a comment that echoes Salas's description, the writer Jorge Luis Borges once described a game of truco in a café as "allow[ing] us to forget our destinies" in a space of "stolen time." In her introduction to Salas's book, the writer Victoria Ocampo alluded to the exclusionary effect of these gendered spaces. Cafés had long been important places in which political decisions were made, literary groups were formed—they were, as Salas put it, "the center" of Buenos Aires life; yet Ocampo—a key member of the city's cultural scene—noted that she had "never set foot in one." She knew of what went on inside only by listening to the raucous sounds of men arguing and cups and saucers clanging from the street. By the 1960s, cafés were more democratic spaces; over the following decades, gender divides vanished, and, far from disappearing, cafés multiplied, becoming more universal spaces for long conversations, or time alone.

Sounds and Scenes of the Porteño *Café (1955)*
Alberto Mario Salas

The value of the café is just as great as the two other poles of the city: soccer and the racetrack . . . Two or three windows determine the preferred seats in the house, for those who look to stare out the window, distracted, or wait patiently for women to walk by. Other café-goers, on the other hand, look for the shadowy corners, far from the noise, avoiding distractions, keeping a distance from one another. As is standard, the floor should be wood, with a little bit of sawdust when it is raining. Plank floor, probably pine. Floor tiles or other supposedly hygienic materials, used so often these days, disrupt the social dynamic of the café, making the floors cold to the feet and taking out the dense rich sound of the place. The tables are wood, either rectangular or round, but always, without a doubt, lacking any decoration, no tablecloth, no flowers. [. . .] They are simple wooden chairs, naturally comfortable, which is all that the regulars need. The back of the chair, untouched by those deep in thought or in an intimate conversation, become used when one leans back, itching to eavesdrop on a far-off argument, preparing one's own, or, when playing cards, to eye slightly at one's neighbor's hand. [. . .] A grand and serious espresso machine sits on top of the bar, opulent, with shining chrome. Behind the bar space there are shelves filled with bottles, and crowning it all, a clock, stopped and totally useless. When the place fills up, at the end of the café, they turn on the lights of the pool table, a game that combines well with the nature of the café. [. . .] Until a few years ago the café also had another element of incredible importance: an object that still lingers in all of our memories: the Victrola. In some central location, usually higher than the tables, in order to acquire the correct perspective, a "young lady," vulgarly known as the *victrolera*, changed records. [. . .]

The café, like all things, has a certain known schedule, each set of hours beholden to their own characteristics. The morning hours are calm and relaxed. [. . .] Retired men read the newspaper, and people on the move or youth still lacking direction occupy a few tables. [. . .] Halfway through the morning, the vermouth or the simple coffee begins to flow, and before lunch, a few play dice. [. . .] This dim life continues until five or six o'clock, when the place fills up. The air, then, fills with smoke, conversations, of the sounds of billiards breaking, of the joyful scattering of the dice. This is all overtaken by the regular shouts of the waitstaff: "an espresso," "one more makes two" [. . .]. It can go on until the early morning hours. Saturday, day of vespers, the place comes to life immediately after lunch and continues during a night that has virtually no end. On the tail end of the night, an everlasting night, comes Sunday, the day that excitement culminates. [. . .] The café can be the negation of time, or, if you like, the availability of time, without tardiness or urgency. [. . .] In the café, time has its own value, diffuse, unexpected, which cannot be measured by the man who delays drinking the contents of his cup. It is measured by friendship, by conversation, by controversies that come up, or in the desire to be alone and in a quiet corner.

Translated by Liliana Frankel

Anonymous, 1943. Courtesy of the Archivo General de la Nación Argentina Dpto. Doc. Fotográficos. Inv: 327998.

Pizza

Norberto Folino

Like many cities with an important Italian heritage, Buenos Aires has its own very specific pizza culture. In this essay, Norberto Folino reflects on the pizza and its rituals. He recalls that Italian immigrants set up bakeries near the port and gradually branched out to use their ovens for more complicated delicacies, like fugazzeta and fainá—local versions of foods enjoyed in Italy. Over time, pizzerias erupted in popularity. They sold cheap, filling, and popular fast foods. Classic pizzerias feature two separate eating areas: a bar-like counter where passersby or people in a rush can stop in for a slice, fainá, and a glass of wine, all enjoyed while standing; and, in the back, a larger space with families and friends who sit and order whole pies.

Pizza at the Counter (1999)

Norberto Folino

Eating pizza standing at the counter is the quintessence of eating pizza. It all started at one sitting where a number of things were invented: the rectangular pieces of paper to hold the slice in your hand; slices of the house's specialties cut just the right size for eating on foot (though we suspect that the size of slices has gotten smaller with time, as if our grandparents and parents had had bigger mouths); the wastebaskets for the pieces of used paper crumpled into the ugliest birds ever fashioned by man. The standing pizza eater, taking it all in slowly with a lost, metaphysical gaze that looks at nothing and everything. While scarfing it down, he looks at the pizza maker, he looks at what's left on his tray, he looks at the oven door in case a curious new combination of toppings appears, he looks at the street, he looks at the other pizza eaters. He also reads all the signs and posters that his wandering eye happens upon. [. . .] That is what we mean by pizza and culture.

Translated by Wendy Gosselin and Jane Brodie

Food and Nostalgia

Julio Cortázar

The choripán *is the city's most emblematic street food—a simple roll with a sliced grilled chorizo topped with chimichurri (a sauce made with garlic, parsley, oil, vinegar, oregano, and other spices) or* salsa criolla *(a sauce made of red pepper, green pepper, tomato, onion, oil, and vinegar). It can be found at most events hosted outdoors, is a starter for an* asado, *and can also be enjoyed at many street fairs and political events. If the* choripán *had a physical home within the city, it would be the Costanera, a street and strip of sidewalk along the river and near the city's docks, ecological reserve, and local airport. There, a scattering of small food carts and trucks offer a similar grilled menu. In this segment of Julio Cortázar's most famous novel,* Hopscotch, *the story's protagonist, Traveler, greets an old friend as he returns to Buenos Aires from Paris. The two head to the Costanera to enjoy chorizos and entrails by the water, and they discuss the difference in the food offerings of the two cities. The text highlights three pastimes—enjoying chorizo by the waterfront, drinking wine with soda, and drawing comparisons and contrasts between the local culture and that of Europe.*

Food and Nostalgia (1963)

Julio Cortázar

Talita was not sure that Traveler was happy about the return of his childhood friend [. . .]. In any case, [Traveler] went down to the port to wait for him. [. . .] Oliveira was just out of customs, carrying a single, light suitcase, and upon recognizing Traveler he raised his eyebrows in a mix of surprise and fascination.

—What do you say, *che.*

—*Salú*—said Traveler, grasping his hand with more feeling than he anticipated.

—Look—said Oliveira—let's go to a *parrilla* near the docks and eat some chorizos. [. . .]

At the *parrilla,* Oliveira began to drink red wine and eat chorizos and *chinchulines* [chitterlings]. Since he wasn't being talkative, Traveler told him about the circus and how he had married Talita. He gave him a rundown of Argentine politics and sports, slowing to talk about the rise and fall of Pascualito Pérez. [. . .] Traveler started to get hungry and ordered some *chinchulines*. He was glad Oliveira accepted his first Argentine cigarette with a smile and smoked it appreciatively. They started in on another liter of red wine and Traveler talked about his work and how he hadn't lost hope of finding something better, which is to say with less work and more money, all the while waiting for Oliveira to say something, he didn't know what, just something that might take them back after so much time.

—All right then, you tell me something—he proposed.

—The weather—said Oliveira—was really varied, but every once in a while, there were good days. [. . .]

—All right, all right—said Traveler—. You don't have to say anything if you don't want to.

—One day I dropped a lump of sugar under the table in a café. In Paris, not in Vienna.

—If all you want to talk about is cafés there was no point in crossing the pond.

—You know—said Oliveira, as he carefully cut into a string of *chinchulin*— This really is something you can't get in the City of Lights, man. The number of Argentines who've said as much. They'd weep for meat, and I even met a woman who nostalgically recalled *criollo* wine. According to her, French wine was no good for mixing with soda water.

—That's a barbarity—said Traveler.

—And, of course, the tomato and the potato are better here than anywhere.

—I can see—said Traveler—that you were rubbing elbows with the upper crust.

—Once in a while. In general, they didn't take kindly to my elbows, to keep with your metaphor. It's so humid out, brother.

—Ah, that—said Traveler—. You are going to have to get acclimatized again.

They carried on for another twenty-five minutes.

Translated by Lisa Ubelaker Andrade

The *Bodegón*

Nicolás Olivari

Cantinas and bodegones are informal eateries that form a sharp contrast with elegant and formal fashionable restaurants: at both, the cooking is simple, the plates are abundant, the style is informal, and the menus center on traditional fare. In "Cantinas and Bodegones," writer Nicolás Olivari captures this, happening upon a bodegón on a dark corner of a neighborhood street, arriving with a band of friends and feeling welcomed by its humble eclectic menu and the diversity of the patrons, rich and poor, young and old.

Cantinas and Bodegones (1966)

Nicolás Olivari

We like to eat well. We *porteños* give each other the scoop (". . . on the corner of such and such street there is this amazing cantina . . .") and it's a done deal. We remember the address and, that same evening, a group of friends—poets, journalists, playwrights—wanders toward that corner where the lights of an old house with bars on the windows beacon out into the sleepy neighborhood. The decor of a *bodegón* verges on sublime. Sausages hanging down from the ceiling glitter, damp with the holy oil of cooking; mushrooms under a scattering of walnuts; chestnuts; jars of wine wrapped in wicker for Dionysian inebriation. Local color is everywhere, for in that lies the appeal, and people come from all corners to receive the satisfying blow to their appetites. They don't grow impatient if, as happens in the office of a doctor who works miracles, they have to wait in line for a table, write their names on a list, etc. Everything is endured in that shameless desire that fattens citizens' hunger. And so, we see ladies in fine attire and gentlemen with bulging bank accounts rub elbows with the proprietor's rowdy truck-driver friends, who display the impressive appetites of those that have never known indigestion. Meek girls with Napoleon-style bangs take gulp after hearty gulp of a deep violet wine from a wide glass, wine that, in keeping with local custom, is poured out of a barrel by the counter. Name after name of dishes illustrated with memories from southern Italy. After the strategic rollout of the appetizers, which are so varied and so nourishing that, at first bite, they would satisfy even a starving

Bedouin, comes the imposing chicken à la Calabrese—the house specialty and a must—and then the steamy platter of noodles bathed in common tomato sauce or in byzantine alle vongole, sophisticated anchovy extract, or the decidedly baroque pesto whose *aji olio* in the breath of the beautiful women that eat in the cantina swirls into a novel perfume. [. . .] The cantina on that now-famous corner of the city earns admiration from big and small, from young and old, from rich and poor, all of whom mingle at a long table, where the back and forth of jaws lays the basis for what is, in the end, the great universal brotherhood.

Translated by Liliana Frankel

A Twenty-First-Century Culinary Scene

Lis Ra

The food scene in Buenos Aires erupted with new flavors in the twenty-first century. Relatively low start-up costs, talented culinary professionals, a market for new flavors and tastes, and a strong culture of dining out have made the city fertile ground for experimentation. It has also created spaces for new generations of immigrants to make their mark and challenge notions of what makes up "Argentine cuisine." In this text, Lis Ra, an Argentine chef whose parents emigrated from Korea, recounts her journey to open her Michelin-awarded restaurant and reflects on the new cultural mixtures afoot in Buenos Aires cuisine.

Milanesa *and* Kimchi *(2023)*

Lis Ra

My mother was part of the one of the first groups of Koreans to emigrate to Argentina in the 1960s; she arrived by boat at the age of three, so perhaps unlike other kids in the Korean community in Buenos Aires, I grew up with a mother who spoke fluent Spanish. My parents worked during the day and studied at the Universidad de Buenos Aires at night. I sometimes felt quite different from other Argentines but also from the Korean community here. For example, growing up, I never had a 100 percent Korean meal. Our standard dinner at home was *milanesa*—an Argentine dinner staple—but with ketchup, kimchi, and sticky rice on the side. [. . .] It was in culinary school that I really found a shared culture; the one thing I had in common with other Argentines was a love of food. When I finished culinary school, I had to ask myself, what differentiates me? I returned to this mixture of foods I grew up eating, a mix that happened organically: I couldn't eat a *milanesa* without kimchi; I loved Korean food, its saltiness, funkiness, spice, but I also loved the flavors of French food, using herbs, cheese, and I loved to balance textures. At first Argentines didn't want to try kimchi; some knew of the health benefits of fermented foods, but back in the early 2000s, the offerings at restaurants were a rotation of meat, sauce, empanadas, *milanesas*, pastas, salads, pizza. But then the restaurant scene started to change: there was much more variety, people started to open up, they traveled, saw foods on social media, they were more curious and realized, "I like sushi, I like curry." Tastes changed. Back then, Korean food in Buenos Aires was also closed off to the rest of the city. Korean restaurants were traditional spots in a [Korean] neighborhood where the dinner shift was over at 8:30. Meanwhile, Argentines sat down for dinner at 9. After culinary school, I was hired to work in a new Asian-fusion restaurant, Niño Gordo. It was a popular spot, a line out the door, and I had the liberty to play with flavors. Then I opened my own restaurant, Na Num. The idea in my kitchen is to present Korean staples but differently. I have to tell people that it is "Argentine Korean" cuisine, but I hesitate to put the food in these categories, or as a fusion; it is just food; it is not traditional Korean, it has Korean and Argentine bases; but Argentine food is not just Argentine food, it is Spanish, Italian, French; with Argentine ingredients, it evolved. We made it our own. We say, "Hey, this is our food," but food evolves; my food is just a part of this process. Our [Korean] community is smaller, so it perhaps doesn't have the influence of Italians in Argentina, but everyone's cooking ends up being shaped by their experiences, the ingredients available, and what we grow up eating. Today, with a different taste, new plates become a part of this cultural process of mixture.

IV

Hinchas, Cracks, *and* Potreros

in the City of Soccer

There is no Buenos Aires team, no singular soccer club that evokes city pride. There are thirty-six soccer stadiums in Buenos Aires and its suburbs; each can seat at least ten thousand fans, and the largest, El Monumental, can seat eighty thousand. Several can sit over fifty thousand at full capacity. Eleven local teams regularly play in the national first division. Rivalries run deep.

What began as a game introduced by a small British immigrant community in the nineteenth century quickly evolved into something far more significant. Unlike other sports imported from abroad, soccer gained popularity in a more bottom-up fashion, becoming the pastime of boys who played in the street, finding a home in neighborhood clubs, and then erupting into a massive commercial spectator event, complete with its own media, legends, and stadiums. Today soccer's influence is enormous: it is a source of power for local politicians, a subject of social debate, and arguably the most thrilling spectacle in the city.

British Origins, Local Style, Neighborhood Roots

The origin of Buenos Aires soccer is not that different from other sports that have been taken up by *porteños*. Polo, horse racing, car racing, field hockey, basketball, fencing, rowing, boxing, rugby, and tennis all offer colorful histories and are important in their own right and at different moments in the city's history. Many of these sports followed a similar path to popularity: introduced by British expatriates in the late nineteenth century, they gained the interest of the upper classes—the sectors of society that had the time and wealth to spend on leisure and made a habit of adopting pastimes that were fashionable in Europe. Members of the elite promoted organized sports as a component of gentlemanly education, arguing that regulated sports would help to uphold social order; would improve the health, strength, and character of the nation's citizens; and would, over time, have a civilizing effect on the masses. (See "Health, Civilization, and Sport," the first selection below.) Yet few of these sports saw real and enduring resonance among the working and middle classes. Horse racing proved to be one of the first exceptions—it drew enormous audiences, even though for most, the races were a spectacle to be seen rather than played. (See "Social Classes Converge at the Racetrack.")

As with other sports, soccer was first played by young men in the British community, and it reached a younger generation when it was brought into the curriculum in British schools. Yet British soccer clubs were exclusive; when local players attempted to join in on games, they were refused. Rejection made for bitter rivalries: before long, the first local clubs were created, and local players proved to be eager to go up against British teams. The first non-British club, Argentinos de Quilmes, quickly replaced British traditions with *criollo* ones—during halftime, for example, when the British often paused for tea, it is said that the Argentine team took to sipping *mate*. Argentine clubs multiplied over the next twenty years. Still, British influence left a mark; the city's two largest sports clubs (and rivals), River Plate and Boca Juniors, use English words in their names (although they are pronounced with local accents); likewise, a number of words with English origins populate the local sports vocabulary, among them *crack* (a great player), *gol* (goal), and *corner* (corner kick).

Soccer made its biggest impact among the lower and middle sectors. The reasons for this are likely several. Timing may have been key: the game became popular at a moment when the city's laboring classes—including children—were enjoying more free time. Workers in the early twentieth century benefited from important advances in labor legislation, like the eight-hour workday, Sunday rest, and child labor laws, which permitted working sectors to have new pastimes. Unlike other "elite" games being played in the city, soccer also required little in the way of equipment or space. It was the perfect street game. At the turn of the century, the city's landscape was not yet filled out or defined. New neighborhoods were under development, and many had large, empty, open lots (known as *potreros*) and quiet streets.

Young people (particularly boys) living in these neighborhoods-in-the-making did not need the approval of adults, much less the British sports clubs, to make the game their own. They sought out a stretch of street, or a dusty abandoned lot, and set up their own games by marking out the goals with sweaters and bags thrown on the ground; they pointed out trees that lined the street to serve as borders. Those who could not afford an inflated leather ball played with a *pelota del trapo*—a ball made up of bags or rags tied tightly together. In these spaces a new version of play known as *fútbol de potrero* (backlot soccer) came into being.

Fútbol de potrero became an iconic part of urban life. The image of scrappy neighborhood boys playing on a makeshift urban field became the stuff of nostalgia and legend. Gradually, neighborhoods across the city also estab-

Argentina's supposed unique style of playing soccer is said to have originated in street games. In this photograph taken at midcentury, the urban portraitist Sara Facio captures a typical game in the streets of Buenos Aires. *Source: Fútbol*, by Sara Facio, previously published in Alicia D'Amico, Sara Facio, and Julio Cortázar, *Buenos Aires, Buenos Aires* (Buenos Aires: Editorial Sudamericana, 1968). Courtesy of the photographer.

lished clubs where youth could compete in soccer and other sports. These new clubs, each a center for neighborhood life, served as incubators for intense identities. They also organized the practice of the sport, introducing regulations and more formal training. Nevertheless, street ball endured. For some, it was in the backlots of the city's developing landscape that local boys conjured an innovative style of play, one that was rugged and creative; there, it was thought, British "football" became *criollo fútbol*.

The Pibe, the Crack, and the Business of Soccer

As clubs cropped up across the city map and rivalries became more intense, a burgeoning popular press also blossomed. Sports journalists followed every local game, reported on players, and galvanized fans with information and purple prose. (See "The Philosophers of Local Sport.") A new local lore took form. In search of an explanation for the incredible popularity of the game and the notable skill and style of the city's players, observers and journalists returned to the city's street game. Two related figures emerged as the embodiment of local play: the *pibe* and the *crack*. The *pibe* was a neighborhood kid; his lack of discipline, rustic appearance, and love for the game made him an emblematic character of working- and middle-class neighborhoods. The most talented neighborhood players—creative, cunning, untrained, with remarkable footwork—were nicknamed *cracks*. (See "El Pibe.")

For most, the *pibe* (and the *crack*) were beloved icons of *porteño* culture. For others, however, including many educators, politicians, and social commentators, the image of the *pibe* and the *potrero* where he played was not a cause for celebration. They questioned the game's social value and argued that these young players, and the sport they loved, were signs of "barbarity" inserting itself in urban culture. Sports like soccer, some said, were the pitiful fate of an unguided youth who dropped out of school and was raised in the uncivilized habitat of the street. In 1953, the Peronist magazine *Mundo Peronista* echoed this sentiment, deriding the empty lots and games ("los potreros y el juego de pelota") as, along with café-bars, "primary schools for delinquents." Peronism, in its various renditions, also made use of the sport's popularity among children, and Perón himself made it a point to receive the adulation of crowds at local games. Nevertheless, the questionable reputation of soccer was sustained in many sectors. Its association with indecent street life, and even violence, meant that for decades it was not fully embraced as a part of physical education in city schools, where young boys were taught the supposedly "civilizing" and more "gentlemanly" games. It went without saying that, in contrast to sports like field hockey, tennis, or *pelota al cesto* (discussed in the first selection, "Health, Civilization, and Sport"), most sectors of society considered soccer completely inappropriate for young girls. This notion was quite pervasive until relatively recently. (See "The Right to Play: Women and the Game.")

The *crack* also came to be seen by many as a rather paradoxical symbol of Argentina itself—he was the creative genius who invented a unique style of play, and, at the same time, lacking the refinement of formal instruction, he spoke to the city's off-the-cuff style. This dual characterization was revived years later when Diego Maradona, arguably one of the best in the world to ever play the game, emerged on the scene in the 1970s. Maradona had a rather humble upbringing in a typical working-class neighborhood in Greater Buenos Aires; he grew up poor and learned to play soccer in an open lot, and his exemplary talent was said to be the epitome of the *criollo* style. He possessed innate skill with fast, tight dribbling, and he played (and seemed to live his life) with a sense of spontaneity and bravado. When Maradona took over the global game, the image of the *pibe* reemerged along with him. Through his own personal and professional ups and downs, he stood as a symbol of the dreams, triumphs—and shortcomings—of Argentina itself. (See "Maradona, Maradonear.")

By the time Maradona rose to fame, *fútbol de potrero* was not nearly as common as it had once been. The sport had begun to be institutionalized (played in organized clubs) in the 1920s. A few decades later, skilled players that in another era would have spent their childhoods playing informally with neighborhood friends began formal training in the club circuit at any early age. In the 1930s and 1940s, as the city's empty lots became fewer and farther between, the streets filled with cars and soccer migrated from streets to plazas, parks, and neighborhood sports clubs. It was not long before enormous stadiums that filled with thousands of fans came into construction; these cathedrals of sport bore little resemblance to what once were small, modest neighborhood fields used by men and boys of working- and middle-class families.

If a *criollo* style of play was born in the *potrero*, it was harnessed and developed in these kinds of neighborhood clubs where the *pibe* learned to compete. There, the neighborhood *crack*—a player with particular talent—could become a competitive player. Between 1901 and 1910 the "big five" teams—River Plate, Independiente, Racing, Boca Juniors, and San Lorenzo, all of which are in Buenos Aires and its suburbs—took form, and over the next two decades, the sport came into its own. By 1931, athletes were no longer amateurs; they were trained, professional players who received regular salaries and were "bought" and "sold" between clubs. River Plate, which moved out of La Boca and into the northern neighborhood of Nuñez in 1938, was nicknamed the millionaire's club in 1931 not because of its location in a wealthier neighborhood (the club was still in La Boca at the time) but because it paid thirty-five thousand pesos for Bernabé Ferreyra in 1932—an enormous sum that marked the degree to which club sports had changed in just a few decades. Clubs had far outgrown the small neighborhood feel that marked their roots, and the sport was now a lucrative enterprise with thousands of fans; games were reaching new audiences, discussed in specialized press, and broadcast by radio into the living rooms of listeners across the city and beyond its borders. In 1935, the big five teams had more than 100,000 official "members," and the rest had nearly 50,000 together.

By the 1940s, soccer was not just a pastime—it was a commercial juggernaut. The best athletes obtained a star status that allowed them to negotiate increasingly high salaries. This confirmed a new idealization of soccer as a path for social and economic ascension. In the film *Los tres berretines* (*The Three Obsessions*, 1933), the father of an immigrant family comes to grasp—with resignation—that soccer and tango (two of the city's obsessions, the third being film) could be promising professional careers. In a 1948 film, *Pelota de trapo* (*Rag Ball*), the poor boys of the neighborhood dream of becoming professional soccer players and helping out their families. Today, a similar mythology—that soccer could serve as a path from poverty to fortune—endures in the city's poorest neighborhoods, where the saying "En los potreros están los 10" (The 10s are in the *potrero*) can be found scribbled on concrete walls (in soccer, the number 10 jersey is usually reserved for the team's star attacker). The dream has also crossed class lines: as fortunes grew, soccer stardom became an aspiration for boys in the city's middle classes.

At the end of the twentieth century, the belief that soccer could be one's ticket to fame and fortune was still prevalent. Yet it included a rather important addendum. As in days before, talented young boys are scouted by the city's clubs and, if selected, begin to train in hopes of eventually advancing from age group squads up through various levels of play. The highest level is the club's "first team," which draws thousands of fans to the stadium on game day. Some travel from their homes in other provinces, arrive in the city alone, and live in dorms, attend school, and grow up within the club. Although many young boys still aspire to become local *cracks*, the decades of economic ups and downs in Argentina have relocated the dream of success abroad. For young players today, the end goal is not to play locally but to be sold to the European leagues. (See "The Dream.") In the early 2000s, some joked that Argentina's greatest export was no longer beef but, instead, soccer players. Conversely, as more and more players went abroad at younger ages, large local teams entered an international market, "buying" players from neighboring Latin American countries. The increased globalization of the sport opened new questions about the meaning and destiny of local soccer culture.

The Hinchada: Passions at Play

As the sport globalized, a new local protagonist emerged. Spectators asked, Was the legacy of the sport still to be found in *pibe del potrero*, in the players who trained at the stadium and wore the team's jersey? Even the most impassioned of these, the rare talents who professed commitment to and love for their original club, were—at most—expected to return and play a final few seasons as a senior player with their team after retiring from a successful career in Europe. At a time in which local players were quick to move abroad, and the sport had become a monetized business, many argued that the true custodians of the sport were instead the *hinchada* (the fans), who never changed teams, who stayed and suffered alongside their club regardless of wins, losses, or money at play. (See "The Fans: *La Hinchada*.") For most, if not all, it was the fans who bore the burden and sacrifice of maintaining the spirit of *porteño* soccer. As the importance of a team's fan base became more pronounced, the *hinchas* became more boisterous and involved, and their role became more complicated.

Team allegiances in Buenos Aires may be fractured, but fans of each team share a common sense of tribalism. Club membership is entangled in sense of self—"belonging" to a club is such an assumed and integrated part of identity that little boys and girls are expected to be able to answer the question "De qué cuadro sos?" (What club are you from?) as soon as they can talk. (See "An *Hincha* Is Born, Not Made.") Their *cuadro*, or team, is not something they choose but, rather, a trait inherited, passed down, from a father to his children. Even *porteños* who do not regularly watch matches or consider themselves among the most avid *hinchas* often grow up aware that they are

Fútbol is an emotional sport for its fans. In this photograph taken in 2020, a fan lights fireworks in an act of homage and during a national day of mourning following the death of Argentina's legendary player, Diego Maradona. *Source: Hinchas*, by Erica Voget, 2020. Courtesy of the photographer.

"from" a specific team. Their team is an immutable trait carried with them for life, so enduring that one popular saying goes, "You can change your nationality, your civil status, your religion, your gender, and your sex, but you can never change your soccer club." For devoted fans, the game, and specifically their team, is one of the most important parts of social and emotional life, a reservoir of powerful feelings that inspires nearly clichéd declarations of romantic love, devotion, suffering, and ecstasy. For many, the idea of club loyalty also offers a sense of certainty, particularly in times of economic, political, and personal crisis. In 2001, just following the economic crisis that plummeted much of the country into poverty, a fan painted a sign addressing his small club team outside its field: "Gallo, you are my only hero in this chaos." That call was all the more resonant given the precarious financial position of neighborhood clubs since the 1990s.

Members of a team's *hinchada* are insistent on displaying their total devotion to their team. In so doing, they demonstrate what they call *aguante*. As one fan put it, "*Aguante* means to accept your role as a person who will suffer with the team you love unconditionally, no matter what. To live this way makes one wonder what it could be like to be able to just enjoy a sport." Fans at the stadium often refer to themselves as the twelfth player on the field: during the game they relentlessly jump in place and sing chants in unison, stopping only long enough to watch apprehensively as their team looks for an open shot and to mourn or celebrate the results. The stadium erupts in a common response, and fans celebrate with affection—they embrace each other, kiss each other's faces at the sign of victory, and cry over a lost game. Emotional responses to defeat and victory are understood as sincere displays of loyalty.

These ideas are captured vividly in many of the songs that the *hinchas* sing at the stadium. While songs and chants that openly declare the depths of the *hincha's* devotion to his team are key components of soccer culture, they also include lyrics and ideas that reflect the sport's cultures of exclusion: racism, homophobia, and sexism have long been entangled and reflected in the cultures of sport, and particularly in soccer chants. (See "Stadium Songs.")

Rivalry is what most defines and invigorates the passion of soccer fans. The most torrid rivalries set in the city is that between River Plate and Boca Juniors, the two largest clubs. Most *hinchas* insist that the only thing more important than their own team doing well is their rival doing poorly. In the past, scheduled games in which these two rivals met face to face, called *clásicos*, were the most anticipated events of the calendar year. (See "The Thrill of the Superclásico.")

Clásicos are billed as exciting events, but over the course of the twentieth century, they also often showcased a disturbing level of violence. In the first decades of play, episodes of violence were few and far between, ranging from accidental deaths to heated moments when rivalries boiled over into physical fights. By the late 1950s, threats became more routine, and home team fans began to organize to defend themselves against visiting fans. In 1958, the local press used the term *barra fuerte* to describe these new organized groups who vowed to protect their own teams' fans and rile visitors at their own stands. By the 1980s, these groups were called the *barra brava*, and they had grown considerably; their influence was greater, their capacity for violence was more extreme, and their role was also far more integrated. Rather than being ostracized, they had become part of the club economy, culture, and politics. The *barra brava* also set the tone of excitement at the stadium—sitting in a section of bleachers known as the *popular*, they bring in banners, drums, bands, and streamers and lead the rest of the *hinchas* in songs they wrote. They also intervene in the club's underground economy, controlling the street sales of unofficial merchandise and scalped tickets, and managing parking near the stadium as well as the illegal trafficking of drugs. Their power stems from their threats of violence, as well as their network of allies in the police and the club's administration. (See "Violence.")

In recent decades, the power of the *barra brava* has also extended beyond the stadium into union, municipal, and national politics. At the end of the 1990s, one local politician told the newspaper that it was "impossible" to win an election without contracting the services of these groups. For his own campaign, he hired River's *barra brava* (nicknamed "los Borrachos del

Tablón," or, "the Drunks of the Bleachers"), and they covered his district in favorable graffiti and posters, brought in banners to games, showed support at political events, and ensured "security" at public speeches and acts. It is alleged that *barras bravas* from each team are paid to recruit voters from the poorest sectors of a club's fanbase on election days, but other types of support more closely resemble paid advertising that plays to club allegiances. The Boca Juniors' *barra brava*, known as "La Doce," or "the Twelve" (as in the twelfth player on the team), hung banners with a politician's name in the middle of a game and received a hefty sum in turn.

As these deals suggest, the magnetism and mass appeal of the sport has made it a prime setting for political campaigns; on occasion, the sport has also been the site of protest. Although club loyalties have never neatly translated to political partisanship with all fans of a club backing a single candidate, club politics has often served as a training ground for national politics—a way for an individual to gain exposure and a public following before running for office. Soccer's nature as a massive spectator sport and its ability to congregate diverse audiences has also made the stadium a forum for public issues to come to a head—a site where all types of political leaders can seek out a public, and in turn, where a public can condemn or condone leadership. (See "Soccer, Politics, and Protest.")

Far from the dusty open lots where, as legend would have it, the cunning, rebellious *crack* invented a new style of play, the massive cathedrals of sport that dot the city's landscape are more complex theaters of Buenos Aires culture—stages for pitted rivalries, sites for the advance of social inclusion (see "Toward an Inclusive Future"), markers of commercial and political empires, and the home of the most celebrated figure, the relentless *hincha* and his scores of devoted companions.

Health, Civilization, and Sport

Enrique Romero Brest and Anonymous

At the end of the nineteenth century, leaders in the field of education viewed sports and physical education as part of a larger project to instill civilized culture among city residents. Organized sports brought over from Europe, it was said, trained the individual body and reinforced societal concepts of order. In the first decades of the twentieth century, exercise was also understood to be part of personal hygiene and public health. Among the most important proponents of this idea was Enrique Romero Brest, often credited as the founder of Argentina's physical education program. Brest promoted sport as capable of strengthening both the body and soul and suggested that it be used as a tool in disease prevention. In the photograph (1930), girls at school play pelota al cesto *(cestoball), a game Brest invented in which teammates pass a sand-filled ball with the aim of landing it in the opposing team's basket. For many years, the game was a key part of physical education curriculum. By contrast, soccer was not—it was thought to be a street game that had little positive social value. Brest himself was adamant on this point. In the monthly publication* La higiene escolar *he suggested to readers that orderly outdoor exercises should "replace the anachronistic and unhealthy game of soccer, which shares traits with the barbarity of the primitive era." While efforts to keep soccer out of schools were partially successful, educators could do little to stop young boys' growing passion for the game; gradually, the sport became an accepted part of education.*

Physical Education (1939)

Enrique Romero Brest

It is our belief that strong and healthy young individuals can be developed to their fullest through sport and athletics, and this must be preceded by a sound gym system such as our own, and not the reverse. And as these activities are of a rather extracurricular application, they clearly lie outside of the official teachings of the institute under its current organization. All of the teachers who have graduated from the institute know and are convinced of the disadvantages of violent sport and athletics in the formation and development of children and adolescents.

Translated by Leslie Robertson

Girls Play Pelota al Cesto *(1930)*

Anonymous

Courtesy of the Archivo General de la Nación Argentina Dpto. Doc. Fotográficos. Inv: 157167.

Pelota al Cesto *and the Dangers of Soccer (1938)*

Enrique Romero Brest

Pelota al cesto (cestoball) has all of the characteristics of an intense sport, yet its precise rules have been established in order to set it apart, as much as is possible, from the dangers presented by other sports that are played in school settings (soccer, basketball, etc.) by young students at prepubescent and pubescent ages.

Translated by Leslie Robertson

Social Classes Converge at the Racetrack

Modesto Papavero and Last Reason

In the nineteenth century, horses were so numerous in Buenos Aires that they had become nearly a universal form of transportation. They were also used by locals to play a game called pato. *Country-style horse racing was also popular, though these were often informal, linear races on a stretch of land. European-style horse racing on an oval track was introduced by British immigrants. The flat terrains of the pampas suited the sport, as did the growing wealth and prosperity of the Buenos Aires upper class. The elite enjoyed participating in a sport associated with European royalty and took to the pompous displays implied in raising and breeding purebreds; the expensive hobby became a marker of status.*

At the same time, however, watching (and betting on) horse racing emerged as a major pastime among the city's working and middle classes. Tango music, also in its golden age, captured the sport's appeal and drama. "Por una cabeza" ("By a Head"), possibly one of the most famous tangos of all time, is one example: it compares the grief of losing one's money on a tight race and to the anguish of a lost love. In the 1920s, the rise of star jockey Irineo Leguisamo, who came from humble origins and found success, further propelled enthusiasm. The tango "Leguisamo Solo!" ("Only Leguisamo!") takes note of the seating divisions between classes at the racetrack—the "boys" are seated in the cheaper "popular section," while men and women of the elite are watching from the oficial. *Nevertheless, both sectors celebrate the hero jockey. In "The Man Who Bets at the Races," a horse racing commentator who went by the pen-name Last Reason notes the eclectic mix of fans at the racetrack on any given Sunday.*

Only Leguisamo! (1925)

Modesto Papavero

Only Leguisamo!
yell the boys in the *popular*.
Leguisamo, pick it up!
retort the people in the *oficial*.
Only Leguisamo!
El Pulpo [Leguisamo's horse] overtakes the front runner.
Leguisamo gallops on!

el Pulpo is the first to cross the finish line.
There's no doubt, it's in his wrist,
it's in his grand, serene heart
winning by a head
with such style and precision.
He leads the *pingos* (horses) to victory
a master at his trade
they hold him up in his glory,
a mix of wonder and admiration.

Translated by Wendy Gosselin and Jane Brodie

The Man Who Bets at the Races (1925)

Last Reason

If the entire human race were, blessedly, regulars at the racetrack, class struggle, racial strife, and party conflict would immediately come to a halt. [. . .] Give us a hefty lineup, a sunny day, a worthy starter, and a spot-on steward who plays fair—with that and a little luck, all our troubles are gone. You'll see soon enough that gambling is no vice. If governments truly want to work out the vexing conflicts that poison human existence, all they have to do is build more racetracks, spread love for equine struggles, and open schools to train bookies. The rest will follow. Where, after all, do equality and brotherhood reign if not in the racetrack stands?

Translated by Wendy Gosselin and Jane Brodie

The Philosophers of Local Sport

El Gráfico *and Dante Panzeri*

Since its debut in 1919, El Gráfico has been one of the important media outlets de-
voted to sports journalism. As the selection of its early covers illustrates, it did not
simply cover soccer: its pages introduced audiences to a range of new athletes—men
and women—and traced local talents in swimming, bicycling, and boxing, among
other sports. Journalists like Dante Panzeri wrote in enormous detail about what
they called a distinct Argentine style of play. Some drew a connection between tango
and soccer. When one player faced criticism for his partying, he reasoned, "They
don't understand the importance of dancing: at a milonga you learn to control your
body; you work your chest and legs while dancing. Maybe I was such a good player
because I danced tango every night." Journalists also invented characteristics that
colorfully romanticized each club's style (truthfully or not). They described River
Plate as having stunning goals and elegant passes and maneuvering: their ability to
synchronize and circulate the ball was hailed as the essence of beauty. Boca Juniors
was lauded for its energy and "playing the ball like a violinist played his instrument."
As the sport became more commercialized and players were bought and sold with
greater frequency in the 1960s, El Gráfico debated how this context affected the game.
Some criticized that coaches focused too much on strategy and too little on creativity:
"Modern soccer doesn't permit men [to play]. It asks for pieces. Dolls. Robots," one
reporter wrote. Through the decades, sports journalists—some were dubbed soccer's
"philosophers"—paid attention to the slightest changes in the game, emphasized the
elements of Argentine style, and argued endlessly about players, club decisions, and
gossip on and off the field.

El Gráfico: *(clockwise, from upper left)* no. 562, April 19, 1930; no. 749, November 18, 1933; no. 883, June 13, 1936; no. 995, August 5, 1938.

In this 1926 painting by Pío Collivadino, automobiles line the busy streets of a modern Buenos Aires, depicted here as under construction. For more on Collivadino's representations of the city, see "Visual Cities," the first selection in part VII. *Source: El Banco de Boston / Diagonal Norte*, by Pío Collivadino, 1926. Courtesy of the Museo Nacional de Bellas Artes (Argentina) and photographer César Caldarella.

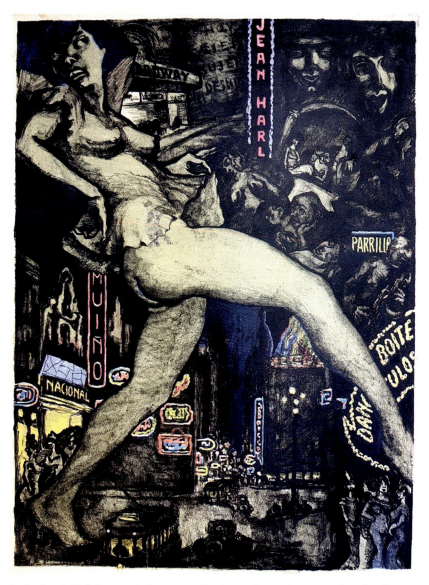

In the first half of the twentieth century, Corrientes Avenue became a place for all kinds of nocturnal delights—brightly lit and lined with theaters, pizzerias, bookstores, and cafés; *porteños* strolled its sidewalks and marveled at the vibrant entertainment of the modern city. This lithograph by Guillermo Facio Hebequer depicts the excitement, sexuality, and many temptations of Corrientes. For more on the city's legendary nightlife, see part VI, "The City at Night." *Source: Calle Corrientes*, by Guillermo Facio Hebequer, n.d. (ca. 1930). Lithograph. Courtesy of the Archivo Taller Albino Fernández.

Benito Quinquela Martín's colorful paintings focused on his neighborhood, La Boca: its laborers, characters, and port-centered culture. Quinquela Martín's work offers a romantic glimpse at a side of Buenos Aires often ignored in fine art—the urban working class and the beautiful hustle of its ports and industry. *Source: Elevadores a pleno sol*, by Benito Quinquela Martín, 1945. Courtesy of the Fundación Benito Quinquela Martín and the Museo Nacional de Bellas Artes (Argentina).

Using collage and mixed media, artist Antonio Berni created a series
of works that told the story of "Juanito," a young working-class
boy in the industrial suburbs surrounding the capital city. These
artworks, sometimes dystopian, contrasted the innocence of the
protagonist against the pollution and inequality of his surrounding
landscape. For more on Berni and his representations of Buenos
Aires, see "Visual Cities," the first selection in part VII. *Source:
Juanito va a la ciudad*, by Antonio Berni, 1963. Wood, paint, industrial
trash, cardboard, scrap metal, leather, and fabric on wood, 129 × 79
× 15 in. (327.7 × 200.7 × 38.1 cm). Courtesy of the Museum of Fine
Arts, Houston. Museum purchase funded by the Caroline Wiess
Law Accessions Endowment Fund, 2007.1167. © Luis Emilio De
Rosa, Argentina. Photograph © The Museum of Fine Arts, Houston;
Thomas R. DuBrock.

Painter Luis Felipe Noé, a member of the vanguard group Otra Figuración, sought to break away from traditional categories of painting. In this work, *Introducción a la esperanza*, people in a crowd hold up signs, illustrating the street as a space of both protest and celebration: one sign reads "Campeón" on a Boca Juniors soccer club flag; another, "Christ speaks in Luna Park" (Luna Park is an indoor event venue). As discussed in part II, "Taking to the Street," protests and celebrations appear here as defining attributes of the Buenos Aires landscape. *Source: Introducción a la esperanza*, by Luis Felipe Noé, 1963. Courtesy of the artist and the Museo Nacional de Bellas Artes (Argentina).

As detailed in part III, "Eating in Buenos Aires," the Argentine *asado* is an important food ritual. It is a simple but plentiful meal in which several cuts of meat, as well as accompanying sides, are served to guests in a sequence. Because of its abundance, it is often seen as a sign of economic "good times" as well as a celebration of family and friendship. In this photograph, artist Marcos López highlights the traditional masculine tenor of the meal but also hints at its cultural association with the country's economic ups and downs: made in the image of *The Last Supper* and photographed in the year 2001, the work evokes a sense of foreboding as the country neared one of its most severe economic crises. *Source: Asado en Mendiolaza*, by Marcos López, 2001. Courtesy of the photographer.

Painter Marcia Schvartz captures the likeness of a popular and idiosyncratic character, the city bus (or *colectivo*) driver. As detailed in part I, "The Living City," Buenos Aires has hundreds of bus lines crisscrossing its urban grid; the *colectivo* has a long and storied history in urban culture. *Source: Con música de Tito Rodríguez*, by Marcia Schvartz, 1982. Courtesy of the artist.

At an event known as the Superclásico, rival soccer teams River Plate and Boca Juniors meet. The match draws such intense passions from the crowd that playing at home can offer an important advantage. *Top:* River Plate fans launch smoke bombs and streamers at their stadium, El Monumental, in the Nuñez neighborhood. *Bottom:* Boca fans color the stadium with confetti at La Bombonera, in La Boca. For more on the event, see "The Thrill of the Superclásico" in part IV. *Sources:* Sergio Goya, *Superclásico at the Monumental*, October 25, 2009. Courtesy of *Clarín*; Aníbal Greco / *La Nación*, *Superclásico at the Bombonera*, May 4, 2008. Courtesy of *La Nación*.

The contemporary feminist movement has been perhaps one of the most impactful social mobilizations of the twenty-first century. Beginning with a march against domestic violence and the recurrence of femicides in 2013, it has since evolved into a multigenerational movement for gender diversity, sexual education, and legalized abortion. In this photograph, marchers show their support for the campaign to legalize abortion by demonstrating with green bandannas in what organizers call a "#pañuelazo" (a kerchief demonstration). Like many of the movement's major marches—including #NiUnaMenos, #QueSeaLey, and #8M—this one was first organized online and then erupted into a massive street presence. The green bandanna has become an international feminist symbol. During this campaign, it was worn daily by supporters, tied around bookbags, on purses, and on wrists. The bandanna pays homage to a longer history of mobilized women's movements, including the Mothers of the Plaza de Mayo, who wore white scarves to evoke their maternal search for their disappeared children. *Source: Pañuelazo*, by Sol Avena, February 19, 2019. Courtesy of the photographer.

Fútbol *and Improvisation (1967)*

Dante Panzeri

Soccer is all about improvisation. [. . .] The only thing that can be organized in soccer is what happens before and after the games. What happens on the field depends on hap and circumstance. [. . .] Many books could be written on soccer, giving shape to the past and explaining it, even figuring out why certain things happened. But honestly, there is no way to make a reasonable guess as to what will happen. Here's what one player said in 1967 when looking back on his career: "I scored some goals with my left leg and others with my right. [. . .] I always try to score, that I can say for sure, but I don't know how I did it. [. . .] In soccer, you can talk about your past plays but there is no way to prepare for the ones to come." Many people are captivated by the supposed importance of technique [but] don't stop to remember that soccer is a sport governed by the dynamics of the unexpected. [. . .] Naturally, those who've never played place much more faith in tactics than those who have. Those who have played place their faith in the players. This is how a systematic and pretty well-organized disdain developed for "improvised play" [. . .]. I suppose, though cannot be certain, that this industrial psychology process began in Great Britain. [. . .] This kind of disciplined soccer was introduced to Latin American playing fields by the soccer players from Río de la Plata living in Italy who returned to their homelands as war loomed between '39 and '45. [. . .] These players introduced South America to the same alleged technical guidelines they had seen as a novelty in Italy, a country inclined to believe in discipline due to a lack of soccer naturals. [. . .] Around that time, Europe started "selling 'playbooks'" to South American soccer. Books on tactics and drills, formations for one's team and others to counter the rival team's formation. It marked the arrival of the "Industrial Revolution" for Argentine, Uruguayan, and Brazilian soccer, which were then entrusted with conveying the push to modernize in their neighboring countries. [. . .] This is how a remote control of soccer players was instilled, a trend that attempts to embody the progress that soccer has made as a game of speculation brimming with anguish. And South America continued selling players without any book training to Europe, players who knew about spontaneity, allowing European countries that played soccer poorly—like Italy and Spain—to come close to the highest levels of beauty and efficacy in the sport worldwide, provided that South American soccer lowered itself to the level of the ones who sold them the books in exchange for players.

Translated by Wendy Gosselin and Jane Brodie

El Pibe

Billiken *and Pedro Orgambide*

In Buenos Aires folklore, el pibe *(the kid) invented a local style of play. In the first document, the image of* el pibe *is featured on the cover of the very first issue of the children's magazine* Billiken. *Here his most typical characteristics are on display: he is rebellious, grungy, beat-up, and mischievous, with a spark of creativity and cleverness; he holds a rustic leather ball in his hand. His is a sport unregulated by adults; he hones his talent in the empty lots of a modernizing city, rather than its more orderly and celebrated institutions. In "Backlot Soccer," urban chronicler Pedro Orgambide nostalgically recalls these roots, describing old neighborhood games. He also observes that by the mid-twentieth century, the game was changing—the sport was professionalizing and the city's growth was leaving fewer and fewer empty lots for spontaneous play.*

El Pibe *(1919)*

Billiken

Billiken, November 17, 1919.

Backlot Soccer (1968)
Pedro Orgambide

Back then the neighborhood was a wasteland, a vast *potrero* that covered a number of blocks and opened up on to streets lined with row houses, alleyways, and dead ends. Finally, by the train tracks just beyond, there was an abandoned mill. Though the confines of that landscape blur into the countenance of childhood, it had a name of its own: Matos' fields, famous as the seat and hometown of soccer.

Players from other neighborhoods would often come there, donning colorful jerseys and cleats with spikes—luxuries available only to the wealthiest teams—I can still recall the scent of the leather of the round number five ball. We more modest locals practiced with a ball made of rags (in our case, a sock stuffed with newspaper) or a rubber ball always at risk of deflating amid all the glass and tin. The anonymous onlookers often included a famous neighbor, a professional player who, when not at his team practices, would take in the games on the Matos soccer fields for the sheer fun of it—just as we would. I remember having vied for the ball against the guys who, on Sundays, would run out of the tunnel while we, in the bleachers, chanted their names. Back then, there was none of the inhibiting distance that some researchers have claimed is characteristic of soccer. We were not passive spectators before an all-powerful idol.

Still, the club, the badge, represented then, as it does today, a sort of community, a clan, a group closed in its passions and interests. Notwithstanding—and this is something that, in my view, Argentine soccer sociologists have failed to grasp—the professional player is just an extension of ourselves. Indeed, anyone who knows how to play soccer passably—and most Argentines are decent players—can experience from the stands what is happening down on the field. And that participation is by no means an illusion or a minor question. It is akin in many respects to what happens at a play or a concert. The Gestalt that takes hold in the stadium during a memorable game is not all that different from other mass spectacles, be they artistic or political.

But one thing—I think we all agree—is clear: a dramatic change has been underway with the disappearance of the *potrero*, with the end, starting in the forties, of a more provincial lifestyle. As soccer has been professionalized and consumer society expanded, the sport has been stripped of its improvised and wild festivity. Without succumbing to the melancholy of "soccer isn't what it once was," anyone can tell how much has changed: just consider the million-dollar trades and the financial strategies of the major teams.

Translated by Liliana Frankel

The Right to Play: Women and the Game

Mónica Santino and Emilia Rojas

Women athletes have long figured as a part of city sports culture. Luciana Aymar (field hockey) and Gabriela Sabatini (tennis) have risen to the status of national sports icons, and in previous generations, El Gráfico *magazine featured Noemí Simonetto (track and field, 1940s), Ingeborg Mello de Preiss (field, 1940s), and Jeanette Campbell (swimming, 1930s) on its covers. Yet women and girls were historically excluded from soccer—a reality that has been loudly challenged in recent years. Despite obstacles, women's participation has grown substantially, and calls for a professional women's soccer league have been included in demands in the twenty-first-century feminist movement. In this interview, Mónica Santino, a feminist activist and a leader of La Nuestra–Fútbol Femenista, a club made up of more than 150 girls, women, and the* LGBTQ+ *community in the Villa 31 / Barrio Mugica neighborhood, discusses why, in a city where soccer is central to everyday culture, playing the game as a woman is a struggle.*

Soccer, Gender, and the Right to Play (2018)
Mónica Santino and Emilia Rojas

ER: How did soccer come into your life? It is one of the most popular sports, but it still has strong roots in machismo . . .

MS: I was born into a soccer household, as happens to many of us—men and women—and soccer came into our house from every angle. We are a country that breathes soccer; soccer is a cultural good for our people; to then continue pretending that women are somehow outside of a phenomenon with characteristics like these, [that] form the backdrop of our daily lives—on every street corner you can find graffiti that makes reference to soccer, there are entire neighborhoods that explain their histories around soccer—women cannot be outside of something like that; we are more than half of the population.

Soccer has sexist roots because it was a game devised by men, in a time and society where women attended much more to housework and housekeeping, which means we were not permitted to play. [It is] an idea of a society in which women behave in one way and men in another and playing a game is something permitted for men more than for women. [. . .] In soccer, I believe that the questions of machismo and patriarchy are bestial—that we cannot play, we cannot make commentary, we can hardly be spectators. And I think for some time now, and especially given today's women's movement, it seems to me that soccer is also contributing to the fourth wave [of feminism]; we realize that we have bodies that can kick, perspire, jump, elbow, and if you do all this from the time you are a *pibita* [a little girl], when you are bigger you can play very well, just like a man.

[. . .] At the beginning it was a battle, body to body, and we were gaining ground and we were convinced that it was our right, and every time we went back there were more of us. The tradition is that a little boy arrives home from school, throws his backpack down and goes to the field, and that the older guys play for money or for the *asado,* forming championships that are well known in the neighborhood; and the women have to take care of the children, and the young girls have to take on adult behaviors at a very young age. This last March 8 [International Women's Day] women went on strike in some sectors of the neighborhood, and [Villa 31 / Barrio Mugica] was like a ghost town, and that is when you realize that women are the base of work and the cradle of the neighborhood. When you realize that you too have the right to play, then you begin to see life in a different way and think that perhaps motherhood is not our only goal.

Translated by Wendy Gosselin and Jane Brodie

Maradona, *Maradonear*

Eduardo Galeano and Jorge Giner

If there is one player who came to symbolize porteño soccer, *it is Diego Maradona. Many soccer fans worldwide argue that Maradona is the greatest player to have ever played the game; he is, no doubt, the best to have ever come out of Buenos Aires. The highlights of his career had him, time and time again, dribbling past defensive players to make sharp goals, leaving announcers and audiences stunned. In one particularly controversial play, Maradona scored with an illegal hand ball that somehow evaded the eyes of the referee (when asked about it later, he responded to the press that it was "the hand of God" that intervened). Four minutes later, he scored again in a second play nicknamed the "goal of the century"—Maradona weaved through the defense of the British team in the quarterfinals for the World Cup, effortlessly avoiding them and popping a goal, bringing Argentina to victory. The television announcer was caught off-guard by the beauty of the play and began to weep on air. For some the win felt like a salve after a traumatic few years: Argentina had just lost the Malvinas/Falkland Islands War to the British and ended years of violent rule by its own military; Maradona, for a moment, converted the pain of war into a vindication.*

Maradona's life story is one of incredible wins punctured by episodes of addiction, defeat, and seemingly countless comebacks, always held together by an unapologetic personality; he consistently defended the poor, questioned authority, and vociferously opined on any topic. He has emerged as such a powerful icon that his name has become a description: the term maradoñano *is used so commonly in speech that some consider it a new addition to local slang. It is also a word that has almost no clear definition and is present far beyond the world of sports commentary: to* maradonear *is to prevail, to ride a comeback, to betray, to confront authority with gusto, or to do something awe-inspiring and with incredible skill. In "The Hand of God," the writer Eduardo Galeano reflects on Maradona's contradictions and meanings for his fans; in "Verb: To Maradonear," soccer fan Jorge Giner reflects on the multiple meanings of the word in sports vocabulary.*

The Hand of God (2017)

Eduardo Galeano

No other major soccer player had ever so plainly criticized the heads of the soccer industry like that before. He was the most famous and popular athlete of all times, the one who defended to the bitter end players who were neither famous nor popular. This generous and righteous idol had, in just five minutes, scored what are inarguably the two most contradictory goals in the history of soccer. His fans worship him for them both: he not only earned their admiration for his goal as an artist, the one crafted by his mischievous legs, but also—indeed mostly, perhaps—for his goal as a thief, the one his hand swiped. Diego Armando Maradona was adored because of his dazzling stunts and because he was a dirty god, a sinner, the most human god of them all.

Translated by Wendy Gosselin and Jane Brodie

Verb: To Maradonear (2017)

Jorge Giner

Though it is not in the RAE (Real Academia Español) dictionary and there is no one definition that encapsulates everything it means, *maradonear* has become a common term to describe an extraordinary act. *Maradonear* means to score the goal you have dreamed of scoring since the time you were a kid; it means that straightforward dribble that, though not particularly masterful or wily, baffles the defense (then they try to come up with a physical explanation for how you got through); it can even mean when you turn your back on your team and single-handedly lead your teammates to glory—just as Diego did thirty-one long summers ago in Mexico's stadiums. *Maradonear* means, then, something like making human an act only the gods are capable of.

Translated by Wendy Gosselin and Jane Brodie

The Dream

Reinaldo Yiso and Lucio Arce

As the sport professionalized and began rewarding players with high salaries, soccer was perceived to offer a promise of social mobility. The global popularity of the sport inspired a new dream, in which skill and success brought recognition far beyond national borders. One might consider Lionel Messi an example of that dream: he was an otherwise ordinary boy with an extraordinary talent, one that helped him achieve an early career in Europe and unparalleled global success and recognition. Messi's story was quite different (he left Argentina as a young boy rather than as an adult player), but he is far from alone in taking off for Europe—as the roster of Argentina's national team often suggests, the very best players in local teams are regularly scouted by European leagues. In this way, the dream of soccer has changed over the course of the last century. This can be seen in these two tangos; in the first, "El sueño del pibe" ("The Dream of the Pibe*") from 1945, a young boy from a poor neighborhood dreams of finding wealth and fame as a player in the local league; in the second tango, "El pibe nos va a salvar" ("The Boy Will Save Us"), written nearly fifty years later, a father dreams that his son will be "exported" to play in the European leagues—here, soccer remains an imagined path of social mobility, but the dream's geography has changed.*

The Dream of the Pibe (1945)

Reinaldo Yiso

They knocked on the door of the humble home,
the voice of the postman could be clearly heard,
and the *pibe* went running with all of his nerve,
by mistake he stepped on his little white dog.
"Mamita, mamita" he ran up yelling;
the mother, busy washing, left her tub,
and the boy told her through laughter and tears,
"The club today sent me a call."
Mamita, my dear,
I'll make money,
I'll be a Baldonedo,
a Martino, a Boyé;

the boys of Oeste Argentino,
say I have more pull than
the great Bernabé.
You're gonna see how beautiful
It'll be on the field.
They'll applaud my goals,
And I am triumphant.
I'll play in the fifth team,
Then in the first,
I know what's in store
My sanctification.

The boy went to sleep and that night had a dream,
The most beautiful dream that one can have,
The stadium full, a glorious Sunday,
Playing first team, they'd see him at last.
A minute to go, the score zero-zero,
He took the ball, calm in his step,
He dribbled past until the goalie he faced,
and with a firm kick, broke the tie.

Translated by Wendy Gosselin and Jane Brodie

The Boy Will Save Us (2007)

Lucio Arce

I've got a *pibe* who handles the ball, caresses the ball, wears it down
he's a dream that's already come true.
And with the future ahead of me, I don't need no job
with all his talent, I'll never have to work.
He's just twelve but you should see him rip it up
I'm taking him into town Friday morning.
He'll live the player's dream, he'll play for Boca or River
and over in Spain and Italy, we'll make some bucks.
Mark my words.
Leave it to me, cause I know,
we're going straight to Madrid
I can already see him coming out of the Bernabeu.
You'll see how your troubles fly away
When the kid sets foot on the field
and the bleachers tremble.
So tell the butcher
to give you the meat on credit

'cause one of these days
the *pibe* is going to save us!
You keep him healthy, plenty of steak and pasta,
before sitting down to watch videos of Diego playing with the national.
Then I'll take him to the *potrero*,
let him practice for a while
with the rag ball I made out of socks tied.
Stay strong, be patient, if there's not enough money
this kid is our hope, he's got the soul of a champ.
You'll see soon enough, when the world shouts "olé,"
with the goals he scores,
the kid's export-quality.

Translated by Wendy Gosselin and Jane Brodie

The Fans: *La Hinchada*

Roberto Fontanarrosa

Roberto Fontanarrosa was one of Argentina's most beloved storytellers and cartoonists, as well as an avid soccer fan. His essays and short stories about soccer are celebrated descriptions, always laced with humor. Using his understanding that the true protagonists of the game are the fans, not the players, the drama of this classic story is set in the popu—*the lowest-priced, "popular" section of the stadium. The game described is the semifinal of the National Tournament in 1971, Rosario Central beat Newell's Old Boys; both teams are from the city of Rosario, but the game was played at the River Plate stadium in Buenos Aires. The game is real, although the scene described by Fontanarrosa is fiction. In the story, fans (*hinchas*) decide to invite an old man who had never seen Rosario Central lose a game to come to Buenos Aires as a sort of good-luck charm. When the old man resists, citing bad health, the fans decide to kidnap him and bring him to Buenos Aires. After a gripping game, Rosario Central wins the match 1–0, and the old man suffers a heart attack. Rather than regret their decision, the fans admire his end, declaring that there would be no better way to die.*

December 19, 1971 (1987)

Roberto Fontanarrosa

I know that now lots of people say we were some sons of bitches for what we did to old man Casale. I know, there's always someone who'll talk, but now it's easy to say it, now it's easy. You had to be there those days in Rosario to really get it, man. Now it's easy to talk it to shit, now anyone will talk. I don't know if you remember what Rosario was in those days before the game. [. . .] But look, I'll keep it brief. When the old man saw that there was no way out of it, that there wasn't the chance we'd let him get off the bus, he surrendered. But he surrendered-surrendered, eh. 'Cause to start off, we came up to him and he went off on us. He said we were irresponsible, bad news, that we had no conscience, that we should be ashamed. What do I know, all the stuff he said to us. But after, when we told him that he was perfect. That he was strong as an ox. That if his heart had survived the shock of the bus, it meant it could survive anything. And he began to calm down.

[. . .] Long before we were getting into Buenos Aires, that old man was the happiest of mortals. I'm telling you, and I swear on the health of my children. The old man sang, swore, drank *mate*, ate pastries, yelled out the window. And at the field he got out wrapped in a flag!

There was no man in the fandom happier than him. He came with us to *la popu* [the "popular" section or bleachers]. He sat through all the waiting for the game, which was longer than the bitch that bore him. And after that he sat through the game itself. He was green, that's true, and there were moments when it seemed like, you pricked him with a pin, he'd blow up like a frog—'cause I kept tabs on him every moment. And after Aldo's goal, I looked for him, I looked for him, because the melee and the mess after Aldo sent it inside was such that I don't even know where we fell, between the avalanches and the hugs and the fainting and that shit. But afterward I looked to the old man's side and I saw him hugging a giant in a muscle shirt, almost on top of him, crying. And that's when I said to myself: if he didn't die here, he'll never die. He's immortal.

And afterward [. . .] we were praying, walking in circles, there were people sitting down in the middle of all that chaos 'cause they didn't even want to look. 'Cause we fucked up big time, by the second half the thing was already theirs, and you know what was the worst, the most terrible part? That if we tied, they beat us, brother, because that's justice! Those sons of bitches would beat us! They tied us, we went into overtime, and then they were gonna give us a shock to the ass 'cause they were in better shape, and they came like an ambush, the bastards!

Such a way to worry! I said that day, dear God, I don't know what got into el Flaco Menotti who tried everything, tried everything, you don't wanna believe what he tried that day, that sickly Flaco who looked like he'd break into pieces with every play. He got a magnificent running header out of Silva that all of us saw going in, brother—that was reason for us all to make a parade and kiss el Flaco on his ass—what a play he got out of Silva! That moment we were all having a heart attack, there were five minutes left and if we tied, I repeat, we were dead in overtime.

I remember that I looked back and I saw the old man, white, pale, with his eyes popping out poor guy, but alive. And now I tell ya, I tell ya and I'd like them to answer me, everyone who now says that it was dumbfuckery what we did with old man Casale that day. I'd like one of those losers to answer me, if one of them saw him like I saw old man Casale when the referee called the end of the game, brother.

One of them should tell me if, by fucking chance, he saw old man Casale the way I saw him when the referee called the end of the game and the field became an inferno that can't be described in words. I tell ya I'd like someone to tell me if they saw him like I saw him. The face of joy on that old man, brother, the craze of happiness on the face of that old man! Someone tell me if they saw him cry, hugging everyone, like I saw that old man crying, 'cause I can assure you that day was for that old man the happiest day of his life, but beyond-beyond the happiest day of his life, because I swear the happiness of that old man was something impressive!

And when I saw him fall to the ground as if struck by lightning, 'cause he died suddenly, the poor old man, we all thought a little: "What does it matter!" What more had that man wanted than to die like this! Would he have stayed alive? For what? To last two or three halting years more, just like he was living, inside a closet, trashed by his wife and all his family? It was better to die like this, brother! He died jumping, happy, in arms with the boys . . .

Translated by Liliana Frankel

An *Hincha* Is Born, Not Made

Juan Sasturian

*The writer Juan Sasturian reflects on what it means to be a fan (*hincha*) and how he came to be "from" Boca Juniors. As he notes, just as a person does not choose their family, most never choose their team allegiances. This idea of origin and identity is also embedded in the language that* hinchas *use to talk about their teams—one is not "a fan of" or "for" a particular team but rather "from" the team. The essay also describes how team identity is often passed down from generation to generation, particularly from father to child.*

A Boca Fan from Birth (2014)

Juan Sasturian

I had just turned three when, scavenging for information about a topic older boys had interrogated me about, I asked my young parents a question: "What soccer team am I from?" That's literally how I put it. "We are from Boca," they told me. "So am I, then," I said. And that's how it went: I didn't choose Boca, I was from Boca, because my family was from it.

It can be assumed that at the origin of the original question lies, albeit tacitly, elusively, the word *hincha*: What team am I (*hincha*) from? But I'm not entirely sure. I think that the Latin construction of the genitive case (to be of) is absolute; it is a sign of prior possession and belonging, one broader than the relationship established or at play in the fanciful status of being a fan. Insofar as the response is objective, it is closer to the question "where are you from," which asks after a geographic location. In other words, being from Boca [. . .] is a possessive case (I belong to), a partitive case (I am part of), and a mark of origin. All at once.

Looking back, I remember that the question "what team are you from" was, among boys, the one asked immediately after "what's your name." And the content of neither answer was—at least not in my case or in my house—something one chose, but rather something one learned and embraced unquestioningly. [. . .]

I want to pinpoint in time and in space another event: it was late spring '49—I had just turned four. [. . .] With Boca on the verge of falling to the minors—it had been at the bottom of the ranking all season—and my father on the verge of collapse, Xeneize [a way to refer to Boca in the Genoese dialect] beat Lanús—their greatest rival—at their home stadium, and managed to get out of a jam the likes of which it had never seen before and has not seen since. Sheer madness. As an act of superstition, an exorcism, or a pledge, the following Monday my old man bought me my first Boca jersey. And he put it on me. Family folklore had it that I wore it at all times, and I was able to see so for myself many years later, in the '90s, when my mother died. Among her letters and old bills, I found the V-necked piqué jersey with most likely Ricoltore-brand oil stains on it. I didn't take it off to go to sleep at night, let alone to eat the wildly greasy fried eggs from a time before indigestion was known—just another of that era's many treasures. In other words, I was a *bostero* [Boca fan] by birth. I am one, I didn't become one. And I didn't put the team's blue and gold on my own back, it was put on me.

Translated by Wendy Gosselin and Jane Brodie

Stadium Songs

River Plate Fans and San Lorenzo Fans

Porteño *soccer fans are well known for their ironic, caustic, emotional, and loud songs and chants at the soccer field. The songs are usually written by members of a team's* barra brava *and circulated to the fans so that the entire crowd can sing along in a rhythmic tone on game day. These two songs from River Plate and San Lorenzo clubs highlight the importance of rivalry and loyalty at the stadium. They demonstrate a competition that focuses not only on what happens on the field but also on what happens between fans: chants sometimes read more like love songs or odes, they recount fans' own experience of suffering alongside their team, and they compete with other* hinchas *for being the loudest, the most devoted. Although stadium culture has changed over the years, many songs also contain sexist, racist, xenophobic, or homophobic lyrics. Some fans choose which parts of a song they will sing. In the first example, fans of River Plate, rather than taunting the players of Boca Juniors, take aim directly at their* hinchas (called bosteros) *for being weak-minded, giving up and "leaving the stadium" before a game is over when things do not go well. They lob insults, calling them police, thugs, cowards, and* chamuyeros (fakes). *In a similar tone, but emphasizing their own pride and dedication, fans of San Lorenzo chant that they are the most faithful* hinchas *and imitate statements one might make to a lover—singing, for example, that San Lorenzo is their "reason for being" and promising the team that "no matter what we've been through, I'll always be at your side." Here the fans of San Lorenzo make reference to their team's descent to the B-league, but they do so in order to show their true devotion to the team, in good times and bad. They call themselves their team's guardians; they vow that they will keep the team from selling out.*

That's How Boca Fans Are

River Plate Fans

That's how *bosteros* [Boca fans] are,
they're the most bitter people on earth,
when they aren't the champions,
they fly black flags.
Boca, stop telling lies,

with this talk of your devotion,
when things start to go badly
"the 12th" [Boca fans] bow out in the first period.
You wet yourselves in fear,
You are just like cops,
The *federal* [police] has to escort you everywhere,
You can't take it,
and after what happened in Mar del Plata
you ran away as fast as you could.

Translated by Lisa Ubelaker Andrade

Let's Go, Ciclón

San Lorenzo Fans

From the cradle I've carried you
In my heart,
You are my reason,
Nothing would make sense
if one day you weren't there.
That's why I am with you, in the good and the bad,
Whether you win or lose I don't even care
Because despite everything we have been through
My dear San Lorenzo, I will always be at your side.
There is something that they will never understand
That the Glorious will be wherever you play
This is your people, the ones who stayed when you fell [to the B-league],
The ones that kept San Lorenzo from selling out.

Translated by Lisa Ubelaker Andrade

The Thrill of the Superclásico

Héctor Negro

The Superclásico is one of the most anticipated events in the city's calendar; twice a year Boca and River play each other, usually once at each stadium. In years previous, the match would also mean that each team's fans had the chance to confront each other at the stadium, a thrilling, tense encounter, heavy with meaning for the fans. Visiting fans have been excluded from games since 2013 due to episodes of violence and riots after the game. In "River and Boca—a Poem," the journalist and poet Héctor Negro captures how the rivalries of a River-Boca match can hold the attention of the entire city: he sees a city partitioned in two.

River and Boca—a Poem (2005)

Héctor Negro

Two rivers: El Riachuelo and La Plata
have two jerseys,
their waters may blend nearby,
But River and Boca do not.
Boca and River, a lightning bolt of nerves,
a hundred neighborhoods, a hundred cities on alert.
No one is neutral, no one deaf, no one can sleep.
River—Boca, they measure up and get ready,
they float out on edgy transistors,
wrapped up in banners.
cross forests and feverish roads
pass over rooftops, jumping into antennas,
Way beyond the buzz of the city,
through slums and towns,
they attack borders.
Boca, River, they cross paths.
It's not about eleven vs. eleven,
loyal or unruly fans.
It's about bells, about drums,
about faraway sirens.

They're going to climb impending thunderclaps
the fire of the goal's fuse has been lit.
Unanimous throats will sprout wings,
Unanimous silences will turn to stone.
One side of the stadium will break the afternoon,
the other will clench its jaws and wait.
And wherever it burns,
the window ceremony,
there will be joy, clenched rage,
and no one will be alone.
River and Boca: "THE CELEBRATION."

Translated by Wendy Gosselin and Jane Brodie

Violence

Clarín

Violence at soccer stadiums has been so pronounced in recent decades that some com-
mentators continue to suggest that violence and soccer are simply inseparable. The
passions and culture of rivalry, these critics say, are too unbridled and run too deep
to avoid violent outcomes. But expectations of violence at soccer matches have risen
over the decades. During the 1940s, physical confrontations were rare, but by the end
of the 1960s a series of conflicts provoked discussion over whether the sport inspired
violence. In a game between Vélez Sarsfield and River, River fans descended on the
popular section of the home team; a fight broke out; when tear gas was fired, the crowd
dispersed. One man was found dead. At that time, the death of a fan was shocking,
but as commentators noted, it had become quite common for the visiting team to be
cornered by a group of home-team fans at an away match; the police often turned a
blind eye. After these initial events, groups of each team's fans began to act as mafias.
Known as the barras bravas, *these fans vowed to defend their turf and their team*
by "protecting" fellow hinchas *at away games, and in turn, standing guard during*
home games. Over the course of the following decades, violence only became more
entrenched and regular. Still, little was done about the central role of the barra brava
in club life. As soccer became an arena in which political alliances and money changed
hands, violence became more recurrent. In 2000, the newspaper Clarín *printed a sev-*
eral part series exposing the role of the barra brava *in the sport, and in the political*
and social world beyond.

The Secret Threads of Violence (2000)

Clarín

Almost no one dares speak up about the *barra brava*, about the leaders who
uphold them, about certain politicians and union members who use them
as a hit force, or about the authorities who don't do a thing about any of it.
Sometimes they remain silent because they fear that the rage of a violent
power will overtake them. In other cases, their silence is even more compulsory: they have no moral authority to cast the first stone.

There is nothing novel about saying that the *barra brava* aren't the only vil-
lains in the story: it's certainly not a question of them against the world. On

the contrary: they hobnob with every single one of the sectors that, paradoxically, give life to soccer in the first place.

"Enough; it's time to do something," public discourse implores whenever the topic returns to the front-page news. A few recent measures have been taken, but they were clearly insufficient. In 1985, following the death of teenage Adrián Scaserra (a Boca supporter), the De la Rúa law was established. In 1992, in response to another surge of violence, the law stiffened with Ricardo Levene Jr.'s reform. In 1998, the judge Víctor Perrotta halted tournaments to demand better security. But soccer and violence carried on, hand in hand; administrations came and went and everything remained half-finished.

Today, it's unusual when a team in any division doesn't add any injuries or arrests to the long list of incidents. Who, how, and why are such disturbances provoked? If you intend to conduct serious research, there's often no other way than to turn off your recorder and swear eternal anonymity to your sources. Only in this way has the hermetic circle of soccer begun to crack open. And incredible things come to the surface . . . This afternoon, in the Bombonera [Boca's stadium], Boca and River players will dispute three more points in the closing tournament. In the stands, most paying fans will cheer on their team. But others, the violent ones, will be there, too. Known as "La 12" [Boca's barra brava, the twelve] and "Los Borrachos del Tablón" [River's barra brava, the Drunks of the Bleachers], they're highly trained and used to acting as a group. It's just that they no longer care much about soccer as a sport in itself. And widespread passivity and complicity will probably continue to feed the statistics.

Translated by Robin Myers

Soccer, Politics, and Protest
El Gráfico

Soccer and politics have long been intertwined. Juan Perón, despite his personal disinclination for the sport, often made an appearance at games; candidates for elected office regularly campaign at stadiums and seek support at the clubs. Former president Néstor Kirchner made waves when he announced that he would make all matches free on state television: Fútbol Para Todos (Soccer for All) *aired from 2009 to 2017. The program was cut under the administration of president Mauricio Macri, who himself began his political career as the elected president of Boca Juniors club. Election to a leadership post in a major Buenos Aires soccer club is considered a sound path to a political career.*

The political power of soccer was also palpable during the 1976–83 civic-military dictatorship. In 1978, Argentina was scheduled to host the World Cup, a major undertaking that the military junta believed would be good for its image. Months before Argentina was scheduled to host, however, word began to spread internationally that the Argentine military was illegally detaining thousands of dissidents. Some prisoners were being held at the military barracks known as the Escuela de Mecánica de la Armada (ESMA), a mere mile from El Monumental stadium, where international crowds would attend games. Critics of the violent regime at home and abroad organized a boycott and contended that the cup was a distraction and method of propaganda. During the games, the Mothers of the Plaza de Mayo demonstrated; thousands of family members lined up outside the Organization of American States offices to question the whereabouts of their loved ones. International protestors, galvanized by exiled Argentines, formed a committee "with the very simple idea that soccer can't be played next to a concentration camp" and brought international attention to the human rights violations. In a counter-campaign, the military government and its allies decried the efforts to "slander the nation" and circulated bumper stickers and signs that read, "In Argentina we are right [correct/conservative] and we are human" (somos derechos y somos humanos), a wordplay on rightist politics that was intended to counter protests regarding ongoing human rights (derechos humanos) violations.

State-directed media and outlets publishing in a climate of censorship supported the military campaign. El Gráfico, for example, published this letter, which was later shown to be completely falsified. In it, the Dutch player Ruud Krol supposedly writes to his daughter at home in the Netherlands (in English), lauding the Argentine military as protectors of peace. Krol spoke out against the false, error-laden, and blatantly forged letter; El Gráfico came under fire for committing such an over-the-top fabrication. "A Letter from Argentina" showcases the lengths to which the military and its allies went to frame the World Cup as a peaceful event, and to answer the growing global criticism—and suspicion—of Argentina's violent civic-military dictatorship.

A Letter from Argentina (1978)
El Gráfico

Monday, June 11, 1978

My Beautiful,

Your mom will read this letter to you. [. . .] Mom said the other day you cried a lot because some little friends of yours told you very bad things about Argentina. Those things are not true at all. They are just infantile lies without any importance. Dady is allright [*sic*]. Here in this country everything is quietness and beauty. This is not the "World Cup" but the "Peace Cup." Don't be scared if you see some pictures of the concentration showing green little soldiers standing by us. They love all the people in this country, whom from the very first moment of our arrival showed their affection to us. [. . .] Smile, please, I'll soon be there. Don't be scared, Daddy is OK and has your doll and a couple of little green soldiers who take much care of him, their guns only shoot flowers. Tell your friends the truth: Argentina is a land of love. Some day when you'll be grown up you'll be able to understand the whole truth. I love you, take much care of Mom and wait on me with a big smile.

A big kiss to you,

Daddy

Toward an Inclusive Future

Inés Arrondo and Analía Fernández Fuks

The feminist movement has been a critical agent of change in twenty-first-century Argentina culture and politics, and the world of sport is no exception. Soccer has long been entrenched in ideas of masculinity and machismo, and fans have been known to deploy homophobic, racist, sexist, and xenophobic ideas on and off the field. Anti-LGBTQ+ slurs, in particular, are a common and unquestioned part of game-day parlance in mainstream soccer circles. Queer, feminist, and antiracist advocates, fans, and athletes have become vocal about this hostile culture and have mobilized to alter exclusionary aspects of the sport. In "A Collective Effort" the first female national secretary of sports (and retired field hockey player), Inés Arrondo, reflected on her role in government, efforts to promote gender inclusion in clubs, as part of physical education and at the professional level.

A Collective Effort (2019)

Inés Arrondo and Analía Fernández Fuks

AFF: *What does it mean to be the first women at the helm of the Secretariat of Sports, a position historically occupied by men?*

IA: It is not just me arriving, this is a fight of all [women]. I feel that there are spaces that all of us women are winning in this fight that we are taking on together. It is not something that represents me individually. [. . .] Before the Ni Una Menos [movement], between 2013 and 2014, I did a study on the participation of women in [sports] clubs, and one of the conclusions we made was that there were infrastructures, resources, and a lot of people participating in these athletic spaces, but that women and girls had no place there. [. . .] Hockey was valuable for women to find a place where they could be athletes but not for signifying a discipline in which one had to be feminine. [. . .] I always felt a discomfort regarding our limits in society; I see things from the perspective of what it means to be a woman who has coexisted with the structural problem of this society in terms of gender. Our subjectivities are constructed within all of this.

AFF: How did your coworkers respond to working from this perspective?

IA: It was complicated. It was a job in neighborhoods where there were no activities for girls and soccer was only played by boys. I underlined the need for spaces for girls. But they told me that there was opportunity for everyone. And I responded that until girls were [granted a place], boys should not be participating in the activities. [. . .] Sports and activity are health, education, and security resources that fight addiction for everyone, not just boys. Athletic activity in public space strengthens community.

AFF: And what about women's soccer?

IA: Just as our revolution with hockey was to get women onto the field, the soccer players must combat the stereotype that associated soccer players with the male athlete. We have to work against this naturalized violence of "not having a place." Soccer is a valuable tool that can empower that symbolic battle.

Translated by Lisa Ubelaker Andrade

V

Reading, Watching, and Listening in Buenos Aires

Buenos Aires is a city of readers. It is a place where the printed (and digital) word still finds a captive and avid audience, where street book fairs draw crowds. Although there was a time when reading was a rather exclusive tool of a lettered elite, educational campaigns in the nineteenth century expanded literacy, and by the early twentieth century there was a vast urban readership that extended across the divides of social class. Print media—magazines, periodicals, books, and pamphlets—flourished. All types of presses and publications met the demands of a vast urban readership and diverse sectors of society. Residents' appetite for other kinds of media has been similarly strong. In addition to serving as a major epicenter for Spanish-language publishing, Buenos Aires also became a key location for the production of Argentine—and Latin American—radio, film, television, and digital media. In the process, the sights and sounds of the city have been projected into homes and theaters across the country and the region. In this way, the city's mass media became one of the cornerstones of a shared cultural and social experience—as well as a powerful political outlet. At specific points in the city's history, media has also been heavily regulated, utilized, and censored by the state. In print, on air, and on the reel, a diverse, contested culture took form.

Expanding Literacy

As in many other cities in Latin America, publishing and reading in Buenos Aires was once a practice of the few. The Nicaraguan poet Rubén Darío, who lived in Buenos Aires between 1893 and 1898, recalled that when he was there, the act of publishing a book was something reserved for members of the city's wealthiest families. Other writers noted that a lack of local publishing houses thwarted the development of Buenos Aires literati. In the twentieth century, much changed: a plethora of newspapers, books, and magazines were displayed on kiosks on every corner of the city, and local writers such as Jorge Luis Borges and Julio Cortázar rose to the canon of global literature.

This cultural transformation took form at least in part because of early actions by intellectuals, political leaders, and entrepreneurs, who saw universal literacy as a priority. In the early decades of the republican period, and then again when thousands of immigrants arrived at Buenos Aires's port between 1870 and 1930, Argentina's political elite saw education as an essential tool to "civilize" and generate a sense of national identity in its growing population. Just after independence, some hoped that a standardized school curriculum would "destroy the animosities engendered by ignorance." Key members of the local elite saw public libraries and new educational curricula as tools to inspire a sense of belonging to the nation. As the nineteenth century advanced, universal education campaigns became entangled in a much wider insistence that in order for Argentina to progress, a literate civil society must prevail. (See "Education and Civilization," the first selection below.) But for much of this period, actual access to education was fairly limited—in 1865 a mere one in twenty-five young people were enlisted in school in Buenos Aires, and most parents pulled their children out of school once they achieved basic literacy. As the immigration boom continued, campaigns for state-run education gained traction. Finally, in 1884, Congress enacted a law to provide free, secular, universal basic education.

Nevertheless, a culture of reading and writing changed the way Buenos Aires's residents interacted. As literacy rates in the city rose to near-universal numbers (though reading levels varied) in the first decades of the twentieth century, the printed word became a forum for competing political ideas and community building. The country's two major dailies, *La Prensa* and *La Nación*, were founded in 1869 and 1870, respectively, and their growing circulation over the next decades illustrated this change. *La Prensa* printed 125,000 copies by the start of the twentieth century, making it, along with *La Nación*, a national interpreter of current events. Variety magazines like *Caras y Caretas* (with a circulation of 200,000 copies in 1910) used fiction, caricature, and editorials to trace the quirks of urban experience and convert them into a shared culture among a vast readership.

Meanwhile, as these major press outlets lassoed audiences into a shared national conversation (one strongly localized in the nation's capital), more fractured and diverse communities of readers developed their own, alternative press outlets. Smaller periodicals cropped up quickly, filling up newsstands with copious options and catering to a range of subcultures, including major immigrant groups. *La Patria degli Italiani*, founded in 1860, served Italian-speaking residents, and by 1914 it reached a regular circulation of sixty thousand. Papers like *El Eco de Galicia*, *Di Presse*, the *Buenos Aires Herald*, and *Argentinische Tageblatt* each interpreted Argentine society in their readers' native language, reported on news from abroad, and served as a forum for

Reading was an early and critical component of workers' movements. In this photograph taken in 1904, members of a local union pose with their paper while on strike. *Source: Marineros y foguistas*, by *Caras y Caretas*, 1904. From the *Caras y Caretas* collection. Courtesy of the Archivo General de la Nación Argentina Dpto. Doc. Fotográficos.

local community members to register complaints and opinions. Divisions in political society also began to see their representation in print: Catholic conservativism found its voice in *El Pueblo*; socialists were heard out in *La Vanguardia*; anarchists circulated news via *La Protesta*, founded in 1897. By the twentieth century, literacy—both reading and writing—was no longer an exclusive device for elite dominance or maintenance of the status quo. To the contrary, workers' movements and immigrant groups relied on the city's avid and growing readership to promote their messages and organize.

Print Media and Modern Identities

The diversity of modern Buenos Aires and its mass audiences of eager readers also propelled the growth of a new popular mass media. By the 1920s, it was clear that Buenos Aires was undergoing important changes, and these transformations included the diversification of its large, literate, and rapidly Argentinized immigrant population. A new brand of reporting emerged that drew comparisons to US "yellow journalism"; *Crítica* became the flagship example of an emergent category of print media, publishing photography

Cafés, bars, and public transportation became places where people took in their daily reading and discussed news or sports. Here a group of men pose for a photo at a café-bar. *Source: Hombres leen el periódico en un bar*, by Anonymous, ca. 1940. Courtesy of the Archivo General de la Nación Argentina Dpto. Doc. Fotográficos. Inv: 33340.

and illustration alongside catchy headlines. The editors carefully highlighted new emerging popular cultures, running stories about soccer, tango, jazz, horse racing, crime, politics, scientific and technical novelties, and dramatic news that captured the public's attention. By 1930, the paper sold more than 350,000 copies per day, making it quickly one of the most widely circulated dailies in the Spanish-speaking world and an enormous influencer in local cultural life.

The literary world was following suit, plunging forward with new vanguards. The growing middle classes generated a demand for new types of books. Literary entrepreneurs heeded the call. The Cooperativa Editorial Buenos Aires, a publishing house, built a catalogue of sixty-eight titles in five years; the Biblioteca La Nación, the book publisher operated by the newspaper *La Nación*, was also quite prolific, printing 875 titles in the first two decades of the century and selling nearly a million books at accessible prices. While the general readership gained a taste for fiction, writing became a profession in Buenos Aires. (See "Writing Becomes a Profession.") Journalists and other writers gained steady employment with newspapers, magazines, and publishing houses, bringing print out of an era of self-publishing and transforming it into a small industry.

Several of these new publishers grounded their projects in a social mission. The socialist Antonio Zamora, for example, founded Claridad "not as a commercial enterprise but as a university for the people." Aiming to reach and provide a cultural education to the masses, he published a range of titles in Spanish and sold them for roughly the cost of two trolley tickets in kiosks. (See "New Vanguards.") The catalogue was carefully curated; Zamora selected recognized science, social studies, philosophy, theater, sexuality, and crime texts and made them accessible—both in terms of language and price—to working- and middle-class audiences. Other new publishing houses were determined to grant a platform for local authors; Manuel Gleizer Editor was a significant but small press that printed three hundred titles, including the first edition of Jorge Luis Borges's *El idioma de los argentinos*. It served as a launching point for many other authors who became central to the local literary canon, including Macedonio Fernández, Raúl and Enrique González Tuñón, Manuel Gálvez, Leopoldo Lugones, Eduardo Mallea, Nicolás Olivari, Roberto Payró, and Raúl Scalabrini Ortiz.

These smaller enterprises were well received, but their sales paled in comparison to the numbers of books sold by growing commercial presses. From 1916 to 1971 the publishing house Tor produced more than ten thousand low-cost books and magazines on cheap paper with decorated covers. The texts reached avid readers, though the lesser quality of the low-budget publications became a source of debate. Still, the vast catalogue suggests some of the peculiarities of local taste: their bestsellers included texts by Karl Marx, books for children, and a series titled "Freud al alcance de todos" ("Freud for everyone") that peaked in sales amid a growing affinity for psychoanalysis. Tor also became a larger-scale publishing house for novels by Borges, Cortázar, and other local intellectuals. By the 1930s, Tor's success was clear: the company was publishing five thousand copies of most titles and distributing across Latin America, a regional reach that bolstered Buenos Aires's reputation as a center of publishing for the Spanish-speaking masses.

With big publishers like Tor leading the charge, local production of books rose nearly 150 percent in the 1930s; by 1950, 14 million books were published per year, with exceptional variety in form and function. Pocket-sized books became popular, and a new generation of publishing houses expanded under the leadership of exiled Spanish republicans who brought new talent to the industry through the 1940s.

From the 1920s and into the 1940s, print media exhibited an important level of autonomy with respect to the state: unlike the regulated schooling curriculum, mass media became a diverse forum for scattered and alternative visions of the city. Periodicals and publishers also prospered or perished

Kiosks can still be found today on major avenues and many street corners, offering passersby a range of reading material. In this photograph from the 1920s, young and old browse print offerings. *Source: Kiosko*, by Anonymous, ca. 1920. Courtesy of the Archivo General de la Nación Argentina Dpto. Doc. Fotográficos. Inv: 335058.

at the hand of their paying consumers, advertisers, and benefactors. Amid this golden age of print media, kiosks emerged as a stage of local identities. Buyers confronted a range of options, from general magazines like *El Hogar* to specialized ones like *Mundo Agrario*, from *Billiken* (for kids) and magazines like *Ahora* (with more photographs than text), the sensationalist *Aquí Está*, and *Radiolandia* (for radio enthusiasts) to comics that appealed to a general audience, like character comics *Rico-Tipo* and *Patoruzú*. The emergence and transformation of women's magazines signaled important broader cultural changes. (See "Media, Gender, and Feminist Thought.") The world of print media came to mark a fractured but dynamic mass culture filled with diverse constructions of modern life.

Politics, New Media, and the State

The diversity of Buenos Aires's print media also made political and social fractures clearly visible, and this could become a point of contention for the government. At times the disparate opinions expressed in the media inspired brusque interventions, particularly during periods of authoritarian rule. By the late 1930s, Argentina had been marked by a series of corrupt elections, and the government had lost much of its legitimacy; as a result, the degree to which the state could—or should—control the enormously influential world of print media became a subject of debate. By 1943, when the military took over in a coup, control of media messaging was already a pressing issue. Over the next three years, the military junta, including its secretary of labor, Juan Perón, displayed an interest in gaining access to the key influencers of public opinion—and in silencing the most acerbic voices of criticism. Major dailies like *La Prensa* remained critical and, as a result, were regularly sanctioned. The Peronist government quickly developed an apparatus to manage the press. Perón responded to the petitions of press workers and journalists, who for decades had urged for labor rights, and made sure they received recognition and improved working conditions. Meanwhile, a gradual consensus appeared at the newsstand, a sign of the state's increasing pressure and influence: although Perón's rise to power was widely criticized in the mainstream press in 1945, five years later the major media outlets were rather unconditional supporters. While Perón's relationship with the printed press was often quite contentious, his forays into other forms of new popular media were notable, signaling a talent for mobilizing popular culture toward political ends.

Among the most important medium during the first Peronist era was radio—an outlet that, independent of politics, had already become incredibly important to the city's residents. *Porteños* had been early experimenters in radio. The first broadcast was one of a handful of early transmissions in the world, and although there were few listeners then, radio audiences quickly grew. In 1921, there were 50,000 radio receivers in the country; a year later that number had skyrocketed to 600,000. Radios became more readily available, and in a short time the media began to cross social and geographical lines, extending its reach beyond Buenos Aires and finding a vast audience of listeners that spanned the working and middle classes. New cultures became a part of family life: radio theater, soccer games broadcast live from the stadiums, boxing matches narrated from abroad, and music like folklore, jazz, and tango found their way into the living room. (See "The Pampa in the City, via Radio.") For most, this represented a stark change, blurring the lines between public and private life. Some saw the change more negatively and decried it as decadent middlebrow culture; for others, it was a positive sign of a more egalitarian future. In 1938, when the government stepped in to regulate the use of the local slang, *lunfardo*, on the radio, artists protested the measure, marking out a media battle of what types of culture deserved or were appropriate for the national platform. In the 1940s, radio theater programs tended toward the melodramatic. One successful local program, *Los Pérez García*, ran from 1942 to 1967 and depicted the love and life dramas of a middle-class family in the city; when the program moved from a midday broadcast to an evening slot, listening to the show became a family pastime. In shows like these, it was clear that Buenos Aires radio was providing vast audiences with new shared local stories and was reflecting and informing ideas about a common culture. Even those who warned that the technologies were degrading national values marveled at their clear power.

Radio and cinema blossomed together. While radio transformed the private sphere, cinema became an epicenter of social life. Like radio, film had an early start in Buenos Aires—the first moving picture was presented nearly at the same time as in the United States, in 1896, and the first cinema downtown, showing silent films, opened its doors to a 250-seat audience in 1900. By 1922, the public was so taken with going to the cinema that Argentina was ranked the third-largest importer of US movie reels in the world. But the products of the local film industry were also drawing mass audiences. Theaters began to crop up across the city, and before long, more modest movie halls became neighborhood institutions. (See "The Cinema, a Barrio Institution.") The city also began to appear as a prominent character in Argentine film. In the 1930s, major studios like Sonofilm reimagined the urban world of Buenos Aires using studio backdrops of neighborhoods like La Boca, Abasto, Boedo, and the city's downtown. Movies like *Los tres berretines* (*The Three Whims*, 1933) and *Elvira Fernández, vendedora de tiendas* (*Elvira Fernández, Saleswoman*, 1942) projected ideas about the city and its popular cultures of tango, bars, cafés, and the modern downtown around the country and to audiences across Latin America.

Television and Press, in Dictatorship and Democracy

Beginning in the 1950s, television added to the inundation of images of Buenos Aires in national media; bulky television sets took the spot once reserved for radios in the family home, and the kinds of programs that once found popularity on radio waves migrated to the small screen. In the 1960s, programs like *La Familia Falcón,* a situation comedy, projected a vision of middle-class life in Buenos Aires across the nation. (See "The Buenos Aires Middle Class, on Screen.") National celebrities like the jazz singer Paloma Efron, the actress Mirtha Legrand, and cook and model homemaker Doña Petrona made the move from radio and print to daytime television, developing new aesthetics of production. (See "Radio, Television, and Celebrity Culture.") And although star power migrated to the small screen, radio found new ways to reinvent itself. In the early 1970s, FM radio created a space for diverse music and talk options on the dial.

A rise in consumption of new print media also innovated the mediascape. By the mid-1960s, *Clarín,* a tabloid newspaper that had begun production in 1945, was reaching record audiences, and by the 1970s it had a circulation of 700,000. In those years, magazines like *Primera Plana* and the newspaper *La Opinión,* both founded by Jacobo Timerman, renovated the genre. *Primera*

Plana, a glossy magazine that commented on politics, global affairs, and culture, became a primary source for informed middle- and upper-class local consumers; *La Opinión*, a newspaper that looked to evoke a cross section of interests, was designed to be economically conservative and culturally leftist, though in practice these lines could become quite blurred. It introduced a kind of journalism that sought to more deeply contextualize and interpret the news, orienting the reader rather than presenting news as simplistic fact. During the turbulent democratic years of the second Peronism (which ended in the coup of 1976), a number of magazines put competing interpretations of Peronism on display, including *El Descamisado* on the left and *El Caudillo* on the right; others, like the magazine *Crisis,* entered the realms of arts and ideas, elevating discussion of popular culture, artistic vanguards, and national identity from a broad leftist point of view. With a circulation of twenty thousand copies, it reached a sizable readership.

The rise of the civic-military dictatorship (1976–83) changed the course of this media history. In the first two weeks following the installment of the military junta, all publications were required to report to an executive office, submit their products or programs for review, and obtain permission from intelligence services to continue printing; the military junta announced that anyone who circulated information considered "disruptive" or "discrediting of the state" would be subjected to consequences. Social groups or intermediary entities were prohibited from operating radio programs. In the months and years following, the military government aggressively pursued, intimidated, kidnapped, tortured, and disappeared journalists and media producers who strayed from their narrative of events, effectively silencing any criticism with violence. (See "An Open Letter to the Dictatorship.")

This context of oppression had profound effects on the public's relationship with the media. Whereas prior to the dictatorship annual magazine circulation was as high as 235.6 million copies, by the second year of the junta circulation numbers had plunged to just a third of previous levels. Book publishing was reduced to nearly a quarter of its pre-dictatorship numbers by 1977. Cinemas and production facilities closed, in part due to censorship. Audiences turned to television and radio, but these were increasingly controlled by the military and pro-government groups. The armed forces took over each major television channel and supplied dictums and new regulations regarding the "values" promoted on air. Reports on current events were carefully edited to shore up support for the military regime. Changes were gradual: rather than taking regularly scheduled programming off the air completely, censors monitored casts and plotlines and went about blacklisting actors.

A few dissident media outlets continued to produce despite the crackdown. (See "Humor under Censorship.") Underground publications, as well as a small number of publishing houses, such as Centro Editor de América Latina (CEAL), defied censors. Prior to the dictatorship, and in line with a tradition of local publishers who sought to reach a mass audience, CEAL published a series of affordable and accessible books on a wide variety of topics; following the 1976 coup, the company's listings clearly stood outside the military's conservative dictates. Although copies of CEAL books were burned and censored by the regime, the company defiantly continued. Texts were stowed away in the clandestine libraries of leftist militants, professors, teachers, and curious young people, or circulated in secret. The brand emerged as a symbol of resistance, and persistence, in the 1970s and remained so well into the 1990s. (See "Broad Audiences and Burned Books.")

Meanwhile, much of the city's press fell in line with government censorship, generating a culture of silence, complicity, and consensus around state actions. Most portrayed the military government in a positive light; they ran stories of "leftist militants" engaging in violent actions and portrayed military intervention as necessary; they also filled their pages with news from abroad, as well as frivolous stories that suggested that life was carrying on as normal. The acquiescence of the most trusted papers created an opening for a broader public ignorance regarding the scope and details of the ongoing state violence, pushing such information out of sight. The *Buenos Aires Herald*, a local paper that was written in English and had historically served the British Argentine and diplomatic community, was one of the few media outlets that criticized censorship and printed information regarding kidnappings and state terror. Although the paper had coolly entertained the benefits of military intervention early on, its editors became increasingly staunch supporters of human rights, reporting on disappearances, casting suspicion on government claims, and permitting families to publish the names of their missing loved ones. (See "Press under Dictatorship.")

In the months following Argentina's loss in the Malvinas/Falklands Islands War, the military's grip on the media began to wane, and the return of democracy signaled the end of complete state censorship. Over the following decades, Buenos Aires's culture of reading reemerged; the kiosk again brimmed over with new periodicals and reprints of classic literature. A new newspaper, *Página 12*, became known for its investigative reporting, particularly on matters related to political and economic corruption. In the realms of film, fine art, and literature, a sense of liberty of expression was restored. Films like *La historia oficial* (*The Official Story*, 1985) and *Garage Olimpo* (*Olympic Garage*, 1999) brought a new focus on state terror and the stories of the disappeared, while others, like *Tango feroz: La leyenda de Tanguito* (*Wild Tango: The legend of Tanguito*, 1993) and *Pizza, birra, faso* (*Pizza, Beer, and Cigarettes*, 1998), de-romanticized the neoliberal era and brought to light the struggles of the poor, the young, and the disenfranchised. Journalism also saw a revival of investigative reporting, particularly as the violence, and corruption, of the dictatorship came to light.

But new questions about the meaning of a "free press" also emerged. In the neoliberal 1990s, broad deregulation, privatization, and a culture of corporatization empowered media corporations to expand their reach. The particular, the media conglomerate Clarín Group rapidly bought up a series of national and local media outlets and emerging cable networks. As the corporation also developed a clear political posture, new conflicts over the political orientations of a divided press began to take form. These issues converged during the presidency of Cristina Fernández de Kirchner when Clarín Group became an outspoken voice against the administration. Amid the political conflict, the president made a push for media reforms that promised to break up the corporate monopoly, promote state-run media, and redistribute radio and television channels to underrepresented groups. Critics decried that the law disrupted a free press, empowered the administrations' own allies, and represented an assault on dissident media; the law's proponents argued that it created space for more diverse voices.

In this context, media polarization became quite stark. State and corporate television channels, newspapers, and magazines often gave completely different interpretations of everyday events; media viewers could marvel at headlines and television coverage that reported nearly contradictory information on almost every political and social issue.

Yet beyond the press, the impulse and importance of reading, watching, and listening remained a vital part of life. Although some neighborhood cinemas shuttered their doors, and particularly as digital streaming became widespread, there was no question that film continued to use the city as subject, as a site for production, and was a media enjoyed and discussed by a vast public; in 1999 the city began to host an annual independent film festival (Buenos Aires International Festival of Independent Cinema, BAFICI), and by 2010 some 280,000 spectators attended the festival's 1,115 showings. Moreover, even while large corporate media appeared to dominate major outlets and some decried a sense of superficiality on mainstream television, collectives of independent writers, smaller radio stations, and niche publishers continued to produce; new groups emerged on digital media and other platforms, and social media galvanized mass movements. On an ordinary Saturday afternoon, a street fair of small press and zines could still draw a thick crowd of browsers, and used bookstores on Corrientes Avenue still kept their doors open twenty-four hours per day, even as new digital platforms engaged a new generation of consumers. (See "The Bookstore, a Downtown Institution.") The city of readers, writers, and media makers, it appeared, would endure.

Education and Civilization

Domingo Faustino Sarmiento

De la educación popular *is one of the most important writings on pedagogy in Argentine history. The text, written by the founder of public education in Argentina, Domingo Faustino Sarmiento, detailed a plan for mass education in the country, covering topics like the costs of universal public education, the distribution of resources, education for girls, and early education. The text saw public education as a secular, national project necessary for political stability and social cohesion. For Sarmiento, primary education had a political function that exceeded its economic benefit: the assimilation and integration of arriving immigrants was considered a priority. In this excerpt, Sarmiento describes how education is a key element of a republican project to cultivate a moral, civil, and productive nation.*

Education for the People (1849)

Domingo Faustino Sarmiento

[. . .] Until two centuries ago, education was available to the ruling classes, to the clergy, to the aristocracy; but the people, the masses, were not, strictly speaking, an active part of nations. [. . .] In a republic, the equal rights afforded to all men, even in those countries governed by tutelary systems, are a fact that serves as a foundation for social organization, no matter how they may be accidentally altered by national precedents or other causes. Today, this imprescriptible tenet yields the obligation of every government to provide future generations with an education, as it cannot compel all individuals of the present to receive the intellectual preparation entailed by exercising the rights attributed to them. The social conditions of men often depend on circumstances beyond their will. A poor father cannot be responsible for educating his children, but society as a whole has a vital interest in ensuring that all individuals who help forge the nation over time have been sufficiently prepared, by virtue of the education they receive as children, to undertake the social functions to which they shall be called. A nation's power, wealth, and strength depend on the industrial, moral, and intellectual capacity of the individuals who constitute it; and public education must have no objective other than to expand these forces of production, action, and direction, continually increasing the number of individuals who possess them. The dignity of the state, the glory of a nation, can now be measured only by the dignity enjoyed by its subjects; and this dignity can only be obtained by elevating moral character, developing intelligence, and directing that intelligence toward the organized and legitimate enactment of man's every faculty. There are, too, objectives of foresight to be considered in assuming responsibility for public education, in the sense that the masses are less inclined to respect lives and properties insofar as their reason and their moral sentiments are less cultivated. [. . .] If education does not prepare future generations for the necessary adaptations of the methods of labor, the result will be poverty and national obscurity, amid the development of other nations marching forward with the combined assistance of science and industry long since inaugurated, as well as the contemporary development generated by the public instruction that promises them progress and the growth of greater productive forces. [. . .] Available statistics on the degree of morality obtained by those who have received some elementary education further confirms the spirit's aptitude for improving individual condition solely by virtue of having been exercised. It suffices to observe what is apparent in armies and factories: that those who know how to read will dress themselves more tidily and are more orderly and methodical in all of their actions, and constantly aspire to better their lot. [. . .] Children's attendance at school generates the moralizing effect of occupying certain periods of time that would otherwise be spent in idleness and in neglect. Acculturating the spirit to the idea of regular, continuous obligations provides a child with regular habits; and incorporating an authority other than that of his parents, which does not always function consistently in shaping children's morals, helps mold the spirit to the idea of an influence beyond the household.

Translated by Robin Myers

Writing Becomes a Profession

José González Carbalho

The prolific print culture of the early twentieth century meant that the arts became an accessible pastime, if not necessarily a paying profession. In a short essay that speaks to the popularity of reading and writing during this period, José González Carbalho describes his childhood aspirations to be a famous poet and his disillusionment when he discovered that his favorite poet sat behind the desk at the kiosk down the street. Despite this early disappointment, Carbalho lived to see the career options for writers change considerably—he was a prolific poet and journalist who published in numerous Buenos Aires publications by the 1930s.

From a Castle to a Cash Register (1943)

José González Carbalho

In my avid reading at fifteen I would look over, week after week, the confessions of poets in a section that, more than its intimate attitude toward poetry and life, published the photograph of the author and one of their most characteristic poetic compositions.

[. . .] The story that Fernández told of his soul, of his dreams and aspirations, coincided with the idea that I formed of him as a person [. . .] an idea marvelously anachronistic and essentially poetic. [. . .] Thus, it was impossible to describe my surprise and anxiety when my sister, who also devoured the section called "Our Poets" told me one day after eating:

"Fernández lives on Bolívar Street, in front of the San Telmo market."

It was a surprise to think that such a person could live so close to our home, and I felt anxiety because right then and there I wanted to run out, fly to his home, and admire with my own eyes the gentleman, the page, hero, or poet that had deserved the honor of figuring in the anthology section. And so we went the next day. As we walked my sister told me:

"It's a little store."

"A store?" I asked.

I had thought of fortress walls and the drawbridges of a castle or a city house that had at least a tower. It was a tiny storefront, with a ramshackle counter.

. . . We had to enter the store to come face to face with Felipe H. Fernández, drinking in all of the intensity of emotion of coming so close to a poet and speaking with him. Arming ourselves with valor, we entered. The poet, very casual, was dressed in a striped shirt, slumped pants, and, we saw later, was wearing shoes like sandals; he raised his eyes at us, as if to ask a question. They were the visionary eyes of a poet . . . We stayed silent and he asked,

"What do you want?"

And my sister, with feminine resoluteness, spoke:

"Shoestrings."

Translated by Liliana Frankel

New Vanguards

Martín Fierro *and* Revista Claridad

For many generations, the intellectuals of Buenos Aires published niche magazines that reached small but influential audiences at home and abroad. Although the city had fostered a number of important writers in preceding decades, by the 1920s and 1930s a new generation of intellectuals from a broader range of social backgrounds was emerging on the scene. Their writing reflected new perspectives. In the 1920s, two parallel literary groups emerged: the Florida Group and the Boedo Group. Although they have been characterized as rivals, their members often collaborated. The Florida Group took its name from regular meetings held on the grand Florida Street downtown. The writers were avid vanguardists, eager to challenge tradition. Although their magazine Martín Fierro *never had anything approaching the number of readers of commercial presses, it made its impact in intellectual circles. By contrast, members of the Boedo Group were of more modest backgrounds; they took their name from the working- and middle-class neighborhood where they regularly met. The Boedo Group developed a realist style that foregrounded social issues, and in concert with the publishing house Claridad, its members emerged as public advocates for socially progressive thought.*

Martín Fierro *Manifesto (1924)*

Martín Fierro

"MARTÍN FIERRO" knows that "everything is new under the sun" if everything is seen with some up-to-date pupils and expressed with some contemporary touch.

"MARTÍN FIERRO" thus finds itself more comfortable in a modern transatlantic ocean liner than in a Renaissance palace, and it sustains that a good Hispano-Suiza is a WORK OF ART much more perfect than a chair from the time of Louis XV.

"MARTÍN FIERRO" sees architectural possibility in an "innovation" trunk, a lesson in synthesis from a "marconigrama," the mental organization of a "rotary press"; not that this impedes it from possessing—like the most important families—a portrait album, which it pages through, every so often, to discover itself through its forebears . . . or to laugh at its neck and its necktie.

"MARTÍN FIERRO" believes in the importance of America's intellectual contribution, before any scissor-cut to the whole umbilical cord. To accent and generalize other intellectual statements and the independence movement begun in this language by Rubén Dario, however, doesn't mean that we pretend to ignore that every morning we use Swiss toothpaste, towels from France, and English soap.

"MARTÍN FIERRO" has faith in our phonetics, in our vision, in our modes of being, in our ear, in our ability to digest and to assimilate.

Do you sympathize with "MARTÍN FIERRO"? Then join "MARTÍN FIERRO"! Subscribe to "MARTÍN FIERRO"!

Translated by Liliana Frankel

What Is Claridad (1926)
Revista Claridad

Claridad aspires to be a magazine whose pages reflect all the concerns of leftist thought, in all of their expressions. We wish to be closer to social problems than to purely literary statements. We believe that these struggles will be of more use for future humanity than literary disputes—not that we don't recognize that from a literary dispute, a new school might form which could interpret human expressions in a way more concordant with the reality of our times.

Translated by Liliana Frankel

Media, Gender, and Feminist Thought

Grete Stern and Feminaria

The women's magazine Para Ti *first appeared on city kiosks in 1922. Its subject was the local "modern girl," a new identity illustrated in fiction and consumer culture. New women's media shortly followed:* Idilio, *launched in 1948, mixed high culture with pop culture and generated a space for more sophisticated interventions. A section entitled "Psychoanalysis Will Help You," for example, remains one of the most original culture productions of this era. Women wrote into the magazine with accounts of their dreams and nightmares, and the psychologist Enrique Butelman, the sociologist Gino Germani, and the surrealist photographer Grete Stern offered interpretations. The result was a collection of texts and photographic collages that both represented and challenged the role of women. In particular, Stern's collages offered rather acerbic critiques of tensions and preoccupations surrounding "modern" femininity. In this image, Stern interpreted a reader's dream of being an electric appliance; she is portrayed as a physical object—a bedside lamp that could be turned on and off by her husband.*

In the 1960s, the mass magazine Claudia *arose as a novel representation of the modern woman, playing with the limits of social acceptability and gradually calling into question the basis of domesticity, but without straying too far from traditional ideals. Like many of the magazines that flourished in Buenos Aires, it also concerned itself with keeping up with the most contemporary cosmopolitan trends. At the end of the twentieth century, smaller feminist publications like* Feminaria *gained a place in the cultural pantheon by outlining new provocative feminist thought, grounding it in local experience.* Feminaria *also foreshadowed the importance of journalism and niche outlets for the circulation of feminist ideas. In this text, the editors of* Feminaria *describe language and publishing as part of an emancipatory project. These two ideas—the need for a feminist perspective in the press, and the power of language—remained key aspects of the contemporary feminist movement.*

Dream No 1: She Dreamed She Was an Electrical Appliance (1949)

Grete Stern

Sueño No 1: Artículos eléctricos para el hogar, by Grete Stern, 1949. Courtesy of the Galería Jorge Mara–La Ruche.

Language and Power (1988)

Feminaria

Feminaria is feminist but does not limit itself to a single concept of feminism. It is published three times a year and includes any type of writing that is not sexist, racist, or homophobic or does not express other kinds of discrimination. The magazine reserves the right to emancipate the language of submitted articles from any sexist element—for example, use of the word "man" as a synonymous for humanity. We believe that the relationship between power and knowledge is also expressed through language.

Translated by Lisa Ubelaker Andrade

The Pampa in the City, via Radio

Andrés González Pulido

Just after World War I, a handful of locals brought radio tubes and receivers to Buenos Aires from Europe. Three of those aficionados decided to set up a station in the Teatro Coliseo; they successfully broadcasted the opera Parsifal *and called themselves Radio Argentina. Despite having very few listeners, this early local adoption of new media technology drew interest. Over the next decade, radio audiences grew, and by the 1930s, radio access was close to universal in the city. New local genres of radio emerged. In 1934, the radio theater program* Chispazos de Tradición *(Flickers of Tradition) made its debut. Bringing a longer tradition of theater to the airwaves, the scripts told stories from the pampa, of heroic and villainous gauchos and ladies in distress, and often did so using stereotypical rural accents. The program also compelled urbanites, including recent migrants, to connect with national rural culture. Thus, while media produced in Buenos Aires often served to bring the capital city culture into homes across the country, radio also became a means for urbanites to imagine rural folkloric and gaucho culture as cornerstones of their own national identity. Shows like this one also made radio a new arena for the dramatic arts.*

Flickers of Tradition (1933)

Andrés González Pulido

[Sounds of horse galloping]

Doña Pancha: My old man!

Jacinta: Father!

Don Segundo: Din't you hear what I 'aid, Nazareno . . . Go'on and cut that ol' useless horse in pieces . . .

Rosaura: Wa'ch it, Nazareno, nobody touches tha' horse! Nobody!

Don Segundo: Move 'side then, Rosaura, I'll handle this!

Churrinche: My sister jus'aid that nobody touch the horse and nobody'll touch it. Not even you, father, 'tho I know y'would!

Don Segundo: Move aside, you li'l brat!

Doña Pancha: Segundo! This won't brin' 'appiness to our ranch. Be reasonable, my old man. Listen to yer Pancha, yer old lady, the one you've given all the years o' your life to.

Don Segundo: Pancha! . . . My old lady.

Translation by Wendy Gosselin and Jane Brodie

The Cinema, a Barrio Institution

José Pablo Feinmann

By the 1930s, neighborhood cinemas were a key part of city life. They were important spaces for families to go out and socialize, to see their neighbors, and be seen. Regardless of social class, moviegoers recall the outing as something of a "ceremony," a cause to dress up in one's most fashionable clothes. The writer José Pablo Feinmann recalls what it meant to go to the neighborhood cinema when he was a teenager. National and imported films first debuted in the more extravagant theaters downtown; two weeks later, they would make their way to neighborhood venues.

Villa Urquiza (2000)

José Pablo Feinmann

In Villa Urquiza there were movie theaters and pizza parlors, in Belgrano R there weren't—back in the '50s, that is. Belgrano R went from the train station back to Donado Street, and included—and this is key—San Patricio church. That meant that in the '50s a kid who lived near that church had two options if he wanted to go to the movies and get a few slices of pizza afterward: Cabildo Avenue or Villa Urquiza, where Edén Palace was not the only choice, but the obvious one . . . Us guys from Belgrano R would choose Villa Urquiza . . . It was a small theater (but in none of our memories is it remotely small) with a lot of doors, a poster for a movie on each. And the posters were full of bright colors, the actors' names in yellow letters clashing with bright red fires, shootouts, and explosions. That was where us guys from the '50s would watch cowboys movies (which most of us pronounced *kon-bois*), gangster movies (which is where we learned to say *hahns-ap*—it was not until much later that we learned, to our amazement, that it was "hands up"), and pirate movies. [. . .] And then, after the triple-feature matinee, we would cross back over the tracks to go to a pizza parlor on the corner where the Grand Bourg movie theater was. They made this thick-crust pizza that we would lift to our mouths on pieces of paper. It was so greasy that reddish oil, like the shrapnel in *The Black Swan* or *The Golden Falcon* or—even—*Red Eagle* (all of them pirate ships) would run down the palms of our hands onto our—if I am not mistaken—almost always blue shirts. And later, at dusk, we would come back down Olazábal Street, turn on Estomba until we would get to San Patricio church, near our homes.

Translated by Wendy Gosselin and Jane Brodie

The Buenos Aires Middle Class, on Screen

Atlántida

By the early 1960s, the television audience in Buenos Aires was sizable. One of the first popular series to re-create porteño *domestic life on the small screen was* La Familia Falcón, *a show sponsored by Ford Motor Company. Early advertisements for the program represented the Falcón family as "a family like all families, like yours, like any family in your neighborhood, that lives the life of all* porteño *families." The show depicted a "typical" middle-class Buenos Aires lifestyle; it played on local stereotypes but also reinforced a sense of middle-class identity. As the show's creators recount here,* La Familia Falcón *represented an important moment in Argentine television as it showed how the television drama could perform and dramatize shared experiences of current events on national television while capturing and circulating ideas of the so-called middle-class city.*

The Secret of La Familia Falcón *(1965)*

Atlántida

One day [writer and director Hugo Moser] had a great idea: to paint the portrait of a family and appeal to the middle class—the target audience—in such a way that everyone could identify with this painting in its *costumbrismo*, we could call it. And that's how the Falcón Family was born, a family that represents an incredibly curious phenomenon. It was a TV hit ever since its premiere on February 4, 1962. And its contract extends to 1966. A family that, in a slightly magical way, began to affect the lives of everyone who had any contact with them. [. . .] The story focused on direct plotlines, on scenes that may have been very commonplace, but which become extraordinarily compelling to a considerable mass of viewers whose attachment to the program, according to the statistics, never waned at all. [. . .] A competing channel scheduled a high-impact American show, *Combat!*, at the same time. Moser felt a chill come over him. "Relax, my boy," said Belilla [a colleague], patting him on the back. "Maybe men will watch [*Combat!*], but women will stick with us." To a certain extent, his prediction was wrong: much of the male audience continued to watch "the family." [. . .] Gradually, Moser intensified his "engaged" scripts, trying to express Argentine reality through the everyday ups and downs of "the family."

Translated by Robin Myers

Radio, Television, and Celebrity Culture

Carlos Ulanovsky, Clarín, and Beatriz Sarlo

The rise of commercial radio, a national film industry, and, later, television created new generations of local celebrities. The wealthy elite, who had previously appeared on newspaper social pages wearing the latest fashions, were gradually replaced by images of new heroes and starlets, many of them exceptionally talented individuals from modest backgrounds who rose to new status.

A few of these early stars retained their relevance for decades. Mirtha Legrand is the most iconic example: born in 1927, she emerged as a young radio star in the 1940s, appeared in films in the 1950s, and then found her way to television in the late 1960s. There she became host of the longest-running and most-watched talk show on national television, Almorzando con Mirtha Legrand *(Having Lunch with Mirtha Legrand); Legrand stayed on as host well into her nineties. For decades, viewers have tuned in to watch Legrand break bread and engage in prodding conversations with a table of illustrious guests—a mix of politicians, sports stars, actors, and other prominent figures. The photograph illustrates a typical scene from the show in the 1980s, and the accompanying texts by prominent cultural critics give two different perspectives on the show. In 1972, writer Carlos Ulanovsky ruminates on the show's growing audience and its conflicted reputation: it was a massive hit, a "must" for important guests, but many who awaited an invitation nevertheless criticized it as a flashy, unserious, and superficial display of elite hobnobbing televised to a mass audience. Nearly fifty years later, when the show remained an on-air success, Beatriz Sarlo contemplates Legrand's unparalleled stretch as a television celebrity.*

Lunch with Mirtha Legrand (1972)

Carlos Ulanovsky

She has had lunch with almost five thousand people over her 1,085 shows; even those who criticize her want to be invited to have lunch on television; even those who saw it as "trashy"; even those who laughed at her or spoke poorly of her behind her back accepted an invitation, probably because they knew "the whole country would be watching." [. . .] She had lunch on television at one o'clock in the afternoon. An hour of day when thousands of women in thousands of homes were performing—in a less sophisticated universe, with the smell of fried food instead of Chanel—the same ritual. [. . .] What would be the intrinsic interest of these lunches? [. . .] The interest was to see her and the acquaintances who visited her, to spy on them [. . .] to imagine oneself entering into the intimacy of a world that was far out of reach. To increase these fantasies, she always invited people who were "somebodies," people who had something to say. She never invited someone on the margins of society. She never rubbed elbows with outcasts, with people who were bad or simple. [. . .] Once, among her guests sat the director of the Neuropsychiatric Institute. Lunch was in full swing and several guests had already spoken. In an attempt to strike an informal tone, Legrand decided to discard the questions that had been prepared for her and to ask the doctor: "What's up, doctor? How are your loonies doing? Is it true that there are more and more crazies in Buenos Aires?" Annoyed, the guest only answered: "Yes, ma'am, and they are the ones watching your program right now."

Translated by Lisa Ubelaker Andrade

Mirtha Legrand and a Table of Guests on the Set of Her Show,
Almorzando con Mirtha Legrand *(1986)*

Clarín

Courtesy of *Clarín.*

Public Intimacy (2018)

Beatriz Sarlo

Her secret is a disciplined repetition. Read the news every day, go over her guests' biographies, decide on her dress and jewelry, which she changes various times over the course of a show, personally write up the list of guests [. . .] every week for four decades. Repetition like this could drive someone crazy if they did not have the strength to endure it. [. . .] She governs her body like a dancer or a top tennis player. No one has ever seen her get up from a table or interrupt a conversation to go to the bathroom. [. . .] An athlete has to be tough, unilateral, obsessive, unforgiving with herself, and Mirtha Legrand has been all of these things.

Translated by Lisa Ubelaker Andrade

An Open Letter to the Dictatorship

Rodolfo Walsh

*While the violent and damaging effects of state terror during (and in the years im-
mediately prior to) the 1976–83 civic-military dictatorship were felt immediately in
politically active circles, those stories were silenced in the media, which, at most, reported on "shoot-outs" between "leftist terrorists" and state agents, and said nothing
of the late-night arrests and disappearances taking place at increasing rates. Journalists who strayed from the official line were threatened with violence. Objectors, aware
of the costs of speaking out, struggled to find formats to transmit information about
what they knew to be occurring. Among them was Rodolfo Walsh, a journalist and
member of the Montonero group. Walsh began ANCLA, a clandestine news agency in
which people passed along information about who had been disappeared. The reports
included the plea "Reproduce this information, circulate it by any means at your
disposal: by hand, by machine, by mimeograph, orally. Send copies to your friends:
nine out of ten are waiting for them. Millions want to be informed. Terror is based on
lack of communication. Break the isolation. Feel again the moral satisfaction of an act
of freedom. Defeat the terror. Circulate this information." A year later Walsh penned
an "open letter to the military dictatorship" in which he addresses the authoritarians
directly and calls them out for their practices of torture, violence, disappearances,
and an economic policy that he correctly forecasted would leave the country in debt
and the people in poverty. After writing the open letter, a portion of which is included
here, Walsh was abducted and never seen again.*

Open Letter to the Military Dictatorship (1977)

Rodolfo Walsh

Press censorship, the persecution of intellectuals, the raid on my home in
Tigre, my dear friends who you have murdered, the loss of a daughter who
died in combat against you. [. . .] These are just some of the incidences that
has forced me, after freely expressing my opinion as a journalist and a writer
for nearly thirty years, to engage in this clandestine form of expression. The
first anniversary of this military junta gives cause to measure this government's actions and its official discourses and documents, where what you all
call certified facts are mistakes, and what you are willing to admit as your

mistakes are in fact your crimes, and events that you have omitted entirely are calamities. [. . .]

Fifteen thousand disappeared persons, ten thousand prisoners, four thousand dead, tens of thousands left landless—these are the bare numbers of this terror. The common prisons already overflowing, you turned military barracks into what are essentially concentration camps, camps where no judge, lawyer, journalist, or international monitor is permitted entry. The martial secrecy of these procedures, a silence invoked as necessary for investigation, has made most detentions abductions, permitted torture without limits, and executions without trial. There were more than a thousand requests for habeas corpus refused in the past year. For thousands of other disappearances, no request was filed in court, either because it seemed futile or because, after fifty or sixty lawyers who filed such claims were themselves abducted, it became nearly impossible to find a lawyer willing to do so.

In this way, you all have dusted off torture from its limit in time. As the detainee does not exist, there is no way of presenting him before a judge within ten days as is mandated by a law that has been respected even by the most repressive dictators of the past. [. . .]

This junta's order against publishing the names of those detained is in itself a cover-up of the systematic execution of hostages that takes place in deserted areas in the early morning hours; these have the pretext of bogus battle-scenes and made-up escape attempts. Reports about extremists spreading pamphlets across the countryside, painting over the irrigation channels, and then supposedly riding by the tens in cars that spontaneously catch on fire are based in stereotypes that are straight out of a propaganda leaflet, material that is not intended to be believable but only to mock the international outcry against these mass executions and underline the brutal, disproportionate nature of your retaliations.

Translated by Lisa Ubelaker Andrade

Humor under Censorship

Humor Registrado, *Andrés Cascioli, and Tomás Lüders*

*Humor Registrado was a magazine that built on a long tradition of Argentine com-
ics, using caricature and humor to comment on local society and politics. During
the civic-military dictatorship, critical commentary was violently suppressed by the
state. The magazine focused on economic and cultural issues in its initial editions,
but as its audience expanded, it grew bolder in its critiques. In this interview with
journalist Tomás Lüders,* Humor Registrado's *editor Andrés Cascioli describes the
conditions that helped the magazine grow and survive amid an era of violent repression. A magazine cover provides example of its sardonic commentary as the country
transitioned to democracy: its headlines read " . . . And They Told Us There Were No
More Kidnappings"; "Prohibited: To See, to Speak, to Listen."*

The Magazine Humor Registrado *Openly Mocks the Military
Dictatorship (1983)*

Humor Registrado, no. 98, February
1983, cover. Courtesy of Juan Izquierdo
Brown.

Laughter and Threats (2005)

Andrés Cascioli and Tomás Lüders

TL: It's been said that Humor *was able to publish what it did because it seemed to be a satirical magazine. That said, it published very sharp works of investigation into [the civic-military dictatorship]. How did you manage to withstand the pressure?*

AC: I think they warned us too late. As we grew and started to publish journalistic material condemning [the military government], we were already selling almost 200,000 copies. Besides, dissent within the government was widespread; to an extent, that's what stopped them. We know, for example, that Minister of the Interior Harguindeguy wanted to destroy us, and others told him that would be a scandal, because the Carter administration and the OAS [Organization of American States] were disgusted with the human rights violations. In any case, though, it wasn't easy, as you can imagine: there were incidents of harassment by phone, in the offices and at journalists' homes; we were "invited" for "friendly" chats, which we once attended; I had a car ram into me on the road; they confiscated an issue at the press—things like that.

Translated by Robin Myers

Broad Audiences and Burned Books

Amanda Toubes, Ricardo Figueira, Boris Spivacow,
and Delia Maunás

The publisher Centro Editor de América Latina (CEAL) was among the most impor-
tant to emerge in the 1960s. During the dictatorship of Juan Carlos Onganía, Boris
Spivacow, the founder of CEAL, describes this initial venture as part of a tradition of
reaching out to a broad readership, this time in the context of censorship and oppres-
sion. During the civic-military dictatorship (1976–83), the books served as symbols of
resistance. In turn, CEAL was targeted by the regime and was accused of publishing
subversive and dangerous material. On June 26, 1980, a judge ordered the publisher
to take twenty-four tons of CEAL books out of storage, drive them to an empty lot
and burn them. The photograph presented here is part of a series taken by Ricardo
Figueira and Amanda Toubes, two CEAL editors who were present at the burning
and were required to gather evidence that they had complied with the order. Figueira
offered to go himself, not wanting to expose a photographer, and Toubes volunteered
to come along, admitting later she wanted to "see the faces of those who burned our
work." Toubes can be seen in this photograph, walking through the piles of books.
Ownership of the banned books could be seen as a subversive action, and many stu-
dents and academics began to hide their own copies in secret locations.

Truckloads of Books Arrive to Be Burned by the Military Regime (1980)

Ricardo Figueira

Courtesy of the photographer.

Memoirs of a Publisher (1995)

Boris Spivacow and Delia Maunás

On September 21, 1966, we founded CEAL with the group that had revived EUDEBA, transforming it within just a few years into one of Latin America's major publishing houses. [. . .] In 1967, CEAL published the first weekly children's book collection to be sold in newsstands. [. . .] Since we didn't have the money to produce a big collection for bookstores, where sales are slow and it takes even longer to get paid, I thought of the kiosks. [. . .] That same year, we published "Capítulo: Historia de la literatura argentina" ["Chapter: The History of Argentine Literature"], the first weekly collection for adults—and, I think, the first collection in the world to sell both an installment and a book together. The installment accompanied the author's book, contextualized it. [. . .] it was an incredible success. We sold 100,000 copies of each of the first issues. [. . .] Other collections soon appeared, with varying degrees of success. [. . .] They included "Mi país, tu país" ["My Country, Your Country"], "Polémica: Historia integral argentina" ["Controversy: Comprehensive Argentine History"], "Transformaciones en el tercer mundo" ["Transformations in the Third World"], "Historia del movimiento obrero" ["History of the Labor Movement"], "Enciclopedia del mundo joven" ["An Encyclopedia of Youth"]. There were tens and tens of thousands of issues and books published, which always cost less than a kilo of bread, a pack of cigarettes, or a bottle of cheap wine . . . Both EUDEBA and CEAL published Argentine and international writers. The collections showcased thinkers from all over the world. That was an unusual thing. The French, the English, the Germans— they have incredible cultures, but they often scorn other cultures; they think they invented the wheel. Argentina knows it didn't invent the wheel. So it was a question of translating everything, translating from fifty different languages.

Translated by Robin Myers

Press under Dictatorship

Robert Cox and Luis Bruschtein

During the military dictatorship the press was heavily censored, and journalists who strayed from the political script were threatened, kidnapped, or killed. The English-language paper the Buenos Aires Herald *was a centrist paper that had long served the English-speaking community of Argentina; at first it did not disparage the military coup, but eventually it became one of the few publications to openly criticize the dictatorship and even print names of persons who had been disappeared. Many surmise that the paper was left largely unscathed because it was held in such high esteem in international and diplomatic circles, and it was also a rather niche publication, without a large local audience. Yet it was not left completely alone. Faced with threats of violence to themselves and their families, the paper's editors, Robert Cox and Andrew Graham-Yooll, both went into exile by 1980. Up until that time, Cox bravely printed what no other paper dared to, and several prisoners were released as a direct result of his editorial choices and advocacy. As Cox describes in this interview, the* Herald *staff was regularly threatened and monitored; the military appeared at the* Herald *offices to intimidate and interrogate them, detained Cox, and threatened with letters and explosives that sought to connect the paper to the antidictatorship groups*

Reporting Disappearances (2014)
Robert Cox and Luis Bruschtein

LB: When the dictatorship started, did you think you would have to close the newspaper?

RC: Not necessarily, but it was a risk. And it had been before, during Isabel [Perón]'s administration. That was when they showed up at the newspaper with machine guns and handguns. We'd built a new building near Customs. The first floor was open, under construction. Everyone was working when they showed up. We had a music critic named Fred Murray who'd fled Nazi Germany. He kept writing with all those armed guys pacing around. "What are you doing!" they demanded of him. And he answered in his German accent, "I'm writing about music." They couldn't control anything at all. The commander of the operation, who was dressed like a Scotland Yard detective, was surprised: "We were told this was a terrorist den," he said. They were looking for our editor Andrew Graham Yooll and I told them no problem, I'd call him. "Don't do that," he told me; "You'll alert him." I called Andrew and he came in with his wife. I insisted on accompanying him. They put us into those famous unmarked green Falcons and took us to the Federal Headquarters, which was later called the Superintendency of Federal Security. I waited while they interrogated Andrew and heard screaming down below, obviously from people being tortured, with the radio up all the way. That was 1975, under López Rega [before the military coup]. There were lots of episodes like that one.

LB: *Did you have those kinds of visits on the day of the coup?*

RC: No, because I think the military thought well of the newspaper before the coup. On the first page we'd publish the names of the victims of violence every day. We wrote who knows how many articles about the Triple A, the infamous Falcons without license plates. Once, we published a joke that went, "I went by the Casa de Gobierno and all I saw were six unmarked green Falcons; they're making progress, because the day before yesterday there were ten." On the day of the coup, they called us to say we were forbidden from publishing anything related to attacks, guerrilla activity, or bodies found in the street. We learned that the violence was unrelenting and getting worse. And people started showing up at the newspaper to report things. We also had our sources and foreign agencies. When the massacre of the Pallottine priests happened, foreign publications correctly reported that a far-right group was responsible, but here all the newspapers were saying that it had been an act of terrorism, the Montoneros. When people came to the offices to report things, I'd always ask them to present a writ of habeas corpus. The military forbade us from publishing news on kidnappings or dead bodies without official confirmation. We'd take a writ of habeas corpus as confirmation.

LB: *It wasn't long before they took you away, too . . .*

RC: When they came, I was working on an issue about the Dutch queen's birthday. I made them wait for me to finish, and I called Maud, to let her know. [. . .] They entered the Federal Headquarters through an underground route, and as soon as I got there I saw a huge swastika on the wall. They put me in a cell, naked, a sort of tube. It was a very difficult experience. I didn't know this at the time, but when they arrested me there was a major international backlash. I had contacts. Tex Harris, who was a fantastic guy, an American diplomat sent by Jimmy Carter and Patricia Derian, put in a lot of effort.

LB: Did they interrogate you about what they accused you of?

RC: They asked me ridiculous questions. They wanted to know what the newspaper's editorial line was, and I said it was "liberal," but European-liberal, centrist. Then they took me to the Sheraton, which is where the VIP prisoners were. I wasn't there for long. It was very useful, like going into the belly of the beast—I heard the screams of people being tortured there, too. I was there for three days. Their investigation was still ongoing when I was released; my father-in-law had to give up his 9 de Julio bonds as bail, and I got out. But the pressure continued.

Translated by Robin Myers

The Bookstore, a Downtown Institution

Jennifer Croft and Rubén Vela

Bookstores are a Buenos Aires tradition. Tourists still flock to some of the city's more impressive stores—the Ateneo Grand Splendid, for example, a converted theater, has been likened to a kind of cathedral of reading. Other bookstores offer a humbler setting but a nonetheless storied reputation. Used book fairs in Plaza Rivadavia and near Plaza Italia draw collectors and bargain hunters. The bookstores that line Corrientes Avenue are often open late into the night; shelves of used books, new books, and treasured antiquities run from floor to ceiling; tables are lined with cheap offerings. "Booksellers in Buenos Aires" offers a depiction of these types of stores in 1956. Though the twenty-first century has marked a decline in book reading, many of these institutions still draw crowds. Buenos Aires remains, by some counts, the city with the most bookstores per capita (twenty-five stores per 100,000 residents). Writers and readers have also found new venues; at cultural centers and street fairs, zines and small-press and self-published books are bought and sold. Once a year, the city celebrates the continued cultural importance of bookstores by restricting long stretches of Corrientes Avenue to pedestrians and allowing booksellers to extend their bookshops out into the street. As the photograph illustrates, crowds gather to peruse the offerings, listen to writers read from their work, and find bargains into the early morning hours.

Booksellers' Night on Corrientes Avenue (2016)

Jennifer Croft

Courtesy of the photographer.

Booksellers in Buenos Aires (1956)

Rubén Vela

Buenos Aires sometimes opens out into imaginary places. A city of unexpected destinations, it has kept for itself in every neighborhood, and with a final, secret pride, the deep individual preoccupation of its poets; the half-real, half-imagined world of its writers; and, in a general sense, the permanence-through-literature of the city itself. This is its most generous destination. Walking into each of the city's bookstores means walking into chaos. But into a different kind of chaos, something like the din of organized thinking. And that's where the bookseller is, ever-locked into a faintly lit smile. Because our city's booksellers are, with few exceptions, solemn-faced men who smile rarely, if at all. (Surely, they've been infected with the city's ancient face, the early colonial face that yielded a Buenos Aires teeming with candlewicks and shadows.) And the booksellers' lack of laughter—or, better put, their nearly priestly bearing—is their most praiseworthy feature. In this city, we love solemn men as we love gestures, ceremonies, and gray suits. And these are the very same characteristics that make certain bookstores settle into the intellectual inclinations of every neighborhood, opening branches in other states of things.

Translated by Liliana Frankel

VI

The City at Night

There are two Buenos Aires. One exists in the daytime. Another comes out at night and lives until the early morning, offering a parade of nocturnal traditions, from the rebellious to the mundane. There are hundreds of bars and clubs that open their doors as late as 2 a.m. and end their "night" at 8 or 9 a.m. There is also a tamer nocturnal city, lit up by twenty-four-hour flower shops, restaurants, theaters, and bookstores. While the darkness has long been a haven for thrill-seekers, there are diverse options of leisure for all, young and old. *Porteños* hone their ability to stay awake at all hours from an early age—family dinners can begin as late as ten in the evening, preteens are used to staying out until after midnight, and weddings, which include even the eldest generations, continue until seven or eight the next morning. Tourists are often shocked to find some of the city's restaurants still closed at 7:30 p.m.—considered too early to begin an evening out—or to find the elderly out on the town at 1 or 2 a.m. For some, the city at night is a playground of music, dance, sex, and drink; for others, it serves as host to the spectacles of opera, or more humble outings at a neighborhood theater or social club. Certainly, there have also been moments when this nocturnal city spun into a more austere darkness: times of dictatorship and repression when the night served as a cover for a far more ominous threat of state violence. Yet as democracy returned, the cultures of the night were again reinvented; while a few nocturnal customs are new, Buenos Aires's nightlife remains an enduring and essential component of its culture. (See "The City of Fury," the first selection below.)

From the Tango to the Colón

When did these nocturnal habits begin? Since the days predating the revolution for independence, cafés—as well as spaces like *pulperías* (rustic bars) and *fondas* (popular eateries)—stayed open through the night, drawing a faithful clientele.

At the end of the nineteenth century, cafés and other illuminated spaces used for dancing remained open late. During this era, the tango was also born on the outskirts of the city and in its poorest sections, popularized within the culture of the *conventillo* (tenement housing). The tango's stylistic heritage reflects the kind of cultural mixture that went on in nocturnal spaces of the city's periphery, known as the *arrabal*. The tango mixes the Afro-Argentine styles of *candombe* with musical instrumentation brought in by the city's immigrant communities; it also included a somber, lamenting lyricism.

As its popularity grew, a much-noted aspect of tango was the way it was danced: in an embrace, with both arms and pelvis in contact. The dance found its initial audiences in bars and brothels, but even by the end of the nineteenth century, its geography began to expand, prompting discussion of sexuality and "indecency." Even more than the sadness conveyed in tango's lyrics or the popular culture of which it was born, it was the overt sexuality of the dance's movement, at a time when sex was entering the public discourse (talked about in media, in literature), that set it apart from other kinds of music.

The dance became a part of cabarets in the city center and some nocturnal clubs. Cabarets were restaurants where orchestras played during the day, but at night they turned into a place where more transgression was possible: some came to indulge in sexual fantasies and, as the trend caught on, to dance tango. Young women did participate in these spaces—some as workers, but others as patrons, enjoying the thrills of the night, though not without raising questions regarding their moral character. (See "Tango and the Melodrama of the *Milonguita*.")

At the other end of the cultural map of Buenos Aires's nightlife at the turn of the century stood the adorned world of the city's historic high culture. The present-day Teatro Colón, a ravishing opera theater that *porteños* often reminded visitors was considered "one of the grandest in the world," opened its doors in 1908. Its regular schedule drew the wealthiest sectors out for glamorous nights, dressed in their finest imported suits, gowns, and furs. For the elite, the Colón was not only a key social center of high society but also, at least in their eyes, a testament to their arrival to the global stage. (See "Nights at the Colón.")

The dramatic arts were not only popular among the elite, nor were they exclusively found in venues that showcased Buenos Aires's accumulating wealth and prestige. In other less extravagant venues like the Politeama Argentino and the Coliseo, theater and opera found much broader audiences. In 1905, more than 2.5 million tickets to stage performances—dramas, comedies, operettas—were sold. On weekend evenings, larger venues offered elaborate productions, while in the city's neighborhoods, small stages hosted simpler performances. The diversity of venues made the theater a nearly

This photograph, taken on New Year's Eve in 1904, captures the city's well-to-do enjoying the night at a café on one of the city's major arteries, the Avenida de Mayo. Elegantly dressed men and women sit at café tables on the sidewalk, some accompanied by their children; a young working boy stands by, while another child, about the same age and dressed in a bow tie, sits with his parents. Although Buenos Aires's nightlife was yet to see its true heyday, one can already observe a lively street as well as the ways economic and social class divided experiences. *Source: Fin de año en la Avenida Mayo*, by Anonymous, 1904. Courtesy of the Archivo General de la Nación Argentina Dpto. Doc. Fotográficos. Inv: 153542.

universal enjoyment; this was particularly true before the age of film, but even in the decades after, theater retained its relevance, evolving into new formats and exploring new subjects. (See "Evening Theater, on Stage and in the Street.")

As electricity spread further across the city map in the first decades of the twentieth century, a more extensive nightlife expanded along with it. The timing was rather poignant: citizens and workers were making new (often forceful) strides toward greater political participation, organization, and with it, had more time to dedicate to leisure; the wealthiest sectors were enjoying a golden age of prosperity. Amid all these parallel changes, the night exploded as an interest—housing new more universal thrills, a growing entertainment industry, and new cultures of music, art, and dance.

The photographer Horacio Coppola became known for his images of the modern streets of Buenos Aires in the 1930s and '40s. Coppola's downtown Buenos Aires was busy, vibrant, modern, and seemingly in constant movement. His scenes set the darkness of the sky and the silhouettes of buildings against the grand illumination of street signs, a visual testament to the still relatively new electric nightlife. This photograph depicts the famous Florida Street at 8 p.m. *Source: Calle Florida a las 20:00 horas*, by Horacio Coppola, 1936. Courtesy of the Galería Jorge Mara–La Ruche.

The Erotic Night

These habits also pointed to the rise of robust mass-entertainment industries that began to populate the Buenos Aires night with options in the early twentieth century. Between the 1920s and the 1950s, the city's nocturnal offerings multiplied. Persons of all ages flocked to theaters and cinemas on the brightly lit Corrientes Avenue; they walked the avenue and ate at pizzerias and cafés, perused offerings at its many bookshops. By the 1920s, a new generation of middle-and upper-class youth also began to rebel against the typical conventions of high culture, turning away from the opera and toward new musical styles.

A poster announces what would be tango singer Carlos Gardel's final two shows in Buenos Aires, on September 9 and 10, 1933, in a theater in the neighborhood of Villa Urquiza. Not long after the show, while on tour, Gardel would die in a plane crash. Gardel remains the most popular and revered tango artist of all time. His image can be found emblazoned on photographs, paintings, and décor across the city. The poster reads, in part, "On Saturday the 9th (at night) and Sunday the 10th (vermouth and night) at the Cine 25 de Mayo. See the formidable debut of the greatest national singer, Carlos Gardel, accompanied by his guitarists Pettorossi, Barbieri, Riverol and Vivas. Carlitos Gardel will say goodbye to the public of Villa Urquiza before leaving for Hollywood and Europe." *Source:* Anonymous, Concert poster, September 1933.

Early tango had flourished in the brothels of the *arrabal*, but by the end of the 1910s and 1920s, young people who lived far from those neighborhoods were also beginning to travel to spaces where they could dance, hear music, and enjoy the cultures of the night without their decency being called into question. Lyrics were added to small orchestra tangos, and the genre erupted in popularity, launching new talents like Carlos Gardel into the limelight. By 1920, Gardel's music and his story captured the imagination of fans: he was an immigrant born into poverty on his way to international fame; he would soon become the most iconic tango singer of all time. The growing availability of the phonograph and the radio extended the tango's reach outside the downtown dance halls and into homes, as well as spaces far beyond Buenos Aires's borders. These sentimental tangos exalted the spirit of the Buenos Aires nightlife and made Gardel an enduring symbol of *porteño* identity. (See "The Iconic Gardel.")

Tango never lost its connection with the nightlife of the Buenos Aires underworld, but as it became popular in Paris and much of Europe, it (in turn) became well accepted among wealthier sectors in Buenos Aires. Jazz, an import from the United States via Paris, was also thriving among sectors of the elite and upper middle classes, while the tango was becoming more mainstream. In the 1930 and 1940s, *milongas* (tango dances) were held in more "respectable" dance halls, in neighborhood clubs, and at gazebos in public parks. (See "Decent Tango.") In the 1960s, as tango continued to change, spaces also opened where audiences could listen to the music without dancing at all. (See "Piazzola and the Reinvention of Tango.")

The sustained popularity of tangos and cabarets also gave way to another form of erotic, mainstream entertainment: the *revista* show. These variety shows made their debut in the 1920s at the Teatro Maipo, and they experienced various moments of heightened popularity over the following decades. The shows offered a mix of theater, dancing, and lewd jokes and were headlined by dancers with sparkling, sparse costumes. Patrons were not just men—to the contrary, some of the shows' most avid fans were women who headed out to enjoy its raunchy humor. The dancers, called *vedettes*, rose to become celebrities of pop culture; each show was headlined by a *supervedette*, who occasionally made the move from the stage to the silver screen, staring in tango-themed movies in the 1940s and 1950s, and films in the 1960s and 1970s. Such was the case of Nélida Roca, known as the "Venus of Calle Corrientes." Roca was "discovered" singing jazz at a nightclub and found quick stardom as the headliner of a *revista* show. Her fans, eager to see her sing and perform in bejeweled bikinis and extravagant feathered headdresses, sold out her performances. The kitsch sexuality of her *revista* performances catapulted the once-marginalized eroticism of the city's nightlife onto public billboards and into the realm of the acceptable. Moria Casán, a *supervedette* who headlined shows in the 1970s, also built a career in show business. She moved from the stage to television, where she built a multidecade career as a bold commentator; her unforgiving quips and outspoken public views also fueled her reputation as an advocate for sexual liberation and LGBTQ+ culture.

In these ways, Buenos Aires's nightlife forged rather accepted spaces for expressions of sexuality. Another ordinary part of this scene was the *telo*—a pay-by-the-hour hotel that provides *porteños* with an escape to engage in semi-clandestine sexual encounters. The *telo* is both a place of exciting nocturnal transgression and a rather mundane and accepted part of urban life. Although more than a few patrons hide away in *telos* to engage in affairs, most are lovers with no other place to go: adolescents and young adults still living with their parents, parents still living with their young children. Even the name *telo* reflects a joint sense of transgression and acceptability: while it is a known part of local vocabulary, *te-lo* is *hotel* spoken in reverse, or *vesre*,

The night offered entertainment options for all types of thrill-seekers. *Revista* shows were no exception, often drawing mixed crowds of women and men of many ages. These cabaret shows featured bejeweled dancers and a comic host who worked through a series of sketches with erotic endings. The theater program for the show *Aleluya Buenos Aires* at the emblematic Teatro Maipo sets the scene. *Aleluya Buenos Aires*. Program cover, Teatro Maipo, Buenos Aires, 1975.

a popular and very informal local code of speaking in which the syllables of common words are rearranged in order to allude to hidden meaning. (See "Sex, *Telos*, and Regulation.")

Oppression and Resistance

For much of the city's history, the night offered many spaces that toed the line between transgression and "decency," but ideas of what was moral or acceptable behavior was also made an issue of policy. During the 1930s, for example, the authoritarian government cracked down on the city's brothels and gambling houses, making both illegal. Brothels continued to operate in clandestine spaces known as *amueblados*; gambling was hidden from view. Other forms of sexuality and sexual expression also became heavily regulated by the state. Queer cultures existed across the urban map, though not without judgment, a history of restrictive policies, and oppressive policing. (See "Queer Nights, Policed.") In the 1960s, for example, conservative media heightened rumors that the number of gay men, referred to as *amorales,* was increasing alongside a culture of late-night orgies and "sexual deviancy"; in previous years, President Juan Perón had reacted to similar rumors by calling for the city's brothels to reopen, contending that the lack of female prostitutes was "to blame" for the "spread" of homosexuality. During the 1976–83 civic-military dictatorship, authorities made damaging links between open sexual expression (and particularly homosexuality) and a broader list of "behaviors" they deemed objectionable and politically "subversive"; during that era, the perception or rumor that an individual was not heterosexual became evidence of "deviance" and was noted in the files of several of the state's civilian targets.

The night also served as a cover for broader state violence and oppression. Military agents who kidnapped, tortured, and killed leftists and those they deemed "subversives" often began their operations at night. Nocturnal kidnappings became a regular occurrence. The state's grupos de tarea (task forces) would locate targets and often bring them out of their houses, or in the street, in the middle of the night, transporting them to clandestine detentions centers in unmarked Ford Falcons. (See "State Terror in the Dark.") Yet just as the night served as a cover for the state's terrifying acts against its people, so too did it provide shelter for ongoing acts of resistance. Night colors the memories of defiance: one local artist recalled gathering with friends to plan interventions of visual resistance in darkness, placing a memorial for the disappeared in the central plaza of her neighborhood and then fleeing so as not to be caught or recognized.

For others, it was music that allowed for the expression of resistance. In the 1960s and 1970s, the rise of rock and the reemergence of folk music marked the Buenos Aires night as the domain of the city's youth as never before. Though rock initially seemed to imitate US and British beat and youth cultures, local artists quickly found ways to define a unique style; their lyrics, in Spanish, began to contend with the city at their feet and its particular stories. As it came into its own, the geography of the new rock nacional (national rock) also changed: at first rock was seen as a bohemian, underground music played in specific cafés and bars—among them the legendary La Perla bar in El Once—but its popularity gradually pushed it into more transited venues: concert halls, parks, and even stadiums. The new sound's growing presence, and artists' ability to use lyrics to communicate personal poetic explorations as well as a generalized youth discomfort with the city's new realities, invited the observation that it was displacing the tango.

During the civic-military dictatorship, rock concerts persisted, although some popular haunts and gathering places were also closed and albums deemed "subversive" were removed from music stores. The state forced musicians to submit song lists for approval before any public shows. Nonetheless, lyrics of protest were obstinately produced by artists in exile; those still in Argentina used subtle allegories to color their lyrics. Songs were also reproduced by a public who memorized the melodies and lyrics and sang them at private gatherings. Much of *rock nacional* stayed on the periphery of politics, but near the end of the dictatorship, some of the most famous bands gave more adamant and daring testament to the cruelties of an era. *Rock nacional* has since become one of the cultural markers of the return to democracy, a massively popular genre that celebrated the resilience of rebellious spirit, launched new icons, and became an integral part of local identity. (See "Rebellious Rock.")

Folk music had a different trajectory, though it, too, became a form of resistance during the 1960s and 1970s. Rather than youthful rebellion, its emergence in Buenos Aires more closely reflected a history of migration; it accompanied the wave of migrants and laborers who had left provinces in the country's Interior and settled in the city's outskirts since the 1930s. The genre reached a wider audience when national radio programming featured key artists in the 1940s. From there its popularity skyrocketed: by 1948 the popular radio magazine *Sintonía* told readers that records by folk artist Antonio Tormo were outselling tangos. Around this time, spaces for folk dances known as *peñas* became incorporated into the city's nightlife, first in neighborhood clubs on the outskirts of the city and later in spaces closer to the city center. At these informal gatherings, folk musicians played and patrons danced *chacareras, zambas*, and *chamamés* while enjoying simple food and drink. By the 1960s, the genre was revived again when left-leaning youth held *guitarreada* gatherings, singing traditional acoustic songs as well as new tunes with lyrics that reflected a spirit of social justice. (See "Sounds of Folk Cross Social Lines.")

The Twenty-First-Century Night

In the wake of dictatorship, a reemergent nightlife stood to prove that the legendary Buenos Aires night would not just persist—it would flourish. *Rock nacional* was in its heyday. By the 1990s, new subgenres had also emerged; bands from working-class neighborhoods developed a new style known as *rock barrial* (neighborhood rock) in which a powerful lead voice sang slang-laced lyrics that referenced neighborhood identity and personal experiences of struggle in the neoliberal era. Unlike *rock nacional,* this new genre spoke to divided social experiences.

At the same time, in the 1980s and 1990s, *cumbia* regained an important role on the radio and in Buenos Aires nightlife. Argentine *cumbia* developed as a fusion of sounds that had been circulating in Greater Buenos Aires, brought together by new cultures of mixture and by waves of migration and immigration that had taken place over previous decades. As noted, migrants from the provinces of Argentina had brought the *cuarteto cordobés* and the folk style *chamamé* to Greater Buenos Aires, and in the 1950s and '60s these two musical styles mixed with *cumbias* played by immigrants from Bolivia, Peru, and other Latin American countries; a new music laced with local slang emerged, dubbed the *movida tropical*; dances in Greater Buenos Aires played the music in the 1970s, and the genre erupted into mainstream by the early 1990s, when *cumbia argentina* (Argentine cumbia) began to dominate the dance scene. The singer Gilda provided radio listeners with a less controversial rendition of the music; her hits became anthems at massive *bailantas,* dance parties held in converted garages or empty lots near railroad stations in Once, Retiro, and Constitución, points of connection between Buenos Aires's downtown and the greater metropolitan area. These parties were not without precedent: the first *bailantas* were held in smaller venues in Greater Buenos Aires long before they gained fame in the capital city. City concerts were more heavily policed and larger. In some, thousands of partygoers danced until the morning hours.

In the early 2000s, a new sound known as *cumbia villera* emerged in Greater Buenos Aires. Far from the romantic themes of Gilda's dance tunes, it described scenes of poverty, drugs, and street life in visceral terms. In the 2010s this local sound continued to mix with other globalized music styles like reggaetón—creating the *cachengue*—and hip-hop, which became reinterpreted into the innovative sounds of Argentine trap. Youth began to gather in plazas to rap, and by the late 2010s, rap battles in places like the central Parque Centenario became an anticipated event for artists. While local crowds gathered to watch, fans tuned in via social media from around the Spanish-speaking world. Global connections were instant: local artists went viral on social media, putting both their music and the Buenos Aires scene in the international limelight. (See "Global/Local Sounds: *Cumbia Villera* and Argentine Trap.")

These recent hits have also returned to a longtime theme: the all-night scene in contemporary Buenos Aires. In a 2022 collaboration between the Spanish singer Quevedo and Buenos Aires native Bizarrap, the singer tells of going out in Buenos Aires, and the chorus clicks, "We went out at one, the hits came fast and then it was three, we danced all night and fell asleep at ten"—it was a timeline *porteños* knew well (and became a fast hit at clubs). By the 1990s, *boliche*—a word once referenced in the world of the tango— was used to refer to a massive nightclub that hosted thousands. Clubs like these showed up across the city map. To name only a few, Paladium, located in Retiro, was known for a liberated bohemian style in the postdictatorship 1980s; in the 1990s, Morocco, a three-story club, hosted celebrities and thousands of patrons; in the early 2000s, The End, in Flores, offered cheap drinks and entry to all; multifloor Amerika in Almagro became an enduring site for LGBTQ+ nightlife; meanwhile a scattering of large venues cropped up along the Costanera, a riverside area in Palermo.

Most of these clubs followed a similar schedule, opening their doors after midnight, filling up at three, and staying open into the morning. Although class, genre of music, and *onda* (vibe) fragmented nights out, most young people shared similar habits: after eating dinner at nine or ten, they gathered for a pre-party, known as a *previa*, to drink cheap drinks like Fernet and Coke around midnight; then, they headed to a club of their liking no earlier than two and danced until they found their way home after daylight. (See "The *Boliche.*") Younger kids, ages twelve to fourteen, went out too, going unaccompanied to *matinés*, under-eighteen clubs that closed at the "early" hour of midnight.

In 2004, this widely accepted practice of all-night partying was temporarily put on hold when a tragic accident occurred at Cromañón, a club in the neighborhood of Balvanera. The venue was hosting the *rock barrial* group Callejeros, performing in front of a crowd of three thousand people, when someone lit a flare and the highly flammable ceiling caught fire. Several of the doors were chained shut; the patrons stampeded out of the ones that were still unlocked, and 194 died from carbon monoxide poisoning. The tragedy spurred national debate.

Notably, the conversation that ensued did not criticize the young people's nocturnal habits. No one questioned whether the Buenos Aires night should go on. Rather, the debate centered on a sense of disgust at the state and the club's owners: the former had approved the precarious construction materials; the latter had built and packed the club without regard for safety. The event emerged as a symbol of deregulation and failed infrastructure following the neoliberal 1990s and the 2001 economic crisis. As debate ensued over culpability and a city mourned its youth, it was clear the nocturnal "city of fury" would carry on.

The City of Fury

Manuel Romero and Gustavo Cerati

These two odes to the Buenos Aires night were written decades apart, but they both capture the feeling that the city has a double life—one takes place during the day, and the other is found in the pleasures and escapism of its after-hours. The first text, "Buenos Aires Nights," is taken from the tango "Noches de Buenos Aires," written in 1937, and describes the night to be a place of pleasure and pain. The second, "In the City of Fury" is an excerpt of a rock hit ("En la Ciudad de la Furia") performed by the band Soda Stereo and written by Gustavo Cerati in 1988; it was also mentioned in the introduction to this Reader. *The two writers describe feeling captivated or seduced by the Buenos Aires night, as part of a nocturnal crowd but also alone; they allude to the eroticism and notions of transgression that the night makes possible, and at the same time, they find a sense of peril there: a poison for Romero, and, for Cerati, the mixed thrill of flying above the night, and then—as in the legend of Icarus—falling when the rising sun burns his wings.*

Buenos Aires Nights (1937)

Manuel Romero

Buenos Aires nights,
your captivating spell
burns a seal of emotion,
in my song.

With your mysterious perfume
I feel a strange palpitation,
Buenos Aires nights,
[in my] heart.

You have always held pleasure
right along with pain,
happiness the sibling of sorrow.
Beneath the glitter
of your colorful lights,
the air intoxicates and poisons.

The illusion of youth is tied
to the bitter old age of Don Juan,
and the one who cries for bread
and who cries for love,
bound together, forever.

Buenos Aires nights,
so much pain
in your courtesan's laughter
in the bitterness of every kiss.
The nightly caravan passes
wrapped in shadows and shine,
Buenos Aires nights,
looking for love . . .

Translated by Wendy Gosselin and Jane Brodie

In the City of Fury (1988)

Gustavo Cerati

You'll see me fly over the city of fury;
where no one knows who I am
and I'm part of all of them.
Nothing will change,
with the warning of curves ahead.
In their faces, I see the fear
There are no more fables left to be told.
In the city of fury, you'll see me fall
like a bird of prey.
You'll see me fall onto deserted terraces
You'll be undressed by the blue streets.
I'll take refuge before they all awaken. [. . .]
A winged man longs for the earth
you'll see me fly across the city of fury.
Where no one knows who I am
and I'm part of them all.

In the sunlight my wings melt
Only in the dark of night
do I find what binds me
to the city of fury. [. . .]

Buenos Aires looks so vulnerable,
it is the destiny of the fury
that lingers on their faces.

You'll let me sleep at sunrise between your legs;
You'll hide me well and disappear in the fog
A winged man prefers the night
And you will see me return
to the city of fury.

Translated by Wendy Gosselin and Jane Brodie

Nights at the Colón

El Mosquito *and Manuel Mujica Lainez*

The new Teatro Colón was inaugurated in 1908, just in time for the celebration of the centennial of Argentina's independence, in 1910. Its design drew comparison to the great concert halls of Paris and Vienna; evening shows were known for their grandeur. As these documents show, while the building spoke to elite aspirations, the theater and the opera both drew audiences and performers from a wider cross section of society. Smaller performance houses were also flourishing, attracting less elite audiences. In "The Politeama Theater," the magazine El Mosquito *observes a diverse audience at an opening night in 1879. In "To Colón," a fictionalized narrative by the writer Manuel Mujica Lainez, the narrator discovers the elitist lexicon of the Teatro Colón in the 1940s. The theater remained a place where the middle and lower classes were in attendance but also where the wealthy and elite made their status known.*

The Politeama Theater (1879)

El Mosquito

Above the box seats are the balcony galleries, likewise, occupied largely by ladies, though not attired in evening gowns, but rather dressed for a stroll or for receiving guests . . . Higher still, a small row of gradated seats with nearly equal numbers of gentlemen and ladies. Here, the categories are less distinct; the clean, simple garb of the wife of the clerk or the humble worker brushes against the somewhat more costly attire of the bourgeoisie, and the neighbor's frock coat fraternizes easily with the master craftsman's new jacket . . . Paradise: a homogeneous row of men garbed in various manners, dominated nonetheless by somber colors.

Translated by Robin Myers

To Colón (1979)

Manuel Mujica Lainez

"We say 'to Colón,'" María Zuñiga added, with the definitive emphasis of someone putting an end to a debate . . . and this time she emphasized the *we.* The teenager went mute. *We,* he thought. *We* would mean the Gonzálvez and the Zuñigas? And there will be some others. Those who don't say *to the Colón* (as it should be) but *to Colón* (like *we* say it). Do *we* say it this way to distinguish ourselves? Is it code? Do we talk in code? And Salvador promised himself that from that moment on he would keep an eye on who said "to Colón." This would help him classify them. Still, he was ashamed he had not been initiated into this particularity by his own clan, his own people, his *we.* He gazed around and wondered if those around him were part of the *we.*

Translated by Claudio Bezencry

Evening Theater, on Stage and in the Street

Leónidas Barletta, Clarín, and Carlos Somigliana

When theater became a popular venue for entertainment in the nineteenth century, it gave rise to an important subculture that reached broad audiences. Neighborhoods began hosting small productions in the first decades of the twentieth century, and as venues became more numerous, writing plays and acting also became a common pastime. Performances also reflected changing demographics and culture. Early theater was characterized by the gauchesque play, a genre that foregrounded the legendary rural Argentine horseman, the gaucho, as a protagonist. The zarzuela madrileña highlighted local cultural connections to Spain. New styles, including the criollo sainete and the criollo grotesque, replaced the gaucho protagonist with the figure of the immigrant: the gallego, the turco, the ruso, and the tano all took to the stage, speaking in lunfardo (local slang) and cocoliche (a style of speaking with mixed languages). Theater's popularity grew— companies put on three shows every night of the week: a matinee, a vermouth, and a night show; scripts could be bought at any bookstore or kiosk. Over the following decades, the independent theater movement was founded at the Teatro del Pueblo (The People's Theater), offering shows that its writers believed would "counter" the commercial theater movement that had taken off on flashy Corrientes Avenue. In the first text, "The People's Theater," playwright Leónidas Barletta, an organizer of the Teatro del Pueblo, describes the group's mission. By the 1960s, the theater was a complex space for cultural expression; during dictatorships, it was pushed underground. In 1981, the opening of Teatro Abierto (Open Theater) at the Teatro del Picadero (Picadero Theater) marked the aboveground debut of a theater movement that had been, until then, meeting in secret to circulate ideas and writings, despite state repression. The group organized a series of shows that would take place in the early evening. This act of rebellion and expression was not tolerated by the civic-military dictatorship. At four in the morning, a week after their grand opening, the theater was set on fire. The fire drew the attention of international artists and writers, creating a backlash that mounted support for the project. When it resumed at another location shortly thereafter, it was a powerful symbol of resistance. In "Teatro Abierto," its leaders declare its purpose; in the photo, actors from the group parade in the streets amid the transition to democracy, celebrating the return of a vibrant independent nightlife.

In the postdictatorship era, theater again began to thrive; some productions had great commercial success, like Bertolt Brecht's Galileo Galilei, *which sold 200,000 tickets when it was performed at the Teatro San Martín; San Telmo's Parakultural became a hub for experimental theater. Today, city residents make use of over three hundred theaters—historic theaters, large-commercial theaters, and independent venues, many located in residential neighborhoods.*

The People's Theater (1938)

Leónidas Barletta

When we decided to establish the Teatro del Pueblo (People's Theater) to counter the effects of an artless theater scene twelve years ago, we did not ignore the fact that we were confronting an enemy superior in number and in resources that would not hesitate in going to all extremes to block our initiative. At first, they ignored us. And when it was evident they had to recognize our existence, they did so with a guarded irony. We worked in silence, in obstinance, with the understanding smile of someone who had foreseen, measured, and weighed everything. Our will and our optimism grew stronger as we discovered in the burning eyes of anonymous spectators that we were not wrong, that the people embraced this theater of youth with a loving bond, without the failures that had taken the virtue out of this art and transformed it into a kind of grotesque instrument of commerce.

Translated by Lisa Ubelaker Andrade

Actors from the Theater Group Teatro Abierto Parade Down a City Street (1983)

Clarín

Courtesy of *Clarín*.

Teatro Abierto (1981)

Carlos Somigliana

Why are we creating Teatro Abierto? Because we want to demonstrate the existence and vitality of the Argentine theater, so often denied; because the theater is a cultural phenomenon that is above all social and community-based, we are attempting to recover its mass audience through high-quality shows offered at a low cost; because we believe that all of us together are more than the sum of each of us individually; because we want to exercise our right to freedom of speech in a mature and responsible way that liberates us from confines of commercialism; because we believe that our fraternal solidarity is more important than individual competition; because we painfully love our country and this is the only homage that we know to give it; and because, above all other reasons, we are happy to be together.

Translated by Lisa Ubelaker Andrade

Tango and the Melodrama of the *Milonguita*

Samuel Linning

Tango lyrics often referenced a city nightlife made up of bars, brothels, and improvised dance halls. In these songs, characters like pimps, lady's men, and tough guys became part of an urban mythology. The milonguita *was one such persona. In the real world of tango,* milonguitas *were women who danced tango. Many engaged in sex work, and some were called* queridas *(lovers); others were simply tango singers, or regulars on the dance scene. When represented in stories and in tango lyrics, however, the* milonguita *was a melodramatic character. This tango by writer Samuel Linning offers a common storyline: a young, innocent woman from a "good" and humble home exhibits a rebellious and adventurous spirit; she seeks to escape the rather strict moral gaze of her family and neighborhood. Hers, like many youthful stories of nightlife, was told as a journey of transgression and plight: she was seduced by the night and became a* milonguita. *In many such tales, she fell from grace, ending up on the margins of society, a poor prostitute sick with tuberculosis; the disease represented both a physical and moral punishment. This storyline—always written by men—warned young women of the perils of nightlife while revealing male anxieties about changing gender norms. In reality, however, things did not always end so disastrously; for some women, tango offered not only the lure of rebellion but also the chance for independence, even some wealth, or, at least, a pleasurable escape.*

Milonguita (1920)

Samuel Linning

Milonguita, do you remember? You were
the prettiest girl on Chiclana Avenue.
with your short skirt and braids,
your sun-kissed braids.
And on those summer nights, woman,
what was your little soul dreaming of
when on the corner you'd hear some tango
whispering to you of love?
Little Esther,
today they call you Milonguita,

flower of the night and pleasure,
flower of luxury and the cabaret.
Milonguita,
men have done you wrong
and today you'd give your soul
to wear a simple cotton dress.
When you emerge at dawn,
Milonguita, from that cabaret
your soul trembling from the cold,
you say, "Oh, if only I could love!"
And between the wine and the last tango
A rich guy whisks you off to his room . . .
Oh, little Esther, you feel so all alone!
If you cry . . . they say it's the champagne!

Translated by Wendy Gosselin and Jane Brodie

The Iconic Gardel

Edmundo Eichelbaum and Juan José Sebreli

Not long after the tango took off as a popular music and dance, lyrics became an important component of the genre. It was Carlos Gardel who most marked this change. Gardel's life story also resonated with audiences: his fans saw in him the success story of an ordinary man who grew up poor and, thanks to his voice, talent, and drive, found fame, fortune, and universal respect. He was known for his suave masculinity, his generosity, his humility, his iconographic dress, and his voice; unlike other icons of Argentine culture, Gardel was embraced by all social sectors as a kind of timeless soul. One popular saying insists, "Gardel sings better every day," suggesting he has become immortal. In this excerpt, journalist and critic Edmundo Eichelbaum and essayist Juan José Sebreli contemplate how Gardel became synonymous with urban folklore culture—they note that Gardel's talent, combined with his modest origins, allowed him to forge and represent a unique local identity.

Gardel and the Elite (1977)

Edmundo Eichelbaum

[Gardel] was interested in individual advancement, and as an artist on his own. In that sense, too, he did not distinguish himself from the average type of person he had encountered in the *conventillo*—the type of person who aspires to overcome his class through personal success, economically or vocationally speaking. If he was sensitive to certain collective dramas (and tangos mention these things, sometimes in protest but always as an inevitable fatality in society), this was a manner appropriate for the self-made man of those times, incapable of conceiving social protest movements from the viewpoint of the masses. He had accepted the paternalism of others, to help him in his rise to fame, and later on he too was paternalistic, when his means permitted.

Translated by Liliana Frankel

Gardel as Symbol (1964)

Juan José Sebreli

Gardel is the symbol of the hallucinatory dreams of underdogs, who hate the rich because they themselves cannot be rich. He is someone who has "arrived" and by arriving has avenged those who never could or did. He is someone who has risen from the tenements of Abasto to the dazzling banqueting table of the great international bourgeoise.

Translated by Liliana Frankel

Decent Tango

Clara Gertz

*During a brief economic dip in the 1930s, the city's entertainment offerings dimin-
ished and then revived. When they resumed, the tango gathered new momentum. Radio played an important role. The new technology was already popularizing artists
like Gardel, but by the end of the 1930s new programs called* bailables *(for dancing)
hosted larger orchestras and drew bigger audiences. Scheduled after soccer matches on
Sunday, the shows offered hours of tango music and changed the geography of tango
by permitting its sounds to move from the late-night bar scene and into the family living room and the neighborhood social club. In this transition, tango became "decent."
Some saw this mass popularity as a point of decline—the writer Ezequiel Martínez
Estrada recalled the talent of artists from the previous era and lamented that the
modern tango, in reaching its apex of popularity, lacked its former expression. "Decent tango" was accessible and inclusive of those who were not expert dancers, and
its appearance in neighborhood social clubs and family events meant it lost some of its
former spirit of transgression. Dancers established new codes about touching. There
were also other innovations: some neighborhoods developed their own styles, making
their tango unique. In this interview, a lifelong fan of tango who grew up in La Paternal neighborhood in the 1920s and '30s recalls hearing it on the radio and at dances.*

Dancing Tango (2018)

Clara Gertz

When I started going out to dance the orchestras were already well established. This would have been in the '40s. There was [Juan] D'Arienzo's orchestra, [Aníbal] Troilo's, and many others. Each with a more or less defined
style of its own. At first, I liked [Carlos] Di Sarli's, but then I became more
partial to [Osvaldo] Pugliese's. You had to be a follower of one orchestra or
another. Almost like with a soccer team, but without all the competition. It
was a matter of taste and loyalty; it wasn't about winning or losing. I think I
became a follower of Pugliese more for the rhythm than for the lyrics. I also
liked some of his singers. When Pugliese's orchestra finished a piece, we supporters would religiously applaud and shout "To the Colón [Theater]! To the
Colón!" Everyone shouted it, both those of us who'd come to dance and the

others who'd just come to listen. It was a way to acknowledge the quality of his performance, and to emphasize that he deserved to play there, in the very same place as the great classical music orchestras. [. . .] I grew up listening to the radio. My brother taught me to dance tango in the yard, in La Paternal neighborhood, listening to the radio. On the radio, I found all the most important orchestras with their male singers. But you could also hear the female singers. They were the center of it all. Some of my girlfriends in the neighborhood liked Libertad Lamarque. But I didn't. I found her too shrill and she put on airs. I liked Tita Merello better. She sounded more down-to-earth, more real.

Translated by Robin Myers

Piazzola and the Reinvention of Tango

Diana Piazzola

The musician and composer Astor Piazzola bridged the genres of tango, classical music, and jazz. Along with a handful of musicians of his generation, he transformed tango; it became a type of music that audiences could gather and listen to without dancing. Amid this reinvention, the tango was also facing disinterest from younger generations. In 1963, the magazine Primera Plana *confirmed that few young people knew how to dance tango anymore; folk and rock were more popular in clubs and bars across the city. By the end of the 1980s, tango enjoyed another revival, restoring it to a role in the Buenos Aires night. In this reinvention, tango became an intergenerational dance, bringing together old and young. Today tango is both a dance enjoyed by locals at milongas, a musical scene with regular concert performances, and an international attraction: the world championship of tango has been hosted in the city since 2003, drawing hundreds of thousands of competitors from around the world. Here Astor Piazzola's daughter and biographer, Diana Piazzola, recounts how her father discovered new sounds within an old genre.*

Astor (1992)

Diana Piazzola

As he progressed in his classes with [Alberto] Ginastera, as he discovered new sounds and modern harmonies in [Béla] Bartók and [Igor] Stravinsky, Astor started to feel that something was splitting in half inside him. His tango-fate tugged at him, hurt him, dragged him into the night. His counterpart—dreaming of sonatas and grand pianos, ashamed of tango music and the bandoneón [a kind of accordion]—grew up and sought out the day . . .

"Ginastera stimulated me, shook me, showed me the way. [. . .] He taught me composition, orchestration, harmony, theory. [. . .] And I started resenting the cabaret, the musicians who didn't study the night. They noticed and a secret conflict began. [. . .] They were bothered by the fact that I was studying [. . .]."

One day Astor stood up in front of Aníbal "Gordo" Troilo—the conductor of the orchestra—and told him, "I want to write arrangements for your orchestra." Gordo said no, don't even think about it. [. . .] But Astor persisted.

[. . .] Later, on the occasion of a radio contest, he told Gordo that he wanted to arrange the *candombe* "Azabache." Troilo said no, that he didn't have enough experience. Astor said yes, he could do it. Troilo finally relented. [. . .] Piazzolla's arrangement won first place in the contest. After he received the prize, Troilo said, "It was fine, Gato, but that's enough now. I liked it, but those violins doing high scales—they don't belong there. The musicians can't pull it off; they muddy the waters. Besides, people want to dance, not sit and listen to a concert." [. . .] Ultimately, Astor decided to leave the orchestra: "I can't stand it anymore. I'm going to start my own orchestra, and no one will change my arrangements there."

Translated by Robin Myers

Sex, *Telos*, and Regulation

Fernando S. and César A.

An iconic space of the Buenos Aires night, telos *are pay-by-the-hour hotels, used for sexual escapes. The word* telo *is a play on the word* hotel, *spoken in a local urban slang that rearranges the syllables of words. Though widely used for many decades,* telos *were not always openly embraced elements of city culture. In 1960 and 1961 the federal police conducted over seven hundred operations in* telos *in what they called a "morality" campaign—the police detained thousands of couples for engaging in relations without a marriage license, even calling the husbands of married women to inform them of their wives' infidelity. The morality campaign was extended into other public spaces; women were detained in the street if they were found wearing miniskirts, or were asked to lower the hem; young men with long hair were subjected to haircuts. As noted in the following selection in this part ("Queer Nights, Policed"), gay spaces were particularly targeted. In "Memories of Telos" and "Sex and Discretion" a man who frequented* telos *and a* telo *operator recall their experiences.*

Memories of Telos (2018)

Fernando S.

When I was a teenager in the early 1970s, *telos*—both the ones in my neighborhood and the ones I would see out the bus window on my way downtown, where my high school was—were something looked at from afar. Minors were not allowed in, which meant that they had to find somewhere else to go, usually the homes of friends with tolerant or absent parents. Because of that restriction, *telos* were intriguing places, places to give free rein to our imaginations, to imagine ourselves as adults. *Telos* with their elaborate furnishings—the walls and ceiling lined with mirrors, the strange lighting—were an essential part of a teenager's fantasy world. TV and the movies did their part as well, especially since scenes that took place in *telos* were beginning to appear. Later, when age was no longer an issue, *telos* became much more mundane, places where sexuality was experienced rather than fantasized about. I remember that the first one I visited had very few mirrors; it was shabby and in no way lived up to the rooms I had imagined. I soon learned that there were *telos* to suit all pocketbooks, and that it was best to check in late at night so that paying for just two hours would get you a room until the next morning. During the military dictatorship activists would go to *telos* because it was thought they were safe places to spend the night, but there were plenty of raids where undercover cops would knock on the doors of rooms asking couples to show their IDs.

Translated by Wendy Gosselin and Jane Brodie

Sex and Discretion (2018)

César A.

In the '60s, *telos* were a sanctuary for secret love. In the '70s, despite military rule, they became widespread. They were usually places for heterosexual couples only, though. In the late '80s and '90s, they began to offer novel attractions like hot tubs and theme rooms. Now they offer Wi-Fi. But what has always mattered most, then and now, is discretion, and for that covered parking spots directly outside the room are essential. Twenty or thirty years ago, *telos* were a place for two-timing, a place where lovers would meet or prostitutes turn tricks. That's still true, but *telos* are also frequented by married couples that want to mix things up a bit. Some say that *telos* will soon disappear, that they are no longer a viable business because they have ceased to stir desire or a sense of transgression. Or simply because customs have changed. They are no longer very profitable—it's true—and where there were once *telos* there are now apartment buildings. The business, I think, is just undergoing a restructuring. Because people have always screwed—that's not going to change.

Translated by Wendy Gosselin and Jane Brodie

Queer Nights, Policed

Luis Troitiño, Juan Queiroz, Cristian Trincado, and María Luisa Peralta

In 2007 the New York Times *hailed Buenos Aires as a "beacon" for gay tourists, and in 2011 Spain's* El Mundo *echoed that the city's inclusivity made it "paradise" for gay tourism in Latin America. Legal and social advances sparked this international reputation: in the early 2000s, Argentina passed some of the world's most progressive laws regarding gender and sexuality. Gay marriage was made a legal right in Argentina in 2010, and laws were later modified so persons could easily change their recorded gender or elect a nonbinary option on state identification. Although experiences of discrimination remain a part of daily life, a large, diverse* LGBTQ+ *community and a long history of queer activism had made significant inroads in local culture, where acceptance had become quite common.*

The city's nightlife, in particular, offered many spaces for community building, joy, and expression. But as the testimonies included here also recall, it was as recently as 1998 that law enforcement was finally stripped of the legal power to raid gay cultural spaces, police gender expression, and make arrests on the grounds of regulating "morality." These accounts, compiled and published by the queer archive Moléculas Malucas, *describe how* LGBTQ+ *peoples in the 1950s, 1980s, and 1990s enjoyed the Buenos Aires night while also navigating oppressive encounters with the police. In the first, Luis Troitiño, a cofounder of one of the first gay rights groups, describes, in a conversation with archivist Juan Queiroz, both the spirit of a night at the theater in the 1950s and regular encounters with police; in the second, the dancer and* DJ *Cristian Trincado describes how a nightclub became a site of resistance in the 1980s; and in the third, María Luisa Peralta, an activist and writer, describes the scene when police raided a lesbian bar in the 1990s.*

Policed Nights in the 1950s (2020)
Luis Troitiño with Juan Queiroz

We went often to Teatro Avenida, a theater in the city center where the big Spanish companies would perform. We were always up in the high seats, in what is called "the *paraíso*" [paradise] section, it was full of gays, and when the castanets began to click, those *locas* [crazies, a slang term meaning "queer men"] with their Manila shawls bothered everybody, and the public down below, furious, would ask us to be quiet [*laughs*]. The Paraguayan *marica* [slang for "queer man"] La Mendieta was always there and was obsessed with the Manila shawl and stood up on tiptoes because she was so small. She had a beautiful voice and we'd make her sing "Galopera" by Cardozo Ocampo, so she might run out of air but she always did it full of gusto [*laughs*]. At the exit we would go to the Politeama *confitería* [café], which was next to the theater, or to El Cortijo, a bar at the intersection of Avenida de Mayo and Santiago del Estero, where all the Spaniards from the theater troupes went, and it was just full of *maricas* that made such a scandal inside and on the street. [. . .] Sometimes outside of the theater there would be arrests but you have no idea how much self-confidence they had as they confronted that situation, each of them getting in a police car with their heads held high and sure of themselves, their faces done up and their shawls.

Memories of "Area" in the 1980s (2021)

Cristian Trincado

The return to democracy was incomplete for dissident, nonheteronormative communities. One had to be brave and courageous to face the night in those years. Up until 1998, the police decrees were still in place [and one could be arrested] under the pretext of inciting a carnal act or wearing clothes of the opposite sex. The Morality Division of the Federal Police would ambush places where *maricas* [slang for "queer men"], *tortas* [slang for "lesbians"], or *travestis* [a Latin American term meaning "trans women"] were gathering, they would put their jail cars right at the door to load them up with *amorales* [unmorals], as they called us in the press back then, and send them to the police precincts. In this light, and for those of us who had the fortune of being there, the Area nightclub (1985–89) occupies a place in our memory as a site of resistance during a repressive time. It was a place where our struggles converged, in the place of individual liberties and activism by and of itself, without flags. It was at Area, which was inaugurated in March 1985, where what would be later labeled as an "underground" scene really emerged: polysexual, multi-social, and multicultural.

The Last Raid on a Lesbian Bar (2021)

María Luisa Peralta

On April 15, 1995, there was a police raid. They still occurred relatively regularly at the gay clubs and in those for gay and trans persons. This one, nonetheless, was a remarkable raid because it would be the last one at a lesbian club in Buenos Aires; later [lesbian bars] would have their economic ups and downs but would open largely without police threat (even though they would continue to have to pay the police bribes). [. . .] [The police] would turn off the music, turn on the lights, and separate men on one side and women on the other and put us in a line. Besides the Morality [police division], the neighborhood police would also come, even though we paid them the monthly bribe that they demanded. They would enter in the middle of the night, completely unprompted, and there was nothing you could do then; when they came, they came [. . .].

Liliana Furió [. . .], who often went to the bar and was there that night, remembers it like this: "The night in Boicot began divinely, dancing, drinking something, we introduced [some Paraguayan girls we met] to some friends and the more formal one had never been in a lesbian bar and was completely obsessed. All of a sudden, while we were dancing with our drinks in hand, we started to hear shouts, there were strange movements, furniture being moved: "The *cana* [slang for police] got in! Run, the *cana* got in!" In a second of distraction, I lost sight of the Paraguayan girls and then I desperately started looking for them because I felt a sense of responsibility. All of a sudden, I see the police twisting the girls' arms and putting them against the wall to take them."

Translated by Lisa Ubelaker Andrade

State Terror in the Dark

CONADEP (National Commission on
the Disappearance of Persons)

During the 1976–83 civic-military dictatorship, the night was laced with new dangers: not only were the streets placed under military vigilance, but the darkness had also become a cover for state abductions and disappearances. This selection from the 1984 report on the military regime's violent strategies and methods, Nunca más *(Never Again), recounts how the military officers would often pursue their victims in the middle of the night when they could find them asleep in their homes. After the raid, these civilians were placed in secret detention cells where they were tortured, jailed, or, in many cases, sent to their deaths.*

Anonymous Groups Forced Their Way into Homes at Night (1984)

CONADEP

The first act of the drama involved both the victim and their families and began when the group of abductors abruptly stormed the victim's home. The thousands of testimonies collected in the CONADEP archives show that these operations of abduction followed a consistent procedure; they took place late at night or in the early hours of morning and generally at the end of the week so as to delay the possibility of a response on the part of the victim's family.

It was usually one *patota*—a group of five or six individuals—that raided the home. On occasion, several groups were present, and in some special cases, up to fifty people took part in the abduction.

The members [of the *patota*] were heavily armed, disproportionately so given the threat posed by their victims. They carried small guns and larger arms and used them to threaten their targets, their families, and the neighbors. Prior to their arrival, they would often trigger a blackout, cutting off electricity in the area surrounding the home.

The number of vehicles used [in an operation] varied; in some cases, they were unmarked cars (usually with no license plate); in others, it was the armed forces, some in uniform, who used trucks or vans marked as belonging to one of the three branches of the military; in some cases, helicopters flew overhead.

Translated by Lisa Ubelaker Andrade

Rebellious Rock

Jorge Hipólito Meijide and Charly García

During the 1960s and into the 1980s, rock nacional, *the term for the localized style of rock, harbored a culture of rebellion. A cartoon from the magazine* Humor Registrado *makes light of the youthful rebellion (and its characteristic style), the popularity of rock concerts, as well as the ominous presence of government oppression in connection to both of those trends.*

 One of most emblematic lyricists to emerge in this era, Charly García, penned many songs that articulated counter-narratives to that of the dictatorship. Listening, sharing, and singing songs like García's provided a way for young people to collectively question life (and death) under dictatorship. Today this canon of songs still evokes shared memories of a variety of experiences during that era. Lyrics written from 1976 to 1982 were carefully worded, but their declarations of pain and protest were not difficult to decode. A selection of lines from García's songs are illustrative: 1977's "Hipercandombe," for example, written just a year into the military authoritarianism, is already suggestive of the pain and silence surrounding military control—after declaring that there is "no hope in the city" and referencing a decaying body, García plays on the notion of complicity and censorship, telling listeners that if they are scared by his song's message they can turn the radio dial; "Los sobrevivientes" ("The Survivors," 1978) evokes the language of survival in its title and makes reference to the experience of exile—a people losing their home who are "tired of escaping"; "Encuentro con el Diablo" ("Encounter with the Devil," 1980) powerfully alludes to confrontation with a truly vile and evil power, suggesting that the devil is alive, present, and feeding off of a fearful people; and "La canción de Alicia en el país" ("The Story of Alicia in the Country," 1980) uses the story of Alice in Wonderland (specifically, a scene in which Alice is unfairly tried by the Queen) as an allegory for the prevailing injustice and violence under military rule. Songs written at the close of the dictatorship are more explicit in their reckoning. "No bombardeen Buenos Aires" ("Don't Bomb Buenos Aires," 1982) reacts to the Malvinas/Falklands War with Great Britain; it references warnings on the news that the city could be bombed. In response, García seems to scream into a void, "Don't bomb Buenos Aires, we can't defend ourselves" above a tight, danceable beat. The call resounds as an expression of perplexed, rebellious exhaustion set against the strange energy of what was initially a popular war. Finally, the song "Los dinosaurios" ("The Dinosaurs"), released in 1983—amid the transition to democracy—names the crimes of the government outright, sets the song's repetition around the many who have "disappeared," and uses a slang term for the military (the dinosaurs) in the song's title and refrain, insisting that they will one day also be made extinct.

Rock (1982)

Jorge Hipólito Meijide ("Meiji")

Young man leaving: "Bye Mom, I'm going to the Buenos Aires Auditorium to see a rock show." Mother: "Which [police] station should I pick you up at?" *Humor Registrado,* January 1982. Courtesy of the artist.

*Hyper-*candombe *(1977)*

Charly García

. . . This is no hope in the city
My love is far from here
in a hypernatural country;
When the raining gas and tar
covers your decaying body
your conformist-yuppy face, friend,
loses its meaning;
And if this last song scares you
if you can't find its reason,
you can turn the dial,
and listen to something entertaining.

The Survivors (1979)

Charly García

. . . We are blind to see
tired of walking so long
sick of escaping
in the city
we'll have no roots
we'll never have a home.

An Encounter with the Devil (1980)

Charly García

I never imagined an encounter with the devil,
as alive and well as you or I,
his laughter has grown over the years
as has his confidence, from the fear

Song of Alicia in the Country (1980)

Charly García

We are in the land of no one, but it is mine,
The innocents are the guilty,
says his highness, the King of Spades.
Don't reveal what's behind that mirror,
You will have no power,
No lawyers. No witnesses.

Don't Bomb Buenos Aires (1982)

Charly García

Don't bomb Buenos Aires, we can't defend ourselves.
. . . I am scared of the blond one now,
I don't know who I will fear next
Terror and distrust by the games . . .
By the rancid cribs of power, cribs of power, cribs of power

The Dinosaurs (1983)

Charly García

Friends in the neighborhood can disappear
The singers on the radio can disappear
The people in the newspaper can disappear

The person you love can disappear
The people in the air can disappear in the air,
The people in the street can disappear in the street,
Friends in the neighborhood can disappear,
But the dinosaurs will disappear.

Texts translated by Wendy Gosselin, Jane Brodie, and Lisa Ubelaker Andrade

Sounds of Folk Cross Social Lines

Anonymous and María Seoane

Folk music has enjoyed several waves of popularity. The genre picked up radio time in the 1940s following a wave of rural–urban migration. The genre broadened its audiences in the 1960s, when it formed part of the new youth culture and the peña, a folk dance event with live music, became a popular outing in the city's neighborhoods. In the photograph, couples dance at La Salamanca, a bar in the neighborhood of Caballito. In the 1970s, the genre also became connected to a spirit of protest. Singers like Mercedes Sosa rose to international fame and spoke out against the civic-military dictatorship from exile; several of her songs reference survival and disappearance. As the writer and journalist María Seoane recounts, Sosa's arrival in Buenos Aires for a series of shows in February 1982 signaled the impending return to democracy. Known across Argentina as "La Negra," Sosa was joined on stage with other vocal dissident musicians, including Charly García, and she defied regulations by singing, among many other songs, a banned song by Chilean artist Violeta Parra, "La carta" ("The Letter"). Sosa departed again for Europe shortly thereafter when the military authorities issued new threats against her.

Neighbors at a Peña *Dance*
to Folk Music (ca. 1940s)

Anonymous

Courtesy of the Archivo General de la Nación Argentina Dpto. Doc. Fotográficos.
Inv: 7858.

Mercedes Sosa Returns to Buenos Aires (2019)

María Seoane

Carlos Alberto Lacoste had only occupied his new rank in the dictatorship's
Ministry of the Interior for two months when he found out that Mercedes
"La Negra" Sosa had arrived in her homeland, desperate to end her exile
in Europe, in Spain and in France. All of Europe had heard her on its most
important stages since 1979, when censorship and persecution—she had been
detained after a concert—forced her to flee [Argentina], like so many others [. . .] who were hounded by the nocturnal dogs of the terrorist regime.
That February of '82, after her long pilgrimage, "La Negra" could no longer
contain her desire to come back and "sing to the sun," after years "under
the earth, just like a survivor who comes back from war"—just "like the
cicada." ["Como la Cigarra," or "Like the Cicada," one of Mercedes Sosa's
most famous protest songs, can be found in part VII of this volume.] [. . .] For
each verse that "La Negra" powerfully unleashed in that concert at the Opera [Theater], hundreds of voices joined her as she sang "Sólo le pido a Dios"
["I Only Ask of God"], with [rock singer] León Gieco; "María va" ["Maria

Goes"] with [folk singer] Antonio Tarragó Ros; "Sueño con serpientes" ["I Dream with Snakes"], with [Cuban singer] Silvio Rodríguez; or "Cuando ya me empiece a quedar solo" ["When I Begin to Stay Alone"], with [rock band] Sui Generis, together with the great Charly García. And the theater hushed when—all alone—that great mockingbird's lungs bellowed "La Cigarra," like a bird singing for hundreds of voices. It was not enough: she should have given twelve more concerts to quench the thirst of liberty of the thousands of Argentines present in that secular church, so in need of air and sun, like the cicada. But it was too much for the regime to take. One afternoon in that summer of '82, Admiral Lacoste asked the press, "Who gave Mercedes Sosa permission to be in my country?" So "La Negra" left once again, this time with the conviction that what was taking place was a final throe of her separation from *la patria* [the homeland], as she referred to Argentina more and more often. She had to wait until the darkness that reigned was broken by a beam of light.

Translated by Lisa Ubelaker Andrade

Global/Local Sounds: *Cumbia Villera* and Argentine Trap

Daniel Riera, Bizarrap, and Julio Leiva

The twenty-first century witnessed the rise of many new styles of music, among them cumbia villera *and, even more recently, Argentine trap.* Cumbia villera *took the beats of Argentine* cumbia *and mixed it with the slang and rhetoric stylings of Greater Buenos Aires and the capital city. In the first text, journalist Daniel Riera describes the scene at a concert by popular* cumbia *band Damas Gratis. The lyrics of* cumbia villera *songs often refer to its audience as* negros, *a term with a complex history. Though* negro *(black) was used as a racial category since the colonial era, at the beginning of the twentieth century the word's meaning broadened;* negro *began to be used as a nickname of endearment (El Negro, La Negra) for persons of varying backgrounds with black hair or dark features; it can also, however, be launched as an epithet, to mark race and class offensively. The word's multiple meanings became particularly evident when it was deployed by anti-Peronists in the 1940s as a racialized, classist slur for Perón's followers (*cabecitas negras*) but was then reappropriated by Peronists. Today it has also been reappropriated by many people—of diverse racial backgrounds—as a term of identity connected to experiences of marginality, whether due to poverty, race, neighborhood or ethnic origin, or social belonging.*

Over the last decade, trap *and* reggaetón argentino *have emerged as new genres that echo themes of* cumbia villera. *Trap found initial popularity in marginalized neighborhoods, where a mixture of globalized US and Latin hip-hop and trap merged with* cumbia villera *and* reggaetón. *The introduction of local slang and cultural references nurtured a Buenos Aires style. In recent years, events have drawn huge crowds; online platforms catapulted a number of local artists—including María Becerra, Trueno, Bizarrap, and Duki—to regional and international fame. The scene expanded so rapidly, renovating nightlife, that the latter enthusiastically proclaimed Buenos Aires "a global capital of trap, the city that doesn't sleep." In this interview with journalist Julio Leiva, artist and producer Bizarrap—who has since topped the global charts—reflects on the globalization of trap and his first viral hits, which he produced in his bedroom in Ramos Mejía (in Greater Buenos Aires) using basic technology.*

The Rhythm of the Villa (2001)

Daniel Riera

If you're used to rock concerts and you walk out cursing whenever the band plays for less than ninety minutes, then don't go see Damas Gratis or any other *cumbia* group—*cumbia villera* or otherwise. Damas Gratis concerts are programmed to last twenty-two minutes, the exact amount of time stipulated in the band's contract. [. . .] It's always the same. Pablo places a red keyboard on his chest and moves center stage. *"Vamos los pibes!"* [Let's go, boys!], he cries out, and the band starts with its biggest hit, "Quiero vitamina" ["I Want Vitamin"]. When the audience sings along, they change the lyrics and the original allegory becomes even more patent: "I want to take / cocaine / I buy a bag / and I'm revved up" (the public's version of the lyrics). [. . .] Before starting the second song, Pablo almost always raises his arms and says, "I want to see the hands of all the *negros cumbieros* here tonight. This is the Damasss Gratisss show, this is the Damasss Gratisss show." That's how he marks the beat. [. . .]

"I think Damas Gratis and *cumbia villera* are to *cumbia* what punk is to rock," ventures the group's guitar player in the van on the way from Reflex, a club in Solano [in Greater Buenos Aires], to Metrópoli, one in Palermo, as his bandmates sleep. "Check this out: anyone can play *cumbia*, you don't have to be a musician to play it. If it sounds like shit, it doesn't matter. What matters is expressing yourself. That's punk rock, and that's Damas Gratis." [. . .] *Cumbia villera* scares the older women in your family, just like punk rock, but [the difference is] *cumbia villera* doesn't try to incite rebellion. Instead, it describes a harsh reality and invites people to have fun despite it.

Translated by Robin Myers

From the Plaza to Global Trap (2020)

Bizarrap with Julio Leiva

I had been rapping a long time with my friends, in the plaza, after school. [. . .] I thought it would be cool to do a remix of the battles at Quinta Escalón [a rap battle held in Parque Centenario]. [. . .] I did [it] and sent it to friends and they said it was incredible and I thought maybe I would do a video to go along with the battle. I did it but it felt empty. [. . .] then I got inspired with the idea of doing a compilation with funny or interesting things on top of the remix, a remix of a remix. I uploaded it and left with some friends to vacation to Gessel [a beach town a few hours away]; I come back and in two weeks I had like ten thousand subscribers. [. . .] Later, the idea wasn't to do a whole cycle of sessions. [. . .] I was in my studio apartment with a friend of mine and the [rapper] Kódigo and I said he should record a freestyle, people love his freestyles. [. . .] I wanted to record it in my room there, with a phone, record it and put it on YouTube; my channel had like 500,000 subscribers then. I convinced him and I said let's do it here in my room. I knew a kid, from Ramos [Mejía], a neighborhood kid, who took photos, and I asked him to bring his camera and some lights. That's how the first session came out. [. . .] In Argentina [trap] depends on your point of view, it gives off a lot of messages: the bad, the superficial, the *guita* [money], the drugs, all of that is the bad part of the message. It also shows that today you can get to any country from here, you can collaborate, have fans everywhere—as a kid from the neighborhood you can get someplace else.

Translated by Lisa Ubelaker Andrade

The *Boliche*

Olivia Gallo

Buenos Aires's nightlife gets started late—young people begin to move out of their houses at midnight and head out to the city's bars and clubs at two or three in the morning; their night ends only when the sun comes up. In this fictional text, writer Olivia Gallo depicts a typical night out—drinking a cheap drink of Fernet and Coca-Cola while riding the city's buses, going out dancing at clubs followed by a choripán at daybreak, or meeting smaller crowds at clubs, bars, or concerts. Echoing the gendered violence that has become the subject of vocal protest by women in recent years, Gallo's story takes a darker turn when the narrator narrowly escapes street harassment.

Boliches *in Palermo (2019)*

Olivia Gallo

We went to Voodoo with Palo. We almost always went alone, with the hope of making new friends. The rest of our girlfriends would go to the *boliches* [nightclubs] on the Costanera [a part of the city on the river's edge], with their shiny plastic palm trees at the entrance and cocktails with names like "Smurf Sperm." In order to get into those places, we would have to wait in long lines: we spent hours shivering on the sidewalk while cars sped down the avenue. On more than one occasion after waiting for ages and finally getting to the door, the bouncer would refuse us entry because he saw that we were under-age, and so we would go and eat enormous *choripanes* from one of the food trucks.

Palo and I had tired of the whole routine, and so we began to go to Voodoo. There was no waiting in line . . . One night Palo and I met up to drink Fernet and Coke and smoke a joint in the street. Then we got on a bus at Cabildo. We got off at Plaza Italia. We continued drinking the Fernet. We were having a hard time walking, so we decided to take a taxi to Voodoo . . .

At Voodoo, we all danced together and then Palo, Xavi, and I went out to the patio to smoke. We shared a cigarette. Then Xavi took a big drag, filled his mouth with smoke, and blew it into Palo's lips, bringing his face extremely close to hers. Palo laughed, and they kissed for a long time. "Your turn," he said to me. He breathed in the smoke and turned to me. I opened my mouth and he kissed me for a long time. When we broke off, I opened my eyes and Palo wasn't there. Finally, I found her by the door, with her coat on. [. . .] "Where are you going?" I asked. "You're not mad about that, are you?" She had never told me that she really liked Xavi. [. . .]

The streets were empty and poorly lit. I continued talking, sometimes begging, sometimes angry. While I spoke, the dark shadow of a man appeared before us. He had on a blue sweatshirt with the hood up and his pants down around his ankles. He was jerking off, his hand moving up and down furiously. He was thin as a rail. I remember that was the first thing that came to my mind. That he looked like Jesus. My second thought was that he was going to rape us. I didn't think it, I knew. I saw it. I saw both of us, Palo and I, in the news the next day. I saw a reporter in a suit and tie saying our names in front of a camera. I saw our parents crying, feeling guilty, breaking down at the kitchen table. Palo took out her cell phone. She pretended to be talking to someone. "We're on our way to the car," she said. She grabbed me by the arm and forced me to walk quickly. Jesus followed, but did not pick up his pace. At one point, we started to run. We didn't want to turn around for fear that he was following us. My stomach seized, like I was going through turbulence. I fell to my knees on the sidewalk and vomited. And at that moment I felt a hand brush my cheek; it was Palo, holding my hair back from my face.

Translated by Leslie Robertson

VII

Written Cities

The writer Sylvia Molloy once said that she thought of her native Buenos Aires as a "a topography of quotations [. . .] a reservoir of literary invention."[1] Buenos Aires is certainly a city that has been returned to as subject time and again: since its founding, writers of all kinds—essayists, academics, novelists, planners, journalists, and poets, both locals and foreigners—have taken up the task of writing about the city, engaging in a sort of dispersed, disconnected conversation over its character, its future, its idiosyncrasies, and its problems. Visual artists and filmmakers have added to the chorus of representations. (See "Visual Cities," the first selection below.) The resulting vast array of ruminations are diverse in tone, topic, and origin. At times they can seem to offer nearly contradictory accounts; some are quite oversimplistic, even essentialist, in their descriptions. Nonetheless, many of these texts have collectively shaped the popular imagination, influencing how residents think and talk about the place where they live. Several topics stick out as repeated subjects of debate and exploration: the idea of order; a likeness to Europe or a more unique local identity; neighborhood life and its cast of characters; the idea of a "middle-class" city; and the experiences of struggle and resilience in the face of recurrent crisis.

The Ordered City

Independence from Spain marked an opportunity for writers to rethink the city of Buenos Aires, its future and its possibilities. Amid a spirit of reinvention, many contemplated ways to diminish signs of colonial life and rebuild under new terms. The city map became a point of focus for change, a concrete way to think about the city's future. Under Bernardino Rivadavia (1826–28), the city's elite wrote of their vision to remake Buenos Aires using a grid street plan, which they believed would shore up support for the new republic by making Buenos Aires an example of enlightened, rational living; they heralded the city as the "Athens of the Río de la Plata." It was not long before changes in the political tide dulled their sense of optimism. When Juan Manuel de Rosas came to power in 1829, his opponents took to their pens to depict what they viewed as a reversal: they wrote of a city that was becoming more backward and rural under his regime. (See "The City Abandoned.")

In the 1880s, amid a new wave of changes in which Buenos Aires had grown in size, was receiving thousands of immigrants, and was filled with commercial and bureaucratic activity, some elite writers began to record more nostalgic renderings of early nineteenth century. José Antonio Wilde and Lucio V. López recalled a small and self-contained city, filled with personalities and picturesque scenes; they celebrated, in retrospect, the city's austerity, domesticity, and sociability. These romanticized reminiscences of a city that no longer was (and perhaps never had been) seemed to contrast with the reality that by the mid- to late nineteenth century, Buenos Aires was a medium-sized city in a process of expansion and modernization.

The Cosmopolitan City

Every city mirrors others in some ways, but the idea that Buenos Aires is a copy or an imitation of Europe is one of its greatest clichés. Even today, the moniker "the Paris of South America" appears in countless tour books and guides. It is, however, a disputed reputation. (See "Buenos Aires as Paris.") The idea that Buenos Aires resembles a "European" city has certainly shaped narratives of nation-building, perceptions of race, lessons on national history, and the writings of countless observers. Some have protested this as a rhetorical distancing from Latin America; others have sought to recover a more local vision of modernity that pays greater attention to the uniqueness of the city and attempts to decenter the typical Euro-centrist storyline. A third perspective has celebrated the city as a great Latin American metropolis, a port city shaped by colonialism and in permanent tension with the country's vast Interior.

Beyond mere imagination, the idea that Buenos Aires somehow resembles Europe is also a reflection of the impact of intentional architecture and design by those who built its plazas, streets, and most iconic buildings. The city's European leanings can also be justly attributed to the enormous (and simultaneous) influence of large waves of immigration. Although these two processes—architectural and demographic—occurred during a specific period in the city's history, the profound impact of both created a lasting effect on the city.

Well into the twentieth century, the sense that Buenos Aires was in some way a European city transported to South America continued to frame many writers' points of view. The Italian writer Vasco Pratolini, for example, wrote of Buenos Aires, "The impression I have had is of finding myself in an imaginary province in the south of Italy; imaginary, because I wouldn't know where to place it."[2] Similar commentaries abound from earlier in the century. Jules Huret, a French writer and journalist who visited Buenos Aires during its centennial celebration, wrote that he had none of "those feelings of exoticism [. . .] that give one the sense of [being] far away."[3]

Locals also spoke to this tension between Europeanness and Americanness. In 1941, the writer María Rosa Oliver reminded her colleagues in a dialogue published in the literary magazine *Sur* that "our soul is American as well, not just European."[4] Discussions like these sometimes called up the idea that Buenos Aires was a city of people with European heritage; some authors also spoke of the city in terms of its whiteness. In his 1945 *Geografía de Buenos Aires,* for example, the doctor-turned-essayist Florencio Escardó wrote of Buenos Aires as "a white city in a mestizo America."[5]

For their part, traditional nationalists offered a strong critique of what they saw as "Europeanization." Some members of the local elite also charged that cosmopolitanism—which they saw as a result of the massive arrival of immigrants as well as the international focus of the city's port commerce—were threats to national culture. In 1910, Manuel Gálvez saw Buenos Aires as a mercantile and materialistic city that he contrasted to the Interior of the country, with its more virtuous, pure countryside: "Buenos Aires . . . with its cosmopolitan character, materialism, customs of a town lacking personality and the contemptible morality of a tentacular city," he wrote.[6]

By contrast, other writers insisted that the mix of cultures prevalent in the early twentieth century was creating, or could create, a unique local character. (See "Local Identity and Cosmopolitanism.") In 1935, the writer and editor Victoria Ocampo urged her city, "Liberate yourself of the temptation to imitate the old, magnificent cities of Europe, or you will always seem like a gross caricature."[7] José Ceppi (writing under the pen name Aníbal Latino) wrote of *porteño* cosmopolitanism by emphasizing emergent customs, habits, and forms of everyday speech.

The *porteño* accent and its vocabulary were often cited as example of a homegrown invention that has borrowed intonations, words, and style from a myriad of cultural origins. At the end of the 1920s, urban chronicler Roberto Arlt published the essay "Nuestro idioma reo y cosmopolita" ("Our rough and cosmopolitan language"); Borges, took up the question of the local and the cosmopolitan in many of his writings, and his 1925 *Luna de enfrente (Moon across the Way)*, spoke of "the heterogeneous vernacular tongue of *porteño* chatter"; in 1949 Julio Cortázar added, "We are making a language . . . turbid and hot, clumsy and subtle, but an increasing attribute of our need for expression."[8]

As the next sections explore, in the twentieth and twenty-first centuries, writers would move away from generalizations, delve deeper into their depictions of local culture, and challenge some of these earlier constructions. New forms of thinking about the city's relationship with the rest of the world would also emerge. Outward migrations of persons departing the city became formative to its representations. Experiences of exile and emigration framed several contemporary writers and artists' perspectives on their home city (see "Arrivals and Departures"). Others contemplated the city's global reach and the ways in which Buenos Aires thinkers made their mark on the world (see "The City of Psychoanalysis").

The City of Neighborhoods

Writers and artists approached the idea of local identity by focusing on the cultures and character of the city's neighborhoods. Throughout the twentieth century, photographers, in particular, would turn their gaze to urban scenes. Portraits of everyday residents at work, at play, or engaging in political action became a favorite subject for artists like Sara Facio, whose large body of work seemed to propose that it was in the gaze of its people that the city's dynamic textures could be best understood. (See "Portraits of Buenos Aires.")

Historians James Scobie and José Luis Romero saw the relationship between the city's center and its growing neighborhoods as pivotal to tracing the stories of modern Buenos Aires. Romero emphasized the particularities of the two spaces but also saw them as influencing one another. (See "The Neighborhood and the City Center.") In other, less academic writings, realism intersected with a budding local mythology; descriptions and odes to neighborhoods were filled with picturesque landscapes and poetic, folkloric archetypes. The poet Evaristo Carriego described early twentieth-century neighborhoods as emotional spaces, refuges colored by the hospitality of the home, and the tranquility and warmth of childhood. A few decades later, taking a more nostalgic tone, tango writers recalled the neighborhood as a cordial space overtaken by modernity. (See "A New Urban Folklore.")

The early twentieth-century neighborhood was also adopted as a theme in literature, but through very different prisms of imagination. Jorge Luis Borges described both the cosmopolitan city and the *arrabal*, its outskirts. There he found a setting for a heroic past, of valor, fighting, parties, and *malevaje* (ruffians). Raúl González Tuñón also took up the nostalgic tenor, celebrating the neighborhood as a community space, though pointing out new threats to that local character—Americanization, apartment buildings, shantytowns, and a new impersonal culture were just a few of the changes he saw underfoot.

Essayists who set out to describe the changing city also took a more realist tone, unpretentiously describing the ordinary markers of modern life. José Juan Soiza Reilly was one of the first of these chroniclers, writing of the city's elemental spaces—its plazas, kiosks, theaters—as if the true character of the city could be found only in the everyday. Roberto Arlt took this kind of writing to new heights in his famous *Aguafuertes* (*Sketches*), which detailed everyday characters and corners of Buenos Aires as they faced the unforeseen consequences of modernity. (See "Sketches of Buenos Aires.")

For other writers the layout of the city inspired contemplation. In the 1910s, urbanists like Benito Carrasco promoted a rational development of the city's less populated areas with a network of parks and public buildings that could facilitate civic and community life. Some writers optimistically suggested that this even grid would offer a neat, orderly and promising model for city growth; yet the notion of a tidy map of small, nearly identical neighborhoods was disconcerting to others, who warned that a flat city with identical blocks extending infinitely into the pampa would harbor a culture of conformity. (See "The Beautiful and Mundane Urban Grid.")

The City, Invaded

Although depictions of Buenos Aires neighborhoods could make urban growth appear quite quaint, there were writers who viewed it as a painful process ridden with internal tension. These narrators, writing in different eras and protesting the arrival of different groups of people, interpreted waves of growth as a threat to the status quo.

At the turn of the twentieth century, for example, nationalist writers lashed out against the influence of the recently arrived immigrants from Europe, rejecting the celebrations of demographic mixture and modernization. In his *La restauración nacionalista* (1922) Ricardo Rojas lamented that the "Athens of the Río de la Plata" had become a cosmopolis, arguing, "Just as the state can intervene for health and moral reasons, it should also intervene for reasons of nationality and aesthetics . . . regulating [street] signs to be in the language of the country, suppressing the motley scene that ostentatiously displays our spiritual misery."[9] On the other side of the political spectrum, the socialist Mario Bravo saw a geographical divide taking form. In 1917, he observed a city that offered social mobility but was clearly divided: "the city of the north and the city of the south; the city of rich neighborhoods and those of poor neighborhoods; the well-lit streets and the streets without electricity; the hygienic city and the city that slowly receives public health services."[10]

By the late 1940s, the sense of geographical and class fragmentation had not disappeared; rather, it took on renewed importance. A new wave of arrivals was again changing the city's self-image and its demography. In the wake of economic adjustments, a large number of migrants from the country's Interior moved to the city and settled in large numbers in its bordering neighborhoods. Many writers who came from the city's elite and middle classes (some of them the children and grandchildren of immigrants who had been similarly criticized a generation before) demonstrated their irritation and disapproval of the new urbanites. The derogatory term *cabecitas negras* (little black heads)—which racialized the migrants regardless of their actual backgrounds or even their appearance—became a common, ugly way of rejecting their presence. A renewed discussion emerged around class, race, and politics in the city. Some defended the city as a place of ongoing mixture. Others described the period with a sense of disgust and, particularly in regard to the political mobilization of workers under the leadership of Juan Perón, as a story of political and social interruption. Julio Cortázar's *Casa tomada* (*The House Taken Over*) and *El examen* (*Final Exam*), as well as the *La fiesta del monstruo* (*The Monster's Party*) by Jorge Luis Borges and Adolfo Bioy Casares, alluded to the new residents as a nameless danger, strangers who arrived without invitation and took over. The conservative press echoed this sentiment with their own descriptions of city streets filled with a new, unwanted public. (See "Catholic Encounters with the Peronist City.") The story "Cabecita negra" by Germán Rozenmacher also articulated the sense of brewing conflict. The old *porteños*, the story suggested, had to come to terms with the fact that the city that they believed belonged to them was in fact no longer theirs alone. (See "*Cabecita negra*.")

As the decades went on, questions over racialized and classist divides in the city were revisited in a variety of ways. In 1957, the writer Bernardo Verbitsky published his novel *Villa Miseria también es América* (*The* Villa Miseria *Is Also America*), a portrait of the city's poorest informal neighborhoods that sought to show how a spirit of familial and community ties were the backbone of survival. Verbitsky had coined the term *villa miseria* while describing the precarious settlements in the paper *Noticias Gráficas* years before.

By contrast, between 1976 and 1983, the civic-military dictatorship emphasized what they called "order" by fueling racist and classist discourses that suggested that only certain sectors—white, acquiescent, and well-off—"belonged" in the city. While undertaking operations to violently remove all those they deemed undesirable, they razed *villas*, disappeared dissidents, and instated policies that led to a militarization of daily life. (See "The City under Military Control.")

In the decades that followed, and at the heels of repeating economic crises, the notion that the city must contend with its important inequalities was more acute. Amid the return to democracy and into the neoliberal era, writers dedicated renewed attention to the stigma of poverty and unemployment. The sense of concern heightened further after the 2001 economic crash. While in mass media representations of *villas* as hotbeds for drugs, crime, and violence prevailed, a number of writers called into question this depiction by contemplating the structural and cultural contexts that reinforced their marginalization. Even more recently, writers and artists from the *villas*, like César González, challenged the presumption its stories could be narrated by curious middle-class outsiders, and instead offered a more nuanced portrayal of struggle and everyday life from within. (See "The *Villa*, from Without and Within.")

The Middle-Class City

Discussions of poverty and inequality were often set against an implicit and prevailing perception that Buenos Aires has long been a city with a vast middle class. By the early twentieth century the idea of the "middle class" was only beginning to emerge as a theme—the playwright Federico Martens, for example, spoke to the existence of the middle classes in his productions *Gente bien* (*Decent Folk*, 1906) and *Las de enfrente* (*The Neighbors across the Street*, 1908). Far more common was a narrative of social mobility. (See "Social Mobility.") By the 1930s the notion of a middle economic, social, and cultural sector became a clearer component of urban identities. Hastening this change was the development of the city's neighborhoods, education system, and new professional jobs. Writers reflected on this with descriptions of white-collar workers, a sector that seemed to be flourishing in the 1920s. (See "White-Collar Workers.")

Over the following decades, the perception that Buenos Aires was characterized by a vast middle sector became more prevalent. The sociologist Gino Germani began to study Buenos Aires's middle classes around the same time, characterizing the city as one in which a pattern of social mobility predominated, and opening up a broader conversation among social scientists about how to define the middle class, the process by which the middle sectors grew, and whether that growth would continue.

By the early 1960s, representations of the so-called middle class became more contentious. Juan José Sebreli described the sector as overly interested in individualism, moralism, conservatism, anti-Peronism, and imitation of the upper classes. (See "Critiques of the Buenos Aires Middle Class.") Although these characterizations stuck, there were voices that pointed out that the middle classes were quite diverse and that many of the young people who were challenging these very norms were products of middle-class households themselves.

Resilience and New Realities

The rather precarious state of economic life at the turn of the twenty-first century chipped away at the notion of Buenos Aires as "a middle-class city." While aspects and identities of middle-class culture often endured, repeated experiences of inflation and political and economic crisis generated an entrenched feeling that economic decline was almost an inevitability. Contrasts between the capital and the more unequal Greater Buenos Aires have framed new questions about the degree to which the "middle-class city" still exists—or how it will endure. (See "Writing the Middle Classes.")

Migration and immigration to Buenos Aires from the Interior and neighboring countries have also generated new cultural shifts. Cultural critic Beatriz Sarlo observed a new era of cosmopolitanism by the early twenty-first century, noting that "Buenos Aires has always been a city of foreigners, of immigrants hailing from near and far; these days from South America, [migrants] from the Argentine provinces, and Asia; in the past, from Europe." More recently, Identidad Marrón (Brown Identity), a collective of writers and artists, have looked to center brownness as a key local racial identity in their works. Writer Chana Mamani has referred to a "double mirror" in which Buenos Aires's so-called white "Europeanness" has long made invisible both Indigenous heritage and the contributions of communities built by more recent immigrants from neighboring countries. Speaking of the growing presence of artists and writers from those communities, she has noted, "Us Brown folks write, we think; we have voices."[11]

In the literature and art that takes it as subject, the notion that Buenos Aires is a city made up of diverse economic, ethnic, racial, and social experiences has certainly begun to displace former discussions that centered on Buenos Aires as a mirror of Europe. At the same time, as residents tirelessly navigated a series of economic struggles, there emerged a second narrative that life in the city required a kind of rugged toughness and creative readiness. Embedded in this reflection is also a characterization of Buenos Aires as a place of resilience. The city's writers and artists continue to note that its residents learn and adapt, finding new ways of navigating—or playing—the system through the ups and downs of political and economic crises; despite enormous change, a spirit of continuity endures. (See "Enduring City.")

Notes

All translations are the authors' own.

1. Silvia Molloy, "Afterword: The Buenos Aires Affair," PMLA 122, no. 1 (2007): 353.

2. Francisco Urondo, "Senta, signor Pratolini," in *Obra periodística: Crónicas, entrevistas y perfiles, 1952–1972* (Buenos Aires: Adriana Hidalgo, 2013), 118.

3. Jules Huret, *La Argentina: De Buenos Aires al Gran Chaco* (Paris: Bibliotèque Charpentier, 1911), 25.

4. María Rosa Oliver, in *Sur: Revista Mensual* (December 1941): 100.

5. Florencio Escardó, *Geografía de Buenos Aires* (Buenos Aires: Editorial Losada, 1945), 18.

6. Manuel Gálvez, *El diario de Gabriel Quiroga* (Buenos Aires: Arnoldo Moen, 1910), 59.

7. Victoria Ocampo, *Testimonios, segunda serie, 1937–1940* (Buenos Aires: Sur, 1984), 217–18.

8. Jorge Luis Borges, "Al tal vez lector," in *Luna de enfrente* (Buenos Aires: Editorial Proa, 1925), from *Textos recobrados: 1919–1929* (Buenos Aires: Emecé, 1997), 219; Julio Cortázar, "Leopoldo Marechal: Un Adán en Buenos Aires," in *Realidad* (March–April 1949): 233.

9. Ricardo Rojas, *La restauración nacionalista* (Buenos Aires: Ministerio de Justicia e Instrucción Pública, 1922), 323.

10. Mario Bravo, *La ciudad libre* (Buenos Aires: Ferro & Gnoatto, 1917), 17–18.

11. Chana Mamani, interviewed on *La Siesta Que No Fue*, "Marrones escriben," aired October 5, 2022, Radio Kermes (La Pampa, Argentina).

Visual Cities

Laura Malosetti Costa, Antonio Berni,

and Marta Minujín

The urban experience has been a prominent theme for many of Buenos Aires's artists. Three works that take up the city as subject—Pío Collivadino's El Banco de Boston *(1926), Benito Quinquela Martín's* Elevadores a pleno sol *(Dockloaders under a Full Sun, 1945), and Antonio Berni's* Juanito va a la ciudad *(Juanito Goes to the City, 1963) can be found in the color insert. In* El Banco de Boston, *Collivadino depicts new high-rise buildings next to older edifices, which seem to stand in for a quainter version of the city, one that is gradually being overtaken. The avenues, street lamps, the cars on the road, and the people on the sidewalks are all markers of novelty. In the text "Collivadino, Buenos Aires under Construction," art historian Laura Malosetti Costa reflects on the artist's depictions of an unevenly modern urban landscape in paint. Quinquela Martín's bright depiction of the port in La Boca also takes up the city as landscape, but captures a sense of vibrancy by bringing focus to the port's laborers, and by extension, the working-class world of La Boca. Berni's* Juanito va a la ciudad *offers a more contemporary interpretation of inequalities; the protagonist of this painting, a boy named Juanito Laguna, appears in a series of works. Here he traverses a junkyard landscape to get to the capital. In the text "Juanito," Antonio Berni discusses his choice to use recycled materials and collage to represent a rather dystopic modern metropolis.*

Marta Minujín's urban intervention "El Obelisco de Pan Dulce" ("The Obelisk of Fruitcakes") also reflected on the idea of crisis. The intervention, a photograph of which appears below, re-created an iconic city landmark using ten thousand packages of pan dulce, *which were then distributed to the public. In the accompanying interview Minujín reflects on her numerous interventions in iconic urban spaces, and in particular, the city's Obelisk, a gift to Argentina amid crisis.*

Collivadino: Buenos Aires under Construction (2013)

Laura Malosetti Costa

Pío Collivadino was an artist who, with a light palette and divisive technique, brought to the easel the modern urban landscape of a city whose contradictions had thus been emphasized in the written word and in photographs (its drive for progress and destruction of the traditional ways of life) but had not yet been seen as a motif worthy of the prestigious art of painting. He built an urban landscape consisting of scenes of ports, power plants and industrial buildings, grain elevators, high-rise buildings, and major avenues of the city center, the bridges over the Riachuelo, and he also represented the contradicting progress seen in the slums, the nostalgia of traditional houses in the once rural outskirts of the city. [. . .] In the nineteenth century, the city had not had any painters who presented a view—whether critical or celebratory—of urban modernity in their works. The pampas, rural landscapes, and gaucho customs remained the focus of works that sought out and took up the national character of art. Collivadino's Buenos Aires is the counterpart to that tradition. He is the first modern urban landscape artist.

Translated by Leslie Robertson

Juanito (1975)

Antonio Berni

Juanito marked a return to collage, but it was totally determined by my express interest. I was looking for a certain density in the work, that directly related to that character and the scope of that character. To be precise, the idea of using leftover materials came from when I was in the slums, in the *villas*, I saw all those people there, in misery, taking advantage of the leftovers from consumer society, the waste: old boxes, burlaps, cans, rusted steel sheets. For me, these became the narrative elements for the character that needed—that asked—to be part of my creation. [. . .] I am a painter who is living life. I am holding on to what is ours. Argentina is not Europe or North America.

Translated by Leslie Robertson

El Obelisco de Pan Dulce *(1979)*

Marta Minujín

Courtesy of the artist.

The Iconic Buenos Aires Obelisk (2011)

Marta Minujín and *Clarín*

Anyone who comes to Buenos Aires goes to the Obelisk. Everyone knows where it is; it can be seen from everywhere. People that come from other places may not know where the National Congress or Casa Rosada are located, but everyone knows where the Obelisk is. [. . .] "When I came back to Argentina, I was struck by the rigidity of the military, which I related to the rigidity of society and of the Obelisk. That's why it occurred to me that we should tilt it, and then lay it down," explains Minujín. One year later, she decided to gift to an "Argentina in crisis" *El Obelisco de Pan Dulce (The Obelisk of Fruit Cakes).* Her most recent installation was in 2009, when she presented the *Obelisco Multidireccional (Multidirectional Obelisk).* With four monuments falling, she tried to convey the many directions in which we Argentines are moving. "That is how we are, we go up and down constantly. [. . .] I like monuments, but I want to lie them all on their sides. Because then everything can be seen from a different angle. If you see the Obelisk leaning on its side, it becomes dislodged, and in doing so, it grows. Because all of my life I have been used to the perpendicularity of the Obelisk. And today we are in a world where that no longer works. There is such a thing as multidimensionality. Because that is how we Argentines think, that there are no rules; here it seems that anything goes."

Translated by Leslie Robertson

The City Abandoned

José Mármol

In the early republican era, stark political conflicts over the organization of the nation set the backdrop for writers' depictions of Buenos Aires. In the canonical novel Amalia, *nineteenth-century liberal writer José Mármol describes a deserted city, a cemetery of living souls that had been taken apart by Juan Manuel de Rosas, who dominated the political landscape from 1829 to 1852.*

Amalia (1852)

José Mármol

The silence was funereal in the city. The monotonous sound of our heavy carts driving to the markets, the footsteps of the workers, the milkman's song, the water carrier's bell, the bread thumping in the baskets: all of these particular sounds of the city of Buenos Aires at dawn have not been heard for four or five years now. The city was abandoned: a cemetery of the living whose souls were present, some in the heaven of holding out hope for Lavalle's triumph: others in the hell of waiting for Rosas'.

"[. . .] He wants us all to remain in Buenos Aires," said the man with the sword, "because the enemy that we must fight is in Buenos Aires, not in the armies; he is making a precise calculation to prove that, when the revolution breaks out, fewer of us will die in the streets than in the battlefield . . . But we should not speak of this any longer; in Buenos Aires the air hears, the light sees, the stones and dust reprise our words to those who seek to take our freedom.

Translated by Lisa Ubelaker Andrade

Buenos Aires as Paris

Adolfo Posada, Marcel Duchamp,
and José María Vargas Vila

Buenos Aires is "the Paris of South America": so goes one of the most clichéd descriptions of the city. The idea is often repeated in texts about the city, and particularly in the observations of foreigners who visit. For some the comparison is meant as a compliment; for others the comparison critiqued a city that far too often looked outward, and particularly to Europe, to construct its identity. These excerpts, written at different points in the early twentieth century, are illustrative. The Spanish jurist and writer Adolfo Posada sees Buenos Aires as a city that rivals Paris, while the artist Marcel Duchamp, who lived in the city for a short time, finds Buenos Aires to be in a constant crisis of identity: he famously proclaims that Buenos Aires "does not exist." The Colombian writer José María Vargas Vila criticizes the city as lacking originality or a culture of its own.

Impressions of the Argentine Republic (1912)
Adolfo Posada

Paris is the only Latin city with a larger population than Buenos Aires, and there is no Spanish-speaking city that rivals it. [. . .] Buenos Aires is, remarkably—indeed, oddly—a vast city that can be walked endlessly [. . .] a city that has taken shape on the grounds of all that we have been. It is one of the most pulsating and vibrant centers known to humankind, an ode to greatness, to economic growth.

Translated by Robin Myers

Buenos Aires Does Not Exist (1918)
Marcel Duchamp

Buenos Aires does not exist. It is just a big provincial town full of rich people with absolutely no taste, and everything bought in Europe, right down to the stone they build their houses with. I have even found a French toothpaste which I had forgotten about in New York.

Translated by Robin Myers

An Utter Lack of Originality (1923)

José María Vargas Vila

An utter lack of originality is what distinguishes Buenos Aires. That holds true for absolutely everything: its writers and sculptors, its painters and architects, its revolutionaries and shoe-shiners. [. . .] Nothing original, nothing new, nothing its own . . . Everything imported, everything transported, everything imitation. [. . .] It's the homeland of plagiarized European gestures. [. . .] Copies are the norm. [. . .] From literature to art, it's nothing more than a vast museum of reproductions.

Translated by Robin Myers

Local Identity and Cosmopolitanism

Aníbal Latino and Georges Clemenceau

While some writers contended that Buenos Aires was a mere copy of European cities, others saw its history of mixture as the starting point for a new, unique local culture. The journalist José Ceppi, writing under the pseudonym Aníbal Latino, suggests that Buenos Aires's deepest connection to Europe comes not from its intentional efforts at imitation but, rather, from the fact that immigrants had brought a diversity of traditions and shared those customs with each other. The French politician and writer Georges Clemenceau wrote of Buenos Aires as a "great European city" while visiting on official business, but he underlined that it possessed a clear Argentine-ness.

Customs and Habits in Buenos Aires (1886)

Aníbal Latino

Is the makeup of Buenos Aires unique? Yes, it is! It, like all large capitals, is more and more cosmopolitan in appearance, and some traditional Argentine, Italian, Spanish, and French festivities are still observed. They change with each passing day, though, because, as an individual, no European carries on, or is capable of carrying on, the habits brought over from his country of origin. Nor, for that matter, is there any Argentine who is not drawn to the inclinations of one or another of his guests. While Italians drink *mate* or become generous—well, a few of them do—and spendthrift, some Porteños die for tagliarini and ravioli. [. . .] Such a vast array of people live perfectly well together, if not without friction. Even the ethnic festivities that, for a sizable portion of the population, are a means to distinguish themselves end up evidencing the city's cosmopolitanism: the enthusiasm for such festivities is always matched by the indifference of the majority. [. . .] The city of Buenos Aires is more cosmopolitan than any European city, including London or Paris, because within its confines there is a higher proportion of foreigners [. . .]. If you spend a few leisurely hours on its streets, in its public places and establishments, taking it all in, you will hear languages from each and every European country as well as their dialects, and see people of all colors, representatives of every race, and endless varieties of dress. The study could be taken further, perfected even, but only by following one or more of the families as soon as they have come over from Europe, before their primitive habits are, to a greater or lesser extent, muddled and mixed, transformed and corrupted.

Translated by Wendy Gosselin and Jane Brodie

Argentine-ness (1911)

Georges Clemenceau

While the look of the streets of Buenos Aires is truly European, both for their disposition and the appearance of everything, the dominance of our fashions and the expressions on their faces,—all of this world is Argentina to its core. It is exclusively Argentine. New York is closer to Europe, and New York is North American in its soul, as perfectly so as Buenos Aires is Argentine. The difference is that in New York, as in Boston and even in Chicago, North American–ness is present in what a person wears, his face, his step and his voice, as much as in his sentiments and ways of thinking, while what is piquant about Buenos Aires is that it presents to us, under the veil of Europe, a mistaken Argentinism. And the most curious, perhaps, is that this imitated patriotism, which is born witness in an offensive manner in so many places that I cannot name, here takes such a pleasant form, such a candid form, I would dare say, that we are soon left with the desire to see how it can be justified. Not content to be Argentines from head to toe, this devilish folk would Argentinize us in a blink of an eye, if we gave them occasion to do so.

Translated by Wendy Gosselin and Jane Brodie

Arrivals and Departures

Sylvia Molloy

The story of Buenos Aires is often told in connection to the movement of people: the large waves of European immigration at the end of the nineteenth century, the arrival of internal migrants in the twentieth century, and, over the last several decades, the arrival of new immigrants, many from neighboring countries. At the same time, there have also been emigrations out. Many porteños *have left their city and their country to find themselves as immigrants abroad. Some departed in exile, escaping threats of state violence. Others left in search of employment, opportunity, economic stability. In this text, writer Sylvia Molloy suggests that returning to her home—as a visitor—has framed her writing and her reencounters with the city.*

Returning to Buenos Aires

My second novel, *El común olvido*, begins with the protagonist [. . .] arriving in another airport, clutching a bag containing an urn with his mother's ashes, which, in accordance with her last wishes, he is bringing back to scatter in the Río de la Plata. The city, this time, is identified: it's Buenos Aires in the mid-1980s. It was time to come home, for my character and for me, even if we both knew that you only call home that which you leave behind. [. . .] [L]ike New York, Buenos Aires today is made up of a more complex mix. There are few European immigrants—the movement goes in the opposite direction these days—and, as in many Latin American capitals, there are long lines before European consulates. These are the grandchildren of immigrants, seeking to reclaim the nationality of their forebears so they can try their luck in Europe. Besides, as popular wisdom has it, it's always good to have a second passport. For years, many of my friends waited impatiently for Poland to join the European Union so they could claim EU citizenship through grandparents or parents who had fled Poland because they were Jews. As soon as Poland became part of the union, my friends got their Polish passports. With typical *porteño* insight, they appreciated the irony of the situation, its subtle poetic justice. [. . .]

[One of the] most salient recollections I have of Buenos Aires dates from [. . .] just at the end of the dictatorship. Two things stand out in my memory marking that "new" Buenos Aires, the one to which I now return with increasing frequency. One was the absence of young soldiers with machine guns at the airport. The other—I remember this clearly, staring out the taxi window on my way in from the airport—was the walls of the city, literally papered with silhouettes. Every available surface, or so it seemed, was covered with black outlines of human forms on thick white paper, marked with persons' names and the dates of their disappearance. The visual impact of these paper ghosts was enormous—I couldn't stop talking about it, couldn't help looking at them up close, checking names and dates, afraid I might happen on a name I knew. People in Buenos Aires seemed less traumatized by this display than I was. For them it had been an everyday experience; for me it was a blatant reminder of what I had been spared.

The City of Psychoanalysis

Elisabeth Roudinesco

Psychoanalysis, far from stigmatized, is a common—and embraced—practice in Buenos Aires. Rather than being associated with mental illness, it is regarded by many as a completely routine component of living a healthy life. Psychoanalysts have long provided expert commentary on national media outlets, and the language of psychology and introspection pervades popular culture, film, art, and politics. In this text, French psychoanalyst and historian Elisabeth Roudinesco contends that Buenos Aires's particular relationship with psychoanalysis is remarkable in many aspects: for the degree to which its residents have taken to it, for the unique local cultures that have developed around it, and for the impact that the city's psychoanalysts have had on their field.

To Analyze Oneself (2018)

Elisabeth Roudinesco

In the interwar period, Buenos Aires reinvented the love of psychoanalysis, that Freudian passion that had so marked Europe. [. . .] Buenos Aires is none other than the new Vienna, the new Athens, the new Jerusalem, so dreamed of by the Freudian West. [. . .] Its very particular situation conferred a beautiful vivacity to that peculiar academy of Buenos Aires intellectuals—so different from each other, but united by a shared state of exile, by violent passions in the style of the old heroic dynasties. They were the founders of the Argentine school of psychoanalysis, and their heirs later emigrated to Europe and all over the world to form a diaspora, as their European pioneers, forced into exile by fascism, had done before them. But rather than reproducing the hierarchy of the European and North American institutes, in which the teacher/pupil relationship predominated, they formed a "Republic of Equals" [. . .]. It is that topological figure that would have fascinated [Jacques] Lacan if he had had the opportunity to go to Buenos Aires as often as he went to Rome; everything happens as if in a story by Jorge Luis Borges, as a Borgesian cosmopolitan cosmos. [. . .] In all seriousness, among all the places where Freudianism was implanted, Buenos Aires was the only city in the world where a specific expression was invented to designate psychoanalysis treatment, a definition that seemed to exclude transference: one says (*anali-zarse*) "to analyze oneself" and not "to be analyzed," or "to get analyzed," or "to go to analysis." It was never a trend; the love of psychoanalysis ran deep.

Translated by Lisa Ubelaker Andrade

Portraits of Buenos Aires

Sara Facio and Facundo de Zuviría

A long lineage of photographers has created a powerful visual biography of the city and its inhabitants. Artists like Horacio Coppola (see part VI) became known for his pictures of the modern and diverse landscape; Sameer Makarius (see part I) captured everyday life in neighborhoods; Annemarie Heinrich became known for her glamorous portraits of impactful individuals, and Grete Stern (see part V) for her use of collage to represent internal dilemmas at midcentury. In later decades, artists like Alicia D'Amico, Adriana Lestido (see part II), and Eduardo Longoni (see part II) turned their cameras toward a society in protest, toward people experiencing both conflict and joy amid repression. Facundo de Zuviría's work, an example of which is included here, foregrounds patterns and rhythms in the city's streets, houses, and highways. The iconic work of Sara Facio, by contrast, turned to the people of the city. Facio's Buenos Aires is built of rich characters set against local backdrops and contexts; her choice not to use flash, light reflectors, or long-range lenses and instead to favor close-range, often emotional, shots, taken from her position "next to the people" magnified a viewpoint grounded in the diverse realities of urban life.

Lustrabotas,
by Sara Facio.
From *Buenos
Aires, Buenos
Aires*, by Alicia
D'Amico, Sara
Facio, and Julio
Cortázar (Buenos
Aires: Editorial
Sudamericana,
1968). Courtesy of
the photographer.

Peatones en Retiro, by Facundo de Zuviría, 1999, from *Estampas, 1985–2015* (Barcelona: Ediciones Rm, 2016). Courtesy of the photographer.

The Neighborhood and the City Center

José Luis Romero

The historian José Luis Romero saw decades of urban growth as producing various subcultures but also possessing a spirit of shared experience and integration. He, too, compares Buenos Aires in the 1920s to Paris and London, noting in particular that the city's architecture, fashion, and high culture could often make it a bit derivative; yet he also finds that social and economic mobility generated a culturally plural middle class and that a unique, celebrated popular culture grew out of the city's neighborhoods. He finds unity in moments of exchange across subcultures, noting that there existed numerous spaces where the various sectors coexisted and interacted even while remaining separate.

Buenos Aires, Unity and Diversity (1970)

José Luis Romero

In these ways, *porteño* society diversified. Within different sectors of the city were lodged different societies, clearly distinguished from one another, and each disclosed a singular culture that maintained itself in irreducible confrontation with the others for a long time. There was one culture of traditional classes and another of new social formations—the latter split, in turn, into that of immigratory groups keeping their popular European traditions alive and that of the hybrid *criollo* groups.

The culture of the traditional classes fed on its *criollo* roots and adorned itself with the reflection of bourgeois culture typical of Paris and London. It shone in the center, in aristocratic residences, in clubs and dances, in the loges and box seats of the Teatro Colón, in the university, in literary gatherings, in the grandstand for members of the Hipódromo Nacional [National Racetrack], in the compilation of the great newspapers. There resided Parisian fashion, art nouveau, then modernism [. . .] and then Ultraism. [. . .] It was a brilliant culture, without a doubt, but a bit conventional—and, above all, highly dependent on the latest Parisian trends, which were as visible in the window displays at Harrods as in the magazine *Nosotros*; or in the everyday controversies at the Café de los Inmortales, refuge for a bohemian crowd. [. . .] And it wasn't just high-class culture, but also that of the traditional middle classes and that of the new ones as they managed to integrate themselves in traditional society—some readers of *Plus Ultra* and *La Nación*, others of *El Hogar* and *La Prensa*, others habitués of Harrods and still others of the department stores Gath & Chaves or La ciudad de México; magazines, newspapers, stores, pastry shops, all subtly marked by nuances that revealed their corresponding sectors of social stratification. It was an established culture.

In the barrios, on the other hand, an unprecedented culture was developed, belonging to the immigrant and marginal sectors, and it had two distinct shades. The groups of immigrants and immigrants' children constituted a marginal culture, but one that was uncomfortable with its own marginality and showed aspirations toward rapid integration. Signs of their popular European roots persisted: the predominance of Spanish or Italian cooking; the operation of ethical and social norms corresponding to their places of origin, usually villages whose lifestyles were adapted with great difficulty to those of the enormous city Buenos Aires had become. But the aspiration toward social ascent forced the limitations imposed by tradition and pushed the new generations to accept the guidelines established by the dominant classes: they had to abandon their Genoese or their Yiddish; they had to try to enroll in the Colegio Nacional; they had to learn the conventional forms of interpersonal relations. It was a tough education. Those groups seeking social ascent could appear coarse in the eyes of the traditional classes—which could sometimes be overly foolish—precisely because they were developing, in their own way and in order to adapt it to their own needs, the model that the upper classes offered them. Certainly, the elegance of the barrio girls wasn't the same as that of the high-class girls, but it aspired to be, and, little by little, it managed to be. This re-elaboration of the high-class model by the newly formed middle classes amounted to a curious cultural adventure for a two-culture Buenos Aires.

But this wasn't the only unprecedented culture that emerged in the barrios. Beside it, and occasionally mixed in with it, appeared a marginal culture that accepted its marginality, took on its roots and tendencies, and affirmed its particularity. It was produced, in the marginal suburbs of Los Corrales, Barracas, La Boca, Palermo, Nuevo Chicago, or Nueva Pompeya, by villagers from the plains and by Spanish and Italian immigrants who intertwined their emotions and sometimes their ideas, customs, and principles, their atavistic ways of eating and their systems of struggle for living. And their convergence was so vigorous that they generated a language (*lunfardo*); created a dance and a song form (tango); and gave life to *criollo* theater, which quickly culminated in *sainete*, a lovely theatrical expression.

The cultural values of the Center weren't questioned so much as simply ignored; norms were left to the side and replaced with others that responded exactly to the reality of people's actual situations. Viewed in terms of its component parts, it didn't seem like an original culture, but the combination of old elements was unusual, and so was the meaning attributed to that combination. It was a formidable combination, impelled by the presence of and contact among different groups placed into a shared situation, and for whom their segregation acted as a catalyzing agent. This marginal culture that accepted its marginality and persevered in its peculiarity coincided with the marginal culture that did not: neither one could live without the culture of the Center. Therefore, the two were intertwined, and they formed a vague union that responded to the challenge posed by the established culture, which was a powerful one.

Translated by Robin Myers

A New Urban Folklore

Evaristo Carriego and Homero Manzi

New visions and narrations of urban life found a voice in poetry, lyricism, and tango of the early twentieth century. Rather than lauding the modern city or drawing comparisons to far-off metropolises, these odes were grounded in the local; they celebrated the humble and intimate scene of the city's neighborhoods. In Evaristo Carriego's poems the neighborhood is "the emotional geography of the poor"—but it is also a refuge. The writer Jorge Luis Borges said that Carriego was the first observer of these spaces, discovering them and inventing them in representation. Decades later, tango writers like Homero Manzi recalled the neighborhood nostalgically. They sung of a kind of paradise lost, a city of long ago, of quiet intimacy, of people and places that, by midcentury, were no longer part of its reality. In "Sur" ("South"), Manzi contemplates the end of an era, missing the city of his youth.

The Path to Our House (1913)

Evaristo Carriego

We know you so well, like something
that was ours, ours alone
Familiar in the streets, in the trees
that line the sidewalk
in the brimming and passionate happiness
of the boys, in the faces
of the old friends,
in the stories that travel in a whisper
from mouth to mouth across the neighborhood
and in the painful drone
of that whining barrel organ
so loved by our neighbor,
the lady with the sad eyes.

Translated by Wendy Gosselin and Jane Brodie

Sur (1948)

Homero Manzi

The old corner of San Juan and Boedo, and all the sky,
Pompeya and beyond, the flooded lands.
Your girlish mane in my memory
And your name floating in farewell.
The blacksmith's corner, mud and grass,
Your house, your sidewalk, the gutter
And the scent of weeds and alfalfa
That fills my heart anew.

Nostalgia for things past
Sand that life has swept away
the gloom of neighborhoods no longer the same
And the bitterness of a dream that has died.

Translated by Wendy Gosselin and Jane Brodie

Sketches of Buenos Aires

Roberto Arlt

The writer Roberto Arlt's Buenos Aires was quite different from more elite renditions of the city. Filled with local characters and grounded in the geography of the city's neighborhoods, it was a world constructed out of everyday observation. In many of his short essays, known as Aguafuertes *(Sketches), Arlt took on a nearly existential tone, contemplating the enormous changes underfoot in the 1920s and 1930s. His descriptions were cherished for being both specific and universal, scenes that could take place in any of the city's many middle- and working-class neighborhoods, thus reaffirming a sense of community identity while at the same time essentializing what it meant to live in Buenos Aires.*

A Chair on the Sidewalk (1933)

Roberto Arlt

The nights of chairs carried out to the sidewalk, of families settled in outside the doors of their homes, have come; the nights of the sentimental love in a "Good evening, Miss," and in a polite and suggestive "How are you, Don Pascual?" And Don Pascual grins and twirls his moustache knowing full well just why the boy asks. The nights are here . . .

I don't know what makes these Buenos Aires neighborhoods so sad beneath the daytime sun, and so lovely when the moon shines down on them from that angle. I don't know what it is about them that makes all of us—whether rough or refined, lazy or hardworking—love this neighborhood with its garden (we'll add on that new room someday) and its girls, always the same and always different, and its old folks, always the same and always different too. A mafia sort of charm, a humble sweetness, a cheap illusion, I don't know what it is about all these neighborhoods! These long Buenos Aires neighborhoods, all cut from the same cloth, all similar with their houses, their gardens with palm tree in the middle and weeds with a flower or two whose scent incites the night to cut loose the passion trapped within the city's souls; souls that know nothing but the beat of the tango and "I love you." Poetic rubbish, that and something more.

A few kids kicking a ball around in the middle of the street; half a dozen men lazing on the corner; a quizzical old lady standing in a doorway; a younger woman avoiding that corner where the men are lazing; three home-owners exchanging numbers in front of the corner bar; a piano playing an old waltz; a dog in a seizure writhing and digging his jaw into the colony of fleas that lives along his tailbone; a couple standing at the dark window of a room: the sisters at the door and the brother joining those half dozen men at that corner. This is everything and nothing more. Poetic rubbish, down-and-out charm, a study—of Bach or Beethoven along with a tango by [Juan de Dios] Filiberto or [Gerardo] Matos Rodríguez.

This is a Buenos Aires neighborhood, a neighborhood profoundly our own: a neighborhood that all of us, rough or refined, carry in our bones like a magical spell that doesn't die, that will never die.

And next to the door, there's a chair. A chair where an old lady sits, a chair where the *jovie* [*viejo*, or "old man," with the syllables reversed] rests. A sym-bolic chair, a chair that is moved thirty centimeters to the left when a worthy visitor arrives, while the mother or father says,

"Bring out another chair, dear."

. . . Beneath the starry rooftop at ten o'clock, that chair in the Buenos Aires neighborhood captures a local way of being.

Translated by Wendy Gosselin and Jane Brodie

The Beautiful and Mundane Urban Grid

Alberto Gerchunoff, Ezequiel Martínez Estrada,

and Alfonsina Storni

In the 1910s, Buenos Aires was undergoing a rapid process of modernization. Although some met these changes with apprehension, many saw it as a sign of immense potential. The writer Alberto Gerchunoff celebrates the urban grid as a beautiful, modern expansion of the city. There are components of his Buenos Aires that are recognizable today: a plan built on a flat terrain allowed for an even and straight grid. These plans for an "exacting" future city reflected a broader idealization of order. By contrast, Ezequiel Martínez Estrada, one of the most important essayists and critics of the twentieth century, raised objections to the city's layout. From his perspective, the city's grid-like spread was connected to a culture that had become damaging to the well-being of the republic. The poet Alfonsina Storni also criticized the city's organization, finding a sense of monotony in her "Sad Lines of Buenos Aires" (1925).

Buenos Aires, Continental Metropolis (1914)
Alberto Gerchunoff

Buenos Aires is not lacking in historical tradition, but in local tradition. There are no medieval castles suggestive of the lives of princes or of legendary love affairs and chilling crimes; there are no gloomy corners, twisting alleyways in dreary neighborhoods that sum up before today's onlooker age-old episodes. [. . .] Everything in Buenos Aires is youthful, everything belongs to yesterday, everything will belong to tomorrow. And to react to that with a scornful grimace is like to deride a healthy and exuberant youth because, in his virile beauty, he bears no signs of age, none of the melancholy of gray hairs or wrinkles.

We are the barbarians, the glorious and rough barbarians of civilization. [. . .] In Buenos Aires, there are none of the quaint winding roads of cities of the past. [. . .] The streets here are ruler straight and long, the city laid out on a perfect checkerboard grid. Is that ugly? No, it's beautiful! A straight line is lovely when it stretches on forever, and Buenos Aires is built on endless straight lines [. . .] because its founders, their heirs, and its current inhabitants envision beauty as endlessness . . .

Translated by Robin Myers

Goliath's Head: A Microscopic View of Buenos Aires (1947)
Ezequiel Martínez Estrada

Buenos Aires has been made from centripetal movement. [. . .] It has concluded by absorbing and enveloping the surrounding populations. [. . .] It is the city of the pampa. Instead of asking ourselves now why its Viceroyal head has grown so phenomenally, we should ask ourselves why the body has remained so stymied. Before the problem never bothered us, but rather was almost a point of pride; because having a phenomenally large head tends to be an index of mental excellence, for those who calculate in meters . . . Gradually we began to realize that it was not an enlarged head, but a body that was completely malnourished and poorly developed. The head was drinking the blood of the body.

Translated by Liliana Frankel

Sad Lines of Buenos Aires (1925)
Alfonsina Storni

Sad straight streets, gray and all the same,
On occasion a piece of sky,
Dark façades and the ground of asphalt
Extinguishing my warm springtime dreams
How often I have wandered them, distracted, soaked
the slow gray mist adorning them.
My soul suffers now from their monotony.
—Alfonsina!—don't call me. I answer to nothing.
Buenos Aires, if I die in one of your houses,
Watching this prison-like cycle on autumn days
The heavy stone will not come as a surprise
As, on your straight-lined streets, which spread
from your clouded, desolate, and somber river,
I wandered and was already buried.

Translated by Lisa Ubelaker Andrade

Catholic Encounters with the Peronist City

Delfina Bunge de Gálvez

In the wake of the first Peronist mobilization on October 17, 1945, the conservative press described the massive crowd that gathered in support of Perón as an invasive, nonwhite threat to the status quo. In this text, Delfina Bunge de Gálvez, a member of the traditional Catholic elite, writes for the Catholic newspaper El Pueblo. *Although she begins by describing the Peronist masses as an invasion from the outskirts of the city, her tone gradually changes; she demonstrates sympathy for the group, whom she says are clearly Catholic, and draws a comparison to the crowds that had gathered to celebrate the Eucharistic Congress. While Bunge de Gálvez aligned with Peronism, many of the paper's readers reacted with dismay to this article's pro-Peronist stance.*

A New Emotion in Buenos Aires (1945)

Delfina Bunge de Gálvez

The streets of Buenos Aires witnessed something truly astonishing. From all directions, groups of workers streamed in from the outskirts: the very poorest of the working class. And they walked beneath our balconies. This was the feared mob. They were—we believed—the discontented mass. Out of an old fear, our first impulse was to close the shutters. But when we looked out onto the street, we were taken aback by what we saw: the mobs had undergone a miraculous transformation. They seemed good-natured and calm, the angry faces and raised fists we had seen just a few years ago nowhere to be found. That first defensive impulse gave way to an empathetic urge to offer the poor walkers a place to rest and a bite to eat. But what would they do once they had gathered in large numbers? What would their intentions be? The surprises were just beginning. When night fell, we sat and listened as multitudes of workers gathered before the Casa Rosada for several emotional hours. The radio told us there were half a million people there. The skeptics among us reduced that to half—still some two hundred thousand. Would all that pent-up hatred explode? Would the hostilities begin? A crowd that size must feel powerful enough to do just about anything. The Cathedral was right on the square: they could have set it on fire. The Cathedral had been the target of anticlerical violence on many occasions. But the multitude has no ill intentions toward the institution. In fact, some of the people marching could be seen crossing themselves as they walked by the church. Some claim that in other parts of the city things got out of hand. It would have been a miracle if they hadn't. These mobs looked Christian, though they didn't know it. To us, they looked like a distant, unintentional, and humble echo of our Eucharistic Congresses.

Translated by Robin Myers

"Cabecita negra"

Germán Rozenmacher

Cabecita negra *(literally, "little black head") is a derogatory and racist term first used in the 1930s and 1940s to express disgust at the thousands of migrants from the Interior who moved to the outskirts of Buenos Aires to work in factories and who ultimately enlivened a political movement, contributing to the rise of Juan Perón. The term racialized Perón's supporters, intermixing ideas about race, class, and politics; they were described as "darker" than the typical "white" porteño, thus both unsettling a predominant narrative of Buenos Aires as a city of European descendants and illustrating an underlying racism. In this short story, written in 1961, fiction writer Germán Rozenmacher depicts this conflict. The story centers on Señor Lanari, the son of immigrants and owner of a successful hardware store. Lanari takes refuge in his home and his modest wealth. In a bout of insomnia, he decides to go to the street, where he encounters a young woman, drunk, alone, and lost; a police officer finds him and seeks his arrest for disturbing public order, insinuating that he had caused a problem. Lanari blames "negros" for upsetting the peace of the street, then realizes the cop is also "dark."*

"Cabecita negra" (1962)

Germán Rozenmacher

He had nothing to complain about. His father, a lowly debt collector for the electric company, was a starving immigrant who had never made anything of himself. Mr. Lanari had worked his fingers to the bone and now he had this third-floor walkup near the Capitol Building. A few months ago, he had bought himself a small Renault that was now parked in the garage below. He had spent a fortune on those gorgeous chrome door knockers. The hardware store on Avenida de Mayo was doing well, and now he had a weekend house as well. No complaints. He didn't deny himself anything. [. . .] Everything he had done in life he had done so that people would call him "sir." And he saved some money and opened a hardware store. You only live once, and things hadn't gone badly for him. No sir, not at all. They might be killing each other out there in the street, but he had his house, his sanctuary, a place of his own where he could live in peace and everything was just as it should be, a place where he got the respect he deserved. The only thing that hounded him was sleeplessness. It was four in the morning, and the fog was at its thickest. A heavy silence had fallen over Buenos Aires. Not a single sound. Motionless. But Mr. Lanari, trying not to wake anyone up, smoked, nodding off occasionally.

Out of nowhere, a woman screamed into the night. Out of nowhere. [. . .]

The wind kept blowing. Nobody stirred. Nobody knew what was happening. So Mr. Lanari walked down to the street and stumbled his way through the fog to the corner. And that was where he saw her. Just a *cabecita negra* sitting at the door of a hotel with a sign out front that read "Ladies Only." There she was, drunk, legs spread, almost like a little girl, her hands resting on her lap, defeated, lost, and all alone. Those legs open under a filthy skirt with big garish red flowers, her head on her chest and a bottle of beer under her arm.

"I wanna go home, mommy," she cried. "I want a hundred pesos for the train to get back home." [. . .] A vague sense of tenderness, of pity, stirred Mr. Lanari. He told himself that's just what these people were like, nothing to be done, life is rough. He smiled, and rolled up one hundred pesos that he then placed in the neck of the bottle with vague thoughts of charity. He felt satisfied. Hands in his pockets, he took her in for a while with slow disdain.

"What are you two doing here?" said a harsh wicked voice. Before he could turn around, he felt a hand on his shoulder.

"Come on, you two, we're going down to the station. For disturbing the peace."

Puzzled and frightened, Mr. Lanari smiled at the cop, his certain ally.

"Look these *negros*, officer, they spend their whole lives boozing, and then they get all worked up and make a racket. People can't get a decent night's sleep."

By the time he realized that the cop was also quite dark-skinned, it was too late.

Translated by Robin Myers

The City under Military Control

Jorge Asís and Ricardo Piglia

During the 1976–83 civic-military dictatorship, the state proclaimed they were creating "order" and suggested they would determine who "deserved" to live in the city. The urban chronicler and fiction writer Jorge Asís probed this imposition of so-called stability, asking if, in fact, the military were not the "unwelcome invaders": "What did they do to our city?"; "For whose order are we so used?" In "ID Cards and Life under Dictatorship," an excerpt from a short story penned while the military was still in power, the narrator is chatting in a café with a US filmmaker when the police begin to question them. When he discusses what is happening with the guest, the narrator begins to reflect on the military's presence and its vigilance over daily life.

Ricardo Piglia's 1992 novel, La ciudad ausente *(The Absent City), was published nearly a decade after the return to democracy. The story presents a dystopic Buenos Aires under authoritarian rule and combines themes of memory and resistance in an alternative reality. In Piglia's work, Junior, a journalist, is attempting to track down "the machine"—a tool that was designed to translate texts but has been found to possess a creative mind, capable of producing original work. The state, which persecutes alternative narratives, attempts to find and destroy the machine. The plot provides opportunity to reflect on memory, violence, and control—but also on the ways military rule shaped everyday life in the city. In this excerpt, Junior comments on the more mundane experience of authoritarian rule: the constant police checks; a pervasive sense of fear, control, violence, and danger; and, simultaneously, an eerie feeling that life was carrying on "normally."*

ID Cards and Life under Dictatorship (1981)

Jorge Asís

Suddenly the cops stormed in. And one surprising thing: they didn't just ask to see everyone's ID, they actually confiscated some of them. Albert showed his passport and they handed it back, but they whisked mine away while some of the officers stood strategically at the doors to make sure no one escaped. [. . .] To distract myself, I struck up a none-too-symbolic conversation about *The Grapes of Wrath*. [. . .] Twenty minutes later, in a sudden act of courtesy . . . an officer began to shout [names, until he got to mine]. I paid for the four whiskeys, we left, and as I walked Alberto to his hotel, he told me he'd never forget this night in Buenos Aires. "They're protecting our right to circulate," I told him. [. . .] [During another visit] Alberto told me that he wanted to meet a group of intellectuals, and I didn't know where to take him. I eventually admitted that the intellectuals no longer gathered, that the custom of sharing thoughts in a group had disappeared. [. . .] When we were about to order a second coffee, the authorities came in again. They went from table to table asking for everyone's ID. [. . .] There was a young man wearing jeans at the table next to us, a guy who stood out from the rest, and a plainclothes cop went through his wallet, asked him fifteen questions, turned the pockets of his jacket inside out, looked inside his cigarette pack, and went through the cards in his little phone book one by one, asking him where he had met a guy whose name began with a B. Alberto looked on, astonished. [. . .] Half an hour later, when the cops had gone, Albert asked us, "You can't go anywhere without your ID, can you?" And I said, "Our ID cards are like a part of our body. When we don't have it on us, we actually experience pain. [. . .] I have it on me even when I'm dreaming. It's the most important thing in my life."

Translated by Robin Myers

La ciudad ausente (1992)

Ricardo Piglia

It was six in the morning and the city had taken up its usual rhythm; one had to be attentive to movement, but without appearing too apprehensive. He watched the subway exit and the hall . . . the police controlled the city and it was important to pay close attention, to stay alert, to follow what was going on. There were constant controls. The police always had the last word; they could take your license to circulate; they could deny you entry to the press conference; they could even take away your work permit. Seeking out clandestine information was prohibited. He trusted Julia. He hoped she would appear. Perhaps she was telling the truth; perhaps she would show up with the police. There was a strange disparity in the awareness of what was going on. Everything was normal and at the same time the danger could be felt in the air, in the murmur of an alarm, as if the city was on the brink of being bombed. Amid the horror of everyday life, things carry on; this helped many maintain their sanity. The signs of death and terror are felt, but there is no change in conduct. The buses keep stopping on the street corners, businesses keep operating, couples get married and have wedding parties; it couldn't be that something so terrible was going on.

Translated by Lisa Ubelaker Andrade

The *Villa*, from Without and Within

Sergio Chejfec, César Aira, and César González

At the turn of the twenty-first century, social and spatial divides evident in Buenos Aires became a more central subject in literature. Many writers looked to imagine and represent the most impoverished communities in the city, the villas—*informal neighborhoods and settlements that had been built up by residents and that in many cases lacked basic public services. Their representations often reflected an outsider's viewpoint and commented on middle-class reactions to poverty. Sergio Chejfec's 1992 novel* El aire *(The Air) describes a fictional dystopic urban landscape in which the poor have begun to construct housing on the rooftops of middle-class apartment buildings; in this excerpt, the narrator contemplates the ways the presence of settlements were begrudgingly accepted by society. A second example is the 2001 novel* La villa, *by César Aira, which also critiqued and illustrated two irreconcilable landscapes—the* villa *and the city beyond. In this excerpt, the middle-class narrator enters the* villa *and views it as a sort of island that has its own rules, impenetrable to outsiders.*

The third text offers a different perspective. Its author, César González, is a poet and filmmaker from a villa—*Barrio Carlos Gardel—whose works reflect on poverty, inequality, labor, and the injustice of everyday life. In this text, a portion of an interview at an event on poetry from the* villa *in 2023, González reflects on the need for self-representation, for artists and poets from the* villas *who can speak to the beauty and violence of inequality, from the perspective of those who have lived it.*

The Air (1992)

Sergio Chejfec

Many years ago, prior generations of self-builders had fought dauntlessly so that the city would recognize their right to live on the land they'd taken; they had been accused of being usurpers, and they had generally drawn law and order against them. But not anymore: the new settlers weren't usurpers because no one reported them. Whether they invaded public or private plots, the plots were usually worth nothing even if they had owners, so no one tried to expel them or accuse them of anything. [. . .] Met with only indifference and marginalization, poverty seemed to be gradually losing its association with a social failure and was starting to be treated as personal incapacity.

Translated by Robin Myers

The Villa *(2001)*

César Aira

He felt privileged, and he didn't know why; it was no privilege to enter that foul-smelling, tin-shack labyrinth, where the poorest of the poor were huddled together. [. . .] He could have wagered that none of his acquaintances from school, from the gym, from his neighborhood, none of his parents' or relatives' friends, had ever entered or would ever enter a *villa*. And they were so close to it! It was just around the corner, really. Which meant both that it wasn't a big deal and that it was. [. . .] Its residents had become invisible [. . .] because they were wrapped in a fold of life that people usually prefer not to see.

Translated by Robin Myers

Poetry in the Villas *(2023)*

César González

The *villa* overflows with poetry, if you understand poetry like I do, as a vital experience, as a way of perceiving the world, of positioning oneself in society. It isn't just a form of catharsis or a strict literary form. Poetry has something unknowable, and at the same time, it is of the earth. That is why there is so much unwritten poetry in the *villas*. There is so much poetry because there is a vitality that is made necessary because it is a place of death—and I refer not to physical death but, rather, to other ways of dying, like not having a vision for the future, like living day to day with mountainous adversities, situations of violence that the people in our neighborhoods have grown accustomed to. Paradoxically, and I would even say miraculously, that vitality perseveres, there is a buzz; there is happiness. There is dancing and enjoyment. That is a poetry that is unwritten; we must claim our right to take up a space that, until now, has been dominated by an aristocratic stereotype of what poetry is; yet we must do so without falling into a romanticization of the world of the *villa*. Because even if we point to all its beauty, we must underscore that it is a beauty that rises from a place permeated by sad occurrences.

Translated by Lisa Ubelaker Andrade

Social Mobility

Tulio Halperín Donghi

Upward mobility, the idea that a person could improve their social and economic position, predated a recognition of a "middle class." In this text, the historian Tulio Halperín Donghi reconstructs the importance and prevalence of the notion of upward mobility during the early twentieth century. In the second half of the century, this sense of possibility was no longer quite so robust, and by the 1970s, there was a growing sense that "social mobility" did not only move in an upward direction: while ascension was possible, experiences of economic crisis, frustration, and "downward mobility" were also quite common. These changes in perception also invited investigation into the idea of social mobility and its fluctuations over the course of the century; while some returned to take a closer look at the notion of the middle class, others turned their focus to those who found their aspirations for prosperity frustrated.

A City Enters the Twentieth Century (1999)

Tulio Halperín Donghi

This is a society whose internal borders—except for the one separating the peak of the proprietary class, with the landowner in its nucleus, from the rest—are still fluid. [In the early twentieth century], the virtues exalted by socialist or anarchist morals sometimes find their prize within the framework of a progressing capitalist economy. No small number of their most militant representatives will one day become entrepreneurs; some will abandon the ideology of the class to which they no longer belong; others will not. [. . .] This is, indeed, a society with borders so fluid that internal locations are often imprecise. Let's describe, with some exactitude, the location of a literary character indelibly carved into collective memory: *la costurerita que dio aquel mal paso*, or "the seamstress who went wrong." An entire body of specialized literature invites us to place her in a tenement room, and to associate her ultimately fatal illness with the sanitary conditions exhaustively examined in such works. But that's not where Evaristo Carriego places her: he makes her part of a family that starts to feel cramped in its quarters. The point isn't to conclude that seamstresses in 1910 were a neglected sector of an expanding middle class. If only Carriego's audience hadn't seemed so nonchalant before a scene—a scene that strikes us as inconceivable today—in which the writer would locate the tragedy of this girl, abandoned and left to die.

Translated by Robin Myers

White-Collar Workers

Roberto Mariani and Alfonsina Storni

The topic of modernity and its effect on urban life was an often-revisited theme during the 1920s and 1930s. The short-story writer Roberto Mariani depicts a downtown filled with offices and, then, a world of neighborhoods filled with a typical family-based social scene. He describes these community spaces as having what for him was a utopian daily life—men traveled to work downtown and returned to their neighborhoods, where they found modern amenities like movie theaters, shops, and their wives virtuously caring for their homes and growing children. This story speaks to a growing trend during this era of visualizing Buenos Aires as a city with a large middle class—one in which residents went to school, saved money, and climbed the social ladder to improve their standard of living. Offering a different perspective on this trend, the writer Alfonsina Storni noted that many women had also taken up professions downtown, as secretaries, teachers, and saleswomen; some were employed as factory workers, and some even rejected the supposed comforts of domestic home life in favor of staying in the workforce.

Stories from the Office (1925)

Roberto Mariani

Ah, how he longed to have found her on a familiar street in a familiar neighborhood, in those neighborhoods of squat houses and rowdy children: [. . .] the daughter of the corner shopkeeper [. . .] educated in the domestic virtues of humble families in Buenos Aires neighborhoods [. . .] a teacher of piano and solfège lessons, or of other labors. [. . .] He remembered having a few sweethearts there, when he was around twenty years old. [. . .] What beautiful girls, and how humble were even the most flirtatious among them, how innocent even the most intelligent. [. . .] All maternal, with a visible tendency toward swiftly abandoning their idylls in the name of settling into the affections of their household tasks, their furniture, their future children. [. . .] On Saturday nights they would go to the movies on the main street of the neighborhood. [. . .] On Sunday they would go to Palermo with the little ones.

[. . .] She would cook, wash the clothes, educate the children [. . .] sweet, lively children in a happy and tranquil household.

Translated by Robin Myers

Women on Their Way to Work (1920)

Alfonsina Storni

If at seven or eight in the morning one gets on the trolley, she will see it partly occupied with women on their way to work, distracting themselves on their commute with something to read. If a young lady reader carries with her a crime novel, we know she is a factory worker or a seamstress; if she holds a popular illustrated magazine close to her chest, she is a secretary or a store worker; if the magazine is of an intellectual character, she is a primary or secondary school teacher, and if she carries with her a casually folded newspaper, no need to doubt [. . .] an accomplished feminist, a brave feminist. [. . .] The typists represent the advance of working women, and number in the thousands. They invade the desks at private offices, houses of commerce, public offices, and private studios. They sway in the monotonous *tip, tip, tiptiptip* of their machines, and range from the poor young girl who writes addresses on envelopes by the cent, to the upper-level employee who knows stenography and is in charge of foreign correspondence.

Translated by Lisa Ubelaker Andrade

Critiques of the Buenos Aires Middle Class

Juan José Sebreli

In 1964, the essayist Juan José Sebreli published Buenos Aires, vida cotidiana y alienación *(Buenos Aires, Everyday Life and Alienation), a book that revived criticism and conversation about the culture of the city's various classes and their origins. Sebreli identified classes by their everyday customs and habits—forms "of loving, of feeling, of having fun, of thinking." He saw each class dealing with the inevitable alienation brought on by modern capitalism and identified the middle classes, in particular, as close-minded, superficial, and anti-Peronist. While this description has since been criticized as overly simplistic, it resonated with readers. In this excerpt, Sebreli narrates how the middle classes in Buenos Aires came to be and describes the group's characteristics in rather essentialist terms.*

The Misery of the Buenos Aires Middle Class (1964)

Juan José Sebreli

Alongside the old run-down neighborhoods, new ones were being built around the industrial establishments or on the vacant lots, sometimes leaving the finishings or plot divisions of the old estates on the outskirts. Workers gathered there who had risen to the lower levels of the middle class and built little houses with their own hands that did not initially resolve the discomforts of the tenement. [. . .] Interminable neighborhoods [. . .] with some solitary movie theater, the display window of a corner store, the fleeting reflection of the bus heading downtown, the grocery store [. . .] the modest Italian builders who constructed their own houses unknowingly restored a solemn classicism. [. . .] These cubist houses—with limestone façades painted white or pink, flat roofs, balustrades, concrete urns, checkered plant-filled yards—turned out to be more aesthetically respectable than the wild, ostentatious eclecticism of the petite bourgeoisie and the gentry. [. . .] Over time, these neighborhoods became imbued with a certain tradition; they were inhabited by the oldest families of the proletariat, the elite of the working class, the descendants of late-century European immigrants. [. . .] At first, the fear of change, as well as the prejudice that associated apartments with tenements, were mental obstacles for the middle class in departing from the old ramshackle mansions and their lack of urban amenities. The upper class had to impose the multistory home so that the middle class would trail behind. This is how the petite bourgeois apartment came into existence—lavish façades and sad, dismal backdrops—for a sector that fed on appearances. [. . .] Sorrow, indifference, fatalism—illustrated by typical Buenos Aires expressions like "stay out of others' business"; [. . .] "go with the flow"; [. . .] "what are you going to do"—instituted by harried interpreters, have ultimately been none other than the psychological reactions of a particular social class [. . .] that saw life as a spectacle, taken in from the sidewalk [. . .] of a class that did not want to participate in history. What mattered to the middle class was reputation, appearances, what everyone else thought of it. It relied heavily on its fellows, lived in terror of what they would say, of rumors, of scandal. [. . .] Everyone ensconced in their homes, securely protected by four walls and free from probing eyes. The petite bourgeois household constituted the refuge ensuring isolation, separation from the outside world.

Translated by Robin Myers

Writing the Middle Classes

Juan Carlos Torre and Guillermo Oliveto

Despite the common refrain that Buenos Aires is a "middle-class city," the exact meaning of what it means to be "middle class" is elusive and the subject of debate. References to a middle class emerged in Buenos Aires theater and cultural productions in the early twentieth century, and academics began to try to quantify and define what it meant to be a part of the middle classes at midcentury; they often saw the structural components of public education, urban infrastructure, commerce, labor regulations, and mass culture as critical to the expansion of white-collar occupations and a middle-class ideal. In the 1980s, sociologists like Juan Carlos Torre attempted to define the characteristics of Buenos Aires life that provided a framework for "middle-class" culture. In a more contemporary take, consumer analyst Guillermo Oliveto describes the idea of middle-class resilience, the perception that, despite repeated crises and economic precarity, an idea of a middle class survives; he suggests that the lower middle class is in a more precarious position than is often understood.

Collective and Individual Mobility (1983)

Juan Carlos Torre

If one wanted to distill the history of Buenos Aires between 1930 and the present into a formula encompassing all of its most distinctive parts, the resulting image is one of massification: Buenos Aires, city of modern masses, city of middle classes. If this was already true in 1930, it was even truer in 1945, and it was certainly so from 1960 onward. [. . .] The transformation at work in Argentina's centenary also encompassed its social actors. The social mobility, both upward and downward, that characterized modernization, contributed—along with the rapid expansion of service and public employment activities—to the formation of a middle class that continued to grow, and that thus increasingly influenced the country's social composition. By 1930, Argentine society was already made up of middle classes, and its capital was the capital of those classes: in the city-dwellers' lifestyles, in their tastes and expectations, in their behavior as consumers and as political beings, and also, unquestionably, in the gravitational path of the social sector whose patterns, needs, and preferences imposed a particular style onto the city as a whole. [. . .] The growth of education illustrates the rise of the middle class. [. . .] In 1939, the population was somewhat over 2 million inhabitants. Between 1947 and 1970, it rose to 2.9 million. Within the same period, the number of students enrolled in primary school increased by over 100 percent, and the number enrolled in secondary school increased several hundreds of times. [. . .] The university population of Buenos Aires barely exceeded 10,000 in 1930, while in 1975 it was over 200,000 students. [. . .] Between 1947 and 1960, middle-class professions increased by 16 percent, while lower-class professions decreased by over 10 percent. [. . .] Far from constituting a prize, mobility was the norm, a way of life. Several generations thus experienced upward social mobility as a goal attainable through minimal effort in just a few years, at almost no cost other than that of a single generation's formal education. Between 1930 and 1955, the remarkable wave of upward mobility was the major engine behind the creation of middle-class sectors and thus the primary influence on Buenos Aires's massification. Collective mobility accompanied individual mobility. The growing economic prosperity started to enable entire sectors of the lower classes, especially the industrial working class, to access middle-class ways of life—without having to abandon their occupations. In the jeans generation of the 1960s, it was difficult to distinguish a worker's son from the son of a merchant or a university graduate.

Translated by Robin Myers

Crisis and Resilience in the Diverse Middle Class (2021)
Guillermo Oliveto

One could say that [despite the crises that have occurred], the middle class managed to sustain itself thanks to its accumulated "stock." [. . .] They have lost the power of consumption but maintained their culture. I find this analysis somewhat superficial and even dangerous. It would be like saying that even if a bomb fell on the Argentine economy that "almost nothing would happen." [. . .] Over the last decade, the gap between the upper middle class and the lower middle class has been widening and the differences between them becoming starker. [. . .] One tends to think in almost binary terms: middle class or poor. And it is not like that. There is something in between. That something is a lower class who is not poor. Their values largely coincide with those of the middle class. The middle class defines itself as the group of the population that is neither rich nor poor; that does not have a driver or private security; that can take care of the expenses of its family; that does not depend on state assistance; that, whether big or small, is investing in a project for the future; and, in particular, that has work, and works to live. That is why 85 percent of the population perceives itself as middle class, although technically many are not. It is a symbolic communion, a shared imaginary, rather than an equality that can be expressed in practice. [. . .] Almost like a genetic inheritance from a country with cyclical crises, [the middle class] developed the mechanisms to process the harshness of a cruel economic context without abandoning their identity in the process. The middle class maintains its soul. It would seem that the violence of economic ups and downs is breaking the resistance of a part of that above-poverty lower class. Those who have fallen are a part of the lower class near the poverty line, who until now have avoided that category. It is a world marked in large part by informal labor [work without a formal contract] [. . .] people who were not used to depending on or do not want to depend on assistance. They are the ones who have lost the most over the last decade. [. . .] They are the ones who have been left fragile but dream of returning [to what they were]. That vocation to find a way around it, in some way, that entrepreneurial spirit, that determination to get ahead by some means, is probably the most valuable reserve that this battered society treasures.

Translated by Lisa Ubelaker Andrade

Enduring City

María Elena Walsh and Bersuit Vergarabat

The song "Como la Cigarra" ("Like the Cicada") by the poet María Elena Walsh was written at the end of the 1966–73 dictatorship. In the following decades it became an important ode to the notions of survival and resilience in the wake of oppression or crisis. Its fame and profound significance were intensified when the exiled singer Mercedes Sosa performed it on the event of her momentous return to Buenos Aires in 1982, just as the civic-military dictatorship was coming to an end. References to disappearance and erasure resonated, as did the lyrics' insistence on the act of return— "singing to the sun, like a cicada, after a year underground," despite facing enormous tragedy, experiences of death and "war." In the decades after, these themes of an insistent return, or endurance, were revisited, their meanings extended to consider how the city (as well as the country) and its peoples would have to continually find ways to navigate and persist despite what felt like relentless, recurring experiences of crisis. While written in a different tone, this idea of resilience is also echoed in the 2004 song by the rock band Bersuit Vergarabat, "El baile de la gambeta" ("The Dance of the Gambeta"). The song uses soccer as a metaphor for a fast-paced defiance for survival: gambeta refers to smart footwork, smooth like dancing, that sharply evades opponents during play; written in the wake of the 2001 crisis, the song also alludes to the need to be strategic and streetwise and to live amid pain, to return from loss and refuse to give in, to navigate survival despite the feeling of imminent defeat.

Like the Cicada (1972)

María Elena Walsh

So many times, they've killed me,
So many times, I've died,
Nevertheless, here I am,
Revived.
I give thanks to hardships,
to the clenched fist,
Because they killed me so poorly
that I keep singing.
Singing to the sun,

Like the cicada,
after a year underground,
just like a survivor,
back from war;
So many times they erased me,
so many times I disappeared,
my own funeral I attended
alone and crying [. . .]
Singing to the sun,
after a year underground,
just like a survivor,
back from a war [. . .]

Translated by Lisa Ubelaker Andrade

The Dance of the Gambeta *(2004)*

Bersuit Vergarabat

I'll play a fantasy of cold strategy
and if there is no victory cup
at least the people will drink theirs, make do,
jump on top of the pain and be born again,
Come on, madmen!

If I have to die
I am not going out like a sheep
that lies down when he's done giving wool

We're going to dance
to change our luck,
we know how to move the ball,
to escape our death.

Translated by Lisa Ubelaker Andrade

Suggestions for Further Reading and Viewing

The works below informed this *Reader* and are recommended for further reading; the list, however, is by no means exhaustive. Readings are organized by theme, though several of the texts are relevant to understanding topics across the *Reader*. Texts included in the *Reader* can be found in the Acknowledgment of Copyrights and Sources.

General

Armus, Diego, ed. *Mundo urbano y cultura popular: Estudios de historia social argentina.* Buenos Aires: Sudamericana, 1990.

Bourdé, Guy. *Buenos Aires: Urbanización e inmigración.* Buenos Aires: Huemul, 1977.

Carretero, Andrés. *Vida cotidiana en Buenos Aires: Desde la sociedad autoritaria hasta la sociedad de masas (1918–1970).* Buenos Aires: Planeta, 2001.

Gardner, James. *Buenos Aires: The Biography of a City.* New York: Saint Martin's, 2015.

Gorelik, Adrián. *The Grid and the Park: Public Space and Urban Culture in Buenos Aires, 1887–1936.* Pittsburgh: Latin America Research Commons, 2022.

Gutman, Margarita, and Jorge Enrique Hardoy. *Buenos Aires, 1536–2000: Historia urbana del área metropolitana.* Buenos Aires: Ediciones Infinito, 2007.

Landau, Matías. *Gobernar Buenos Aires: Ciudad, política y sociedad, del siglo XIX a nuestros días.* Buenos Aires: Prometeo, 2018.

Liernur, Jorge Francisco. *Arquitectura en la Argentina del siglo XX: La construcción de la modernidad.* Buenos Aires: Fondo Nacional de las Artes, 2001.

Molina y Vedia, Juan. *Mi Buenos Aires herido: Planes de desarrollo territorial y urbano (1535–2000).* Buenos Aires: Ediciones Colihue, 1999.

Rapoport, Mario, and María Seoane. *Buenos Aires, historia de una ciudad: De la modernidad al siglo XXI, sociedad, política, economía y cultura.* Buenos Aires: Planeta, 2007.

Romero, José Luis, and Luis Alberto Romero, eds. *Buenos Aires: Historia de cuatro siglos.* Buenos Aires: Abril, 1983.

Ross, Stanley R., and Thomas F. McGann, eds. *Buenos Aires: 400 Years.* Austin: University of Texas Press, 1982.

Sargent, Charles. *Spatial Evolution of Greater Buenos Aires, Argentina, 1870–1930.* Tempe: Arizona State University Press, 1974.

Scobie, James. *Buenos Aires: Plaza to Suburb, 1870–1910.* New York: Oxford University Press, 1974.

Torres, Horacio. *El mapa social de Buenos Aires (1940–1990)*. Buenos Aires: FADU-UBA, 1993.

Vapnarsky, César A. *La aglomeración Gran Buenos Aires: Expansión espacial y crecimiento demográfico entre 1869–1991*. Buenos Aires: Eudeba, 2000.

Vázquez Rial, Horacio, ed. *Buenos Aires 1880–1930: La capital de un imperio imaginario*. Madrid: Alianza, 1996.

Walter, Richard. *Politics and Urban Growth in Buenos Aires, 1910–1942*. Cambridge: Cambridge University Press, 1993.

Welch Guerra, Max, ed. *Buenos Aires a la deriva: Transformaciones urbanas recientes*. Buenos Aires: Biblos, 2005.

Wilson, Jason. *Buenos Aires: A Cultural History*. Northampton, MA: Interlink Books, 2007.

Guides

Bigongiari, Diego. *BUE: Buenos Aires y alrededores*. Buenos Aires: Rumbo Austral, 2008.

Watson, Ricardo, Lucas Rentero, and Gabriel Di Meglio. *Buenos Aires tiene historia: Once itinerarios guiados por la ciudad*. Buenos Aires: Aguilar, 2008.

Part I. The Living City

Adair, Jennifer. *In Search of the Lost Decade: Everyday Rights in Post-dictatorship Argentina*. Berkeley: University of California Press, 2019.

Andrews, George. *The Afro-Argentines of Buenos Aires, 1800–1900*. Madison: University of Wisconsin Press, 1980.

Armus, Diego. *The Ailing City: Health, Tuberculosis, and Culture, 1870–1950*. Durham, NC: Duke University Press, 2011.

Auyero, Javier, and Debora Swistum. *Flammable: Environmental Suffering in an Argentine Shantytown*. New York: Oxford University Press, 2009.

Baily, Samuel. *Immigrants in the Lands of Promise: Italians in Buenos Aires and New York City, 1870–1914*. Ithaca, NY: Cornell University Press, 1999.

Baldasarre, María Isabel. *Bien vestidos: Una historia visual de la moda en Buenos Aires (1870–1914)*. Buenos Aires: Ampersand, 2021.

Ballent, Anahí. *Las huellas de la política: Vivienda, ciudad, peronismo en Buenos Aires, 1943–1955*. Bernal: Universidad Nacional de Quilmes, 2005.

Borrini, Alberto. *El siglo de la publicidad: Homenaje a la publicidad gráfica argentina*. Buenos Aires: Atlántida, 2006.

Bryce, Benjamin. *To Belong in Buenos Aires: Germans, Argentines, and the Rise of a Pluralistic Society*. Stanford, CA: Stanford University Press, 2018.

Cravino, María Cristina. *Las villas de la ciudad: Mercados e informalidad urbana*. Buenos Aires: Universidad Nacional de General Sarmiento, 2006.

Del Nido, Juan Manuel. *Taxis vs Uber: Courts, Markets, and Technology in Buenos Aires*. Stanford, CA: Stanford University Press, 2021.

Fara, Catalina. *Un horizonte vertical: Paisaje urbano de Buenos Aires (1910–1936)*. Buenos Aires: Ampersand, 2020.

Feijóo, María del Carmen. *Nuevo país, nueva pobreza*. Buenos Aires: Fondo de Cultura Económica, 2001.

García Heras, Raúl. *Transportes, negocios y política: La Compañía Anglo Argentina de Tranvías, 1876–1981*. Buenos Aires: Sudamericana, 1994.

Gené, Marcela. *Un mundo feliz: Imágenes de los trabajadores en el primer peronismo, 1946–1955*. Buenos Aires: Universidad de San Andrés, 2005.

Goldar, Ernesto. *Buenos Aires: Vida cotidiana en la década del 50*. Buenos Aires: Plus Ultra, 1980.

Grimson, Alejandro. *Relatos de la diferencia y la igualdad: Los bolivianos en Buenos Aires*. Buenos Aires: EUDEBA, 1999.

Gutiérrez, Leandro, and Luis Alberto Romero. *Sectores populares, cultura y política: Buenos Aires en la entreguerra*. Buenos Aires: Sudamericana, 1995.

Kessler, Gabriel, ed. *El Gran Buenos Aires*. Buenos Aires: UNIPE / Edhasa, 2015.

Korn, Francis. *Buenos Aires 1895: Un ciudad moderna*. Buenos Aires: Editorial del Instituto, 1981.

Lederman, Jacob. *Chasing World-Class Urbanism: Global Policy versus Everyday Survival in Buenos Aires*. Minneapolis: University of Minnesota Press, 2020.

Liernur, Francisco, and Graciela Silvestri. *El umbral de la metropolis: Transformaciones técnicas y cultura en la modernización de Buenos Aires (1870–1930)*. Buenos Aires: Sudamericana, 1993.

Milanesio, Natalia. *Workers Go Shopping in Argentina: The Rise of a Consumer Popular Culture*. Albuquerque: New Mexico University Press, 2013.

Moya, José. *Cousins and Strangers: Spanish Immigrants in Buenos Aires, 1850–1930*. Berkeley: University of California Press, 1998.

Prignano, Angel O. *Barriología y diversidad cultural*. Buenos Aires: Ciccus, 2008.

Rocchi, Fernando. *Chimneys in the Desert: Industrialization in Argentina during the Export Boom Years, 1870–1930*. Stanford, CA: Stanford University Press, 2006.

Sofer, Eugene. *From Pale to Pampa: A Social History of Jews in Buenos Aires*. New York: Holmes & Meir, 1982.

Svampa, Maristella. *Los que ganaron: La vida en los countries y barrios cerrados*. Buenos Aires: Biblos, 2001.

Tossounian, Cecilia. *La Joven Moderna in Interwar Argentina: Gender, Nation, and Popular Culture*. Gainesville: University of Florida Press, 2020.

Wortman, Ana, ed. *Pensar las clases medias argentinas: Consumos culturales y estilos de vida urbanos en la Argentina de los noventa*. Buenos Aires: La Crujía Ediciones, 2003.

Yujnovksy, Oscar. *Claves políticas del problema habitacional argentino, 1955–1981*. Buenos Aires: Grupo Editor Latinoamericano, 1984.

Part II. Taking to the Street

Auyero, Javier. *Poor People's Politics: Peronist Survival Networks and the Legacy of Evita*. Durham, NC: Duke University Press, 2001.

Bonner, Michelle. *Sustaining Human Rights: Women and Argentine Human Rights Organizations*. University Park: Pennsylvania State University Press, 2007.

De Privitellio, Luciano. *Vecinos y ciudadanos: Política y sociedad en la Buenos Aires de entreguerras*. Buenos Aires: Siglo XXI, 2003.

Fraser, Nicholas, and Maryssa Navarro. *Evita: The Real Life of Eva Peron*. New York: Norton, 1996.

Ippolito-O'Donnell, Gabriela. *The Right to the City: Popular Contention in Contemporary Buenos Aires*. Notre Dame, IN: University of Notre Dame Press, 2012.

James, Daniel. *Resistance and Integration: The Argentine Working Class, 1946–1976*. Cambridge: Cambridge University Press, 1988.

Kozak, Claudia. *Contra la pared: Sobre graffitis, pintadas y otras intervenciones urbanas*. Buenos Aires: Libros del Rojas, 2004.

Liut, Martín, ed. *2001: Una crisis cantada*. Buenos Aires: Gourmet Musical, 2021.

Lobato, Mirta. *Historia de las trabajadoras en la Argentina, 1869–1960*. Buenos Aires: Edhasa, 2007.

Longoni, Ana. "Crossroads for Activist Art in Argentina." *Third Text* 22 (September 2008): 575–87.

Macón, Cecilia. "White Scarves and Green Scarves: The Affective Temporality of #QueSeaLey [#MakeItLaw] as Fourth-Wave Feminism." In *Affect, Gender, and Sexuality in Latin America*, edited by Cecilia Macón, Mariela Solana, and Nayla Luz Vacarezza. New York: Palgrave, 2021.

Munilla Lacasa, María Lía. *Celebrar y gobernar: Un estudio de las fiestas cívicas en Buenos Aires, 1810–1835*. Buenos Aires: Miño y Dávila, 2013.

Ozlak, Oscar. *Merecer la ciudad: Los pobres y el derecho al espacio urbano*. Buenos Aires: Cedes-Humanitas, 1991.

Sábato, Hilda. *The Many and the Few: Political Participation in Republican Buenos Aires*. Stanford, CA: Stanford University Press, 2001.

Serulnikov, Sergio. "When Looting Becomes a Right: Urban Poverty and Food Riots in Argentina." *Latin American Perspectives* 21, no. 3 (Summer 1994): 69–89.

Sigal, Silvia. *La Plaza de Mayo: Una crónica*. Buenos Aires: Siglo XXI, 2006.

Suriano, Juan. *Paradoxes of Utopias: Anarchist Culture and Politics in Buenos Aires, 1890–1910*. Oakland, CA: AK Press, 2010.

Torre, Juan Carlos, and Elisa Pastoriza. "La democratización del bienestar." In *Los años peronistas*, edited by Juan Carlos Torre. Buenos Aires: Sudamericana, 2002.

Vázquez, Ayelén. *Paisaje expandido: Ensayos sobre el arte público de Buenos Aires en el siglo XXI*. Buenos Aires: ArtexArte, 2020.

Zanatta, Loris. *Del estado liberal a la nación católica: Iglesia y ejército en el orígenes del peronismo, 1930–1943*. Bernal: Universidad Nacional del Quilmes, 1996.

Part III. Eating in Buenos Aires

Aguirre, Patricia. *Ricos flacos y gordos pobres: La alimentación en crisis*. Buenos Aires: Capital intelectual, 2010.

Armus, Diego, and Lisa Ubelaker-Andrade. "Cibo della mescolanza, menù estesi, riostoranti e pizzeria: Buenos Aires nel secolo XX." In *Identità culinarie in Sudamerica*, edited by Camilla Cattarulla. Roma: Nova Delphi, 2017.

Caldo, Paula. *Mujeres cocineras: Hacia una historia socio-cultural de la cocina argentina a fines del siglo XIX y primera mitad del XX*. Rosario: Prohistoria, 2009.

Cattarula, Camila, ed. *Juana Manuela Gorriti: Cocina ecléctica*. Buenos Aires: La Crujía Ediciones, 2015.

Ducrot, Víctor Ego. *Los sabores de la patria: Las intrigas de la historia argentina contadas desde la mesa y la cocina*. Buenos Aires: Norma, 1998.

Pérez, Inés. "Comfort for the People and Liberalization for the Housewife: Gender, Consumption and Refrigerators in Argentina (1930–1960)." *Journal of Consumer Culture* 12, no. 2 (2012): 156–74.

Pite, Rebekah. *Creating a Common Table in Twentieth-Century Argentina: Doña Petrona, Women, and Food*. Chapel Hill: University of North Carolina Press, 2013.

Poblete, Lorena. "Acceso a la justicia de trabajadores de casas particulares: La experiencia del tribunal de trabajo doméstico de la Ciudad Autónoma de Buenos Aires." Buenos Aires: ILO, 2023.

Porta Fouz, Javier, and Natalia Schejtman. *El libro de oro del helado argentino*. Buenos Aires: Sudamericana, 2012.

Sarreal, Julia. *Yerba Mate: The Drink That Shaped a Nation*. Berkeley: University of California Press, 2023.

Schavelzon, Daniel. *Historias del comer y del beber en Buenos Aires: Arqueología histórica de la vajilla de mesa*. Buenos Aires: Aguilar, 2000.

Schneider, Arnd. "Ethnicity, Changing Paradigms and Variations in Food Consumption among Italians in Buenos Aires." *Altreitalie* 7 (1992): 84–95.

Sorba, Pietro. *Los bodegones de Buenos Aires*. Buenos Aires: Planeta, 2014.

Vazquez-Prego, Alberto. *Así cocinan los argentinos*. Buenos Aires: El Ateneo, 1979.

Part IV. Hinchas, Cracks, *and* Potreros *in the City of* Soccer

Alabarces, Pablo, and María Graciela Rodríguez. *Cuestión de pelotas: Fútbol, deporte, sociedad, cultura*. Buenos Aires: Atuel, 1996.

Anderson, Patricia. "Sporting Women and Machonas: Negotiating Gender through Sports in Argentina, 1900–1946." *Women's History Review* 24, no. 5 (2015): 700–720.

Archetti, Eduardo. *Masculinities: Football, Polo, and Tango in Argentina*. Oxford: Berg, 1999.

Armus, Diego, and Pablo Scharogrodsky. "El fútbol en las escuelas y colegios argentinos: Notas sobre un desencuentro en el siglo XX." In *Del football al fútbol/futebol: Historias argentinas, brasileras y uruguayas en el siglo XX*, edited by Diego Armus and Stefan Rinke, 85–100. Madrid: Iberoamericana, 2014.

Bayer, Osvaldo. *Fútbol argentino*. Buenos Aires: Sudamericana, 1990.

Caparrós, Martín. *Boquita*. Buenos Aires: Planeta, 2005.

Duke, Vic, and Liz Crolley. "Fútbol, Politicians and the People: Populism and Politics in Argentina." *International Journal of the History of Sport* 18, no. 3 (2001): 93–116.

Frydenberg, Julio. *Historia social del fútbol: Del amateurismo a la profesionalización*. Buenos Aires: Siglo XXI, 2011.

González, Florencia. *Ovarios y pelotas: Más que fútbol femenino*. Buenos Aires: Editorial Apasionarte, 2020.

Hora, Roy. *Historia del turf argentino*. Buenos Aires: Siglo XXI, 2014.

Horowitz, Joel. *The Creation of Modern Buenos Aires: Football, Civic Associations, Barrios, and Politics, 1912–1943*. Albuquerque: University of New Mexico Press, 2024.

Karush, Matthew. "National Identity in the Sport Pages: Football and the Mass Media in 1920s Buenos Aires." *The Americas* 60, no. 1 (2003): 11–52.

Mateu, Cristina. "Política e ideología de la Federación Deportiva Obrera, 1924–1929." In *Deporte y sociedad*, edited by Pablo Alabarces, Roberto Di Giano, and Julio Frydenberg, 67–86. Buenos Aires: EUDEBA, 1998.

Rein, Raanan. "'El Primer Deportista': The Political Use and Abuse of Sport in Peronist Argentina." *International Journal of the History of Sport* 15, no. 2 (1998): 54–76.

Scher, Ariel. *La patria deportista: Cien años de política y deporte.* Buenos Aires: Planeta, 1996.

Wilson, Jonathan. *Angels with Dirty Faces: How Argentinian Soccer Defined a Nation and Changed the Game Forever.* New York: Nation Books, 2016.

Part V. Reading, Watching, and Listening in Buenos Aires

Abraham, Carlos. *La Editorial Tor: Medio siglo de libros populares.* Buenos Aires: Tren en Movimiento, 2012.

Aguilar, Gonzalo. *New Argentine Cinema: Other Worlds.* London: Palgrave, 2011.

Cane, James. *The Fourth Enemy: Journalism and Power in the Making of Peronist Argentina, 1930–1955.* University Park: Pennsylvania State University Press, 2011.

Cosse, Isabella. *Mafalda: A Social and Political History of Latin America's Global Comic.* Translated by Laura Pérez Carrara. Durham, NC: Duke University Press, 2019.

Ehrick, Christine. *Radio and Gendered Soundscape: Women and Broadcasting in Argentina and Uruguay, 1930–1950.* New York: Cambridge University Press, 2015.

Elena, Eduardo. "Peronism in Good Taste: Culture and Consumption in the Magazine *Argentina.*" In *The New Cultural History of Peronism: Power and Identity in Mid-Twentieth-Century Argentina,* edited by Mathew Karush and Oscar Chamosa, 209–38. Durham, NC: Duke University Press, 2010.

Falicov, Tamara. *The Cinematic Tango: Contemporary Argentine Film.* London: Wallflower Press, 2007.

Ford, Aníbal, Jorge B. Rivera, and Eduardo Romano. *Medios de comunicación y cultura popular.* Buenos Aires: Legasa, 1985.

Fortuna, Victoria. *Moving Otherwise: Dance, Violence, and Memory in Buenos Aires.* New York: Oxford University Press, 2018.

Getino, Octavio. *Cine y dependencia: El cine en la Argentina.* Buenos Aires: Puntosur, 1990.

Giunta, Andrea. *Avant-Garde, Internationalism, and Politics: Argentine Art in the Sixties.* Durham, NC: Duke University Press, 2007.

González Velasco, Carolina. *Gente de teatro: Ocio y espectáculos en la Buenos Aires de los años veinte.* Buenos Aires: Siglo XXI, 2012.

Graham-Jones, Jean. *Exorcizing History: Argentine Theater under Dictatorship.* Cranbury, NJ: Bucknell University Press, 2000.

Karush, Matthew. *Culture of Class: Radio and Cinema in the Making of a Divided Argentina, 1920–1946.* Durham, NC: Duke University Press, 2010.

King, John. *Sur: A Study of the Argentine Literary Journal and Its Role in the Development of Culture, 1931–1970.* New York: Cambridge University Press, 1986.

Knudson, Jerry W. "Veil of Silence: The Argentine Press and the Dirty War, 1971–1983." *Latin American Perspectives* 24, no. 6 (1997): 93–112.

Lobato, Mirta. *La prensa obrera: Buenos Aires y Montevideo, 1890–1958.* Buenos Aires: Edhasa, 2009.

Mastrini, Guillermo, ed. *Mucho ruido, pocas leyes: Economía y políticas de comunicación en la Argentina (1920–2004).* Buenos Aires: La Crujía, 2005.

Matallana, Andrea. *"Locos por la radio": Una historia social de la radiofonía en la Argentina, 1923–1947.* Buenos Aires: Prometeo, 2006.

Prieto, Adolfo. *El discurso criollista en la formación de la Argentina moderna.* Buenos Aires: Sudamericana, 1988.

Rea, Lauren. *Children's Culture and Citizenship in Argentina: A History of Billiken Magazine (1919–2019).* York: White Rose University Press, 2023.

Saítta, Sylvia. *Regueros de tinta: El diario Crítica en la década de 1920.* Buenos Aires: Sudamericana, 1998.

Terán, Oscar. *Vida intelectual en el Buenos Aires fin-de-siglo, 1880–1910: Derivas de la "cultura científica."* Buenos Aires: Fondo de Cultura Económica, 2000.

Ubelaker Andrade, Lisa. "La revista mas leída del mundo: Selecciones del *Reader's Digest* y culturas de la clase media, 1940–1960." *Contemporánea* 5, no. 5 (2014): 21–42.

Varela, Mirta. *La televisión criolla: Desde sus inicios a la llegada del hombre a la luna, 1951–1969.* Buenos Aires: Edhasa, 2005.

Vezzetti, Hugo. "Viva Cien Años: Algunas consideraciones sobre familia y matrimonio en Argentina." *Punto de Vista* 9, no. 27 (1986): 5–10.

Vila, Pablo. "Tango to Folk: Hegemony Construction and Popular Identities in Argentina." *Studies in Latin American Popular Culture* 10 (1991): 107–39.

Part VI. The City at Night

Acree, William Garrett. *Staging Frontiers: The Making of Modern Popular Culture in Argentina and Uruguay.* Albuquerque: University of New Mexico Press, 2019.

Alberto, Paulina. *Black Legend: The Many Lives of Raúl Grigera and the Power of Racial Storytelling in Argentina.* Cambridge: Cambridge University Press, 2022.

Azzi, María Susana, and Simon Collier. *Le Grand Tango: The Life and Music of Astor Piazzola.* New York: Oxford University Press, 2000.

Beccaria, Luis, ed. *Sociedad y sociabilidad en la Argentina de los 90.* Buenos Aires: Biblos, 2002.

Ben, Pablo, and Santiago Insausti. "Dictatorial Rule and Sexual Politics in Argentina: The Case of the Frente de Liberación Homosexual, 1967–1976." *Hispanic American Historical Review* 97, no. 2 (2017): 297–325.

Bergero, Adriana. *Intersecting Tango: Cultural Geographies of Buenos Aires, 1900–1930.* Pittsburgh: University of Pittsburgh Press, 2008.

Bezencry, Claudio. *The Opera Fanatic: Ethnography of an Obsession.* Chicago: University of Chicago Press, 2011.

Blanco, Oscar, and Emiliano Scaricaciottoli. *Las letras de rock en Argentina: De la caída de la dictadura a la crisis de la democracia, 1983–2001.* Buenos Aires: Colihue, 2022.

Bockelman, Brian. "Between the Gaucho and the Tango: Popular Songs and the Shifting Landscape of Modern Argentine Identity, 1895–1915." *American Historical Review* 116, no. 3 (2011): 577–601.

Bruno, Paula, ed. *Sociabilidades y vida cultural: Buenos Aires, 1860–1930.* Bernal: Editorial Universidad Nacional de Quilmes, 2014.

Caimari, Lila. *While the City Sleeps: A History of Pistoleros, Policemen, and the Crime Beat in Buenos Aires before Perón.* Berkeley: University of California Press, 2016.

Castro, Donald. *The Argentine Tango as Social History, 1880–1955: The Soul of the People.* Lewiston, NY: Edwin Mellen, 1991.

Collier, Simon. *The Life, Music and Times of Carlos Gardel.* Pittsburgh: University of Pittsburgh Press, 1986.

Garrett, Victoria Lynn. *Performing Everyday Life in Argentine Popular Theater, 1890–1934*. London: Palgrave Macmillan, 2018.

Gayol, Sandra. *Sociabilidad en Buenos Aires: Hombres, honor y cafés, 1862–1910*. Buenos Aires: Ediciones Signo, 2000.

Graham-Jones, Jean. *Exorcising History: Argentine Theater under Dictatorship*. Lewisburg, PA: Associated University Presses, 2000.

Guy, Donna. *Sex and Danger in Buenos Aires: Prostitution, Family, and Nation*. Lincoln: University of Nebraska Press, 1991.

Lamela, Marcelo. *Rock Is Here: Buenos Aires*. Buenos Aires: Aguilar, 2014.

Losada, Leandro. *La alta sociedad en la Buenos Aires de la Belle Epoque*. Buenos Aires: Siglo XXI, 2008.

Manzano, Valeria. *The Age of Youth in Argentina: Culture, Politics, and Sexuality from Perón to Videla*. Chapel Hill: University of North Carolina Press, 2014.

Margulis, Mario, ed. *Juventud, cultura, sexualidad: La dimensión cultural en la afectividad y la sexualidad de los jóvenes de Buenos Aires*. Buenos Aires: Biblos, 2003.

Matamoro, Blas. *La ciudad del tango: Tango histórico y social*. Buenos Aires: Galerna, 1982.

McCleary, Kristen. *Staging Buenos Aires: Theater, Society, and Politics in Argentina, 1860–1920*. Pittsburgh: University of Pittsburgh Press, 2024.

Miller, Marilyn, ed. *Tango Lessons: Movement, Sound, Image, and Text in Contemporary Practice*. Durham, NC: Duke University Press, 2014.

Pujol, Sergio. *Historia del baile: De la milonga a la disco*. Buenos Aires: Emecé, 1999.

Roselli, John. "The Opera Business and the Italian Immigrant Community in Latin America 1820–1930: The Example of Buenos Aires." *Past and Present*, no. 127 (May 1990): 155–82.

Salas, Horacio. *El tango*. Buenos Aires: Emecé, 2004.

Sánchez Trolliet, Ana. *Te devora la ciudad: Itinerarios urbanos y figuraciones espaciales en el rock de Buenos Aires*. Bernal: Universidad Nacional de Quilmes, 2022.

Savigliano, Marta. *Tango and the Political Economy of Passion*. Boulder, CO: Westview, 1995.

Seigel, Micol. "Cocoliche's Romp: Fun with Nationalism at Argentina's Carnival." *Drama Review* 44, no. 2 (2000): 56–83.

Taylor, Julie. *Paper Tangos*. Durham, NC: Duke University Press, 1998.

Vila, Pablo. *Youth Identities and Argentine Popular Music: Beyond Tango*. New York: Palgrave Macmillan, 2012.

Part VII. Written Cities

Adamovsky, Ezequiel. *Historia de la clase media en Argentina: Apogeo y decadencia de una ilusión, 1919–2003*. Buenos Aires: Planeta, 2009.

Aguiló, Ignacio. *The Darkening Nation: Race, Neoliberalism, and Crisis in Argentina*. Cardiff: University of Wales Press, 2018.

Escardó, Florencio. *Nueva geografía de Buenos Aires*. Buenos Aires: Américalee, 1971.

Fondebrider, Jorge, ed. *La Buenos Aires ajena: Testimonios de extranjeros, de 1536 hasta hoy*. Buenos Aires: Emecé, 2001.

Foster, David William. *Buenos Aires: Perspectives on the City and Cultural Production*. Gainesville: University Press of Florida, 1998.

Frank, Patrick. *Los Artistas del Pueblo: Prints and Workers' Culture in Buenos Aires, 1917–1935*. Albuquerque: University of New Mexico Press, 2006.

Gorelick, Adrián. *Miradas sobre Buenos Aires*. Buenos Aires: Siglo XXI, 2004.

Malosetti Costa, Laura. *Los primeros modernos: Arte y sociedad en Buenos Aires a fines del siglo XIX*. Buenos Aires: Fondo de Cultura Económica, 2001.

Plotkin, Mariano. *Freud in the Pampas: The Emergence and Development of a Psychoanalytic Culture in Argentina*. Stanford, CA: Stanford University Press, 2001.

Podalsky, Laura. *Specular City: Transforming Culture, Consumption, and Space in Buenos Aires, 1955–1973*. Philadelphia: Temple University Press, 2004.

Sarlo, Beatriz. *La ciudad vista: Mercancías y cultura urbana*. Buenos Aires: Siglo XXI, 2009.

Sarlo, Beatriz. *Una modernidad periférica: Buenos Aires, 1920 y 1930*. Buenos Aires: Nueva Visión, 1999.

Silvestri, Graciela. *El color del río: Historia cultural del Riachuelo*. Buenos Aires: UNQ/ Prometeo, 2003.

Teruggi, Mario. *Panorama del lunfardo: Génesis y esencia de las lenguas coloquiales urbanas*. Buenos Aires: Sudamericana, 1978.

Viñas, David. *Grotesco, inmigración y fracaso: Armando Discépolo*. Buenos Aires: Corregidor, 1973.

Fiction and Urban Chronicle

AAVV. *Buenos Aires: De la fundación a la angustia*. Buenos Aires: Ediciones de la Flor, 1967.

AAVV. *Buenos Aires: La ciudad como un plano; Crónica y relatos*. Buenos Aires: La Bestia Equilátera, 2010.

Abós, Alvaro. *El libro de Buenos Aires: Crónicas de cinco siglos*. Buenos Aires: Mondadori, 2000.

Alarcón, Cristian. *Cuando me muero quiero que me canten cumbia: Vidas de pibes chorros*. Buenos Aires: Norma, 2003.

Arlt, Roberto. *Las aguafuertes porteñas de Roberto Arlt*. Buenos Aires: Corregidor, 1981.

Asís, Jorge. *El Buenos Aires de Oberdan Rocamora*. Buenos Aires: Sudamericana, 2016.

Bioy Casares, Adolfo. *The Dream of Heroes*. Translated by Diana Thorold. New York: Dutton, 1987.

Borges, Jorge Luis. *Selected Poems*. Translated by Alexander Coleman. New York: Viking, 1999.

Carbalho, José Antonio. *Estampas de Buenos Aires*. Buenos Aires: CEAL, 1971.

Casadevall, Domingo. *Esquema del carácter porteño*. Buenos Aires: CEAL, 1967.

Cortázar, Julio. *Hopscotch*. New York: Pantheon, 1966.

Cozarinsky, Edgardo. *Vudú urbano*. Barcelona: Anagrama, 1985.

De la Púa, Carlos. *La crencha engrasada*. Buenos Aires: Corregidor, 1996.

De Soiza Reilly, Juan José. *La ciudad de los locos*. Buenos Aires: Adriana Hidalgo, 2006.

Discépolo, Armando. *Obras escogidas*. Buenos Aires: Jorge Alvarez, 1969.

Fernández, Macedonio. *Adriana Buenos Aires: Ultima novela mala*. Buenos Aires: Corregidor, 1974.

Fogwill. *Vivir afuera*. Buenos Aires: Alfaguara, 1998.

González, César. *El niño resentido*. Buenos Aires: Reservoir Books, 2023.

González Tuñón, Raúl. *A la sombra de los barrios amados*. Buenos Aires: Lautaro, 1957.

Gorodischer, Julian, ed. *Los atrevidos: Crónicas íntimas de la Argentina*. Buenos Aires: Marea, 2018.

Incardona, Juan. *Villa Celina*. Buenos Aires: Norma, 2008.

López, Lucio Vicente. *La gran aldea: Costumbres bonaerenses*. Buenos Aires: Biedma, 1884.

Lukin, Liliana, ed. *Una Buenos Aires de novela*. 2 vols. Buenos Aires: Sudamericana, 1999, 2001.

Marechal, Leopoldo. *Adán Buenosayres*. Buenos Aires: Sudamericana, 1992.

Martínez Estrada, Ezequiel. *La cabeza de Goliat: Microscopía de Buenos Aires*. Buenos Aires: Club del libro, 1940.

Martini, Juan Carlos. *Puerto Apache*. Buenos Aires: Sudamericana, 2002.

Mertens, Federico. *Confidencias de un hombre de teatro: Medio siglo de una vida escénica*. Buenos Aires: Editorial Nos, 1948.

Mocho, Fray, et al. *Los costumbristas del 900*. Buenos Aires: CEAL, 1992.

Molloy, Sylvia. *El común olvido*. Buenos Aires: Grupo Editorial Norma, 2002.

Ocampo, Victoria. "El Archipiélago." *Autobiografía I*. Buenos Aires: Revista Sur, 1982.

Ocantos, Carlos María. *Quilito*. Buenos Aires: Imprenta La Nación, 1913.

Oliver, María Rosa. *Mundo: Mi casa*. Buenos Aires: Sudamericana, 1970.

Petit de Murat, Ulises. *La noche de mi ciudad*. Buenos Aires: Emecé, 1979.

Piglia, Ricardo. *The Absent City*. Durham, NC: Duke University Press, 2000.

Puig, Manuel. *The Buenos Aires Affair: A Detective Novel*. New York: Vintage, 1980.

Ramos, Laura. *Buenos Aires me mata*. Buenos Aires: Sudamericana, 1993.

Sacheri, Eduardo. *Los dueños del mundo*. Buenos Aires: Alfaguara, 2012.

Saldías, José Antonio. *La inolvidable bohemia porteña: Radiografía ciudadana del primer cuarto de siglo*. Buenos Aires: Freeland, 1968.

Terranova, Juan, ed. *Buenos Aires / Escala 1:1: Los barrios por sus escritores*. Buenos Aires: Entropía, 2007.

Verbitsky, Bernardo. *Villa miseria también es América*. Buenos Aires: Kraft, 1957.

Wernicke, Enrique. *Función y muerte del cine ABC*. Buenos Aires: Ed. Francisco A. Colombo, 1940.

Wilde, José Antonio. *Buenos Aires desde setenta años atrás*. Buenos Aires: Imprenta y librería de Mayo, 1881.

Photography

Cóppola, Horacio. *Buenos Aires 1936: Visión fotográfica*. Buenos Aires: Edición de la Municipalidad de Buenos Aires, 1936.

Cóppola, Horacio, and Facundo Zuviría. *Buenos Aires: Coppola + Zuviría*. Buenos Aires: Ediciones Lariviere, 2006.

D'Amico, Alicia, Sara Facio, and Julio Cortázar. *Buenos Aires, Buenos Aires*. Buenos Aires: Sudamericana, 1968.

Fundación Antorchas. *Imágenes de Buenos Aires, 1915–1940*. Buenos Aires: Fundación Antorchas, 1997.

Junior, Cristiano. *Un país en transición: Fotografías de Buenos Aires, Cuyo y el Noroeste, 1867–1883*. Buenos Aires: Fundación Antorchas, 2002.

Karp, Daniel. *Buenos Aires: Un estado del sentimiento*. Buenos Aires: Lugar, 1994.

Makarius, Sameer. *Buenos Aires, mi ciudad*. Buenos Aires: EUDEBA, 1963.

Priamo, Luis. *Buenos Aires al Sur: Fotografías, 1864–1954*. Buenos Aires: Corporación Buenos Aires Sur, 2001.

Zago, Manrique. *Buenos Aires ayer / Buenos Aires Yesterday: Testimonios gráficos de una ciudad / A City in Pictures, 1910–1930*. Buenos Aires: Manrique Zago, 1984.

Films

1930S

Los tres berretines, Enrique Susini, 1933
Puente Alsina, José Ferreyra, 1935
Puerto Nuevo, Luis César Amadori, 1936

1940S

Elvira Fernández, vendedora de tiendas, Manuel Romero, 1942
Pelota de trapo, Leopoldo Torres Ríos, 1948
Rodríguez supernumerario, Enrique Cahen Salaverry, 1948
Apenas un delincuente, Hugo Fregonese, 1949

1950S

Esposa último modelo, Carlos Schlieper, 1950
El vampiro negro, Román Viñoly Barreto, 1953
Sucedió en Buenos Aires, Enrique Cahen Salaverry, 1954
Mercado de abasto, Lucas Demare, 1955
Los tallos amargos, Fernando Ayala, 1956
La casa del Ángel, Leopoldo Torre Nilsson, 1957
Detrás de un largo muro, Lucas Demare, 1958
El secuestrador, Leopoldo Torre Nilsson, 1958

1960S

Alias Gardelito, Lautaro Murúa, 1961
Dar la cara, José Martínez Suarez, 1962
Los jóvenes viejos, Rodolfo Kuhn, 1962
Los venerables todos, Manuel Antín, 1963
Circe, Manuel Antín, 1964
Crónica de un niño solo, Leonardo Favio, 1965
Pajarito Gómez, Rodolfo Kuhn, 1965
Villa Cariño está que arde, Emilio Vieyra, 1967
Carne, Armando Bo, 1968
La fiaca, Fernando Ayala, 1969
Invasión, Hugo Santiago, 1969
Tiro de gracia, Ricardo Becher, 1969

1970S

Juan Lamaglia y señora, Raúl de la Torre, 1970
Mosaico, Nestor Paternostro, 1970
La tregua, Sergio Renán, 1974

1980S

Últimos días de la víctima, Adolfo Airstarain, 1982

Esperando la carroza, Alejandro Doria, 1985

Hay unos tipos abajo, Rafael Filipelli, 1985

1990S

¡Qué vivan los crotos!, Ana Poliak, 1990

Picado fino, Esteban Sapir, 1995

Buenos Aires viceversa, Alejandro Agresti, 1996

Pizza, birra y faso, Bruno Stagnaro, 1998

El mismo amor, la misma lluvia, Juan José Campanella, 1999

Silvia Prieto, Martín Rejtman, 1999

2000S

Nueve reinas, Fabian Bielinsky, 2000

Bolivia, Adrian Caetano, 2001

Sábado, Juan Villegas, 2001

El bonaerense, Pablo Trapero, 2002

Un oso rojo, Israel Caetano, 2002

Los rubios, Albertina Carri, 2003

Cama adentro, Jorge Gaggero, 2004

Luna de Avellaneda, Juan José Campanella, 2004

El custodio, Rodrigo Moreno, 2005

Tiempo de valientes, Damián Szifron, 2005

Derecho de familia, Daniel Burman, 2006

Los paranoicos, Gabriel Medina, 2008

2010S

Carancho, Pablo Trapero, 2010

El estudiante, Santiago Mitre, 2011

Los Marziano, Ana Katz, 2011

Relatos salvajes, Damián Szifron, 2014

El Ángel, Luis Ortega, 2018

2020S

Argentina, 1985, Santiago Mitre, 2022

Cambio, cambio, Lautaro García Candela, 2022

Al borde, Cesár González, 2023

Los delincuentes, Rodrigo Moreno, 2023

Puan, María Alché and Benjamín Naishtat, 2023

Acknowledgment of Copyrights and Sources

Part I. The Living City

"Shopping in the City": "Florida Street," by Ezequiel Martínez Estrada, from *Radiografía de la Pampa* (Buenos Aires: Babel, 1933), 157–60. Translated by Wendy Gosselin and Jane Brodie.

"From Yellow Fever to COVID-19: Epidemics and Inequalities in the City": "Death in the City in 1871," by Benigno Lugones, previously published as "En 1871" in *La Nación*, January 7, 1872. Translated by Liliana Frankel. Used courtesy of *La Nación*. "A Study of *Conventillo* Housing in Buenos Aires," by Guillermo Rawson, from *Escritos y Discursos del Doctor Guillermo Rawson* (Buenos Aires: Compañía Sudamericana de Billetes de Banco, 1885). Reprinted in *Estudio sobre las casas de inquilinato de Buenos Aires* (Buenos Aires: Imprenta de La Vanguardia, 1926), 1–30. Translated by Liliana Frankel. "COVID-19 and Inequality in the Twenty-First Century: A Petition," by Nora Cortiñas and Adolfo Pérez Esquivel, previously published as "Denunciaremos el crimen en la villa frente a la CIDH" in *Tiempo Argentino*, May 4, 2020, https://www.tiempoar.com.ar/politica/perez-esquivel-y-nora-cortinas-denunciaremos-el-crimen-en-la-villa-frente-a-la-cidh/. Translated by Leslie Robertson.

"The *Colectivo*, an Innovation for the Modern City": "The *Colectivo*," by César Fernández Moreno, from *Argentina* (Barcelona: Editorial Destino, 1972), 196–97. Translated by Wendy Gosselin and Jane Brodie.

"New Neighborhoods and the Expansion of City Life": "Memories of Flores," by Conrado Nalé Roxlo, previously published as "Memorias de Flores" in *Borrador de Memorias* (Buenos Aires: Plus Ultra, 1978), 88. Translated by Liliana Frankel. "A Hundred Years in the Neighborhood," interview with Alberto Vázquez by Pablo Riggio, previously published as "Alberto Vázquez: Cien años de vecindad" by Pablo Riggio in *El Barrio: portal de noticias*, May 31, 2017. Translated by Liliana Frankel.

"Green Spaces": "The Neighborhood Park," by Borocotó [Ricardo Lorenzo], previously published as "Placita de Barrio" in *El Gráfico* 20.995, August 5, 1938, 37. Translated by Lisa Ubelaker Andrade.

"Neighborhood Associations": "Creating a Neighborhood," by Corporación Mitre, from *Labor*, February 1927, no. 5. Reprinted in *Mundo urbano y cultura popular: Estudios de historia social Argentina*, edited by Diego Armus (Buenos Aires: Editorial Sudamericana, 1990), 91. Translated by Liliana Frankel. "Love for Boedo," by Boedo Neighborhood Association, from *Boedo*, April 30, 1940, no. 2. Translated by Liliana Frankel. "Neighborhood Unity," from *Unión Vecinal*, February 1946, no. 5. Translated by Liliana Frankel.

"El Once: The Changing Character of an Iconic Jewish Neighborhood": "Enclave in El Once," by César Tiempo, from *Pan criollo: Comedia gravemente cómica o lo que a ud. le parezca, en cuatro estampas y dos desenlaces* (Buenos Aires: Talleres Gráficos Porter, 1937), 39. Translated by Wendy Gosselin and Jane Brodie. "Diversity in El Once," by Marcelo Cohen, from *Diagonal Sur*, edited by Juan Villoro (Buenos Aires: Edhasa, 2007), 12. Translated by Wendy Gosselin and Jane Brodie.

"The Single-Family Home as a Cultural and Political Ideal": "This Is My Neighborhood," previously published as "Este es mi barrio" in *Mundo Peronista*, March 15, 1952, 23–25. Translated by Lisa Ubelaker Andrade.

"Vertical Living": "The Sixth Floor," tango poem by Homero Expósito, 1955. Translated by Wendy Gosselin and Jane Brodie.

"Dictatorship and the Razing of the City's *Villas*": "A City Ordinance," from *Prohibido vivir aquí: Una historia de los planes de erradicación de villas de la última dictadura* (Comisión Municipal de la Vivienda [City Housing Office] del Gobierno de la Ciudad de Buenos Aires, 2001 [original ordinance from 1976]), 39. Translated by Wendy Gosselin and Jane Brodie. "Recollections of a Demolition," interview with Magtara Feres by Eduardo Blaustein, previously published in *Prohibido Vivir aquí: Una historia de los planes de erradicación de villas de la última dictadura* (Comisión Municipal de la Vivienda del Gobierno de la Ciudad de Buenos Aires, 2001), 43. Translated by Wendy Gosselin and Jane Brodie.

"The Permanence of 'Emergency Settlements'": "A Heart Beats in 'Little' Latin America," from an unpublished essay by Dalma Villalba, 2020. Translated by Lisa Ubelaker Andrade. Used courtesy of Dalma Villalba.

"Contrasts in Greater Buenos Aires": "Urban Sprawl and Land Rights in Greater Buenos Aires: An Open Letter to the Mayor of Quilmes," previously published as "Toma de tierras" in *Al Sur*, March 1982. Translated by Wendy Gosselin and Jane Brodie. Courtesy of Jennifer Adair. "Thursday Night Widows," by Claudia Piñeiro, from *Thursday Night Widows*, translated by Miranda France (London: Bitter Lemon Press, 2009), 21–26. Previously published as *Las viudas de los jueves* (Buenos Aires: Clarín-Aguilar, 2005). Used with kind permission of Bitter Lemon Press © Claudia Pineiro, 2005. English translation © Miranda France, 2009.

Part II. Taking to the Street

"Celebrations in the Plaza in the Early Nineteenth Century": "Letters on South America," by J. P. and W. P. Robertson, from *Letters on South America: Comprising Travels on the Banks of the Paraná and the Rio de la Plata*, vol. 3 (London: John Murray, Albemarle Street, 1843), 129.

"The Plaza and the Demands of the People": "From the Café to the Plaza," by José María Tagiman and Vicente Fidel López, 1810. Reprinted in *La Gran Semana de 1810: Crónica de la Revolución de Mayo* (Buenos Aires: Jacobo Peuser, 1909), 20–21. Translated by Liliana Frankel.

"The Streets of Revelry: Carnaval": "Carnaval," by Eustaquio Pellicer, from *Caras y Caretas*, February 18, 1899, 6. Translated by Liliana Frankel.

"Workers Take to the Street": "Many May Days," by various authors, excerpts from *La Nación*, May 1, 1904; *La Vanguardia*, May 9, 1897; *Caras y Caretas*, May 6, 1899. Translated by Liliana Frankel.

"The Church in the Street": "An Incredible Crowd," previously published as "La impo-
nente concentración de hombres" in *Caras y Caretas*, October 10, 1934. Translated by
Leslie Robertson.

"The Plaza de Mayo and Juan Perón": "Perón and Evita Speak," previously published
as "Lo mejor de Perón" in *Mundo Peronista* 1.8, November 1, 1951, 27. Translated by
Leslie Robertson.

"The Writing on the Wall": "Street Art," interview with Tano Verón by Alejo
Santander, previously published as "Quién es el Tano Verón, el artista callejero
que empapeló la ciudad con sus mensajes" by Alejo Santander, *Infobae*, September
3, 2017, https://www.infobae.com/sociedad/2017/09/03/quien-es-el-tano-veron-el-
artista-callejero-que-empapelo-la-ciudad-con-sus-mensajes/. Translated by Leslie
Robertson.

"Public Violence": "On the Ezeiza Massacre," by Fuerzas Armadas Revolucionarias–
Montoneros, previously published as "Ante la Masacre de Ezeiza" [street poster],
June 1973. Translated by Lisa Ubelaker Andrade.

"The Mothers of the Plaza de Mayo": "In the Beginning We Were a Powerless Group,"
interview with Renée Epelbaum by Marjorie Agosín, from *The Mothers of Plaza de
Mayo (Linea Fundadora): The Story of Renée Epelbaum 1976–1985*, by Marjorie Agosín
(Trenton, NJ: Red Sea Press, 1990), 34–35. Translated by Janice Molloy.

"The Plaza as a Site of 'Consensus'": "The Plaza in Dictatorship," previously published
as "Ahora la plaza sí es de todos" in *Revista Gente*, April 10, 1982, 16–17. Translated by
Wendy Gosselin and Jane Brodie.

"The *Escrache*": "*Escrachar*: To Make the Oppressor's Name Known," interview with
Julieta Colomer by Anabella Arrascaeta, from *Nuestras voces*, May 9, 2016. Translated
by Lisa Ubelaker Andrade.

"A White Tent Occupies the Plaza": "After 1003 Days the Teachers Pack Up 'the White
Tent,'" by Luis Bruschtein, previously published as "Clase de fin de año en Plaza
Congreso: Luego de 1003 días los docentes levantaron la carpa blanca" in *Página/12*,
December 31, 1999. Translated by Wendy Gosselin and Jane Brodie. Used courtesy
of *Página/12*.

"Public Kitchens and *Piquetes*": "Community, Food, and Protest at an *Olla Popular*,"
interview with Hilda by Aníbal Kohan, previously published as "Hilda," in *A
las calles! Una historia de los movimientos piqueteros y caceroleros de los '90 al 2002* by
Aníbal Kohan (Buenos Aires: Ediciones Colihue, 2002), 89–90. Translated by Liliana
Frankel.

"Ni Una Menos, Not One Less": "A Manifesto for a Movement," by Ni Una Menos,
2015, http://niunamenos.org.ar/manifiestos/3-de-junio-2015/. Translated by Liliana
Frankel. "Women's Bodies in Plastic Bags," interview with Carolina Yuriko Arakaki
by Verónica Abdala, previously published as "Mujeres colgantes en bolsas plásticas:
Quiénes son las artistas que hicieron la impactante performance en la marcha
por Lucía Pérez," by Verónica Abdala in *Clarín*, June 12, 2018. Translated by Leslie
Robertson. Used courtesy of *Clarín*.

"Streets of Celebration": "A Sea of People and Flags at the Obelisk," by Pedro Lipcovich, previously published as "Un mar de gente y banderas en el obelisco,"
in *Página/12*, July 10, 2014. Translated by Leslie Robertson. Used courtesy of
Página/12.

Part III. Eating in Buenos Aires

"*Mate* as Ritual": "A *Mate* and a Love," by Lalo Mir, previously published as "Un mate y un amor," performed by the author on the radio program Lalo Bla Bla, Radio Mitre (Buenos Aires, 2009). Translated by Wendy Gosselin and Jane Brodie.

"Nineteenth-Century Meals": "My Memories," by Lucio V. Mansilla, from *Mis memorias y otros escritos* (1904; repr., Buenos Aires: Hachette, 1955), 205–8. Translated by Liliana Frankel.

"Anti-imperialism and Beef": "Report to the National Senate Denouncing the Roca-Runciman Pact," by Lisandro de la Torre, from *Diario de Sesiones de la Honorable Cámara de Senadores*, Congreso de la Nación, September 8, 1934. Translated by Leslie Robertson. "Tales from the Proletariat," by José Peter, from *Crónicas proletarias* (Buenos Aires: Esfera, 1968), 172. Translated by Leslie Robertson.

"Food and Crisis": "Food Struggles in the So-Called 'Breadbasket of the World,'" by Juan González Yuste, previously published as "Por primera vez hay hambre en el 'granero del mundo'" in *El País*, November 29, 1982. Translated by Lisa Ubelaker Andrade.

"The *Asado*: A Food Ritual": "Manhood and the *Asador*," by Eduardo Archetti, previously published as "Hibridación, pertenencia y localidad en la construcción de una cocina nacional" in *La Argentina en el siglo XX*, edited by Carlos Altamirano (Buenos Aires: Ariel-Universidad de Quilmes, 1999), 229–31. Translated by Liliana Frankel. "Lunch at a Construction Site," by Nicolás Olivari, from *Mi Buenos Aires querido* (Buenos Aires: Editorial Jorge Álvarez, 1966), 14–15. Translated by Liliana Frankel.

"Patriotic Cooking": "An Introduction to Fine Cooking," by Cía Sansinena, previously published as "La delicia del buen comer," in *Libro de Cocina* (Buenos Aires: Sansinena SA, 1940), 8–10. Translated by Wendy Gosselin and Jane Brodie.

"Domestic Labors": "Juanita Bordoy, the Other Star," by Marisa Avigliano, previously published as "La otra estrella: Juanita Bordoy, 1916–1955" in *Página/12*, May 13, 2016. Translated by Wendy Gosselin and Jane Brodie. Used courtesy of *Página/12*.

"The Chocotorta and Changing Ideas of Women's Work": "Working Women and the Invention of the Chocotorta," interview with Marité Mabragaña by Hernán Firpo, previously published as "Ella inventó la Chocotorta" in *Clarín*, May 8, 2012. Translated by Liliana Frankel. Used courtesy of *Clarín*.

"Anarchist Pastries": "Strike and Boycott of La Princesa Bakery," previously published as "Huelga y boycott a la panadería 'La Princesa'" in *El Obrero*, January 25, 1902. Translated by Leslie Robertson.

"Neighborhood Businesses": "Ice Cream Carts and Bakeries in the Neighborhood," by Bernardo González Arrili, previously published as "Helados en la calle" and "Panaderías" in *Calle Corrientes entre Esmeralda y Suipacha* (Buenos Aires: Editorial Guillermo Kraft, 1952), 63–65, 67–69. Translated by Wendy Gosselin and Jane Brodie.

"The Café": "Sounds and Scenes of the *Porteño* Café," by Alberto Mario Salas, previously published as "El café" in *Relación Parcial de Buenos Aires* (Buenos Aires: Sur, 1955), 96–104. Translated by Liliana Frankel.

"Pizza": "Pizza at the Counter," by Norberto Folino, previously published as "Introducción al estudio de la pizza" in *Café, bar, billares*, edited by Ricardo Horvath, Norberto Folino, and Daniel Divinsky (Buenos Aires: Ediciones Instituto Movilizador de Fondos Cooperativos, 1999), 41–42. Translated by Wendy Gosselin and Jane Brodie.

"Food and Nostalgia": "Food and Nostalgia," by Julio Cortázar, from *Rayuela* (Buenos Aires: Editorial Sudamericana, 1963; repr., Madrid: Punto de Lectura, 2006), 263–65. Translated by Lisa Ubelaker Andrade.

"The *Bodegón*": "Cantinas and *Bodegones*," by Nicolás Olivari, from *Mi Buenos Aires querido* (Buenos Aires: Jorge Álvarez, 1966), 87–88. Translated by Liliana Frankel.

"A Twenty-First-Century Culinary Scene": "*Milanesa* and Kimchi," unpublished interview with Lis Ra by Lisa Ubelaker Andrade, June 7, 2023. Translated by Lisa Ubelaker Andrade. Courtesy of Lis Ra.

Part IV. Hinchas, Cracks, *and* Potreros *in the City of Soccer*

"Health, Civilization, and Sport": "Physical Education," by Enrique Romero Brest, from *Elementos de gimnástica fisiológica* (Buenos Aires: Librería del Colegio, 1939), 412. Translated by Leslie Robertson. "*Pelota al Cesto* and the Dangers of Soccer," by Enrique Romero Brest, from *El sentido espiritual de la educación física* (Buenos Aires: Librería del Colegio, 1938), 64–65. Translated by Leslie Robertson.

"Social Classes Converge at the Racetrack": "Only Leguisamo!," tango lyrics from Leguisamo Solo, music and lyrics by Modesto Papavero, recorded by Carlos Gardel, Odeón (Barcelona), 1925. Translated by Wendy Gosselin and Jane Brodie. "The Man Who Bets at the Races," by Last Reason (Máximo Teodoro Sáenz), previously published as "Elogio del hombre que juega a las carreras" in *A rienda suelta* (Buenos Aires: Gleizer, 1925; repr., Buenos Aires: Biblioteca Nacional: Ediciones Colihue, 2006), from *El libro de Buenos Aires: Crónicas de cinco siglos*, edited by Alvaro Abós (Buenos Aires: Mondadori, 2000), 195–97. Translated by Wendy Gosselin and Jane Brodie.

"The Philosophers of Local Sport": "*Fútbol* and Improvisation," by Dante Panzeri, from *Fútbol: Dinámica de lo impensado* (Buenos Aires: Paidós, 1967), 42–43. Translated by Wendy Gosselin and Jane Brodie.

"El Pibe": "Backlot Soccer," by Pedro Orgambide, from *Yo, argentino* (Buenos Aires: Jorge Alvarez, 1968), 79–80. Translated by Liliana Frankel.

"The Right to Play: Women and the Game": "Soccer, Gender, and the Right to Play," interview with Mónica Santino by Emilia Rojas, previously published as "Mónica Santino y un sueño colectivo: 'El golazo para nosotras sería fundar un club,'" by Emilia Rojas, in *Mundo Villa*, November 20, 2018. Translated by Wendy Gosselin and Jane Brodie.

"Maradona, *Maradonear*": "The Hand of God," by Eduardo Galeano, from *Cerrado por fútbol* (Buenos Aires: Siglo XXI, 2017), 30–31. Translated by Wendy Gosselin and Jane Brodie. Used courtesy of Siglo XXI. "Verb: To *Maradonear*," by Jorge Giner, previously published as "Diego es el baremo" in *Panenka*, February 2, 2017, https://www.panenka.org/miradas/diego-es-el-baremo/. Translated by Wendy Gosselin and Jane Brodie.

"The Dream": "The Dream of the *Pibe*," tango lyrics by Reinaldo Yiso, music by Juan Puey, previously published as "El sueño del pibe," Odeón (Buenos Aires) 7672 14498, 1945. Translated by Wendy Gosselin and Jane Brodie. "The Boy Will Save Us," tango lyrics and music by Lucio Arce, previously published as "El pibe nos va a salvar" in ¿Trajiste la Guitarra?, Fonocal 771, 2007. Translated by Wendy Gosselin and Jane Brodie.

"The Fans: *La Hinchada*": "December 19, 1971," by Roberto Fontanarrosa, previously published as "19 de diciembre de 1971" in *Nada del otro mundo y otros cuentos* (Buenos Aires: Ediciones de la Flor, 1987; repr., Buenos Aires: Planeta, 2012), 71–90. Translated by Liliana Frankel.

"An *Hincha* Is Born, Not Made": "A Boca Fan from Birth," by Juan Sasturian, previously published as "De la bostería original" in *Página/12*, February 10, 2014. Translated by Wendy Gosselin and Jane Brodie. Used courtesy of *Página/12*.

"Stadium Songs": "That's How Boca Fans Are," by River Plate fans, popularly known as "Los bosteros son así," oral recollection, 2018. Translated by Lisa Ubelaker Andrade. "Let's Go, *Ciclón*," by San Lorenzo fans, popularly known as "Vamos Ciclón," oral recollection, 2017. Translated by Lisa Ubelaker Andrade.

"The Thrill of the Superclásico": "River and Boca—a Poem," by Héctor Negro, previously titled "River y Boca (un poema)," previously published in *El lenguaje y la poesía del fútbol* (Buenos Aires: Corregidor, 2005). Translated by Wendy Gosselin and Jane Brodie.

"Violence": "The Secret Threads of Violence," previously published as "Los hilos secretos de la violencia" in *Clarín*, May 14, 2000. Translated by Robin Myers. Used courtesy of *Clarín*.

"Soccer, Politics, and Protest": "A Letter from Argentina," previously published as "Carta a mi hija," in *El Gráfico*, June 13, 1978, 37–38.

"Toward an Inclusive Future": "A Collective Effort," interview with Inés Arrondo by Analía Fernández Fuks, previously published as "No soy yo sola la que llega, es una lucha de todas" in LATFEM.org, December 19, 2019, https://latfem.org/ines-arrondo-no-soy-yo-sola-la-que-llega-es-una-lucha-de-todas/. Translated by Lisa Ubelaker Andrade.

Part V. Reading, Watching, and Listening in Buenos Aires

"Education and Civilization": "Education for the People," by Domingo Faustino Sarmiento, from *De la educación popular* (Santiago de Chile: Imprenta Julio Belin, 1849), 13–15, 21, 24. Translated by Robin Myers.

"Writing Becomes a Profession": "From a Castle to a Cash Register," by José González Carbalho, previously published as "De la almena al mostrador" in *La estrellita del trolley* (1943; repr., Buenos Aires: Centro Editor de América Latina/CEAL, 1967), 101–3. Translated by Liliana Frankel.

"New Vanguards": "*Martín Fierro* Manifesto," from *Martín Fierro*, May 15, 1924, 1. Translated by Liliana Frankel. "What Is *Claridad*," from *Claridad, revista de arte, crítica y letras—tribuna del pensamiento izquierdista*, no. 1, July 1926, 3. Translated by Liliana Frankel.

"Media, Gender, and Feminist Thought": "Language and Power," from *Feminaria* (Buenos Aires), November 1988, 2. Translated by Lisa Ubelaker Andrade.

"The Pampa in the City, via Radio": "Flickers of Tradition," by Andrés González Pulido, in *Chispazos de tradición*, radio program, LR3 Radio Nacional, ca. 1933. Translated by Wendy Gosselin and Jane Brodie.

"The Cinema, a Barrio Institution": "Villa Urquiza," by José Pablo Feinmann, from *El Libro de Buenos Aires: Crónicas de cinco siglos*, edited by Alvaro Abós (Buenos Aires: Mondadori, 2000), 287–88. Translated by Wendy Gosselin and Jane Brodie.

"The Buenos Aires Middle Class, on Screen": "The Secret of the Falcón Family," previously published as "El secreto de la familia Falcón" in *Atlántida*, October 1965, 44–45. Translated by Robin Myers.

"Radio, Television, and Celebrity Culture": "*Lunch with Mirtha Legrand*," by Carlos Ulanovsky, from "El día que Mirtha Legrand almorzó en su casa después de 5 años," *Satiricón* 1, no. 2 (December 5, 1972): 26–28. Translated by Lisa Ubelaker Andrade. "Public Intimacy," by Beatriz Sarlo, from *La intimidad pública* (Buenos Aires: Seix Barral, 2018), 173. Translated by Lisa Ubelaker Andrade.

"An Open Letter to the Dictatorship": "Open Letter to the Military Dictatorship," by Rodolfo Walsh, in Archivo Nacional de la Memoria, Buenos Aires, March 24, 1977. Translated by Lisa Ubelaker Andrade. Courtesy Archivo Nacional de la Memoria.

"Humor under Censorship": "Laughter and Threats," interview with Andrés Cascioli by Tomás Lüders, from "Hoy en Argentina casi no hay humor politico," by Tomás Lüders. *Lote*, no. 97, August 2005, 10–13. Translated by Robin Myers.

"Broad Audiences and Burned Books": "Memoirs of a Publisher," interview with Boris Spivacow by Delia Maunás, from *Boris Spivacow: Memoria de un sueño argentino*, by Delia Maunás (Buenos Aires: Ediciones Colihue, 1995), 66–68, 107–9. Translated by Robin Myers.

"Press under Dictatorship": "Reporting Disappearances," interview with Robert Cox by Luis Bruschtein, from "Las notas del Herald salvaron vidas humanas," by Luis Bruschtein, in *Página/12*, May 1, 2014. Translated by Robin Myers. Used courtesy of *Página/12*.

"The Bookstore, a Downtown Institution": "Booksellers in Buenos Aires," by Rubén Vela, in *El Hogar*, March 2, 1956. Translated by Liliana Frankel.

Part VI. The City at Night

"The City of Fury": "Buenos Aires Nights," tango lyrics by Manuel Romero, music by Alberto Soifer, previously published as "Noches de Buenos Aires," Lumiton (Buenos Aires), 1937. Translated by Wendy Gosselin and Jane Brodie. Used courtesy of Peermusic. "In the City of Fury," lyrics by Gustavo Cerati, previously published as "La ciudad de la furia" on *Doble Vida* by Soda Stereo, CBS Discos (Buenos Aires), 1988. Translated by Wendy Gosselin and Jane Brodie.

"Nights at the Colón": "The Politeama Theater," from *El Mosquito*, July 20, 1879. Translated by Robin Myers. "To Colón," by Manuel Mujica Lainez, from *El Gran Teatro* (Buenos Aires: Sudamericana, 1979), 69. Translated by Claudio Bezencry.

"Evening Theater, on Stage and in the Street": "The People's Theater," by Leónidas Barletta, from *Conducta*, September 1938, 27–30. Translated by Lisa Ubelaker Andrade. "Teatro Abierto," by Carlos Somigliana, from "Inauguración de Teatro Abierto," performed by Jorge Rivera Lopéz, July 28, 1981, http://www.teatrodelpueblo .org.ar/teatro_abierto/. Translated by Lisa Ubelaker Andrade.

"Tango and the Melodrama of the *Milonguita*": "Milonguita," tango lyrics by Samuel Linning, music by Enrique Pedro Delfino, first recorded by Carlos Gardel, Odeón, 1920. Translated by Wendy Gosselin and Jane Brodie.

"The Iconic Gardel": "Gardel and the Elite," by Edmundo Eichelbaum, from *Historia del tango*, vol. 9, edited by Manuel Pampín (Buenos Aires: Ediciones Corregidor, 1977), 1547, 1587. Translated by Liliana Frankel. "Gardel as Symbol," by Juan José Sebreli, from *Buenos Aires, vida cotidiana y alienación* (Buenos Aires: Ediciones Siglo XX, 1964), 125. Translated by Liliana Frankel.

"Decent Tango": "Dancing Tango," unpublished interview with Clara Gertz by Diego Armus, November 13, 2018. Translated by Robin Myers. Used courtesy of Clara Gertz.

"Piazzola and the Reinvention of Tango": "Astor," by Diana Piazzola, from *Tangueando: Testimonios, cuentos y poemas*, edited by Pedro G. Orgambide (Buenos Aires: Ediciones del IMFC, 1992), 99–106. Translated by Robin Myers.

"Sex, *Telos*, and Regulation": "Memories of *Telos*," unpublished interview with Fernando S. by Diego Armus, October 23, 2018. Translated by Wendy Gosselin and Jane Brodie. Used courtesy of Fernando S. "Sex and Discretion," unpublished interview with César A. by Diego Armus, October 3, 2018. Translated by Wendy Gosselin and Jane Brodie. Used courtesy of César A.

"Queer Nights, Policed": "Policed Nights in the 1950s," interview with Luis Troitiño by Juan Queiroz, previously published as "La historia de nuestra historia" in *Moléculas Malucas*, April 25, 2020, https://www.moleculasmalucas.com/post/la-historia-de-nuestra-historia. Translated by Lisa Ubelaker Andrade. Used courtesy of the author and *Moléculas Malucas*. "Memories of 'Area' in the 1980s," by Cristian Trincado, previously published as "Memorias de Área" in *Moléculas Malucas*, March 30, 2021, https://www.moleculasmalucas.com/post/memorias-de-área. Translated by Lisa Ubelaker Andrade. Used courtesy of the author and *Moléculas Malucas*. "The Last Raid on a Lesbian Bar," by María Luisa Peralta, previously published as "La última razzia a un boliche de lesbianas en Buenos Aires" in *Moléculas Malucas*, February 11, 2021, https://www.moleculasmalucas.com/post/la-última-razzia-a-un-boliche-de-lesbianas-en-buenos-aires. Translated by Lisa Ubelaker Andrade. Courtesy of the author and *Moléculas Malucas*.

"State Terror in the Dark": "Anonymous Groups Forced Their Way into Homes at Night," by National Commission on the Disappearance of Persons (CONADEP), from *Nunca más: Informe de la Comisión Nacional sobre la Desaparición de Personas* (Buenos Aires: EUDEBA, 1984), 17. Translated by Lisa Ubelaker Andrade. Used courtesy of EUDEBA (Editorial Universitaria de Buenos Aires).

"Rebellious Rock": "Hyper-*candombe*," lyrics by Charly García, previously published as "Hipercandombe" on *Películas* by La Máquina de Hacer Pájaros, Microfon, 1977. Translated by Lisa Ubelaker Andrade. "The Survivors," lyrics by Charly García, previously published as "Los sobrevivientes" on *La grasa de las capitales* by Serú Girán, Sazam Records, 1978. Translated by Lisa Ubelaker Andrade. "An Encounter with the Devil," lyrics by Charly García, previously published as "Encuentro con el diablo" on *Bicicleta* by Serú Girán, SG Discos, 1980. Translated by Lisa Ubelaker Andrade. "Song of Alicia in the Country," lyrics by Charly García, previously published as "La canción de Alicia en el país" on *Bicicleta* by Serú Girán, SG Discos, 1980. Translated by Wendy Gosselin and Jane Brodie. "Don't Bomb Buenos Aires" lyrics by Charly García, previously published as "No bombardeen Buenos Aires" on *Pubis angelical— Yendo de la cama al living* by Charly García, Interdisc, 1982. Translated by Lisa

Ubelaker Andrade. "The Dinosaurs," lyrics by Charly García, previously published as "Los dinosaurios" on *Clics Modernos* by Charly García, Universal Music Group, 1983. Translated by Wendy Gosselin and Jane Brodie.

"Sounds of Folk Cross Social Lines": "Mercedes Sosa Returns to Buenos Aires," by María Seoane, originally published as "La garganta de la patria" in *Caras y Caretas*, September 30, 2019. Translated by Lisa Ubelaker Andrade.

"Global/Local Sounds: *Cumbia Villera* and Argentine Trap": "The Rhythm of the Villa," by Daniel Riera, previously published as "El ritmo de la villa" in *Rolling Stone Argentina*, July 1, 2001. Translated by Robin Myers. "From the Plaza to Global Trap," interview with Bizarrap by Julio Leiva, previously published as quoted from "Bizarrap: 'Las Bzrp Music Sessions me cambiaron la forma de verme a mí y a la industria,'" *Caja Negra*, October 11, 2020, podcast, 48:05. https://www.youtube.com/watch?v=o7T6flU8xUY. Translated by Lisa Ubelaker Andrade.

"The *Boliche*": "*Boliches* in Palermo," by Olivia Gallo, previously published as "Dientes de leche" in *Las chicas no lloran* (Buenos Aires: Tenemos las máquinas, 2019), 57–62. Translated by Leslie Robertson.

Part VII. Written Cities

"Visual Cities": "Collivadino: Buenos Aires under Construction," by Laura Malosetti Costa, from *Collivadino: Buenos Aires under Construction* (Buenos Aires: Asociación Amigos del Museo Nacional de Bellas Artes, 2013), 17–19. Translated by Leslie Robertson. "Juanito," interview with Antonio Berni by Hugo Monzón and Alberto Szpunberg, from *La Opinión Cultural*, August 10, 1975, 2. Translated by Leslie Robertson. "The Iconic Buenos Aires Obelisk," by Marta Minujín, interview with *Clarín*, "Las Múltiples Miradas de Minujín sobre el Obelisco, un Icono Porteño," February 13, 2011. Translated by Leslie Robertson. Used courtesy of *Clarín*.

"The City Abandoned": "Amalia," by José Mármol, from *Amalia* serialized in *La Tribuna* (Montevideo), December 1851–February 1852; reprinted as *Amalia* (Barcelona: Seix, 1897). Translated by Lisa Ubelaker Andrade.

"Buenos Aires as Paris": "Impressions of the Argentine Republic," by Adolfo Posada, previously published in *La República Argentina, impresiones y comentarios* by Adolfo Posada (Madrid: V. Suárez Editorial, 1912), reprinted in *La Buenos Aires ajena: Testimonios de extranjeros de 1536 hasta hoy*, edited by Jorge Fondebrider (Buenos Aires: Emecé, 2001), 217. Translated by Robin Myers. "Buenos Aires Does Not Exist," by Marcel Duchamp, correspondence with Ettie Stettheimer, November 12, 1918, previously published in *La Buenos Aires ajena: Testimonios de extranjeros de 1536 hasta hoy*, edited by Jorge Fondebrider (Buenos Aires: Emecé, 2001), 233. Translated by Robin Myers. "An Utter Lack of Originality," by José María Vargas Vila, from *Mi viaje a la Argentina*, 1923, reprinted in *La Buenos Aires ajena: Testimonios de extranjeros de 1536 hasta hoy*, edited by Jorge Fondebrider (Buenos Aires: Emecé, 2001), 235. Translated by Robin Myers.

"Local Identity and Cosmopolitanism": "Customs and Habits in Buenos Aires," by Aníbal Latino (José Ceppi), previously published as *Tipos y costumbres bonaerenses* (Buenos Aires: Imprenta y Librería de Mayo, 1886; repr., Buenos Aires: Hyspamérica Ediciones, 1984). Translated by Wendy Gosselin and Jane Brodie. "Argentine-ness," by Georges Clemenceau, from *Notas de viaje por la América del Sur: Argentina, Uruguay, Brasil* (Buenos Aires: Cabaut y Cia., 1911). Translated by Wendy Gosselin and Jane Brodie.

"Arrivals and Departures": "Returning to Buenos Aires," by Sylvia Molloy, previously published as "Afterword: The Buenos Aires Affair" in *PMLA/Publications of the Modern Language Association of America* 122, no. 1 (2007): 352–56. Reproduced with permission of Cambridge University Press.

"The City of Psychoanalysis": "To Analyze Oneself," by Elisabeth Roudinesco, from *Diccionario amoroso de psicoanálisis* (Buenos Aires: Debate, 2018), 81–85. Used courtesy of Penguin Random House Argentina. Translated by Lisa Ubelaker Andrade.

"The Neighborhood and the City Center": "Buenos Aires, Unity and Diversity," by José Luis Romero, previously published as "Buenos Aires, una historia" in *La ciudad occidental: Culturas urbanas en Europa y América* (1970; repr., Buenos Aires: Siglo XXI, 2009), 321–24. Translated by Robin Myers. Used courtesy of Siglo XXI and Luis Alberto Romero.

"A New Urban Folklore": "The Path to Our House," by Evaristo Carriego, previously published as "El camino de nuestra casa" in *Poesías de Evaristo Carriego* (Barcelona: Auber y Plá, 1913). Translated by Wendy Gosselin and Jane Brodie. "Sur" (1948), by Homero Manzi, from *Letras de tango: Antología poética*, edited by Juan Angel Russo (Buenos Aires: Basílico, 1999), 264–65. Translated by Wendy Gosselin and Jane Brodie.

"Sketches of Buenos Aires": "A Chair on the Sidewalk," by Roberto Arlt, previously published as "Silla en la vereda" in *Aguafuertes Porteñas: Impresiones* (Buenos Aires: Editorial Victoria, 1933; repr., Buenos Aires: Losada, 2010), 101–4. Translated by Wendy Gosselin and Jane Brodie.

"The Beautiful and Mundane Urban Grid": "Buenos Aires, Continental Metropolis," by Alberto Gerchunoff, previously published as "Buenos Aires, Metropolis continental" in *Revista de América* (París, 1914); reprinted as "Buenos Aires, la metrópolis de mañana," in *Cuadernos de Buenos Aires*, vol. 13 (Buenos Aires: Editorial de la Municipalidad de la Ciudad de Buenos Aires, 1960), 15–22. Translated by Robin Myers. "Goliath's Head: A Microscopic View of Buenos Aires," by Ezequiel Martínez Estrada, from *La cabeza de Goliat: Microscopía de Buenos Aires* (Buenos Aires: Emecé, 1947), 77, 30. Translated by Liliana Frankel. "Sad Lines of Buenos Aires," by Alfonsina Storni, previously published as "Versos a la tristeza de Buenos Aires" in *Ocre* (Buenos Aires: Babel, 1925). Reprinted in *Poemas* (Buenos Aires: Biblioteca del Congreso de la Nación, 2017), 57. Translated by Lisa Ubelaker Andrade.

"Catholic Encounters with the Peronist City": "A New Emotion in Buenos Aires," by Delfina Bunge de Gálvez, previously published as "Una emoción nueva en Buenos Aires" in *El Pueblo*, October 25, 1945. Translated by Robin Myers.

"Cabecita negra": "Cabecita negra," by Germán Rozenmacher, from *Cabecita negra y otros cuentos* (Buenos Aires: Editorial Anuario, 1962). Reprinted in *Obras completas* (Buenos Aires: Biblioteca Nacional, 2013), 65–67. Translated by Robin Myers.

"The City under Military Control": "ID Cards and Life under Dictatorship," by Jorge Asís, previously published as "La cédula ya forma parte del cuerpo" in *El Buenos Aires de Oberdan Rocamora* (Buenos Aires: Editorial Losada, 1981), 61. Translated by Robin Myers. Excerpt from *La ciudad ausente*, by Ricardo Piglia (Buenos Aires: Sudamericana, 1992), 91–92. Translated by Lisa Ubelaker Andrade.

"The *Villa*, from Without and Within": "The Air," by Sergio Chejfec, from *El aire* (Buenos Aires: Alfaguara, 1992), 139. Translated by Robin Myers. "The *Villa*," by César Aira, from *La villa* (Buenos Aires: Emecé, 2001), 25, 27. Translated by Robin Myers. "Poetry in the *Villas*," by César González, quoted in "Cesár González, la poesía desde los márgenes," Argentina.gob.ar, February 9, 2023, https://www .argentina.gob.ar/noticias/cesar-gonzalez-la-poesia-desde-los-margenes. Translated by Lisa Ubelaker Andrade.

"Social Mobility": "A City Enters the Twentieth Century," by Tulio Halperín Donghi, previously published as "Una ciudad entra en el siglo XX" in *Buenos Aires 1910: El imaginario para una gran capital*, edited by Margarita Gutman and Thomas Reese (Buenos Aires: Eudeba, 1999), 63, 66. Translated by Robin Myers.

"White-Collar Workers": "Stories from the Office," by Roberto Mariani, from *Cuentos de la oficina* (1925; repr., Buenos Aires: Rescate, 1977), 84. Translated by Robin Myers. "Women on Their Way to Work," by Alfonsina Storni, previously published as "Las mujeres que trabajan" in *La Nación*, June 20, 1920. Translated by Lisa Ubelaker Andrade. Used courtesy of *La Nación*.

"Critiques of the Buenos Aires Middle Class": "The Misery of the Buenos Aires Middle Class," by Juan José Sebreli, from *Buenos Aires, vida cotidiana y alienación* (Buenos Aires: Siglo Veinte, 1964); reprinted in *Buenos Aires, vida cotidiana y alienación, seguido de Buenos Aires en crisis* (Buenos Aires: Sudamericana, 2003), 103–5. Translated by Robin Myers.

"Writing the Middle Classes": "Collective and Individual Mobility," by Juan Carlos Torre, from *Buenos Aires, una historia de cuatro siglos*, vol. 2, edited by José Luis Romero and Luis Alberto Romero (Buenos Aires: Abril, 1983). Translated by Robin Myers. "Crisis and Resilience in the Diverse Middle Class," by Guillermo Oliveto, previously published as "Cuánto resistirá la clase media Argentina" in *La Nación*, April 26, 2021. Translated by Lisa Ubelaker Andrade. Used courtesy of *La Nación*.

"Enduring City": "Like the Cicada," by María Elena Walsh, copy of original poem/ lyrics dated 1972. Translated by Lisa Ubelaker Andrade. Courtesy of the María Elena Walsh Foundation. "The Dance of the *Gambeta*," by Bersuit Vergarabat, performed as "El baile de la gambeta" on *La argentinidad al palo*, Surco/Universal Music, 2004. Translated by Lisa Ubelaker Andrade.

Index

civic-military dictatorship, 4, 18, 59, 105, 212–14, 234–38, 241–43, 282, 286–88; and violence, 18, 234–35, 241, 287–88

Central Bank, 79

Centro Editor de América Latina (CEAL) (publishing house), 213, 237–40

Cerati, Gustavo, 1, 259–60

cestoball, 166, 173–74

chacarera, 255

Chacarita (neighborhood), 31

chalet californiano, 54

children, 12, 34, 57–58, 67, 79–81, 93, 101–9, 138, 144–45, 183, 206; and education, 217–18, 337–38; and housing, 57, 65, 71, 72, 337; and hunger, 128; of immigrants, 12, 47, 206, 299, 312, 319; magazines for, 180–81; other media for, 209, 239–40; playgrounds, 29–31, 34, 48–49; and sport, 164–66, 168, 173–74, 183. *See also* Mothers of the Plaza de Mayo; schools

chimichurri, 121, 126, 156

China, 23

Chinese community, 53; and supermarkets, 124

Chispazos de Tradición (radio show), 225–56

chocotorta, 4, 122, 145–46

choripán, 76, 126, 156, 296

chorizo, 54, 76, 120–21, 126, 141, 156

church, 38, 328. *See also* Catholic Church

cigarettes, 124, 340

cinema, 14, 212–13, 215, 227, 250. *See also* film

city council, 9, 13, 15–18

city government, 8, 14, 18, 21–22, 43, 76

city limits, 14–16, 21, 25–27, 119, 126

City of Fury, 1, 5, 247, 257, 260–61

Ciudad Evita (neighborhood), 32

civic-military dictatorship (1976–83), 1, 17–19, 33; clandestine detention centers, 18, 37; coup of 1976, 18–19, 32, 74–75, 138, 213–14, 241–43; demolition of *villas*, 59–60; disappearances and state terror, 18, 67, 74–75, 101–3, 106–8, 138, 213–14, 234–35, 241–42, 254, 280–86, 300, 312–13, 344–45; economy and, 19, 137; literature, 312, 331–32, 344–45; media and, 105–6, 200–201, 212–14, 234–37, 282–86; return to democracy, 19–20, 106–8, 121, 137–38, 264–65, 300; theater during, 264; use of plaza, 75, 105–6; World Cup, 59, 117, 200–201. *See also* disappeared persons; Malvinas/Falklands War; Mothers of the Plaza de Mayo; state terror

civilization, 163, 165–66, 325; and education, 173, 205–6, 217–18; idea of, 48, 205; and sport, 173–74

Claridad (periodical), 221–22

Claridad (publishing house), 209

Clarín (periodical), 138, 198, 212, 215, 230, 232, 263, 265

Clarín Group, 215

class. *See* classism; elite; inequality; middle class; social mobility; working class

classical music, 272

classism, 15, 49, 80, 289, 300

Claudia (periodical), 223

clergy, 7, 217

club, 4, 9, 35, 177; nightlife, 247–48, 252, 254–57, 271–73, 277–79, 292–93, 318; sports, 12, 31–32, 163–71, 182–83, 194–95, 198–203. *See also* soccer clubs

Club Argentinos de Quilmes (soccer club), 163

Coca-Cola, 292

cocoliche, 12, 264. *See also* immigration; *lunfardo*

colectivo, 28–29, 43–45. *See also* buses

colonial city, 7–9, 25, 34–36, 79, 81, 295

colonialism, 8–9, 82, 119, 296–98

colonial landmarks, 25–26

comedores, 121, 137–38. See also *olla popular*

comics, 2, 210, 236

communism, 13, 68, 134

comparison to Europe, 26–27, 156, 175, 262, 295–97, 301, 304, 308–11, 314

Concejo Deliberante, 9. *See also* city council

concerts, 77, 109, 254, 256, 282, 288, 290, 292

condominiums, 20, 32, 34

Confederación General de Trabajo (CGT), 73, 92

confitería, 14, 278

Congress, 18, 76–77, 89, 109, 113, 206, 305

consensus, 74–75, 105, 139, 210–11, 214; idea of, 75, 105

conservativism, 11, 12, 16–17, 21–23, 67, 69, 77, 89, 113, 200, 207, 213–14, 253–54, 299–301, 327

constitution, 19

construction: and images of city, 303–4; of neighborhoods, 12, 28–29; of stadiums, 167; of state housing, 32, 34–36, 54; and *villas*, 59–60, 65; workers, 63, 139–41

consumer culture, 32, 54, 223

consumerism, 17

ice cream, 150
Identidad Marrón, 302
immigration, 9–12, 14, 23, 26, 68, 206,
    296–97, 299, 302, 312–13; from Bolivia,
    23, 34, 53, 63, 255–56; and Brown iden-
    tity, 302; culture of mixture, 10–12,
    23, 68, 310–11, 319; and demographics,
    10; from Eastern Europe, 10; educa-
    tion and, 206, 217–18; food, 63, 123–24;
    impacts of, 11–12, 25, 63, 68, 296–97,
    302, 312–13; from Italy, 9–10, 219; lan-
    guage, 12, 26; from Latin America, 23,
    63, 255–56, 302, 312; from Middle East,
    10; music, 10, 12, 26, 255–56, 319; from
    Paraguay, 23, 34, 53, 63; recent, 68,
    123–24, 302; from Spain, 10, 319; whit-
    ening, 10. See also cocoliche; lunfardo;
    xenophobia
imperialism, 100, 134–36. See also
    anti-imperialism
imports, 14, 19–20, 25–26, 37, 121, 134–35,
    145, 163, 212, 227, 248, 252, 309. See also
    exports; trade
import-substitution industrialization, 14
independence era, 7–9, 67–68, 80, 125, 206,
    222, 247, 262, 267, 295; and governance,
    8, 9, 295
Indigenous peoples, 7–8, 15, 119, 129, 302.
    See also Guaraní
industry, 14, 31, 33, 38, 218, 304; beef, 120,
    134–36; film, 212, 231, 249; in Greater
    Buenos Aires, 14–16, 28, 64, 72, 120–21,
    126; publishing, 4, 209; soccer, 179; wine,
    125
inequality, 2, 14–15, 32, 35, 70, 120–21, 137–38;
    digital, 39–40; and crisis, 35, 65, 121, 300;
    economic, 14, 35, 64–65, 121, 300–301; and
    food, 120–21, 137–38; in Greater Buenos
    Aires, 14–15, 20, 35, 64; and housing, 20,
    32–33, 41, 64–66; sanitary, 39–41; social,
    14, 35, 65, 301, 303, 333
inflation, 1, 19, 20–21, 35, 71, 75–76, 120–21,
    130, 134–35, 137–38, 301–2; and food,
    120–21, 130, 134–35, 137–38
informal labor, 20–21, 39–40, 143, 343
informal settlements, 19, 32–33, 59–61. See
    villas
infrastructure, 9, 12, 18–19, 31, 33–35, 39, 59,
    64–65, 257, 341. See also specific utilities
inquilinato, 26. See also conventillos
Interior, 8–9, 34, 61, 255, 297, 302; migration
    from, 14, 15, 32–33, 299, 329–30; origins
    of word, 8; relationship with capital city,
    8–9, 33, 299–300, 329–30

International Eucharistic Congress (1934),
    71, 89–90, 327–28
internet, 39–40, 53
Italian immigration, 9–10, 206, 310; and
    food, 120–21, 125, 155, 158, 161, 310, 319, 339;
    and language, 1, 12

jazz, 208, 211–12, 252, 273
Jewish community, 31, 52–53, 69, 312
jockey, 163–64, 175–76. See also horse racing
Jockey Club, 38
journalism, 177–78, 207–10, 213–14, 223
junta, 15, 17–19, 75, 200, 213, 234–35. See also
    civic-military dictatorship; military
Justicialismo, 16. See Peronism

kerchiefs, 103, 113
kidnappings, 4, 18, 101, 189, 213–14, 236,
    241–42, 254. See also disappeared persons
kimchi, 160–61
kiosk, 14, 124, 205, 209–10, 214, 219, 223, 239,
    244, 264, 298
Kirchner, Cristina. See Fernández de Kirch-
    ner, Cristina
Kirchner, Néstor, 21, 200
kitchen, 26, 31, 111–12, 121–22, 127, 133,
    137–38, 143–45, 161, 293
Korean community, 53, 160–61
Krol, Ruud, 200–201

La Boca (neighborhood), 26, 29, 31, 68, 167,
    212, 303, 319. See also Boca Juniors
labor, 3, 13, 15, 35, 92, 341, 343; informal, 343;
    laws, 134, 143, 164; organizations, 13, 68,
    72; press, 68, 239; protest, 15, 17, 68–71,
    147; rights, 11, 13, 143, 211; unions, 92, 134.
    See also unions; workers
La Familia Falcón (TV show), 212, 229–30
La Historia Oficial (film), 214
Lamarque, Libertad, 272
La Nación (periodical), 39, 86–87, 206, 319
landscape architecture, 48
language, 1, 2, 4, 12, 68; and cultural
    mixture, 26, 125, 264, 297, 310–11, 319; and
    feminism, 223–24; and print culture,
    205–7, 209, 222, 239–41; of soccer, 184, 192.
    See also lunfardo; and specific languages
La Opinión (periodical), 212–13
La Paternal (neighborhood), 271–72
La Patria degli Italiani (newspaper), 206
La Perla (bar), 254
La Prensa (periodical), 206, 211, 319
La Salamanca (peña), 286
La Siberia (neighborhood), 46–47

and, 252; neighborhoods, 13, 31, 35, 165; representation of, 211–12, 229–30, 333; and sport, 163–67, 175; women, 122, 145, 338

migration, 4, 26, 33–35, 63, 255, 286, 302; to Greater Buenos Aires, 14–16, 26, 33–35, 255; from the Interior, 14, 33–34, 61, 255, 299–300, 302, 329. *See also* emigration; exile; immigration

milanesa, 119–20, 122, 126, 140, 160; *napolitana*, 120

Milei, Javier, 22

military, 14, 16, 80, 130; and Catholic Church, 89; colonial era, 7; coup of 1930, 325; coup of 1943, 15; dictatorship (1966–73), 17, 238; dictatorship (1976–83) (*see* civic-military dictatorship); insurrections, 9, 11; pardons for, 19, 106; Peronism and, 15–17, 73–74, 92; police, 101–2; trials of, 19, 109. *See also* coup; *escrache*; human rights; state terror

milonga, 1, 10, 177, 252, 273

milonguita, 267–68

Minujín, Marta, 303, 305

modernity, 25, 27, 296, 303–4, 337

modernization, 8–9, 11, 20, 27, 46, 179–80, 296, 299, 325, 341

Molloy, Sylvia, 295, 312–13

monoblock, 32

Montevideo, 10

Montoneros. *See* Fuerzas Armadas Revolucionarios (FAR)–Montoneros

morality, 17, 82, 198, 217–18, 253, 267, 275, 277, 297

Morality Division (police), 278–79

Morocco (nightclub), 278

moscato, 125

Mothers of the Plaza de Mayo, 3, 18, 67, 74–75, 101–4, 113, 200

movie theaters, 14, 212, 227–28, 250, 337, 339

Mundo Agrario (periodical), 210

Mundo Peronista (periodical), 54, 56, 92–94, 166

murga, 82

music, 10, 26, 50, 76, 80, 82, 86–88, 175, 211–12, 247–57, 269–74, 282–91; during dictatorship, 247, 254–55, 282–88. *See also* specific types

National Commission on the Disappearance of Persons (CONADEP), 280–81

nationalism, 69, 92, 297–99, 105; and policy, 16, 134–35

neighborhood: and bookstores, 245; and

cinema, 215, 227–28, 247; culture of, 5, 10, 16, 32, 321; depicted in literature, 298, 321–24; expansion of, 9, 13, 17, 27, 29, 46, 301, 318–19; identity, 255, 321, 324; and middle class, 339–40; and music, 255, 271, 286, 289; and nightlife, 248, 255, 257, 275; and plazas, 3, 36, 48, 82, 108; representations of, 229, 298, 300, 316–17, 318–19, 321, 333, 337; and soccer, 4. See also *villas; and specific neighborhoods*

neighborhood associations, 13, 19, 31–32, 50–51

neoliberalism, 19–20, 32; and theater, 255, 264–65

newspapers, 4, 205–10, 231; censorship of, 103, 137–38, 211–15, 241–43, 284; neighborhood, 46, 50; soccer and, 116, 181, 198–99. *See also specific periodicals*

nightclubs, 252, 256–57, 278, 292–93. *See also specific nightclubs*

nightlife, 4, 247–57, 292–93

Ni Una Menos, 77, 113–15, 202

Nordelta (neighborhood), 35

nostalgia, 26, 156–57, 164, 304, 322

Noticias Gráficas (periodical), 300

Not One Less. *See* Ni Una Menos

Nuñez (neighborhood), 167

Obelisk: celebration at, 3, 77, 116–17; as symbol, 303, 305–6

Ocampo, Victoria, 2, 152, 297

Olivari, Nicolás, 139, 141, 158, 209

Oliver, María Rosa, 297

Olivos, 35

olla popular, 111–12

Onganía, Juan Carlos, 17, 238

opera, 225, 247–48, 250, 262, 287

orchestra, tango, 251, 271, 273–74

order: as political ideal, 8, 17, 300, 331–33; and public space, 8, 325–26, 329; and sport, 273–74; and urban design, 295, 299, 325

outskirts, 8, 12, 14–15, 28, 32, 35, 75, 92, 99, 248, 255, 298, 304, 327, 329, 339. See also *arrabal*; Greater Buenos Aires; suburbs

Página/12 (periodical), 214

painting, 79, 98, 251, 303

pampa, 25, 28, 70, 119–20, 139, 175, 225,

pañuelazo, 77, 113

Paraguay, immigration from, 23, 34, 53, 63

Para Ti (periodical), 223

pardon, 19, 106

prostitution, 254, 267, 276. *See also* brothels; sex work

protest, 67–77, 101, 105, 147, 299; and art, 74, 211, 254, 282, 286–87, 316; feminist movement, 77, 113–15, 202, 292; inequality, 64, 59, 111, 126, 137–38; music and, 109, 254, 269, 282–88; soccer and, 116, 171, 200; workers, 70–71, 109–11, 121, 137, 147–49, 207. *See also* demonstrations; Mothers of the Plaza de Mayo; *olla popular*; *piquete*; plaza; White Tent

public expression, 69, 72, 75

public health, 21, 60, 120, 173, 299

public kitchen, 76, 111. See *comedores*

public space, 19, 22, 31–32, 79, 203, 275; debates over use of, 32, 36, 50, 64, 69, 77; protest and, 67–68, 70, 74–75, 98, 111. *See also* order; plaza

publishing, 4, 135, 205, 207–9, 213, 221, 223, 235, 238–39

puchero, 132

Puerto Madero (neighborhood), 32

Pugliese, Osvaldo, 271

pulpería, 8, 81, 247

Pumper Nic, 127

Quechua, 1

queer cultures, 202, 253, 275, 277–79. *See also* LGBTQ+

Querandí, 7

queridas, 267

Quevedo, 256

Quilmes (neighborhood), 35, 64–65, 164

race, 7, 10–11, 15, 68, 79, 170, 194, 289, 296–97, 300, 310, 329

racism, 11, 170, 194, 202, 300, 329

Radical Party. *See* Unión Cívica Radical

radio: broadcasting, 167, 213, 215, 274, 282, 286; listening, 14, 210, 212, 231, 242, 251, 255–56, 271–72, 327; receivers, 211, 225; theater, 211, 225

railroads, 10, 28, 34, 37, 61, 66

Ramos Mejía (neighborhood), 35, 289, 291

Rawson, Guillermo, 39–40

rebellion, 4, 17, 26, 81, 255, 264, 267, 282, 290

Recoleta (neighborhood), 26, 31, 37, 61; cemetery, 26

reggaeton, 256, 289

regulation: of freedom of speech, 213, 286; of media, 213; of public space, 57, 66, 123; of sexual expression, 253; trade, 14–15. *See also* censorship

renters' strike, 71–72

restaurants, 11, 120, 125–26, 138, 158, 160–61, 248; contemporary scene, 32, 124, 127, 247

Retiro (neighborhood), 41, 59, 61–62, 256, 317

revista (show), 252–53

Riachuelo, 196, 304

Rico-Tipo (periodical), 210

Rio de Janeiro, 117

Rio de la Plata, 25, 179, 295, 299, 312; Viceroyalty of, 7

Rivadavia, Bernardino, 8, 295

rivalry: political, 73; and soccer, 170, 194, 198

River Plate (soccer club), 164, 167, 170, 177, 187, 189, 194–99; stadium, 59, 189

rivers, 126, 156, 196. *See also* Riachuelo; Rio de la Plata

roads, 47, 76, 111, 196, 325; construction of, 13

Roca, Nélida, 252

Roca-Runciman Pact, 134–35

rock, 1, 4, 17, 125, 259, 273, 287–90, 344

rock barrial, 255, 257

rock nacional, 254–55, 282–85

Rodrigo Bueno, 32

Rodríguez Larreta, Horacio, 21–22

Rojas, Ricardo, 299

Romero, José Luis, 298, 318

Rosas, Juan Manuel de, 8–9, 295, 307

rowing, 163

rugby, 163

rural areas, 33, 126, 225, 304

rural-urban migration, 33, 225, 286

Saénz Peña Law, 69

Saint-Jean, Alfredo, 105

salsa criolla, 156

San Isidro (neighborhood), 35

San Lorenzo (soccer club), 167, 194–95

San Telmo (neighborhood), 3, 31, 39, 123–24, 219, 265

Sarlo, Beatriz, 231, 233, 302

Sarmiento, Domingo Faustino, 217–18

Scalabrini Ortiz, Raúl, 209

scarves, 113. *See also* kerchiefs; *pañuelazo*

schools, 50, 56, 108, 176; British, 164; private, 35, 53; public, 109; and sports, 166, 173. *See also* education

Scobie, James, 298

Sebreli, Juan José, 269–70, 301, 339

self-representation, 333

Semana Trágica, 69, 76, 99

Senegal, immigration from, 23

sewage, 12, 46

sex, 114, 275–76, 248

sexism, 170, 182–83, 194, 202, 224. *See also* machismo

sexuality, 3, 209, 248, 252, 275, 276, 277–78; and notions of "decency," 248, 253–54; and policing of, 253–54, 275, 277–79. *See also* queer cultures

sex work, 10, 248, 251, 253–54, 267. *See also* brothels; *milonguita*; prostitution

shopping, 3, 22, 123; malls, 20, 37, 123, 127. *See also* markets

single-family home, 31, 54–57

Sintonía (periodical), 255

slaughterhouse, 8, 126

soccer: and local style of play, 165–66, 171, 177–78; and masculinity, 166, 173–74, 182–83, 202–3; neighborhood pastime, 13, 46–47, 163–65, 167, 180–81; origins of, 164; and songs, 1–2, 170, 344; stadiums, 2, 126, 163, 198; and violence, 166, 170–71, 196, 198–99. *See also barra brava*; soccer clubs; soccer players

soccer clubs: and identity, 13, 163, 169; and political campaigns, 200. *See also specific clubs*

soccer players: and European leagues, 168, 179, 186; and social mobility, 167–68, 184–85

Social Catholicism, 68

social hierarchy, 12, 82. *See also* elite; middle class; social mobility

socialism, 11–14, 68, 86–88, 207, 209, 299, 235

Socialist Party, 11–14

social mobility, 64, 299, 301, 335, 341–42

social reform, 8, 15, 19, 26, 48, 54, 113

sociedades de fomento. See neighborhood associations

Soda Stereo, 1, 259

sorrentinos, 125

Sosa, Mercedes, 286–88, 344

soup kitchens. See *comedores*

South Korea, 23

soybeans, 20

Spain, 7, 10, 179, 187, 264, 277, 287, 295

Spanish (language), 1, 4, 12, 125, 160, 205, 208–9, 254, 256, 308

Spanish Empire, 7

stadiums, 2, 126, 163, 167, 185, 198, 211, 254

stadium songs, 2, 170, 194–95

state terror, 1, 18–19, 22, 67, 106, 214, 234, 254, 280–81. *See also* civic-military dictatorship

street art, 2, 75, 95–98. See also *afiche*; *escrache*; performance art

street lighting, 8, 12, 27, 33

strike, 67–69, 71–72, 109–11, 113–14, 147–49, 183, 207, 232

students, 33, 64, 108, 174, 238, 342

subsidies, 22

subte. See subway

suburbs, 14–16, 20, 28–29, 32, 35, 64, 75, 92, 138, 163, 167, 319, 327. *See also* Greater Buenos Aires; outskirts

subversion, 17, 69, 238, 254

subway, 13, 15, 25, 28, 30, 36, 114, 332

Superclásico, 170, 196–97

Taiwan, 23

tango: and decency, 248, 251–52, 256, 259; lyrics and dances, 1, 12, 57, 175, 269, 273; neighborhood, 271–72, 298, 321; nightlife, 4, 247–48, 252; origins, 10, 26, 248, 319; and soccer, 167, 177, 186, 208, 254; and women, 248, 267. *See also* Gardel, Carlos; Piazzola, Astor

Tango Feroz (film), 214

tariffs, 20, 134

teachers, 76, 108–10, 173, 214, 337

Teatro Abierto, 264–66

Teatro Coliseo, 225

Teatro Colón, 25

Teatro del Picadero, 264–65

Teatro del Pueblo, 264

Teatro Maipo, 252, 253

Teatro Politeama, 262

Teatro Politeama Argentino, 248

Teatro San Martín, 265

television, 4, 76, 92, 212–15; shows, 122, 143, 229, 231

telo, 252, 275

tennis, 65, 163, 166, 178, 182

tertulias, 80

Thays, Carlos, 48

theater, 249, 262, 265, 277, 341; on Corrientes Avenue, 14, 250; criollo theater, 319; independent, 264; movie, 212, 227, 337, 339; and political oppression, 278, 287–88; on radio, 211, 225. *See also specific theaters*

Tigre (neighborhood), 35, 234

Timerman, Jacobo, 212

Tormo, Antonio, 255

torture, 18–19, 74–75, 101, 106, 213, 234–35, 242–43, 254, 280

tourism, 3, 22, 26, 32, 34, 36, 123, 244, 247, 277

trade, 7, 9, 20, 134. *See also* exports; imports